THE DESIGNER'S SOURCEBOOK 11

ART FOR THE WALL,
FURNITURE & ACCESSORIES

⋮⋮⋮ THE GUILD®

Kraus Sikes Inc.
Madison, Wisconsin
USA

Published by
THE GUILD
931 East Main Street #106
Madison, WI 53703
USA
FAX 608-256-1938
TEL 608-256-1990
TEL 800-969-1556
http://www.guild.com

Administration
Toni Fountain Sikes, President
James F. Black, Jr., Vice President
Susan K. Evans, Vice President
Theresa Ace, Business Manager
Deb Lovelace, Operations Manager
Emily Lovelace, Administrative Assistant

Production, Design, Editorial
Cheryll Mellenthin, Production Manager
Marcia LaCour-Little, Production Assistant

Katie Kazan, Editorial Manager
Teddy Zehner, Editorial Assistant
Sarah Mollet, Editorial Intern

Susan Cosgrove, Writer • Ellen Kochansky, Writer

DNP America, Inc., Printer

Publisher's Representatives
Karen O. Brown • Tom Christensen
Susan K. Evans
Martha Johnson • Reed J. McMillan

Worldwide Distribution
Hearst Books International
1350 Avenue of the Americas
New York, NY 10019

ISBN (softback) 1-880140-22-5   ISBN (hardback) 1-880140-21-7

Printed in Hong Kong

Cover Art
Dusk II, by Susanne G. Stephenson, 1995, slips plus vitreous engobes on terra cotta,
27"W x 29"H x 10"D, photo by Suzanne Coles. See page 128.

Special thanks to our 1996 Review Committee
Sylvia White • Contemporary Artists' Services
Sue Wiggins • ArtSouth, Inc.

NOTHING LESS

I know, I know, it's a beautiful book. But it's so much more.

We get hundreds of letters; people tell us how much they love it, how it inspires and stimulates them. Patricia Harvey, FASID, writes, "When it arrives, I feel great! When I open it, I look — or try to look — at everything at once. The quality of work is magnificent."

The words of praise, the phone calls, the faxes from around the world make us feel good. After all, we work hard to put all of these resources under one cover.

But our efforts would be for naught if it weren't for you. For our mission is only accomplished when someone calls an artist for more information, or takes this book along to a client meeting, or even sits with it, dreaming of all the possibilities.

Therefore, as we enter our second decade of playing matchmaker to artists and those who work with them, we dedicate this edition of *The Designer's Sourcebook* to the people who help us accomplish our mission. Interspersed throughout these pages are interviews with design professionals and other individuals who put THE GUILD to its intended use, with marvelous results.

We salute them, and the countless others who enhance the places where we live and work. They show us, time and time again, that it is possible to make buildings and spaces worthy of the public's interest and delight.

And, I think, nothing less will do.

Toni Fountain Sikes
Publisher

TABLE OF CONTENTS

FEATURES

RESOURCES

TABLE OF CONTENTS

ARTISTS

Artists by Section
Turn the page for a listing of featured artists.

THE GUILD REGISTERs®
Concise product and pricing information, as well as addresses and phones,
for artists working in three important areas.

ARTISTS BY SECTION

ARTISTS BY SECTION

10 **Great Ways**

to use *The Designer's Sourcebook 11*

1 QUALITY CONTROL. This book begins with an assurance: these artists are reliable and professional. Featured artists in GUILD sourcebooks have been juried in on the basis of experience, quality of work, and a solid reputation for working with architects and designers.

2 MOTIVATION. *The Designer's Sourcebook* is a great resource for client meetings. Clients have been known to reach levels of extreme excitement upon viewing the artistic possibilities showcased here.

3 GO AHEAD AND CALL. If something intrigues you while perusing *The Designer's Sourcebook* — a shape, a form, an exotic use of the commonplace — please, give the artist a call. Serendipity often leads to a wonderful creation.

4 HOW IT'S DONE. A wise guide is a great thing. Look throughout this volume for interviews with design professionals who have commissioned artwork with the help of THE GUILD. Their advice is insightful; their experiences inspiring.

5 MORE IS BETTER. We're always delighted to hear about firms that commission work from a GUILD artist. The Southern Progress Corporation boasts several works from our advertisers in their new corporate headquarters. Look for the story — and photos of the artwork — beginning on page 10.

6 MORE ARTISTS … AND MORE. The right artist, the right media, the right region, and the right price. That's a lot of information, and we've got it. THE GUILD REGISTERs list contact, product and pricing information for hundreds of artists working in fiber, glass and ceramic art for the wall. Don't miss the new section of ceramic tile, starting on page 131.

7 SKINNING THE CAT. There's more than one way to find art for a specific site. Fiber artist Ellen Kochansky, who is something of a visionary in the world of the decorative arts, describes an everybody-wins competition co-sponsored by the American Craft Council and Hines Interests Limited Partnership. See page 152.

8 DESKTOP DIRECTORY. *The Designer's Sourcebook 11* is designed for quick reference, as well as leisurely browsing. The "Index of Artists and Companies" includes artists listed in THE GUILD REGISTERs, as well as those featured in the full-color pages, so finding a current phone number or checking product information is easily done. The information in your rolodex may grow stale; *The Designer's Sourcebook* is fresh each year.

9 ARTISTS THEN AND NOW. Many of the artists whose work you see here are also represented in earlier GUILD publications; look for references on artists' pages. You can order most of these early volumes through our main office; call 1-800-969-1556 for order information.

10 LET US HEAR FROM YOU. This volume of *The Designer's Sourcebook* is filled with stories about design professionals who use THE GUILD. We love hearing these stories and we love passing them on through the pages of our sourcebooks. Let us know about *your* project … perhaps we'll feature it in next year's edition.

Because THE GUILD operates as a kind of matchmaker between artists and design professionals, we have considerable interest in how the matches that begin here turn out. We want to help these relationships work by doing everything we can to make the contact between architect and artist satisfying and profitable.

We also want to make it easier for architects to create new professional alliances with artists. And we'd especially like to reassure those who have been reluctant to try such collaboration because of their concerns about how the process works.

Successful projects result when architects and artists form good relationships with each other, relationships founded on mutual understanding of expectations, clear communication and a willingness of both parties to accept their responsibilities for making a good project.

This article is a how-to guide of the commissioning process . . . how it comes about, who is involved, the steps to take and when to take them, what to prepare for, and how to avoid problems. We hope it answers some questions and offers encouragement to design professionals seeking to work directly with artists and artisans.

By far the most important part of getting great work is choosing a great artist — or at least the right artist for your particular project and pocketbook. This choice is the decision from which all others will flow, so it's worth investing time and energy in the selection process and seasoning the process with both wild artistic hopes and hard-nosed realism. The right choices at this early stage will make things go easier later on.

Some clients will be very interested in helping select the artist, and working closely with him or her once the choice is made. Others will want only minimal involvement, leaving most of the decision-making to the design team.

Whoever is making the decision, there are several ways to find the right artist. Obviously, we recommend browsing through GUILD sourcebooks. Not only do they show a wide range of some of the top work available, they also have the advantage of weeding out people who may not really want to work with designers and architects on commissioned pieces. Every GUILD artist is looking for collaborative work — that's why they're here. And many already have a strong track record of working with designers, architects and their clients. You will gain from their professionalism and experience.

FINDING YOUR ARTIST

If you don't find exactly what you want through THE GUILD, or you want to know who else may be available, there are a number of other routes to take in the selection process.

You may see work you like at a gallery or craft fair. Ask for artists' names and business cards. Design magazines often feature artist profiles, along with contact information. Your own colleagues may offer more names. And if the project is a large one, you may go through a request-for-proposal process that will draw responses from all over the continent.

A qualified art consultant will also have a wide network of artists to choose from. If the complexity of your project warrants using an art consultant in the selection process, make sure the consultant is sophisticated and experienced enough to provide real guidance in working with the artist. This means the ability to help negotiate the technical details of a very specific contract, including issues like installation, insurance, storage, transportation and possible engineering costs.

Your first contact with an artist sets the tone for the relationship to follow. With that contact, via telephone or letter, be prepared to provide information about the size and scope of your project, the budget, the deadlines, and even the details about the building site. This will help the artist tailor his or her response more specifically, giving you a better sense of whether this is the right person for your project.

Make your initial selection on the basis of what you like about an artist's past work. Most experienced artists will be pleased to provide a portfolio — usually on slides, but sometimes printed. Don't, however, expect to see the exact piece you're looking for in a portfolio. Remember, you're choosing an artist at this point, not a piece of art. Look for creativity, command of the materials or technology, and how the work fits the specific environment.

EXPECT PROFESSIONALISM

Once you've made a tentative selection based on a portfolio and the artist's past experience and reputation, it's time to get serious. Even though some designers and architects still believe artists are too 'unbusinesslike' to worry much about such things as building codes, lighting specifications, deadlines and budgets, the great majority of artists who seek commissioned work will be conversant with

Sue Wiggins   Jerome Lukowicz

SOUTHERN FLAVOR
An Exceptional Corporate Collection

This is the first of several 'user' interviews in this edition of The Designer's Sourcebook. *Each of the design professionals we spoke with has used GUILD sourcebooks to commission original artwork.*

Sue Wiggins, president of ArtSouth, Inc., an art-consulting firm based in Philadelphia, and Karen League, a principal with Jova, Daniels, Busby, Inc., an Atlanta design firm, first met in 1989. Their assignment: to build an art collection for the new corporate headquarters of Southern Progress Corporation. Southern Progress is a subsidiary of Time Warner and publisher of Southern Accents *and* Southern Living *magazines.*

Karen League

these and other contract details. Most designers find that the artist's professionalism and knowledge of subject, materials, and details of code, safety and engineering is both complete and reassuring.

MEETING FACE-TO-FACE

Before making your final choice of artist, it's important to set up an initial, no-obligation meeting.

The purpose of this meeting is to find out if the chemistry is right — whether you have the basis to build a working relationship. It's also the time to confirm that the artist has the necessary skills to undertake your project. Be thorough and specific when asking questions. Ask what the artist sees as the important issues or considerations in the project. Evaluate his or her interest. Will your needs be a major or minor concern? Do the artist's style, approach and personality suit the project?

If it feels like you might have trouble working together, it's wise to heed these early warning signs. But if all goes well and you decide to move ahead with the artist, your second meeting will be to agree on a budget and timetable, and sign a contract.

At this second meeting, be resolved that silence is not golden and ignorance not bliss! Be frank. Tell the artist what you expect. Now is the time for possible misunderstandings to be brought up and resolved, not later, after the work is half done and deadlines loom.

A COLLABORATIVE ATMOSPHERE

Bring the artist into the process at the earliest possible stage — at about the same time you hire the general contractor. This is a wise investment for several reasons. From the very beginning, the space is designed with the art in mind, and the art is created to enhance the space. As a result, there are no unpleasant surprises about size or suitability of the artwork to the space. Furthermore, when art is planned for early on, it's far less likely to be cut at the end of the project, when money may be running low.

Early inclusion of the artist also helps ensure that the collaborative effort will go smoothly throughout all phases of the project. If the artist is respected as part of the team, his work can benefit the project's overall design.

The collaboration between interior designer Karen League, art consultant Sue Wiggins, an entire consortium of artists and an enthusiastic corporate client created such synergy that the positive effects of the association continue to be felt even now, several years after the original assignment was completed.

"Our company provides planning, architectural, and interior design services to clients all over the south," Karen League explains. "As we began to work with Southern Progress on its new headquarters, we noticed that they did not have many pieces from regional artists. Because the culture and the flavor of the South is such a focus of the company's publications, we began to look for artwork from their subscription area: Maryland to Texas."

At this point, ArtSouth, Inc. was hired.

"We're a full-service, fine-arts research firm, and though we're located in Philadelphia, our clients come from all over the country," Sue Wiggins says. Working alongside the client, Wiggins and League began the long review process to determine which artists would be represented in the Southern Progress collection.

"We reviewed over 900 artists in all," Karen League recalls, "and we were so impressed with the quality of the people Sue found. Furthermore, her recommendations recognized and respected the budget and parameters of the project."

Naturally, the scope of the project will determine the number of players to be involved with the artist. How will decisions be made? Will a single person sign off on recommendations? Are committees necessary? If so, it's a good idea to designate one person to serve as liaison with the artist to avoid mixed signals.

SEEK TWO-WAY UNDERSTANDING

Be sure the artist understands the technical requirements of the job, including traffic flow in the space, the intended use of the space, the building structure, maintenance, lighting and environmental concerns. By doing this, you ensure that the artist's knowledge, experience and skill become part of the project.

Keep the artist appraised of any changes you make that will affect the work in progress. Did you find a certain material you specified unavailable and replace it with something else? Did the available space become bigger or smaller? These may seem like small changes to you, but they could have a profound impact on an artist's planning and work.

At the same time, the artist should let you know of any special requirements his or her work will place on the space. Is it especially heavy? Does it need to be mounted in a specific way? Must it be protected from theft or vandalism? What kind of lighting is best? You may want to set aside a contingency budget to fund design changes or omissions once the project begins.

Most artists experienced with commissioned work factor the notion of

a continuing design dialog into their fee. There is an unfortunate belief — harbored by some architects, designers and, yes, artists too — that a willingness to change and compromise somehow indicates a lack of commitment or creativity. On the contrary. The ability to compromise on execution, without compromising on artistic quality, is a mark of professionalism. We recommend that you look for this quality in the artist you choose, and respect it by treating the artist as a partner in decisions made affecting his or her work.

Of course, part of working together is making clear who is responsible for what. Since few designers and architects — and even fewer contractors — are used to working with artists, the relationship is custom-made for misunderstanding. Without a firm understanding from the outset — nurtured by constant communication — things can easily fall through the cracks.

"At a certain point, we began talking about including furniture in the collection," Wiggins remembers. "We decided this was appropriate — primarily for the executive areas of the building — and turned to the resources of THE GUILD for recommendations, with great results." The review committee decided it could accept already completed work, or commission new work, but that in either case, the furniture must be useful as well as beautiful.

Stella End Tables, created for Southern Progress by John Clark

Tom Brummett

"We didn't want to compromise the artists' designs, but we felt strongly that this had to be functional art," Karen League says. The committee approached a number of individuals, including GUILD artists John Clark and Ron Puckett. Neither artist had furniture in their inventory that would be appropriate, so work was commissioned.

PUT IT IN WRITING

It is a truism in any kind of business that it is much cheaper to get the lawyers involved at the beginning of a process than after something goes wrong. A contract or letter of agreement will assure you and the client that the artist will complete his or her work on time and to specifications. It will also assure the artist that he or she will get paid the right amount at the right time. That just about eliminates the biggest conflicts that can arise.

Contracts should be specific to the job. Customarily, artists are responsible for design, production, shipping and installation. If someone else is to be responsible for installation, be sure you specify who will coordinate it and who will pay for it — if it is not the artist, it usually is the client. With a large project, it is helpful to identify the tasks that, if held up for any reason, would delay completion of the project. They should be discussed up front to assure that both parties agree on requirements and expectations.

Most architects recognize that adequate compensation for the artist is in their best interest as it assures the type and level of service needed to fulfill their expectations. The more skill you need and the more complex the project, the more you should budget for the artist's work and services.

PAYMENT SCHEDULE

Payments are usually tied to specific points in the process. These serve as check points to make sure the work is progressing in a satisfactory manner, on time and on budget. Payment is customarily made in three stages, although this certainly depends on the circumstances, scope and complexity of the project.

The first payment is usually made when the contract is signed. It covers the artist's time and creativity in developing a design specific to your needs. You can expect to go through several rounds of trial and error in the design process, but at the end of this stage you will have detailed drawings and, for three-dimensional work, a maquette (model) that everyone agrees upon. The artist usually charges a fee to cover the costs of the maquette and design time.

The second payment is generally set for a mid-way point in the project and is for work done to date. If the materials are expensive, the client may be asked to advance money at this stage to cover materials' costs. If the commission is cancelled during this period,

"I think we worked well together because we were clear from the beginning about what we needed," Wiggins says. "The artists responded extremely well and were able to turn the commissions around quickly."

League says it was fascinating to see how differently the artists worked — even in similar media. Clark, for example, submitted a series of intriguing, highly architectural computer-generated images for exploring ideas. Puckett's drawings

Richard Larimere

C.E.O. Cabinet, created for
Southern Progress by Ron Puckett

were elegant, hand-drawn sketches with watercolor. Both delighted the client, as did the finished pieces.

According to League and Wiggins, there has been a wonderful evolution in the way people see and experience one-of-a-kind fine crafts and original art.

"People have educated themselves and become very sophisticated in their tastes," says Wiggins. "At Southern Progress, for example, there the artist keeps the money already paid for work performed.

Final payment is usually due when the work is installed. If the piece is finished on time but the building or project is delayed, the artist is customarily paid on delivery, but still has the obligation to oversee installation.

You will find that most artists keep tabs on the project budget. Be sure that the project scope does not deviate from what was agreed at the outset. If the scope changes, amend the agreement accordingly.

FORGING A PARTNERSHIP

The partnership between artists and designers is an old and honorable one. Many venerable blueprints will indicate, for example, an architect's detail for a ceiling with the scrawled note, "Finish ceiling in this manner." The assumption, of course, is that the artisan working on the ceiling has both the technical mastery and aesthetic skill to create a whole expanse of space from a detail that comes from the mind and pen of the architect.

We believe today's new breed of artist is capable of such relationships, and we're delighted to see increasing numbers of design professionals including artists on their teams. After too many years of the arts being separated from architectural design, we're happy to be a part of a renewed interest in collaboration.

is a great deal of pride in the collection. It reflects the company's editorial considerations, and shows regional artists in a wonderful setting. *Southern Accents* and *Southern Living* often run profiles of artists, with a focus on fine American crafts as well as fine arts. There is a trend toward original art in design throughout the country, and its something the shelter magazines are becoming more and more attuned to."

By the time the Southern Progress headquarters was finished, League and Wiggins had become friends, and they continue to work together. The collection they assembled remains a real source of pride for the company, its employees and the area.

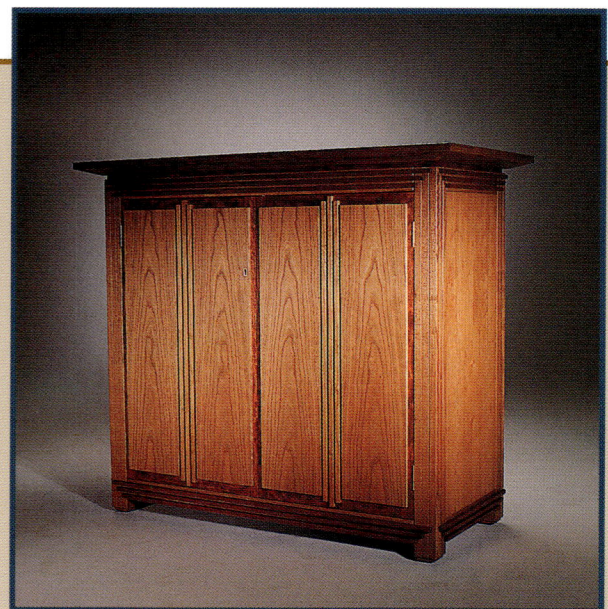

Console Cabinet, created for Southern Progress by Ron Puckett

Richard Larimer

FEATURED ARTISTS

Many of the projects shown on the following pages were commissioned by design professionals for site-specific installation. These ingenious, exhilarating collaborations are an inspiration for future projects.

FURNITURE

Ted Box
Jeff Entner

Ocean Art
PO Box 1764
Edgartown, MA 02539
TEL 508-696-6126

The driftwood pieces of designer Ted Box are sculpted on Martha's Vineyard and reflect the relationship of sea, sand and weathering which is so much the spirit of coastal New England.

These pieces have been successfully marketed to major galleries and private collections throughout Canada, the United States and Japan. A rolltop desk of Box's design is currently in the White House.

The works' versatility and functional durability, and the close collaboration between artist and client, combine to create the heirloom quality of these pieces.

Sweeping Leg Table

Hutch

Eccentric Rolltop, section of cone

Printed in Hong Kong ©1996 THE GUILD: The Designer's Sourcebook

Michael A. Burns

Works in Metal
602 Clemons Avenue
Madison, WI 53704-5508
FAX 608-258-8944
TEL 608-241-7544

Sculpture or furniture? A bit of both, but Michael Burns says it's really jewelry for the home.

With over 20 years experience in both sculpture and jewelry, Burns makes a point of combining elements of each. Carefully worked metal forms harmonize with elegant, polished stone and glass to result in sculpture you can use with little care. Steel gives the work strength and grace but the craftsmanship suggests more noble materials, with details you'd expect to find in jewelry.

With each piece uniquely crafted, this work complements almost every home or office setting.

A Coffee table, steel and granite, 16" x 48" x 28"

B End table, steel and granite, 23" x 22" x 26"

C Floor lamp, steel and glass, 80" x 16" x 12"

D Console table, steel and granite, 36" x 69" x 16"

A

B

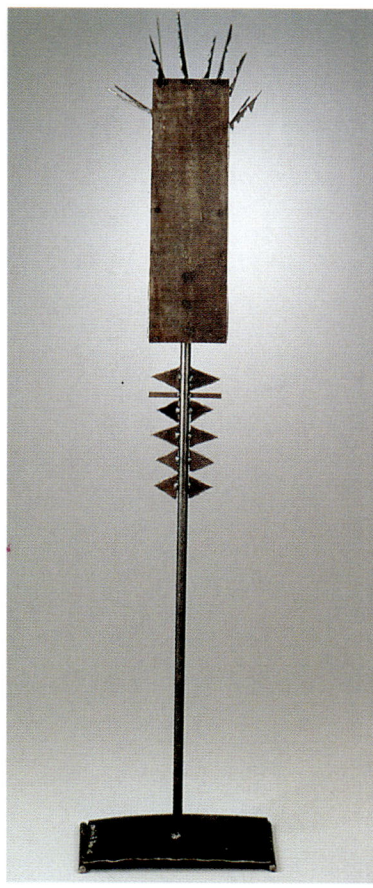

C

D

Photos: Bill Lemke

Christopher Thomson Ironworks

Christopher Thomson and Susan Livermore
PO Box 578
Ribera, NM 87560
FAX 505-421-2618
TEL 505-421-2645
E-Mail: APRV70A@prodigy.com

On the windy pinion-juniper grassland between Rowe Mesa and the Pecos River in New Mexico — painting, flute playing, and swimming in swirling muddy waters — Christopher and Susan strive to creatively merge their own energies with the energies of their daughters, employees and the communities beyond. Their works in hand-forged steel are the outgrowth of and catalyst for this joyous quest.

Make an appointment to visit their restored stone and adobe gallery and tour the forge. Send $7 for a complete catalog, or $15 for a catalog and set of finish samples. Additional information on custom furnishings and architectural works is available on request.

Also see these GUILD publications:
Designer's Edition: 8, 9, 10
Gallery Edition: 2

David O. Marlow

Jeffrey Cooper

Designer of Sculptural Furnishings in Wood
135 McDonough Street
Portsmouth, NH 03801-3978
FAX 603-436-7945
TEL 603-436-7945
E-Mail: jcooper@nh.ultranet.com

"I love it! And everyone who sees it loves it too!"
Lynn Sherr

Jeffrey Cooper gladly works with designers and individuals. His Woodworking Home Page can be viewed on the Internet at http://www.nh.ultranet/~jcooper

Also see these GUILD publications:
THE GUILD: 5
Designer's Edition: 6, 7, 8, 9

A *Giraffe Console Table*, 8'L x 37"H, may be used as a serving buffet in a dining room

B Table lamp and floor lamp, each with three carving sites

C Table base for a glass top with four carving sites, design may be adapted to any size from coffee table to dining table

D Torah scroll stand, Temple Emmanuel, Andover, MA

A   Roger Lemoine, NYC

C   Andrew Edgar, Portsmouth, NH

B   Andrew Edgar, Portsmouth, NH

D   Andrew Edgar, Portsmouth, NH

furnARTure etc.

Charly Stockl
829 North Third Street
Philadelphia, PA 19123
FAX 215-629-3637
TEL 215-592-9669

Self-taught artist Charly Stockl specializes in transforming old furniture into new works of art that are functional, pleasing to the eye and valued collectors' pieces.

Starting with found pieces or the client's existing furniture, and using a wide range of visual references and design influences, Stockl creates one-of-a-kind contemporary —yet nostalgic —furniture and accessories.

Each piece is protected with several coats of extremely durable acrylic polymer, and requires minimal care.

A *Lemon Butter,* 1995, hand-painted armoire

B *Expresso,* 1995, hand-painted coffee table

A

B

Photos: Geoff Verne

Robert Alexander Harman

Upholstered Fine Art
104 East Kirkwood Avenue
Bloomington, IN 47401
TEL 812-333-2244

With over 20 years experience as a craftsman, Robert Harman has developed a distinctive furniture style. He designs one-of-a-kind pieces with each frame individually crafted from maple, then upholstered in fabric, leather, rug or any combination thereof.

Harman is experienced in working with clients and designers to meet their specific needs. His works have been shown in galleries and public spaces, and are in private collections nationwide.

A Painted wood, velvet, jacquard,
   34"H x 30"W x 30"D

B Painted wood, velvet, chenille
   and rug, 30"H x 32"W x 30"D

C Painted wood, leather,
   30"H x 32"W x 30"D

A

Kevin Montague

B

David Dudine

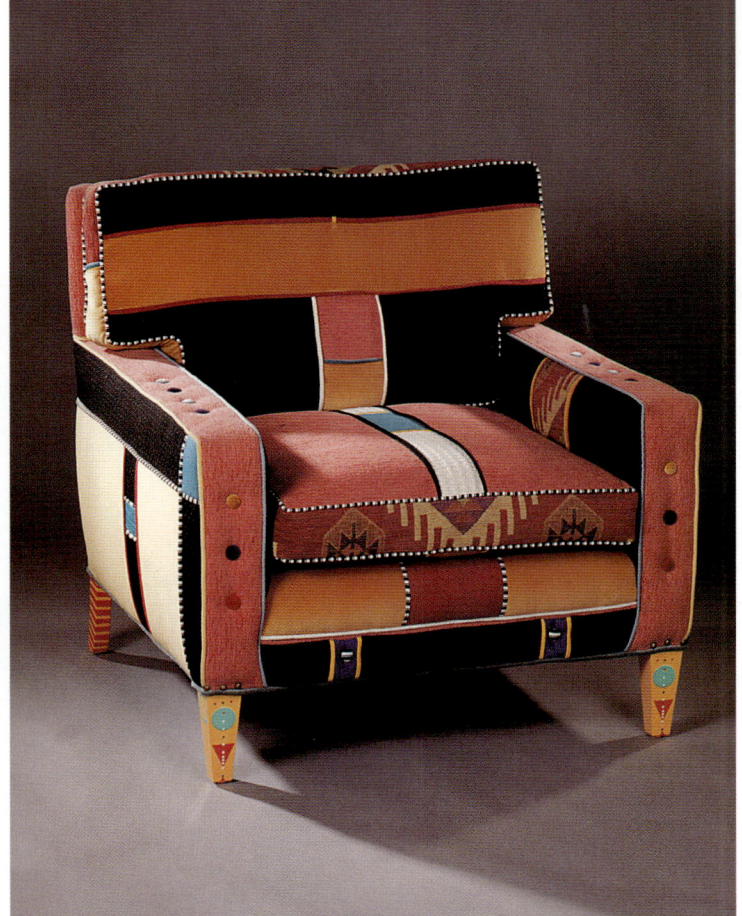

C

David Dudine

Craig Kaviar

Kaviar Forge
147 Stevenson Avenue
Louisville, KY 40206
FAX 502-561-0377
TEL 800-500-3890
TEL 502-561-0377

Kaviar Forge is a sculpture studio that specializes in hand-forged metal work. The work is distinguished by a natural ambiance, with extreme attention to fine craftsmanship and, in the case of furniture, comfort and utility. Craig Kaviar really enjoys working with designers and is able to customize projects, not only through his design and forging skills, but also by providing a large assortment of metals and finishes.

Work is delivered on time and within budget.

A *Perelmuter Memorial Gates,* 8'H x 8'W, forged iron with gold leaf menorah, located at the Jewish Community Center, Louisville, KY

B *Dining Ensemble,* grand chair #505-K, 48"H x 25"W x 27"L; dining table #525A, with glass top, 42" x 66" x 30"H; dining chair #504-K, 36"H x 20"W x 20"L; all pieces of forged iron with leaves and birds.

A

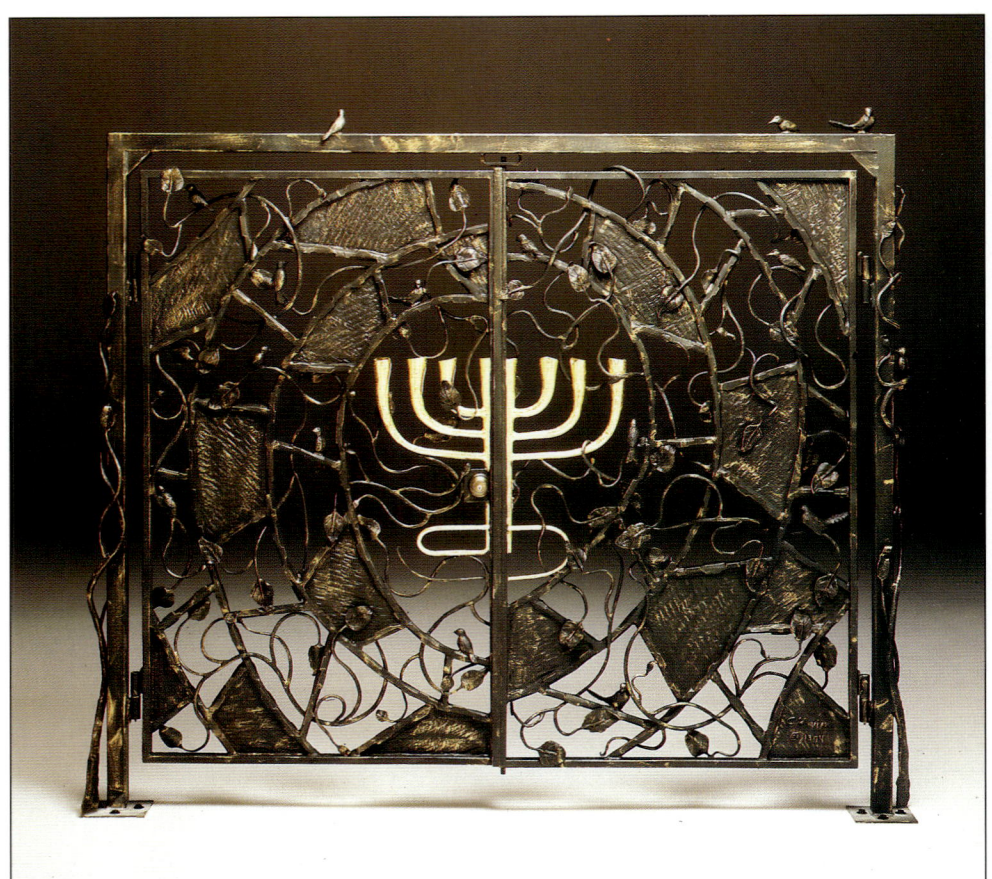

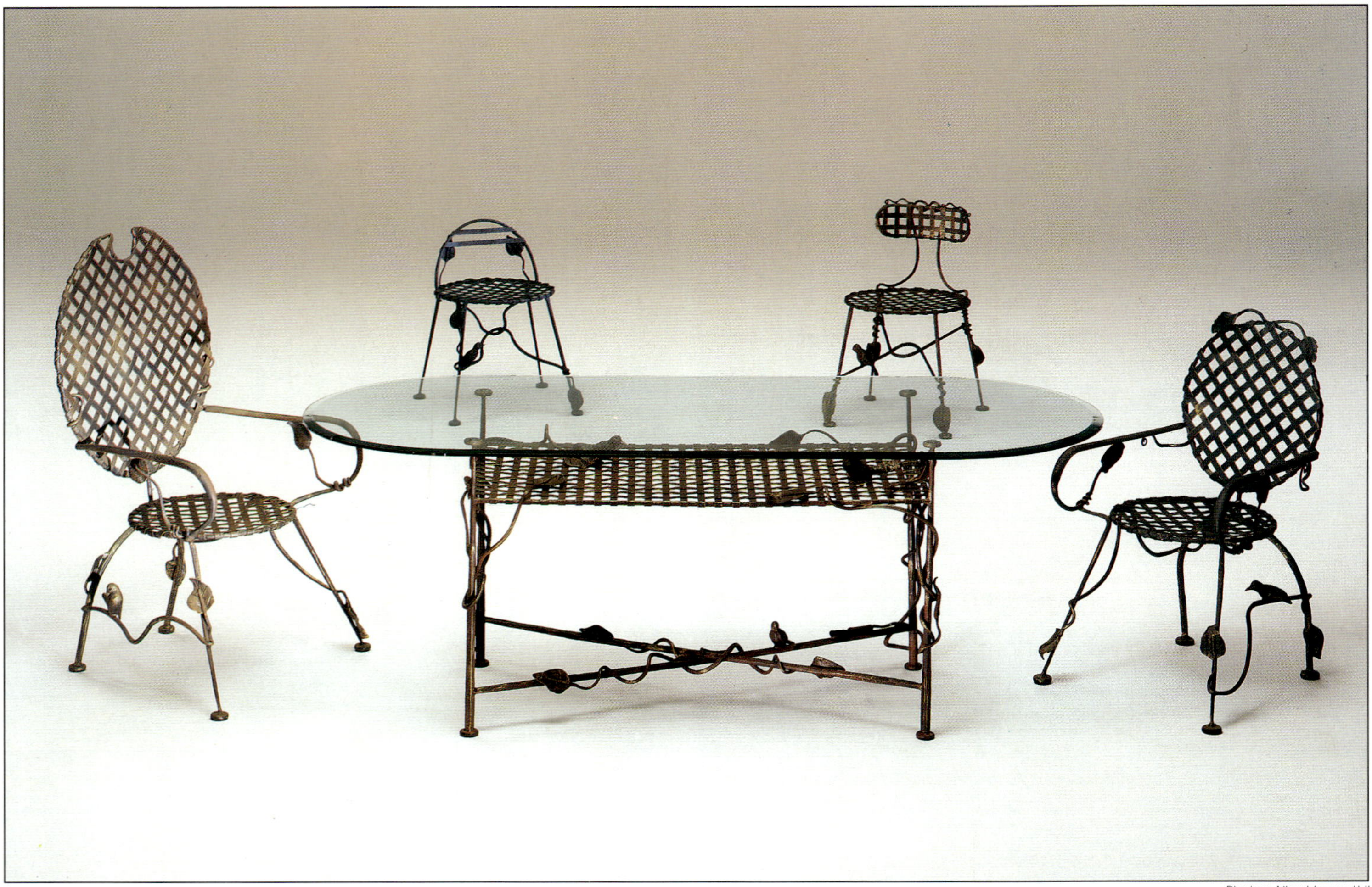

B

Photos: Albert Leggett II

Maggie and Steve Longworth

Wicker Works
Box 169
Gooderham, ON K0M 1R0
CANADA
FAX 705-447-2433
TEL 705-447-2435
E-Mail: 75471.2631@compuserve.com

Maggie and Steve's original twig furniture creates a link with nature and brings a rustic charm to both indoor and outdoor spaces. For seven years, they have consistently created unique and award-winning designs, written magazine articles, and appeared on television. They were recently commissioned by Disney Studios.

The Longworths work with willow, birch, cedar, striped maple, and other woods. Their baskets (both twig and woven) are made from a wide range of natural materials, No project is too big or small and most orders are completed in six to twelve weeks. Prices range from $30 to $3,000.

Completed works are also available. Catalog supplied upon request.

A   Willow staircase with marquetry on posts

B   Willow/birch bark marquetry on coffee
     table, 36" x 36"; willow armchairs/rattan
     seats and backs

A

B

Photos: Lynnie Johnston—Toronto

Doug Weigel

Steel Sculptures by Doug Weigel
PO Box 92408
Albuquerque, NM 87199-2408
FAX 505-821-9696
TEL 505-821-6600

Weigel designs and produces two- and three-dimensional sculptures and furniture in steel. Styles include Southwestern, Western and Art Deco, as well as client-commissioned ideas.

Allow four to eight weeks from design approval and contract to completion. Shipping and handling, FOB Albuquerque.

Selected commissions include the collection of President George Bush, Petrified National Forest, Scottsdale Airport, Sandia Laboratories and the Hyatt Aruba.

A Steel petroglyph hanging pan rack, 24" x 18" x 18"

B *Mimbres Lizard* glass-top game table and four chairs; petroglyph mirror, 20" x 30"; and petroglyph snake floor lamp

C Wall hanging petroglyph circle, 18"; petroglyph high-back chair; quail mirror, 14" x 18"; and wall-hanging petroglyph figure, 22"

A

B

C

SUSAN JAKOBER

Interior Designer—Allied Member A.S.I.D.

"Using original art sets me apart from other interior designers in my area," says Susan Jakober, president of Interior Arts, a small Midwestern design firm. "I enjoy working with artists, and I've found it's good for my business because clients are fascinated with both the artwork and the process."

A designer for 15 years, Jakober has been interested in THE GUILD since it was first published. "A friend of mine had a copy of the first GUILD. I made notes of people in our area and thought, 'wouldn't it be fun to work with these people!' " Over the succeeding years, Jakober has had a number of opportunities to do just that.

One of her most gratifying projects involved GUILD artist Robert Walsh of R. Walsh Forge and Foundry. "My clients had a wonderful project, a grand country house with beautiful dark wood and an Italian marble floor in the foyer. I contacted Bob to create a wrought iron staircase railing for the entry.

"I think the clients were a little anxious at first, until they saw his drawings and suggestions. His design was beautiful, with a lattice and three-dimensional calla lilies. They loved it so much that they added two additional balconies.

"The finished work is spectacular, and gives a remarkable signature to the house. This guy really knows what he's doing!"

Jakober has discovered other artists through THE GUILD as well. "GUILD artists are real professionals and they can work well within a budget," she says. "It doesn't need to cost an arm and a leg. You just tell the artists what you're willing to spend and they tell you whether they can work within that range.

"I think what you get in value is so much more than the cost. Properly selected and properly made, art can pull an entire space into the next level."

Photo by Richard Long

Afrantiquity Design Studio

Vincent White
196 Alps Road, Suite 2-123
Athens, GA 30606
FAX 706-613-1195
TEL 800-307-7782

Afrantiquity is a custom furniture design/build studio and promoter of African art/civilization. Arfantiquity's creative inspirations come from furniture designer Vincent I. White and cultural visionary Gerald S. DeCosta. Their vision and skill have brought together a compelling symmetry of classic design and African art with historic insight.

Afrantiquity's mission is to create the most distinguished artistic designs of our time, and to give the world insights into the soul of African cultures long past.

Shown here are screens from the *Ashanti* collection.

A   *Gye Nyame,* 62"H x 72$^1/_2$"W x 2"D natural bird's-eye maple with wenge posts, solid brass African mask, 23K finials

B   *Sankofa* screen, water-based dye, bird's-eye maple, wenge posts, etched mirror, 74"H x 84$^1/_2$"W x 2"D,

A

B

Andre Richardson

Kathy Mason-Lerner Studios

Kathy Mason-Lerner
471 Coloma Street
Sausalito, CA 94965
FAX 415-381-4101
TEL 415-332-6148

Impressionist scenes by artist Kathy Mason-Lerner are painted in sumptuous colors on birch burl panels edged with black walnut, making portable, harmonious decorative ensembles.

Each panel is hand painted with archival quality oils — no two are alike — embellished with metallic leaf, then covered with multiple layers of amber varnish. The panels will become antique-crackled with age, made in the tradition of the Old Masters, using techniques that have withstood the test of time. Each screen is a treasured work of original, signed art, and delivery is eight to ten weeks.

Custom colors, scenes and dimensions can be chosen in consultation with the artist to compliment any decor.

A *Lascaux Fireplace Screen*, 1995, 30"H x 48"W

B *Waterlilies*, 1995, 72" H x 60"W

A   Kim Stringfellow

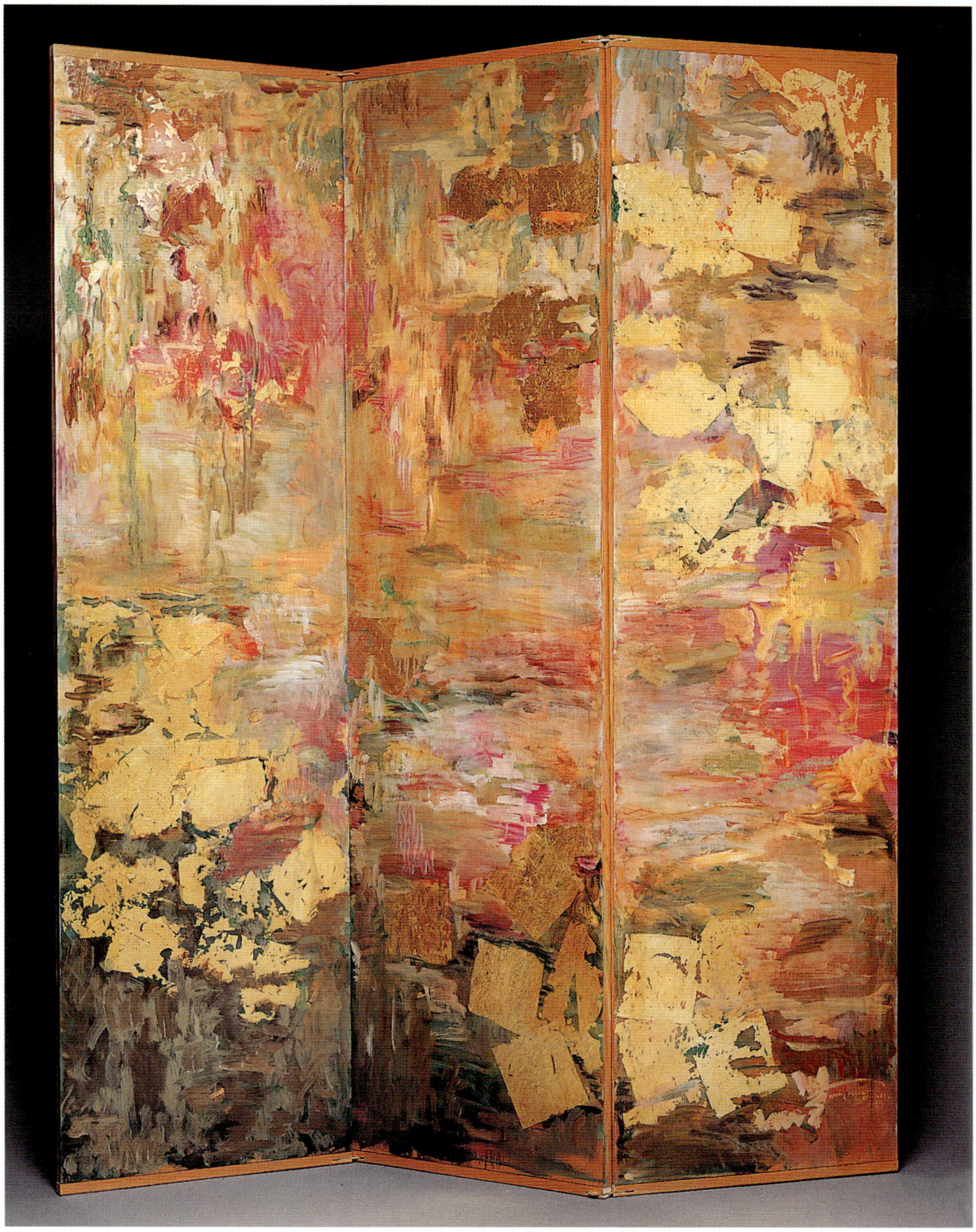

B   Waldo Bascom

Roger Sandes

Grimes Hill Road
Williamsville, VT 05362
TEL   802-348-7865

The jewel-like colors and sprightly detail of the screens of Roger Sandes are as meticulously executed as those in Persian miniatures, yet his style is contemporary and unique.

For 25 years, Sandes has produced original works on nature-based themes for private and corporate collections. These screens feature light-fast acrylic pigments on gessoed panels that are both sturdy and light. Layers of clear acrylic varnish enhance colors and durability, while double-action hinges multiply possible configurations. Reverse sides of simple geometry contrast with the richly patterned fronts to provide additional uses.

Commissions are welcome. Information on screens and site-specific folding triptychs is available on request.

Kingfisher Screen (back), 72" x 48"

Reef Screen (back), 72" x 54"

Kingfisher Screen (front), 72" x 48"

Reef Screen (front), 72" x 54"

Photos: George Leisey, Bellows Falls, VT

Elizabeth Van Riper

Van Riper Designs
1411 East Campbell Road #700
Richardson, TX 75081
FAX 214-470-9268
TEL 214-783-2525

Fresh, sophisticated and whimsical best describe the art furnishings created by Elizabeth Van Riper. A legacy of four generations of female artists precedes Elizabeth into the fine arts. Her unusual heritage and experiences have culminated in the formation of Van Riper Designs.

Elizabeth's decorative and functional art furnishings are inspired by the creative extravagance of nature's flora and fauna. Room divider and fireplace screens, tables, chests, headboards and boxes, as well as custom works, all share a unique artistic interpretation of the natural world. A strong sense of color and style has helped Elizabeth build successful relationships with galleries, museums, designers and clients.

A single Van Riper work stands out as a conversation piece, while complementary elements can create an entire vignette. All major works are signed and numbered.

Photos: Monty Swift, Dallas, TX

ACCESSORIES

LIGHTSPANN
Illumination Design

Christina Spann
5753 Landregan Street
Emeryville, CA 94608
FAX 510-601-8500
TEL 510-601-8500

Christina Spann, owner of LIGHTSPANN, designs and produces fixtures and architectural glass for world-renowned restaurants, residences, and art in public places programs. Projects include work for Kuleto restaurants, Robin Williams, and the San Francisco Federal Building. Ms. Spann received a B.F.A. in art from Arizona State University and completed graduate studies in art at the University of California, Santa Barbara. LIGHTSPANN has been awarded and published nationally.

The work emphasizes glass, but also incorporates metal and painted surfaces. Glass treatments include: cast, slumped, blown, fused and painted. Metal treatments include: forged, brushed patinas, and distressed surfaces.

Studio visits are welcome and prices start at $350. Call for a complete profile and representative projects listing.

Also see this GUILD publication:
Designer's Edition:10

A Custom cuckoo-style pendant, Gary Patrick Salon

B Fused, slumped painted glass sconces, Bolero Restaurant

C Blown-glass table lamp, Bighorn Restaurant

A

Michael Bruk

B

John Sutton

C

Michael Bruk

Printed in Hong Kong ©1996 THE GUILD: The Designer's Sourcebook

Angelika Traylor

100 Poinciana Drive
Indian Harbour Beach, FL 32937
FAX 407-779-3612
TEL 407-773-7640

Featuring one-of-a-kind lamps, autonomous panels and architectural installations, Traylor's award-winning work can be recognized by its intricate, jewel-like composition.

Often referred to as having painterly qualities, the exquisite lamp and charming autonomous panel (shown) reflect an original and intensive design process, implemented with meticulous craftsmanship and an unusually beautiful selection of glass.

Traylor's attention to detail and vibrant colors have resulted in her work being eagerly sought by collectors.

Her work can be found in many publications. Traylor is listed in *Who's Who in America, Who's Who in American Art, Who's Who in American Crafts* and *Who's Who in Contemporary Glass Art.*

Please inquire for more specific information on available work, commissions and pricing.

Also see these GUILD publications:
THE GUILD: 2, 3, 4, 5
Designer's Edition: 7. 8. 9, 10
Architect's Edition: 6

Ron Constantino

Randall Smith

Cleopatra Steps Out

Kate Mellina and Dave Christopher
721 Cookman Avenue
Asbury Park, NJ 07712
TEL 908-774-6306

Fiber artist Kate Mellina has long been drawn by ancient images: the mystery and sophistication of cave paintings; the grace and vitality of ancient Crete; the spirals, whorls and triangles that magically unite cultures and generations.

Now, Kate and artisan/husband Dave Christopher honor these images in *Ancient Icons,* a luxurious collection of hand-tufted wool rugs. Lovingly crafted of high-quality yarns, these dense, cut- and looped-pile rugs are destined to last a lifetime.

Please call for additional styles and price information. Colors and designs can be customized. Our 20th century rug series and artists' rug series are also available.

A *Emergence,* hand-tufted wool rug; color and size can vary

B *Ancestral Memories,* hand-tufted wool rug; color and size can vary

A

B

Photos: Bob Bowné, Neptune, NJ

Jennifer Mackey

CHIA JEN Studio
PO Box 469
Scotia, CA 95565
FAX 707-764-2505
TEL 707-444-6507
TEL 707-764-5877
E-Mail: suziraz@aol.com

Jennifer Mackey produces a high-quality custom line of fabrics for residential and commercial environments. Her use of color is whimsical, delightful and refreshing, with full respect given to use of negative space. This spontaneous approach to design is a Mackey trademark.

All work uses imported and domestic silks, linens and cottons, with frequent use of jacquards and damasks for more texture and depth. She is also known for combining organic and metallic materials for public installations. All materials are environmentally sensitive. The work is always a clever balance of traditional and contemporary elements.

Private and public commissions are encouraged. Completed works are also available. Additional information upon request.

Also see this GUILD publication:
Designer's Edition: 6

A Series of custom upholstery fabrics

B *Cleary* chair with domestic cotton jacquards

A

B

Photos: Scott Chaney

Shawn Athari

Shawn Athari's, Inc.
14332 Mulholland Drive
Los Angeles, CA 90077
FAX 818-787-MASK
TEL 310-476-0066
E-Mail: Glassmaker@aol.com

Shawn Athari's 22 years of experience has given her the opportunity to perfect a variety of glass techniques. The combination of these techniques results in glass sculptures unique in her field. Athari has created a chronology of work depicting an ever-changing evolution of both her skills and techniques. Shawn uses hot glass methods of reforming glass and then layers the individual pieces, melts them together and shapes them.

Most pieces are inspired by images from hisory. The masks pictured on this page are all representative of Pacific Northwest images.

See additional work in the *Work for the Wall* section of this book.

Galleries include:
The Art of Disney, Walt Disney World, FL
Little Switzerland, Alaska and the Caribbean
Neiman Marcus, various cities
Symmetry, Saratoga Springs, NY
Mindscape, Evanston, IL

A *Portrait Mask* (left), *Bear Mask* (right)

B *Wolf Mask* (left), *Wild Man Mask* (center),
Bear Claw Rattle (right)

A

B

Jan D. Gjaltema

3617 A Fairmount Street
Dallas, TX 75219
FAX 214-522-1261
TEL 214-220-3776

Influenced by his education and experience in architecture, Dutch-born Jan D. Gjaltema (1951) produces a most varied and distinctive collection of glass.

After a successful 15-year career in architecture and jewelry design, he has turned his attention and talents to glass.

Jan D. does not show his work at any craft or trade show in the U.S. or abroad, and his work is not sold through representatives. Serious inquiries by mail only.

A Vessel forms, left: 17^1/$_2$" x 4^1/$_2$"; center: 20^1/$_2$" x 7"; right: 13" x 5^1/$_2$"

B Conical vessels, left: 10^1/$_2$" x 8^1/$_4$"; right: 15^1/$_2$" x 8^3/$_4$"

A

B

Deborah Goldhaft

Fire & Ice Glass Studio
11933 SW Cove Road/POB 2292
Vashon Island, WA 98070
TEL   206-463-3601
E-Mail: fireice@wolfenet.com

Deborah Goldhaft's unique glass design work reflects her varied life experience. She incorporates elements of anthropology, Tai Chi, geometric design and Feng Shuei into all her work. Universal archetypes are her aim. Fifteen years experience in glass art gives Deborah's work an extremely three-dimensional and visually satisfying feel.

Goldhaft offers custom-designed art glass for the designer or architect who requires a unique and personal touch. Her specialties are double-sided deep carving and innovative uses of etched mirror. She creates windows and tabletops, as well as standing and sculptural pieces. Gallery work is also available.

The artist welcomes commissions and enjoys working personally with clients. Price list, slides and brochure available on request.

A *Ancient Oryx,* bathroom window, carved plate glass, 6' x 4'

B *After the Ice Age,* sculpture/table prototype, carved glass, 12" x 12" x 12"

A

B

Photos: © Springate Photography

Printed in Hong Kong ©1996 THE GUILD: The Designer's Sourcebook

Michele Savelle

707 South Snoqualmie Street #1A
Seattle, WA 98108
TEL 206-233-0433

Michele Savelle has been working with fused and slumped glass for 15 years. She studied at Pilchuck Glass School and teaches in the Seattle area. Her work is included in corporate and private collections in the United States and abroad.

Works are designed to accent and enliven diverse spaces. Concerns of scale, imagery, price and presentation are tailored to each project on an individual basis.

Also see these GUILD publications:
Gallery Edition: 1, 2

A Bowl, 6"H x 16"Dia

B Free-standing panel, modular units for architectural applications, 22"W x 65"H

A

B

Photos: Jon Savelle

Charles Smith

1410 Melrose Street
Mobile, AL 36605
TEL 334-432-3705

While the size and shape of each piece is unique, it is the hand-carved surface designs that distinguish a Charles Smith pot. Each one, crafted in cone 7 stoneware with a carve-and-sgraffito technique, is laced with Smith's own creative experiments derived from curvilinear Art Nouveau forms, mixed and interspersed with abstract animal imagery. These are the shapes and patterns of nature, and unless Mother Nature finds it necessary to rediscover herself, Smith will remain content following her lead.

Smith's work has appeared in *American Craft, Ceramics Monthly, The International Review of African-American Art* and other national magazines. It ranges in price from $200 to $1,500.

Slides, photos, and pricing available on request. Work averages 6 to 12 weeks to completion.

A Tri-color vessel, 18"H x 9$\frac{1}{2}$"W

B Figure vessel, 15$\frac{1}{2}$"H x 9$\frac{1}{2}$"W

C Tri-color vessel, 16"H x 8$\frac{1}{2}$"W

A

B

C

Printed in Hong Kong ©1996 THE GUILD: The Designer's Sourcebook

Trent Tally

Terra Studios Inc.
12103 Hazel Valley Road
Fayetteville, AR 72701
FAX 501-643-3356
TEL 501-643-3314

Trent Tally produces one-of-a-kind works of art in high-fire stoneware and raku. Combining influences from primitive, ancient and modern cultures, he creates work that reinforces the human experience and enhances our environment.

Specializing in both two- and three-dimensional art, Trent offers designers a wide range of options for interior, as well as exterior, spaces. Work may be selected from current inventory or designed in collaboration with the client. More information available upon request.

Also see these GUILD publications:
Architect's Edition: 11
Gallery Edition: 3

A Artist with big pot commission in progress, 1995, high-fire stoneware to 30" W x 50"H

B Lidded urn, 1995, high-fire stoneware, 18"W x 48"H

C Clay vessel, 1995, raku fired, 12"W x 11"H

D Thomas Hart Benton study, 1995, high-fire stoneware tiles, 4'W x 8'H

A

B

C

D

Juhlin Sculpture Studio

Jean Juhlin
764 North 400 East
Valparaiso, IN 46383
TEL 219-464-0167

Juhlin Sculpture Studio was established in 1965. The award-winning sculpture created there is represented in corporations, libraries, schools and churches, as well as private collections internationally.

Jean works in bronze and casts her sculpture in editions generally limited to 10 or 25. When she is not working in her studio, she is — and has been for 30 years — teaching workshops in sculpture technique across the country.

If you are seeking to enhance a corporate or residential environment, call for a brochure of current sculpture and a price list.

Various patinas available.

A *Together*, 13"H x 12"W

B *Turning Point*, from the *Bearback Rider* series, 14"H x 10"W

C *Friends*, 18"H x 14"W

D *Pueblo Market Woman*, 14"H x 13"W

E *Mystic Journey*, 15"H x 16"W

A

C

D

B

E

Printed in Hong Kong ©1996 THE GUILD: The Designer's Sourcebook

Paul Knoblauch

45 Beacon Street
Rochester, NY 14607
TEL 716-442-3381

Paul creates functional art utilizing metal, glass and wood. While constantly involved with producing new work, he also enjoys the challenges commissions bring.

A, B, C Door knockers, 12"

D Bed, 84"

E Bench, 48"

F Sculptures, 108"

G Chandelier, 120"

A

B

C

D

E

F

G

Photos: Bruce Miller

Sturman Steel Sculptures

Martin Sturman
416 Cricketfield Court
Westlake Village, CA 91361
FAX 805-381-1116
TEL 805-381-0032

Martin Sturman creates original steel sculptures in floral, figurative and abstract designs.

Sculptures range from tabletop to free-standing indoor and outdoor pieces, including sculpted tables and entry gates. These beautiful sculptures are executed in stainless steel, weathered (rusted) steel, powder-coated carbon steel and acrylic-painted carbon steel.

Martin frequently has sculptures available for immediate delivery, but encourages site-specific and collaborative efforts. Depending upon complexity, most sculptures can be shipped within 10 to 12 weeks of commission.

Sizes range from 12 inches to 10 feet high. Prices upon request.

Also see these GUILD publications:
Designer's Edition: 7, 8, 9, 10

Room divider screen, 1995, stainless steel, 70"H x 48"W x 1/8"D

Standing Flowers, 1995, acrylic and steel, 70"H x 34"W x 20"D

Gate, 1995, enamel and steel, 48"H x 60"W x 2"D

Photos: Barry Michlin

Arlene Waxman

29377 Cliffside Drive
Malibu, CA 90265
FAX 310-457-7267
TEL 310-457-3150

Like an alchemist, Arlene Waxman magically transforms heavy, awkward, forgotten steel leftovers into whimsical, lyrical three-dimensional drawings in space. Working with a variety of industrial objects, Waxman's skillful hands assemble the pieces with the ease of a child's tinker toy set.

Most of her current work is constructed from found steel and metal objects collected from properties destroyed in the 1993 Malibu Firestorm. Using high-gloss automotive paints, Waxman transforms everything from structural steel to spatulas into vibrant and resilient sculptures, durable for display indoors or outdoors. Waxman's sculptures appear spontaneous and are filled with a real *joie de vivre*.

Slides, pricing and scheduling upon request.

Firestorm Flower #3, © 1994, painted steel, 71" x 72" x 81"   Ed Glendinning

Gears, Blades & Fan, © 1990,   Sara Kapilevsky
painted steel, 72" x 66" x 20"

Legacy group shot, © 1990   Sara Kapilevsky

Alonzo Davis

2080 Peabody Avenue
Memphis, TN 38104-4237
FAX 901-276-0660
TEL 901-276-9070
E-Mail: ArtAlonzo@aol.com

These highly-textured tar paper shapes are choreographed on the wall with small fetishes and power poles placed at intervals within the space, thus creating a stratosphere of objects in flight, or dancing on air currents.

Layered with color, the shapes are also patterned with designs that have been carved or burned into the surface and which play out as woodcuts. Fetishes and poles are embellished with paint and liquid plastic, then wrapped with twine, leather and tape, and ornamented with stones, feathers, beads and found objects.

SHOWN: *Scatterseed*, wall installation, acrylic on tar paper/mixed media, 96"H x 84"W x 36"D

Hud Andrews Photographer

Mari Marks Fleming

1431 Glendale Avenue
Berkeley, CA 94708-2027
FAX 510-548-3121
TEL 510-548-3121
E-Mail: 102202.3345@compuserve.com

Mari Marks Fleming creates sculptures and wall reliefs using a rich interplay of natural texture and complex pigmented surfaces.

Sculptural houses incorporate burned or distressed elements combined with textures and living plants that convey life.

Wall pieces are composed of paintings on board, using oil and beeswax to form beautiful color and texture. The opening 'doors,' made up of fiber, metals and laminated elements, emphasize the physical and conceptual relationship of doors to paintings. Modules can be constructed in varying sizes or combined to create large installations.

Mari has exhibited nationally for over 25 years. Her wall reliefs and sculpture have been installed in public spaces, universities, museums and private collections. Commissions involving collaboration with architects are welcome. Prices reflect size and complexity.

Also see this GUILD publication:
Designer's Edition: 10

A *Childhood's Shrine,* 14" x 12" x 14"

B *Reliquary XIV,* 20" x 38" x 3" (open),
   20" x 20" x 4" (closed)

A

B

Photos: Kim Harrington

Tim Walker

Pop Cat Studio
28277 Townley
Madison Heights, MI 48071-2846
FAX 810-543-1942
TEL 810-543-1942

Artist Tim Walker creates extraordinary two- and three-dimensional mixed media sculptures that are humorous and refreshing in attitude. Sophisticated in style, satirical in content, and clever in approach, Tim's sculptures express his unique perception of the human condition.

Tim incorporates many technical innovations to achieve archival longevity, internal and external strength, and surface smoothness, and has chosen to draw inspiration from many different sculptural mediums. The result is a hybrid approach to his craft.

The goal is to redefine the medium and to put a whimsical spin on life.

Commissions are accepted.

Portfolio available upon request.

A *Billionaire's Prayer,* 1994, mixed media, 40" x 33" x 19 1/2"

B *The Healthy Jogger,* 1994, mixed media, 47" x 47" x 7"

C *Luciano Pavarotti,* 1994, mixed media, 55" x 60" x 9"

A

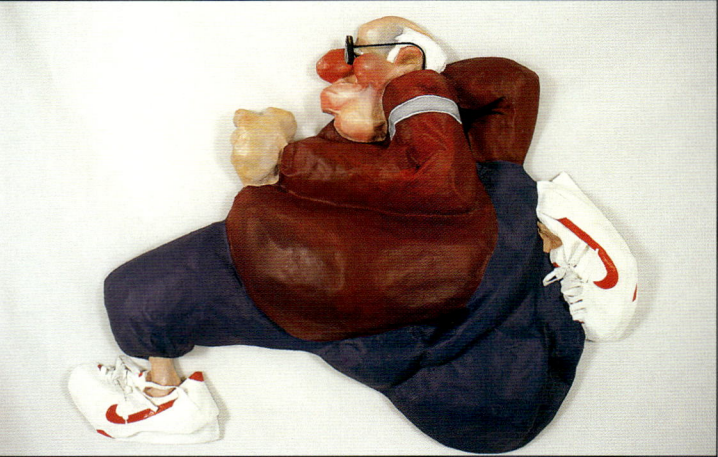

B

C

Zelda Wolock Werner

Z.W. Werner Studio
927 Noyes Street
Evanston, IL 60201
TEL 708-475-1910

Zelda Werner has created for herself a unique place in the world of contemporary sculpture.

Her 35 years of experience with acrylic has taught her great respect for this formidable, pristine material. Because of this, she has been able to venture into complex and innovative techniques, including laser-cutting.

All of her work is commissioned, and there are no editions. She exhibited 12 iconic figures, each eight feet tall, by invitation at *Expo '88* in Brisbane, Australia.

Commissions include:
Capitol Commons Plaza (12 light sculptures, 8')
Winnetka Public Library, Winnetka, IL (*Hi-Tech Tapestry*, 48" x 72" x 3")
Ravinia Music Festival, Highland Park, IL (massive ten-panel sculpture with internal ellipses)
Borg-Warner Corporation
K.P.M.G. Peat Marwick
First National Bank of Chicago
State of Illinois collection

A *Hi-Tech Tapestry,* sandblasted acrylic, 48" x 72" x 3"

B *Pillar of a Thousand Delights,* acrylic, 8' x 8" x 8"

A   Ron Testa

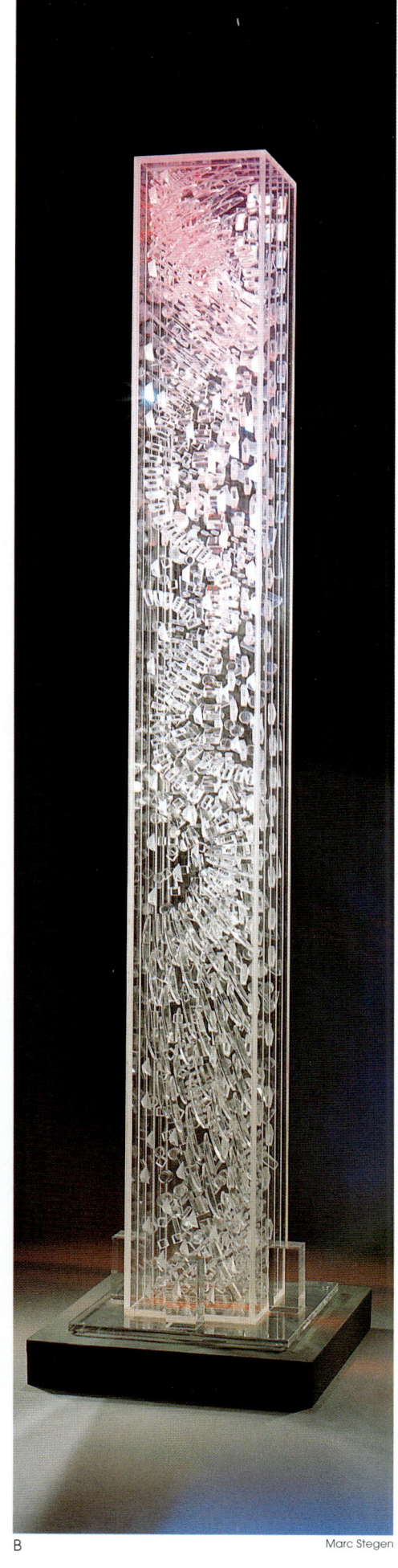

B   Marc Stegen

ART FOR THE WALL

Academy of Portrait & Genre Painters

Columbine Gallery
2683 North Taft Avenue
Loveland, CO 80538
FAX 970-667-2068
TEL 970-667-2015
TEL 800-606-2015

Painters

James Biggers
Linda Cheedle
Charles Cross
Douglas Erion
Cathy Goodale
Lu Haskew
Pat Howard
Liz Todd
Ellie Weakley

Working in oils and watercolor, the painters of the Academy welcome commissions of single or multiple portraits, vignettes of the patron's decorative collections, landscapes — including homes — or combinations of the above.

The experienced painters of the Academy provide varying styles and prices to meet the needs of the client. An initial visit will be made to the patron's residence by the artist to compose the concept for the patron's approval.

Members of the Academy can create a specific, detailed portrait or have it complemented by a requested theme, ambiance or venue.

A Female genre portrait, watercolor, by Cathy Goodale

B Male portrait, oil, by James Biggers

A

B

Leonard Baron

3320 Quebec Place NW
Washington, DC 20008
FAX 202-363-3767
TEL 202-362-5905

Leonard Baron specializes in three-dimensional constructions and large color-field paintings. He has exhibited in one- and two-person shows in Switzerland, Michigan, New York and Washington. The work is in private and corporate collections in the U.S. and abroad.

The paintings are composed of a myriad of brightly colored lines evoking the sensual movement of light within nature. This unique linear style of painting is produced in mediums of both oil and acrylic. Clients as diverse as Chemical Bank, W.B. Doner Advertising and Hotel Kulm in Switzerland are excited by the rich color, texture and pure energy of the work. A complete portfolio of constructions and paintings is available. Commissions are welcomed.

A *Lorelei*, acrylic on canvas, 5' x 5'

B *Caribbean Night*, acrylic on canvas, 5' x 5'

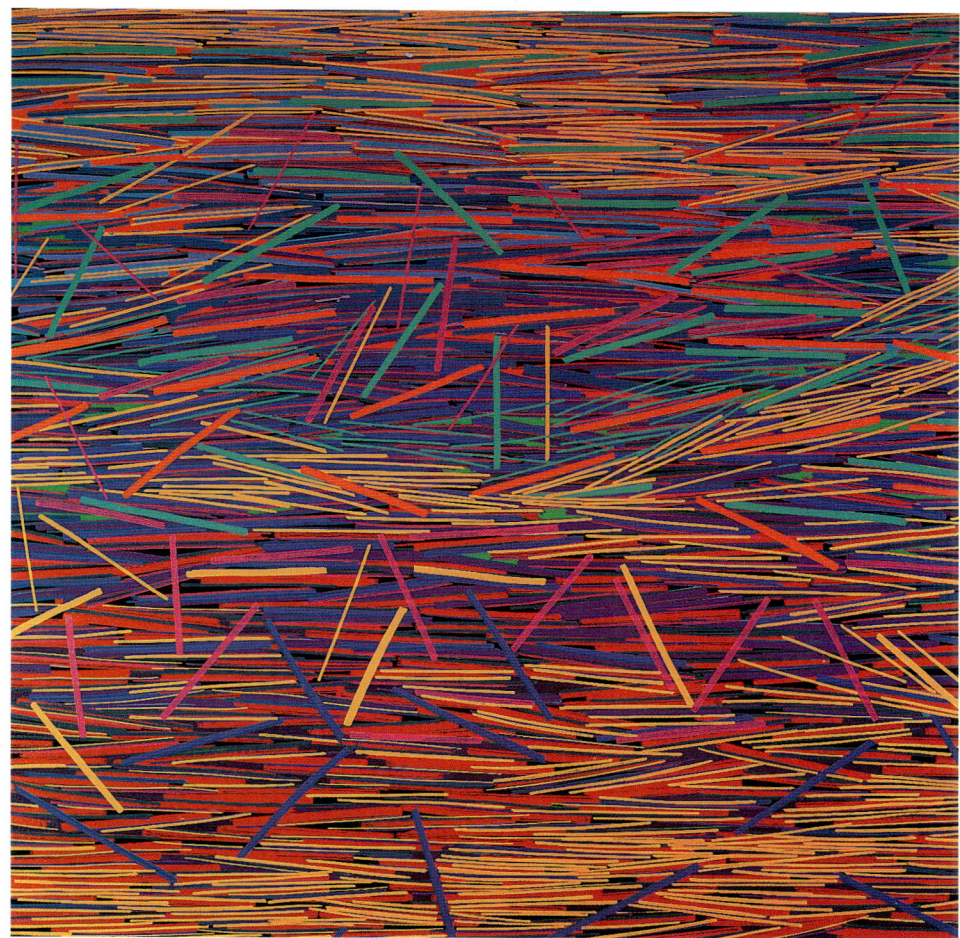

A

B

Rita Blitt

Rita Blitt Inc.
8900 State Line Road, Suite 333
Leawood, KS 66206
FAX 913-381-5624
TEL 913-381-3840

"Rita Blitt's paintings are reflective on both a visual and intellectual level, inviting the viewer to share in their simple beauty."

Program notes
Atlanta Ballet's Dance Technology Project —1996
An arts-meets-science collaboration with the
Georgia Institute of Technology

Blitt's paintings and sculptures have been exhibited in Israel, Singapore, Germany and throughout the United States. She was recently honored with a retrospective at the Kennedy Museum of American Art, Ohio University.

Ms. Blitts's work is permanently installed in many public places and collected by private collectors, institutions and museums. She is listed in *Who's Who of American Women.*

SHOWN: *The Nature Suite,* six paintings on paper, each 30" x 22"

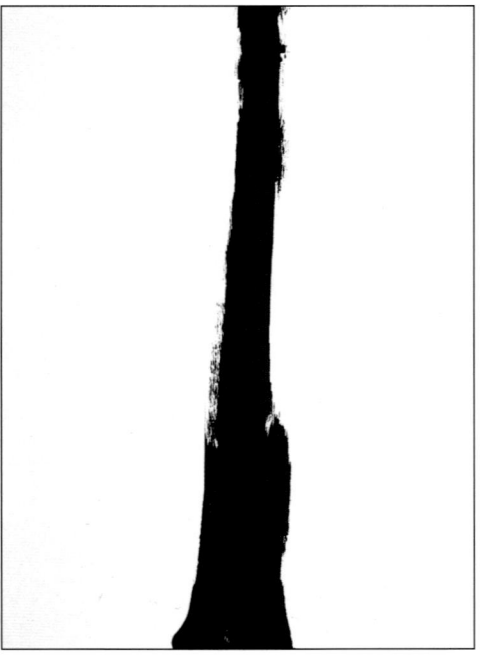

Printed in Hong Kong ©1996 THE GUILD: The Designer's Sourcebook

Brigitte Benzakin

424 3rd Street
East Greenville, PA 18041
TEL   215-541-4238

Brigitte Benzakin creates hand-painted wooden panels and folding screens inspired by the natural environment and mythology — and recast with fanciful innovation.

Each panel is painted with acrylic on wood and sealed with polyurethane.

Her work has appeared in Bloomingdale's, juried art shows, and selective galleries. Commissions are welcomed.

Also see this GUILD publication:
Designer's Edition: 10

A *Summer Time,* 32" x 23"

B *Cornfields,* 23" x 58"

A

B

Photos: Jeff Reeder

Carolyn Blakeslee

Tangier Sound Studios
PO Box 320-G
Upper Fairmount, MD 21867
FAX 410-651-5313
TEL 410-651-0281

Carolyn Blakeslee works realistically in oils.

"My passion is to celebrate the beauty and power of Life in my paintings of flowers and other beautiful subjects. I go for drama, force, and interest — I want each silent subject to tell a huge, dynamic, nearly abstract story."

All work is archival, framed and guaranteed. Sizes range from 11" x 14" to 48" x 72". Retail prices range from $775 to $17,250. Commissions, dealer inquiries, and studio tour appointments are welcome. Catalog, video, brochure, slides and transparencies are available.

Also see this GUILD publication:
Designer's Edition: 10

This page:

A *Domino Effect* (detail), 30" x 30"

B *Crucifix*, 30" x 30"

Facing page:

A *Morning Glory, Night Mood*, 36" x 30"

B *The Twelve*, 30" x 22"

C *The Silent Scream*, 20" x 16"

D *Poker Face*, 36" x 24"

A

B

A

B

C Carolyn Blakeslee, Tangier Sound Studios, PO Box 320-G,
  Upper Fairmount, MD 21867, FAX 410-651-5313, TEL 410-651-0281

D

Veronica Escudero

4201 West Union Hills Drive, #3091
Glendale, AZ 85308
TEL   602-843-8634

Veronica Escudero's art is imaginative; it is a rendering of her conscious mind and unveiling of an internal cry. She does not perceive what the outcome will be until the work has been half executed. Only then is her heart revealed.

Escudero has had various solo exhibitions (NYC), and her work has been included in national and international juried shows. She works with acrylic and oil pastel on paper. Prices of her original art range from $300 to $700.

Slides and pricing available upon request.

A *Devotion*, 1994, oil pastel, acrylic, 22" x 30"

B *Holy, Holy, Holy…*, 1995, acrylic, 22" x 30"

A

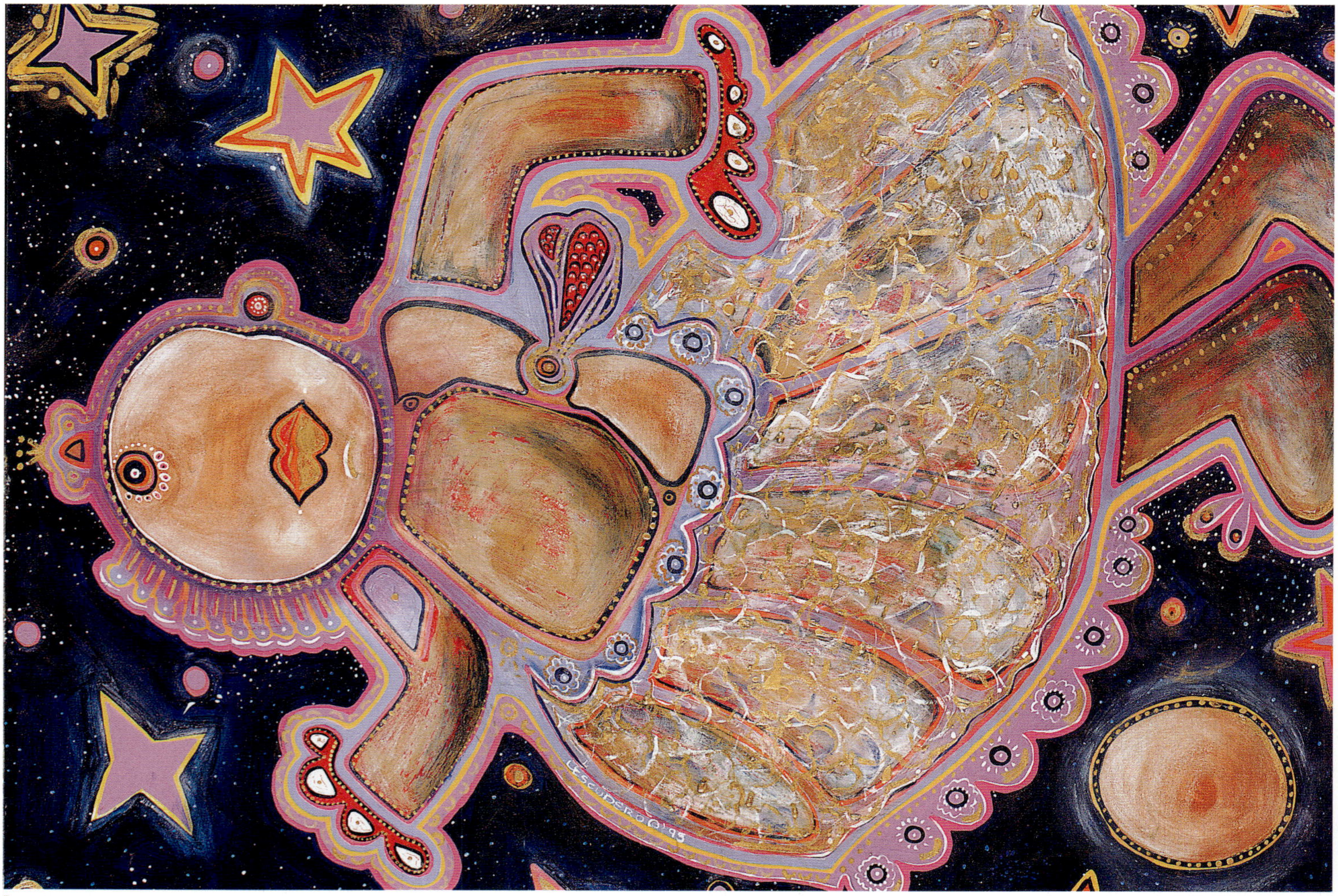

B

Yoshi Hayashi

255 Kansas Street #330
San Francisco, CA 94103
TEL 415-552-0755

Yoshi Hayashi's designs range from very traditional 17th century Japanese lacquer art themes that are delicate with intricate detail to those that are boldly geometric and contemporary. By skillfully applying metallic leaf and bronzing powders, he adds illumination and contrast to the network of color, pattern and texture. His original designs include screens, wall panels, furniture and decorative objects.

Hayashi's pieces have been commissioned for private collections, hotels, restaurants and offices in the United States and Japan. Prices upon request.

Also see these GUILD publications:
THE GUILD: 3, 4, 5
Designer's Edition: 6, 7, 8, 9, 10

A *Early Spring*, 36" x 96"

B *Autumn*, 36" x 72"

A

B

Photos: Ira D. Schrank

ANN AYRES

Corporate Art Advisor

Ann Ayres, a Chicago corporate-art adviser and partner in Ayres-Steinmetz Ltd., has built her business with a careful mix of aggressive marketing, clear thoughtful communication, and an intuitive creativity that helps her understand, define and obtain the kind of work her clients require. Many of her clients are financial institutions or large healthcare providers, and they expect a very systematic approach, she explains. This is certainly true when they are contemplating the purchase or commissioning of highly creative art.

"I think the key to building a successful partnership with my clients, as well as with the artists we use, is an emphasis on clear communication," she says. For this reason, she has found working with GUILD artists particularly satisfying. "I recently had the opportunity to commission a wonderful sculptural wall-piece — a large triptych — from paper and mixed-media artist Martha Chatelain. Martha presented the client with a well-organized approach to the project, and helped to provide a clear, step-by-step explanation of how the commission process moves from preliminary sketches to finished product. She helped make sure there were no unanswered questions, which is, of course, crucial for everyone's comfort level on a large-budget project."

After Chatelain was chosen for the project, she and Ayres worked closely — not just with each other, but with the client as well — to insure that what began as a series of abstract ideas for the space would become a tangible reality that met all expectations.

"We talked early on with the client about the feel of the piece: 'like a billowing drape,' and about the color: 'like the sky at twilight.' Then I provided Martha with some very specific details, things like room light, dimensions, and how close people would be to the artwork when they look at it," Ayres explains.

Working with that information, Chatelain responded with simple, elegant sketches, plus samples of colors and materials she proposed using for the richly textured wall sculpture. The client was delighted as the piece began to take shape through these tangible items, knowing that the artist understood what was wanted.

The finished piece has been well-received, and the client feels very much a part of its success.

Photo by Robert F. Calnen, Calnen of Canada Ltd.

David Johnson

25 West Princeton Circle
Lynchburg, VA 24503
TEL 804-847-5774
FAX 804-847-1279

David Johnson received his B.F.A. from Montana State University, and his M.F.A. from the University of Wisconsin - Madison. His figurative works on wood are highly textured with carving, and richly layered with oil painting. He has shown in solo and group exhibitions in Alaska, California, the District of Columbia, Florida, Georgia, Indiana, Iowa, New York, Tennessee, Wisconsin and Virginia.

Johnson currently teaches painting, photography and drawing in Virginia. Slides available upon request and commission proposals are welcomed.

A *Awash*, 1995, oil on wood, 32" x 48"

B *Split Earth*, 1995, oil on wood, 48" x 64"

A

B

Pamela Joseph

MA Nose Studios
407 Aspen Oak Drive
Aspen, CO 81611
FAX 970-920-2242
TEL 970-920-4098
TEL 970-920-6820 (Studio)

Flip was commissioned by Henry Schein, Inc., a health care company, for its new international headquarters in New York. This 30-foot drawing was painted with sumi ink and a twig onto two layers of paper: handmade Japanese *Okawara* over industrial Tyvek.

The image is of a running figure that leaps, falls and balances on his hands, then lands back on his feet. The company sees this image as symbolic of its sense of innovation and exploration.

The artist also acted as curator for the corporate collection.

Ms. Joseph is director of MA Nose Studios, Inc., Aspen, Colorado, which is capable of a wide variety of artistic creations, including ceramics, painted tiles, glass, wood, painting, computer graphics and printmaking.

Printed in Hong Kong ©1996 THE GUILD: The Designer's Sourcebook

Pamela Joseph, MA Nose Studios, 407 Aspen Oak Drive, Aspen, CO 81611, FAX 970-920-2242, TEL 970-920-4098, TEL 970-920-6820 (Studio)

James C. Leonard

401 Sutton Circle
Danville, CA 94526
FAX 510-736-5968
TEL 510-736-1399

James C. Leonard is a contemporary abstract artist who lives and works outside of the San Francisco Bay Area. Born in Nashville, Tennessee, James brings a great sense of maturity and depth to his work. James characterizes his work as strong, yet sensitive, expressive, yet structured, complex in scope, yet quiet in interpretation. His work is collected both domestically and internationally.

Please feel free to contact the artist. Slides, photographs and catalogs are available upon request.

A *Deva Bardo,* 1996, acrylic on canvas,
   54" x 54"

B *Window 1942,* 1996, acrylic on canvas,
   35" x 53"

C *Time Lost,* 1996, acrylic on canvas,
   48" x 60"

A

B

C

René Levy

40 Mayflower Drive
Tenafly, NJ 07670
TEL   201-569-3934
FAX 201-569-4670
E-Mail: Butch14@aol.com

René Levy's paintings are lush with texture, patterning and layers of paint, some intense, some subtle. The works show variations of color and texture that are coordinated into an expressionistic unity. The imagery is either landscapes or figurative, mostly representational, some abstract.

Ms. Levy has exhibited her work at the Sylvia White Gallery, Santa Monica, and in national juried exhibitions at the St. John's University Art Gallery, NY; Viridian Gallery, New York, NY; and the Art Center of Northern New Jersey, where she won Best in Show in 1994. She also had a one-woman show at the Taner Gallery, Westwood, NJ.

Slides and prices upon request.

A *Provence,* 1995, oil on canvas,
    56" x 56"

B *Power Broker,* 1994, oil and
    collage on canvas, 42" x 32"

A   Craig Phillips

B   Eric Landsberg

Jacques Lieberman

Magic Art Center
170 Mercer Street #3W
New York, NY 10012-3263
TEL 212-219-0939

The artist creates a delightful orchestration of vibrant limited-edition, hand-signed, numbered prints.

Collections: Europe, Asia, North-Central-South America.

Reviews:

"… adversity to predictability …"
William Zimmer, *Arts Magazine*

"… a tangible work of art …"
Leslie Plummer, *New York Arts Journal*

"… lively play, colors, movement …"
Abraham Ilein, *Westsider*, NY.

"… dynamic colors … music visualization … a cheerful song …"
Nina Ffrench-Frazier, *East Side Express*, NY

Collectors' frequent comment: "Vibrant, much presence."

Prints: 27$\frac{1}{2}$" x 36" (image size: 22$\frac{1}{2}$" x 31") and 48" x 36" (image size: 43" x 31"). Catalog available.

SHOWN: Details of various prints

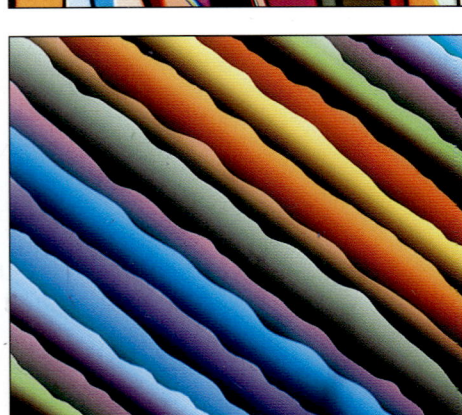

Printed in Hong Kong ©1996 THE GUILD: The Designer's Sourcebook

Ginny Lohr

Greedy for Color—Designs by Ginny Lohr
52 Woodshire North
Getzville, NY 14068
TEL 716-689-4752

Ginny Lohr's designs include lively abstract interpretations of flowers, leaves, and other motifs inspired by nature. Using color to define imagery in a dramatic way, this painter and fiber artist has recently completed commission work based on the themes 'leafscape' and wildflowers.

Designs are available as batiks, using wax resists and fiber reactive dyes hand painted on silk, or as watercolor paintings on archival board. Works are suitable for framing. Pricing begins at $200.

A   Batik (detail),1995, 60" x 15"

B   *Wildflowers,* 1995, watercolor, 40" x 30"

A

Photos: Dorene M. Estrem

Gloria Matuszewski

180 Spring Grove Avenue
San Anselmo, CA 94960
TEL   415-459-5494

Gloria Matuszewski's 'pencil tapestries' are intricately layered drawings ranging from classically rendered sculptures to expressionistic landscapes such as *A Winter Without A Spring*. Quietly textural and complex, the drawings are strongly meditative and peaceful.

A fine-arts graduate from the University of California, Berkeley, Gloria has been doing these drawings for 20 years. They are included in hospital collections, medical and legal offices, and corporations, as well as residential collections.

Slides, pricing and scheduling upon request. Completed works available and commissions welcome.

A   *A Winter Without A Spring*, pencil, sumi ink, 44" x 90"

B   *Paris Sphinx*, pencil, gouache, 44" x 30"

C   *Tapestry*, oil pastel, pencil, 50" x 46"

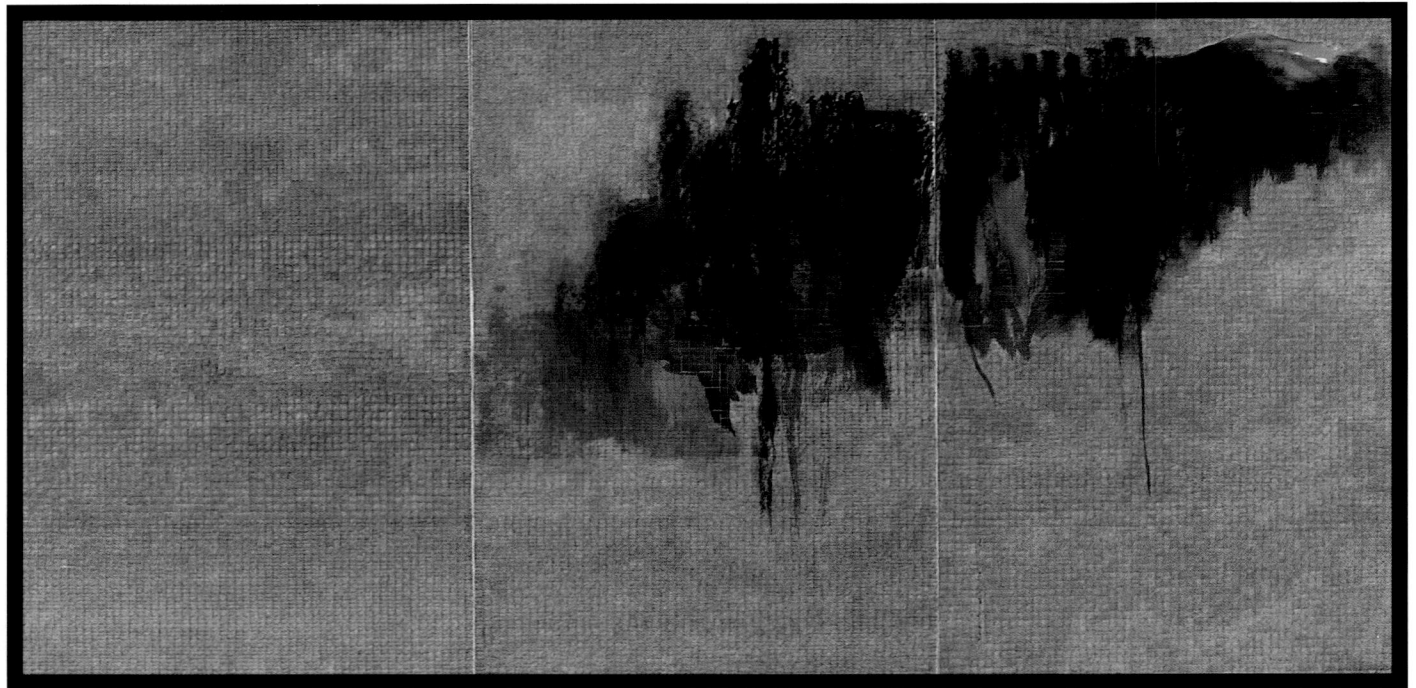

A

B

C

Photos: Jay Daniel Photo

Donna McGinnis

351 Devon Drive
San Rafael, CA 94903
TEL 415-454-4226

Donna McGinnis' brightly colored representational paintings are of common objects from everyday life that have interesting shapes, colors, textures, etc. Her large-scale works make humble objects into heroic portraits. She works with pencils, pastels, watercolors, acrylics and oils. The lightfast watercolors are painted on 100% rag paper.

Donna, an award-winning artist, has worked as a professional in the field for more than 25 years. Selected commissions and collections include the San Francisco Fine Arts Museums, Banco Panamericano in Costa Rica, Lucas Films, Sherwood Hotel in Taiwan, Hilton Hotel in Chicago, Merrill Lynch in Los Angeles, Grand Hyatt Wailea in Maui, and numerous restaurants.

Commissions are welcome. Slides, pricing and other information are available upon request.

A *Sunflowers*, 1996, watercolor,
   29 1/2" x 41"

B *Sweet Red Onions*, 1995.
   watercolor, 60" x 40"

A

B

Photos: Jay Daniel, San Rafael, CA

Saul Polson

40 East 84th Street
New York, NY 10028
TEL 212-861-6957

Saul Polson paints portraits of famous people in a unique contemporary style. This series is called *Legends.*

The artist wants to preserve the memory of people who have made great contributions to society. In addition to portraits shown, he has completed paintings of Shakespeare, Babe Ruth, Benjamin Franklin, Lucille Ball, Golda Meir, Michelangelo, Marilyn Monroe, Einstein, Elvis Presley, Eleanor Roosevelt, Chaplin, Jefferson and Washington. They make fine additions to residential and corporate interiors.

Commissions are welcome and additional information is available on request.

A *Beethoven,* acrylic on canvas, 60" x 64"

B *Lincoln,* acrylic on canvas, 60" x 64"

A

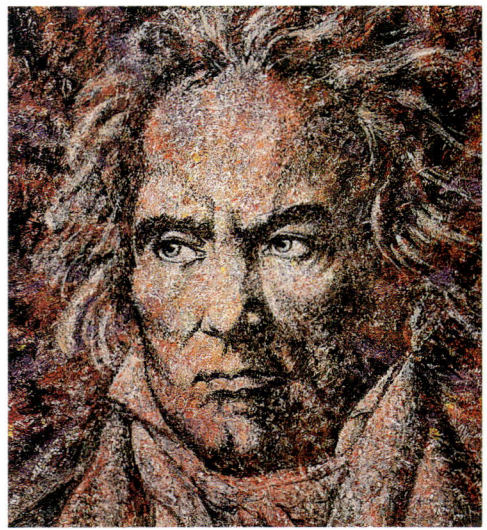

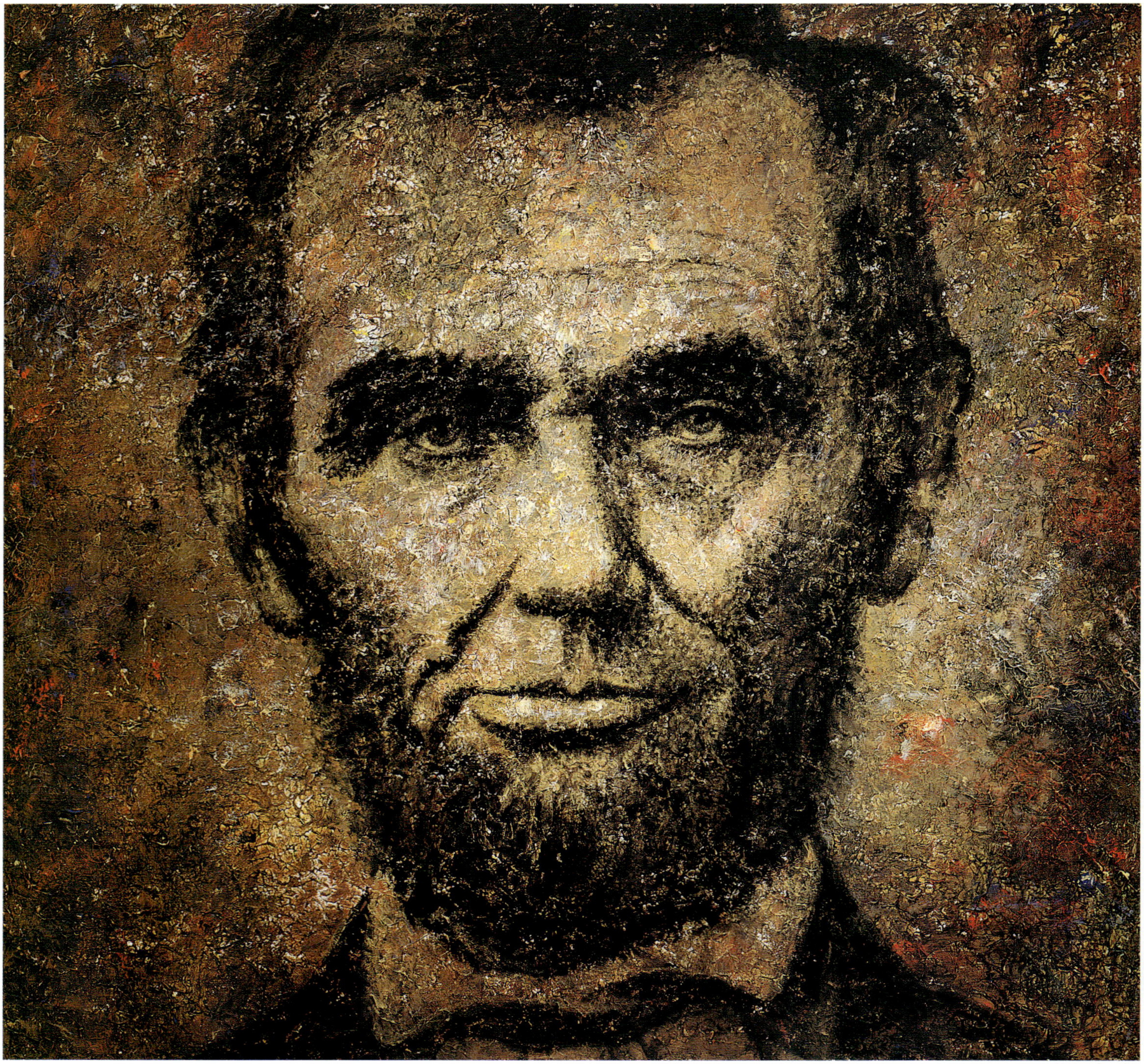

B

Photos: Oren Slor

Barbara Stanley

Painted Traces
PO BOX 2921
San Anselmo, CA 94979
TEL 415-457-5428

Early American colonists used them for carpets. Barbara Stanley paints floorcloths — up to 25 feet wide — to be hung on walls.

Layering rich patinas with iconographic patterns, Barbara creates work that reflects her passion for ancient cultures and her ability to traverse design landscapes ranging from medieval to naturalistic to abstract.

Barbara's painted canvases are lightfast, sealed from moisture and dirt, and easy to install. They are beautiful hung in corporate, public and private settings, and durable enough to place on floors in homes.

Prices range from $1,100 to $15,000.

A *Botanical Tiles,* 6'H x 3'W

B *Copper Oak,* 6'H x 8'W

A

B

Photos: Jay Daniel

Claudia Wagar

Vine Arts Publications and Gallery
301 First Street West
Sonoma, CA 95476
TEL 707-996-7054
E-Mail: Bonnemort@aol.com

Claudia Wagar creates award-winning original paintings of the Wine Country in large and small sizes, watercolors, oils and acrylics. Her corporate murals have received critical recognition, and her prints and notecards are sold throughout the United States. Limited-edition prints of images shown here are available. Commissions welcome.

Also see this GUILD publication:
Architect's Edition: 8

A *Summer Vine*, acrylic, 26" x 25"

B *Cabernet Cluster*, watercolor,
   25" x 24"

C *Blackbirds in a Yellow Spring*,
   watercolor, 18" x 23"

A

B

C

Photos: Custom Image

Mary Boone Wellington

88 Boston Post Road
Amherst, NH 03031
FAX 603-673-2311
TEL 603-673-2311

Mary Boone Wellington has completed numerous commissions for public, private and corporate environments. An expert at working out the final details with architects, designers and owners, she creates a completed work that fulfills aesthetic criteria and expresses the highest vision.

Commissions and collections:
American Embassy, Belise
Bank of Georgia, Atlanta, GA
CocaCola, Salem, NH
Concord Hospital, Concord, NH
Gillette, Boston, MA
Kaiser Medical, San Diego, CA
Kennedy Hotel, Seattle, WA
Kintetsu, Nara, Japan
MCI, Denver, CO
Millipore, Molsheim, France
Plymouth State College, Plymouth, NH
Public Service of Colorado, Denver, CO

Red Lion Inns, Glendale, CA
State of New Hampshire
Union Band, San Diego, CA
Waters Corporation, Milford, MA

A & B *Leaf 1* and *Leaf 2*, oil and gold leaf on canvas, Chevy Chase Federal Savings Bank, Chevy Chase, MD, 24" x 24", liaison: Artists Circle LTD, Potomac, MD

C *Dance*, oil and gold leaf on canvas, Cafe Nuovo, Providence, RI, liaison: Gallery Graphics, Hudson, MA

A

B

C

Mary Alice Wimmer

731 Farwell Drive
Madison, WI 53704
FAX 608-256-3493
TEL 608-241-0821

The large-scale paintings of Mary Alice Wimmer are watercolor still-life works incorporating sensuous organic forms and fabrics, reflecting on surfaces of silver, copper or brass objects. Working primarily on commission, Wimmer may utilize the client's personal pieces in the composition, while also considering individual color and scale specifications.

In addition, Wimmer works in large-scale silverpoint drawing.

A professor of art for over 25 years, Wimmer has been involved in the study of Vanitas still-life painting and the work of Renaissance masters, particularly in Italy. She has exhibited nationally in both juried and invitational shows.

Price range: $9,000 to $20,000.

Slides, scheduling and additional information upon request.

SHOWN: *The Italian Window: Ostia*, first prize, *Watercolor Wisconsin 1995*, 40"H x 60"W

Sharon Yavis

415-B Martha Street
Montgomery, AL 36104
TEL 334-832-9289

Sharon Yavis paints on canvas and half-inch ply-wood which has been cut to form shape-pieces. Her work is figurative and has been described as 'mod-primitive.' It is humorous, whimsical, yet contains the mystery and dignity important in fine art.

Sharon shows in galleries throughout Alabama, and in Atlanta; Richmond; Washington, DC; Hilton Head; Osaka, Japan; and Dania, Florida.

Permanent collections include the Montgomery Museum of Fine Arts, the Parthenon in Nashville, Blount Southern Artist Collection, and Kindercare facilities across the U.S.

Sharon is happy to work with designers to coordinate artwork with a planned decor. Prices on request.

A *Shoppers Five*, 1996, oil on plywood, 48"W

B *Businessmen Five*, 1996, oil on plywood, 48"W

C *Player Pieces*, 1991, oil on canvas, 28"H x 48"W

A

B

C

Photos: Russ Baxley

PHILLIP FRUCHTER

Architect

Architect Philip Fruchter advocates integrating meaningful art into architecture, but cautions that it should be a carefully planned element central to the design, rather than a decorative afterthought.

"We prefer to integrate art into our projects, rather than use it as an appliqué," he explains. This means planning ahead. It also means working with artists who can come into a project early and understand the demands of an architectural construction schedule.

Fruchter, one of three partners at Papp Architects in White Plains, New York, is also a glass artist with a number of sculptural glass installations to his credit. As such, he endorses the use of art within the architectural design.

"I believe a work of architecture is more than just an enclosing shelter, and art and fine crafts can be effectively combined with the design to bring spirit and energy to the project," he says.

Fruchter worked with GUILD artist Katherine Holzknecht on an ambitious three-story, three-building, multi-tenant complex with over 175,000 square feet of space. The design included many long corridors which were created with a series of niches to add visual interest and to provide a space suited to original artwork. Fruchter's firm approached Holzknecht based on her work shown in THE GUILD.

"When she provided portfolio materials, it was clear she had the vision, quality and craftsmanship we were looking for," he says. The artist created a series of five related sculptural pieces using a natural wood grid, brightly colored dowels, raw aluminum sheets and woven wire. Collectively titled *Symbiosis*, the pieces were produced and delivered on schedule, and remain highly respected works of art several years after installation.

"At the time we began working with Katherine, some people questioned whether it was prudent to work with an artist in Washington state when our project was located in New York. That proved to be no problem, however. She was very business-like, and extremely sensitive to commercial construction demands and architectural schedules. We accomplished what we had in mind; we were pleased and the client was pleased."

Photo by George E. Peirce

Cheryl Parsons Designs

6740 Southwest 117th Street
Miami, FL 33156
FAX 305-663-4737
TEL 305-663-3232
E-Mail: CParsons1@aol.com

Imagination, Creativity, Style.

At Cheryl Parsons Designs, fine artists/designers specialize in corporate and residential murals, trompe l'oeil paintings and faux finishes.

Artistic murals are produced on canvas for simple shipping and installation anywhere. Featured below is the Burger King World Headquarters reception area, 50 feet x 12 feet, in oil and acrylic on canvas. Also shown is a residential entrance trompe l'oeil, 15 feet x 8 feet, in acrylic.

Custom, finely painted still lifes, landscapes, and trompe l'oeil framed paintings are available in client-requested styles and sizes.

Fabulous faux inlay wood grains are shown in the tabletop featured below. CPD manufactures customized sizes in faux tabletop styles, including mosaics, inlays, crackle, stencil and trompe l'oeil.

Clients include interior design firms, architects, homeowners and corporations, including Burger King World Headquarters, Spec's Music Stores, and Sunglass Huts International.

References and photos available.

A

B

C

John J. DeVlieger

John J. DeVlieger, Artist
3914 Cedar Lane
Drexel Hill, PA 19026
TEL 215-232-8073 (Philadelphia)
TEL 610-446-2115 (Drexel Hill)

John DeVlieger's technical acumen extends effortlessly from figures to marble to tapestries and beyond. John breathes life into his trompe l'oeil murals with his vibrant sense of color and his mastery of light.

DeVlieger's murals and paintings grace many private estates and commercial establishments throughout North America and abroad. John welcomes commissions, finding that collaboration adds a dynamic and intriguing dimension to his work. Commissions are available as on-site creations or as works on canvas to be installed.

A *Fountainhead,* 8' x 10'

B *Primavera,* 45' x 20'

A

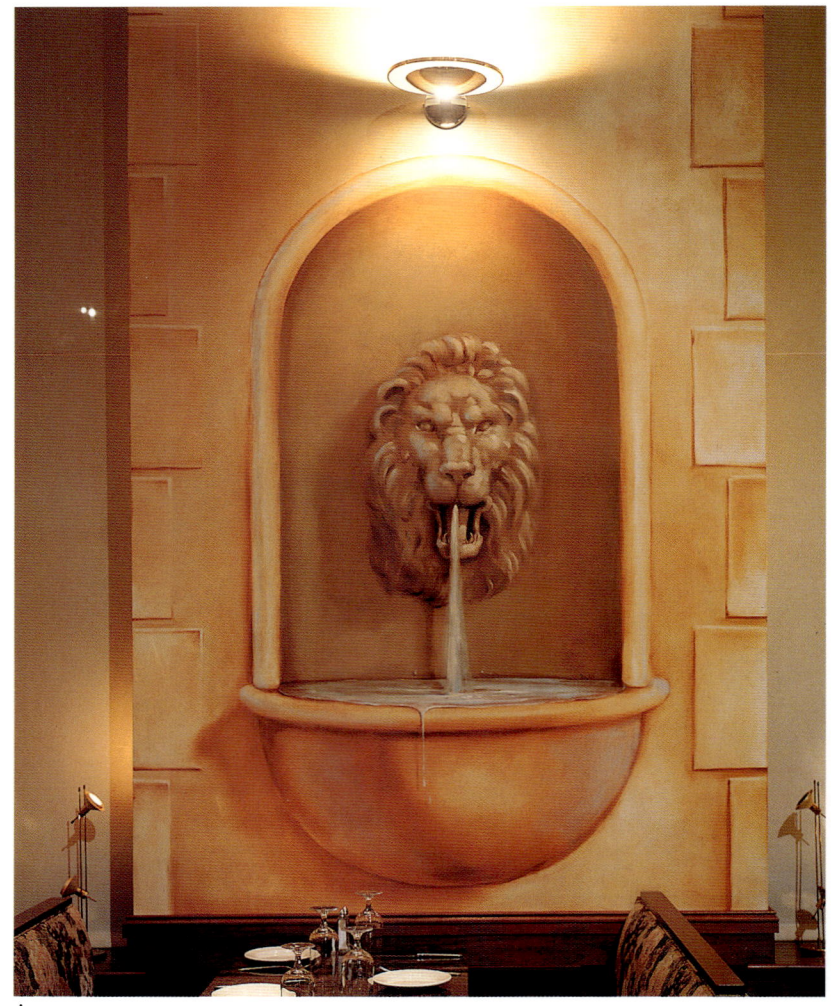

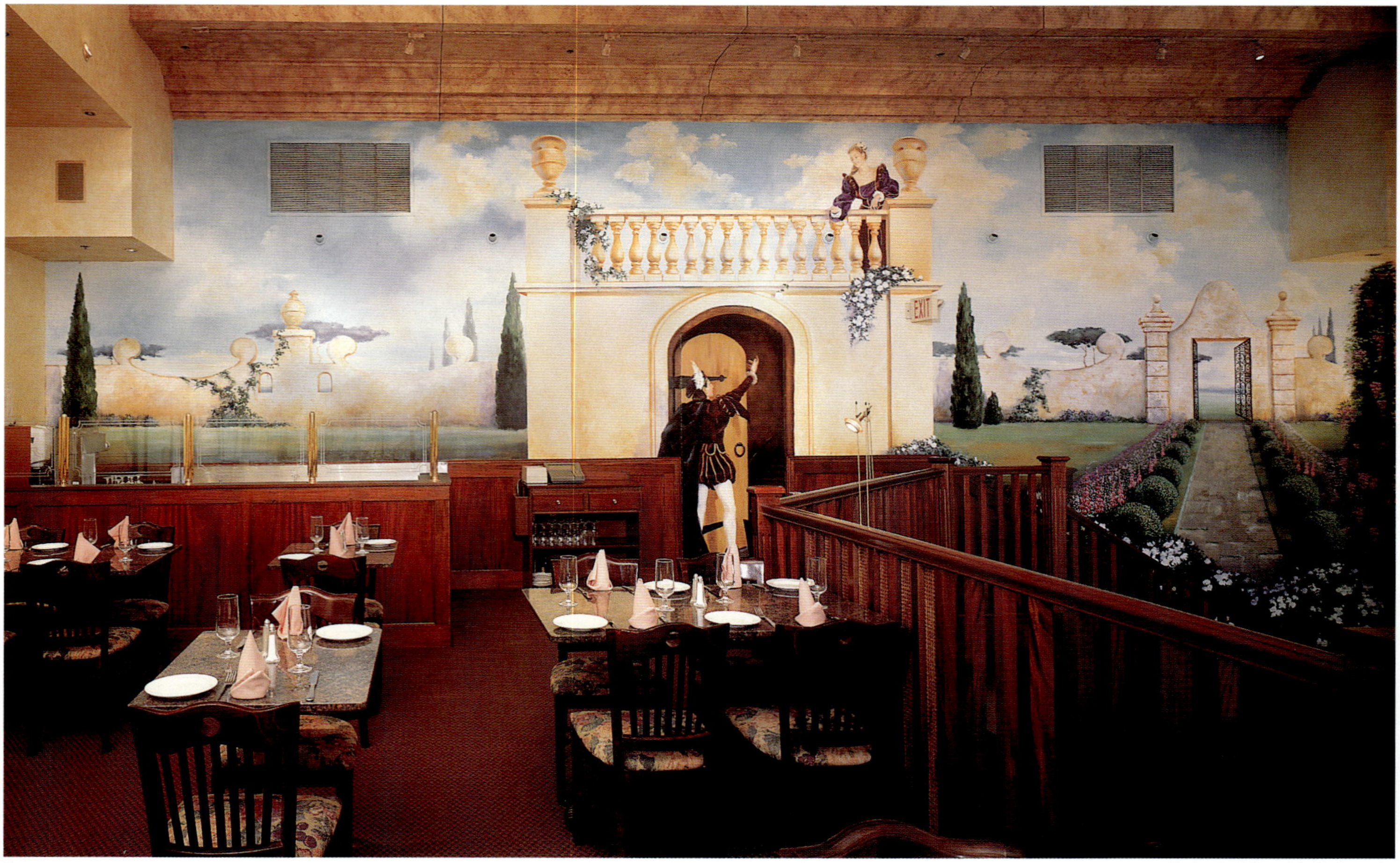

B

Photos: Jack Ramsdale Photography

Pierre Finkelstein

Grand Illusion Decorative Painting
20 West 20th Street #1009
New York, NY 10011
FAX 212-675-2286
TEL 212-675-2286

Mr. Pierre Finkelstein is one of the finest decorative painters in the nation. He was awarded the prestigious title of Best Craftsman of France in 1990. He has just written his second book on step-by-step recipes for finishes: *The Art of Faux: The Complete Sourcebook of Decorative Painted Finishes,* to be published by Watson-Guptill Publication as part of its series entitled *America's Finest Crafts.*

Pierre works for leading decorators and architects, painting faux marbles and woods, and creating textures, patinas, stencils, trompe l'oeils and painted ornaments for some of the most beautiful homes.

He also consults, and gives classes and seminars on decorative painting to painters and decorators.

Also see this GUILD publication:
Architect's Edition: 9

Crotch mahogany wood graining with fake moldings

Black-and-gold marbling

Damask fabric imitation in stenciling

Faux inlayed marquetry in wood graining

Blue-and-white tile imitation with crackling

Photos: Patrick Gries

Jill Kavner

Surfaces
Box 693
Woodstock, NY 12498
TEL 914-679-6555
TEL 212-787-5158 (NYC)

Marble, stone and rare woods: Jill Kavner recreates the beauty and sensuality of these finishes on almost any smooth surface. Her work can disguise damaged areas and blend with the natural materials.

Jill often collaborates with interior designers, architects and furniture designers. Her work has recently been featured in *Marble and Architectural Stone*. Installations include faux walls, floors, countertops, architectural details, furniture, and backdrops for advertisments.

Her most recent show-house installation was the *Kips Bay Decorator Show House 1996* in New York City.

Jill studied with master artist Leonard Pardon in his New York and London studios and at the Parsons School of Design. She now shares her own expertise with others by teaching workshops for such prestigious organizations as the Maine Crafts Association at Haystack.

Featured here are the foyer floor and living room fireplace in the Park Avenue residence of the New York editor of *Traditional Home* magazine.

Also see these GUILD publications: *Architect's Edition: 8, 9*

Photos: Michael Grand

Karl-Heinz Meschbach

The Faux Meister
4901 106th Avenue NE
Circle Pines, MN 55014
FAX 612-784-9201
TEL 612-785-2533

The illusion of trompe l'oeil, the whimsicality of painted furniture, the luxurious look of faux mabre or tortoiseshell ... European decorative art has long been admired but has rarely been available in the United States because of the scarcity of trained artisans who can create the magic designs and are skilled masters of these techniques.

Only a very few traditionally trained artisans reside in the United States. One such artisan is Karl-Heinz Meschbach.

Meschbach began his career as decorative painter and artist over 35 years ago, after completing rigorous European apprenticeship training under the masters of the Berlin Painters Guild.

Works by Karl-Heinz Meschbach have been featured in art galleries, commercial environments and many private homes.

Also see this GUILD publication:
Architect's Edition: 11

Trompe l'oeil ceiling, faux fantasy marbled walls, 1994 PIPP Award, 16' x 12'

Trompe l'oeil ceiling, faux mankato sandstone walls, 1994 PIPP Award, 30' x 20'

Photos: Diane Griffin

Faux mabre glove box, 12" x 4" x 4"

John Pugh

PO Box 1332
Los Gatos, CA 95031
FAX 408-353-3370
TEL 408-353-3370
http://www.illusion-art.com

Book passage into John Pugh's painted illusions. Discover Greece, China or Morocco via the realm of deception, for these life-sized images are flat.

Pugh is a master of architectural trompe l'oeil. Because he fully integrates his art into the existing architecture, the viewer becomes perplexed as to where reality ends and illusion begins. Once captivated, the viewer enters into another dimension of time and place.

John Pugh's creative energy, easy manner, and ability to articulate the client's concepts into a singular solution for each site, make him a favorite choice among private collectors, as well as architects and designers who serve discriminating clients.

Attention to detail — from design through final installation — is John's hallmark.

Ask artist for brochure.

Also see these GUILD publications:
Architect's Edition: 7, 8, 9, 11

Contemplation (detail), Taipei, Taiwan

Dolphin Room Illusion, Menlo Park, CA, 7' x 7'

Ming Vase in Alcove, 40" x 26"   Erik DuBouys

Cross Roads (lower portion of mural), Percent for the Arts award, Palm Desert, CA, 20' x 20'   Chuck Savadelis

DENISE RIPPINGER

Corporate Art Consultant

Chicago-area art consultant Denise Rippinger has built an enormously successful corporate practice in the last ten years. Her secret? Rippinger combines the sales and marketing savvy she learned while working in the highly competitive insurance business with her arts background and enduring contacts with many artists.

"I began with a handful of artist friends, the business contacts I had developed in my sales work, and a very aggressive, business-like attitude. Before I knew it, I'd outgrown my home office and had more business than I could handle," she explains. Today Rippinger juggles accounts from all over the world, employs 16 people, and works with dozens of artists, including many found through THE GUILD.

"I think THE GUILD is an incredible idea," Rippinger says. "Today, companies need to project a distinctive image that defines their corporate identity; it helps them both do business, and attract business. Art, when it's distinctive and appropriate, is an important part of that environment. If an art consultant

can't make recommendations for work that stands out, he or she is doing a disservice to the client. THE GUILD is a great resource for finding art that accommodates the needs of the client."

Recently, Rippinger's company purchased the corporate-art department of Chicago's Merrill Chase galleries, including a vast library of slides and other materials representing, literally, thousands of artists. "Even with this resource, we rely on THE GUILD," Rippinger maintains. "It's the easiest one-stop source for a huge variety of very capable artists."

Rippinger has commissioned work from a list of GUILD artists that reads like a *Who's Who* of fine North American craft: sculptor Joyce Lopez, ceramic muralist Tom Lollar, paper artist Karen Adachi, muralist Trina McNabb, and atrium sculptor Robert Pfitzenmeier, to name just a few.

"The artists I've worked with deserve all the credit in the world for their ability, creativity and patience," she says. "GUILD artists have the experience and the knowledge to help us avoid surprises and keep a project going smoothly. This is the key to their success."

William Baran-Mickle

1237 East Main Street
Rochester, NY 14609
FAX 716-288-8320
TEL 716-288-8320

Baran-Mickle's 15 years of experience forming and fabricating intricate works in metal allows him great flexibility in designing and creating his sculptures. Subjects generally range from nature to subtle observations concerning human relationships and cultural changes. Thematic challenges are most welcome.

Interior works are primarily constructed of non-ferrous metals. Prices are quoted individually based on the degree of intricacy desired and the requirements of the site. The work shown is priced at $350 per square foot.

Baran-Mickle has received numerous awards, including a New York Foundation for the Arts Fellowship and a National Endowment for the Arts/Mid-Atlantic Regional Fellowship. Most recently, he won the Hines Art-in-Architecture National competition with the piece shown below.

Also see these GUILD publications:
Gallery Edition: 1

Along the Way, 1995, wall relief, Chemed Center, Cincinnati, OH, 76" x 72"

Jay Bachemin

Beagle Tiles

300 8th Avenue #3E
Brooklyn, NY 11215
FAX 718-330-0921
TEL 718-965-3654

Ten years ago, Beagle Tiles began creating the first decorative wooden wall tile for corporate and residential use. Over the years, they have expanded the use of tiles to include crowns, baseboards, window sills, cabinetry, back splashes and doors — application as an inlay detail is infinite.

The tiles are available in squares, rectangles and triangles ranging from one-half inch to four inches. Large and custom sizes are available as well.

Tiles are provided stained, dyed or tinted, with three coats of protective sealer. Grouts are all custom-colored; a binder insures vibrancy and stability.

Please write for a sample Beagle Tile kit.

David M Bowman Studio

David M Bowman
Box 738
Berkeley, CA 94701
FAX 510-841-1245
TEL 510-845-1072
E-Mail: dbbowman@hooked.net

David Bowman designs strong abstract compositions in patinaed and etched brass for residential and public spaces.

These wallpieces appear massive, but are actually quite light and can be hung on any type of wall. The patinaed surfaces are durable and weather well out of doors. Designs can be scaled to fit an intimate corner or to fill an entire wall.

David also produces vases, fountains and other accessories for the home or office. He welcomes the opportunity to design wallpieces for specific spaces.

Wallpiece 94.10, 24" x 26", $1,100

Wallpiece 95.15, 23" x 52", $1,600

Printed in Hong Kong ©1996 THE GUILD: The Designer's Sourcebook

Eric Boyer

Eric Boyer Sculptures in Wire Mesh
72 Cotton Mill Hill #A-12
Brattleboro, VT 05301
TEL 802-254-6180

Eric Boyer creates original sculptures in woven wire mesh. The work juxtaposes classical nudes with an exciting industrial material. Formed by hand, these lightweight and resilient figures have been exhibited nationally and collected internationally since 1989.

Works are created for wall-hanging from a single point or free-standing with a wood or masonry base. Sculptures are black, rusted or patinated, and powder-coated for an extremely durable finish. Work may be commissioned in a wide range of sizes and scales with prices starting at around $1,000.

Male torso (left), 1995, rusted steel wire mesh on patinated masonry base, 24" x 8" x 8"; draped female torso (right), 1995, black steel wire mesh, 62" x 40" x 8"

Jeff Baird

Rita Blitt

Rita Blitt Inc.
8900 State Line Road, Suite 333
Leawood, KS 66206
FAX 913-381-5624
TEL 913-381-3840

Rita Blitt's wall sculptures — precise translations of her spontaneous drawings — express her joy of life. They echo the essence of spirit in her paintings and monumental sculpture.

Blitt's work has been exhibited in Israel, Singapore, Germany and throughout the United States. She was recently honored with a retrospective at the Kennedy Museum of American Art, Ohio University. Her work is permanently installed in many public places and collected by private collectors, institutions and museums. She is listed in *Who's Who of American Women*.

A *Flight of Fancy,* wall sculpture, poplar wood, 20" x 72" x 3/4"

B *Silent Energy,* wall sculpture, stained poplar wood, 50" x 40"

A

B

Printed in Hong Kong ©1996 THE GUILD: The Designer's Sourcebook

Beth Cunningham

32 Sweetcake Mountain Road
New Fairfield, CT 06812
TEL   203-746-5160

On the surface of Beth Cunningham's collage paintings is found an overlay of strips, squares or weaving — controlled, and mathematically precise — bound in a square or rectangular format. Beneath the top surface, a pale negative grid of color laces fragments of time and

space together, resulting in a work to be experienced on many levels.

Her atmospheric creations are constructed of heavyweight canvas layered with acrylic paints, polymer, muslin and silk tissue paper. Site-specific pieces may be large or small scale. Paintings are commissioned by collectors, as well as business, medical, banking and hotel facilities.

Completed works available. Gallery inquiries and exhibition opportunities welcomed.

Also see these GUILD publications:
THE GUILD: 1, 2, 3, 4, 5
Designer's Edition: 6, 7, 8, 9, 10

A *Celestial Paths,* 30" x 10"

B *Nebula Vista,* 21" x 10"

C *Disconnected,* 36" x 24"

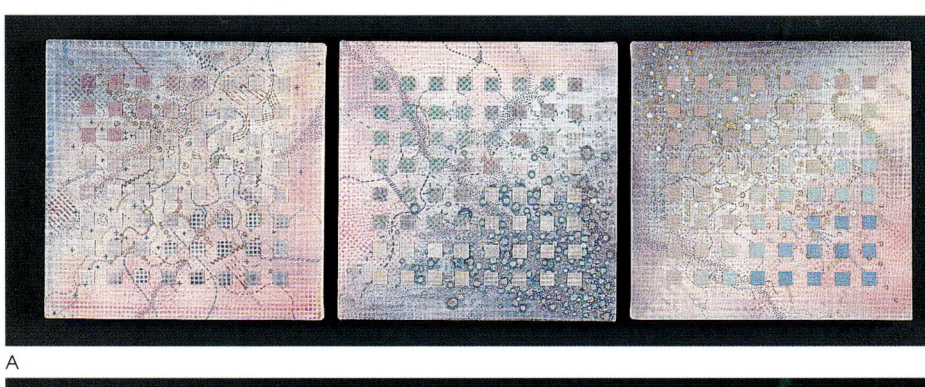

A

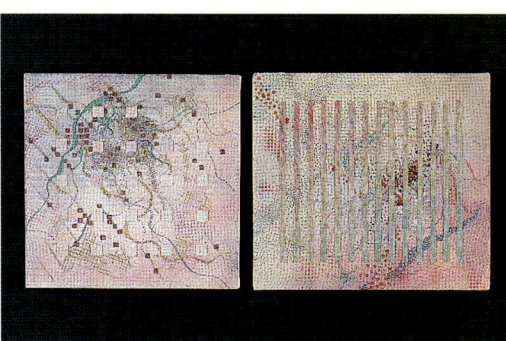

B

C

Photos: Michael Partenio Productions

Jamie Davis

Jamie Davis Sculpture
1239 Mile Creek Road
Pickens, SC 29671
FAX 864-868-4250
TEL 864-868-3302

Having explored clay and other materials in a career which spans 23 years, the artist has recently developed a technique which blends fabric, metal. wood and plastic into visually rich and dimensional layers. Veteran of SC Arts Commission and Rockefeller grants and several solo shows, Davis has also completed many commercial and residential commissions.

Consultation with clients, and the use of videos, photographs of the site, and other auxiliary materials, support the commission process.

List prices range from $150 to $200 per square foot depending on degree of detail. Most commissions can be completed in four to six weeks.

A *Play Ground,* 1995, mixed media
   (metal, fabric, plastic, wood),
   6'W x 4'H x 6"D

B *Step Up,* 1995, mixed media
   (metal, fabric, plastic, wood),
   3'W x 8'H x 6"D

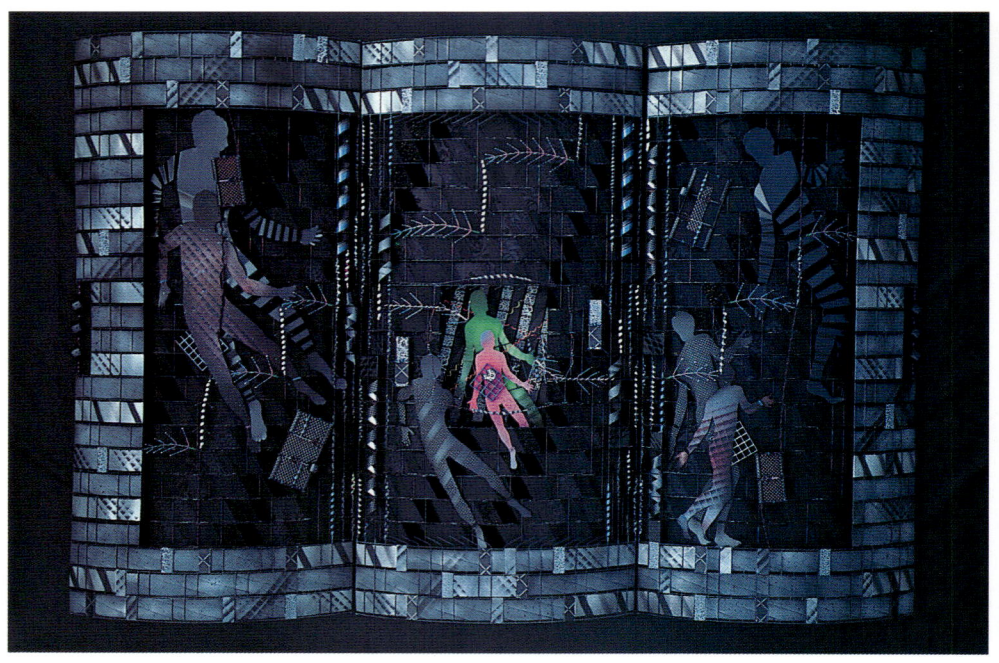

Brian Gassel

Printed in Hong Kong ©1996 THE GUILD: The Designer's Sourcebook

Daydreams by Barry

Barry Sher
3540 Gennesse
Kansas City, MO 64111
TEL   816-561-4833

With 25 years of working in acrylics and resins, Barry Sher has developed fascinating original artwork known as 'Transparent Art.' This signature concept takes form as dyes, pigments and resins are applied to a sheet of clear acrylic.

Whether created for a window or tabletop, or as a stand-alone sculpture, each piece evolves as the light of the environment changes. Works are intended for indoor settings; they are light-weight, movable, and UV/fade resistant. Light boxes are also available.

Each piece is tailored to the client's needs. Sher will work with individuals, designers and/or architects to create designs that capture and express the client's personality and environment.

A   *"Oh My God, It's Full of Stars,"*
    5' x 18" x ¹/₂"

B   *Star Map,* 2' x 2'

C   *Just a Second,* 2' x 2'

A

B

C

Atanas Karpeles

Atanas Karpeles Fine Art
1766 East Vistillas Road
Altadena, CA 91001
TEL 818-794-5963

Atanas Karpeles is a gold-award-winning artist with 30 years of experience. He received his M.F.A. from the Academy of Fine Art in Sofia, Bulgaria.

His paintings, tapestries and mixed-media art can be found in numerous museums, as well as government, corporate and private collections around the world.

For Karpeles, color is a key element through which the creative spirit works onto canvas. The canvas is "battery-charged with color, energy and spiritual vibrations, for man's quest to be in harmony with nature and higher self."

Selected collections include the Karpeles Museum; REIF, Taylor & Taylor, Inc.; ACOF, Los Angeles; Hyundai, Korea; Sofia, Bulgaria; Paris, France.

Brochure available upon request.

A *Mystical Land,* oil on canvas,
   36" x 36"

B *Hiway,* oil, acrylic, sand on canvas,
   24" x 24"

Printed in Hong Kong ©1996 THE GUILD: The Designer's Sourcebook

Silja Lahtinen

Silja's Fine Art Studio
5220 Sunset Trail
Marietta, GA 30068
FAX 770-992-8380
TEL 770-992-8380

Silja Talikka Lahtinen uses images from the myths and landscapes of her native Finland in her large wall panels. With striking combinations of colors and materials, her collages address the "poetry and spirituality that are missing from our modern life."

Lahtinen's other work — paintings of acrylic and oil on canvas, and drums of wood, rope, plywood and fiber — are well known to collectors in the United States and Europe. She exhibits regularly in New York and other U.S. cities, as well as in Paris, France, and Helsinki, Finland.

Commissions are accepted. For more information, please contact the artist.

A   Collage on canvas, silkscreen, paper,
    fiber, etc., 72" x 65"

B   *Eternity Has Ten Dimensions*, collage
    on canvas, fiber, handmade paper,
    silkscreen, 72" x 65"

A

B

DEBRA RHODES

Art Consultant

As an art consultant and appraiser with 20 years experience in the corporate-art business, Debra Rhodes has clearly defined notions about her mission and what she needs to do to help her clients.

"I want to help my customers select work that will endure, work that has the kind of quality that never loses its effect. What I look for is something that goes beyond just decorating. At this level you look for something with a distinctive and unique kind of creativity, as well as a great deal of artistic integrity. I think that's what you find with artists whose work is represented in THE GUILD."

Trained as an artist herself, Rhodes finds that part of her role is to negotiate between her clients — primarily corporations and luxury hotels — and the artists who provide the kind of extraordinary, highly creative work she advocates. When Rhodes was asked to provide a recommendation for artwork for the American Airlines VIP lounge at Philadelphia International Airport, she suggested GUILD artist Karen Adachi of Santa Cruz, California.

"At the time we began working on this project, there was beginning to be a fair amount of interest in cast paper, and there were a certain number of people working within this medium. Karen's work, however, wasn't just cast paper; it incorporated other materials in a fascinating, multi-dimensional way which took it to another level. Work created at this level never becomes dated; it has an enduring kind of value."

Rhodes says she takes prides in seeing both sides of the equation, understanding both the artist's perspective and the client's needs. "I think this perspective helps me find some of the best work," she explains.

"THE GUILD is a wonderful inventory, and a great time saver, as well. Even though I often have a sixth sense about what the client wants, it's a real advantage to be able to use THE GUILD to show a range of quality work in a very accessible, very visual form."

Photo by Peter Wallburg Studio, Inc.

Alexander Mandradjiev

Alexander Studio
12756 Moorpark Street #204
Studio City, CA 91604
FAX 818-762-5598
TEL 818-762-5598

Alexander Mandradjiev has created small- and large-scale mosaics for over 20 years. His favored palette of amethyst, marble, granite, agate, and smalti is employed with equal finesse in natural and abstract depiction.

Mr. Mandradjiev is critically noted for evolving new elements in the language of stone. His challenging innovations richly accompany an ancient tradition as it approaches the new millennium. His art pieces and restorations enjoy an international reputation.

Slides, pricing and scheduling upon request.

A *Comet,* 24" x 26"

B *Sound,* 34" x 25"

A

Foto Hinterman—Germany

B

Oggy Borissov

Sally McKenna

Sally McKenna Sculpture
7050 East Dixileta Drive
Cave Creek, AZ 85331
FAX 602-585-5290
TEL 602-585-7034

Afloat on a ship, or the center of attention while dining, McKenna sculptures make any space more dynamic. Twenty years ago, as a recent art graduate, Sally McKenna took a vocational welding course and began forging a unique combination of media.

Each commission is a mix of precious materials. Welded steel, brass, copper, artist-handwoven exotic yarns and painted, gilded surfaces all combine to create impact. Ms. McKenna works with clients via plans, photos and swatches.

Samples and colored renderings to scale are included in design presentations. International clients include Princess Cruise Lines, Toyota Corporation, Koll Corporation, Carefree Resorts, Penn Central Corporation, Great Western Life, Amoco Corporation and McDonnell-Douglas Corporation.

Brochures, photos and price estimates available upon request.

Canyon River Hawk, Ventana Golf and Racquet Club, rusted steel, woven fiber, brass, copper, 6' x 12'

Radial, Orcutt Winslow Architecture, polished steel, copper, woven fiber, 3¹/₂' x 6¹/₂'

Scheherazade, Bowman and Brooke Law Firms, 4' x 8'   Alex Gray

Solar Crucible and the Crane, Princess Cruise ships, rusted steel, brass, copper, 6' x 12'   Elliot Lincis

Scheherazade (media detail), polished steel, copper, hand-woven fiber, veiled paper   Alex Gray

Bernard J. Roberts

W1952 Roosevelt Road
Oconomowoc, WI 53066
TEL 414-474-4103

Bernard Roberts is an established sculptor working in hand-carved wood.

His forms are inspired by nature and combine the rich natural character of wood with softly textured, painted areas. These beautiful, sensuous sculptures are durable and may be customized for any interior setting.

Portfolio available.

A *Birth Form,* 24"H x 36"W x 2¹/₂"D

B *Growth Form,* 48"H x 21"W x 1¹/₄"D

C *Figure,* 54"H x 24"W x 1¹/₄"D

A

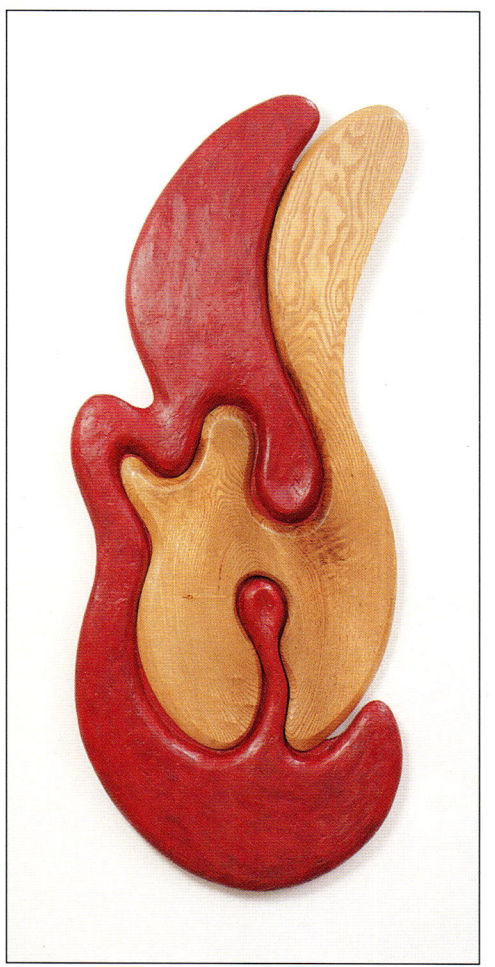

B

C

Sturman Steel Sculptures

Martin Sturman
416 Cricketfield Court
Westlake Village, CA 91361
FAX 805-381-1116
TEL 805-381-0032

Martin Sturman creates original steel sculptures in floral, figurative and abstract designs.

Sculptures range from tabletop to free-standing indoor and outdoor pieces, including sculpted tables and entry gates. These beautiful sculptures are executed in stainless steel, weathered (rusted) steel, powder-coated carbon steel and acrylic-painted carbon steel.

Martin frequently has sculptures available for immediate delivery, but encourages site-specific and collaborative efforts. Depending upon complexity, most sculptures can be shipped within 6 to 12 weeks of commission.

Sizes range from 12 inches to 10 feet high. Prices upon request.

Also see these GUILD publications:
Designer's Edition: 7, 8, 9, 10

A *Pink Flowers,* 1995, acrylic and steel,
   44"H x 33"W x 2"D

B *Tropicals,* 1995, stainless steel,
   34"H x 33"W x 2"D

A

B

Photos: Barry Michlin

Gail Taylor

In the Woods
1639 Cypress Grove Lane
Diamond Bar, CA 91765
FAX 909-861-9722
TEL 909-861-4128
TEL 909-390-0755

Working with a variety of natural organic materials, Gail Taylor creates thought-provoking constructions that ensure distinctive and dramatic impact in both private and corporate settings.

Her subtle, as well as bold, mixed-media assemblages satisfy a broad spectrum of styles and moods, from the serene to whimsical to eclectic.

Taylor's works are designer-friendly, with no limitations of size or color preference. Commissions are encouraged and welcome.

"My work is inspired by, and suggests, quiet walks in the woods."

Call today to discuss your needs.

A Untitled, 1994, mixed media,
    24" x 31" x 5"

B *Seasons,* 1995, mixed media,
    24" x 65" x 4"

C *Walls of Silence,* 1992, mixed
    media, 19" x 48" x 6"

A

B

C

Photos: Ryan Beck

Susan Venable

Venable Studio
214 South Venice Boulevard
Venice, CA 90291
FAX 310-822-0050
TEL 310-827-7233
E-Mail: Copperwyrd@aol.com

Susan Venable's work is non-objective — an exploration of structure and surface. The reliefs are constructed of steel grids and twisted copper wire. The paintings are encaustic and oil. In both, layers are stacked to create a rich and complex surface, maximizing the physicality of the materials.

Venable's wall reliefs have been installed in public spaces as well as private homes and museums. Commissions involving collaboration with architects are welcome, and have included Xerox, Nissan, Hotel Nikko, IBM, and Western Digital, as well as corporations in Europe, Australia, and Asia. The materials are durable and low maintenance, and suitable to installation in public areas.

Also see these GUILD publications:
Designer's Edition: 9, 10

Sur la Mer, 50" x 50"

Fuego Noche, 48" x 36"

Zen Samba, 48" x 63"

Photos: William Nettles

Printed in Hong Kong ©1996 THE GUILD: The Designer's Sourcebook

Bill Wheeler

Studio 1617
1617 Silver Lake Boulevard
Los Angeles, CA 90026
FAX 213-660-7991
TEL 213-660-7991

Bill Wheeler has been creating limited-edition original prints and paintings for public and private commissions since 1970. He also has nearly 20 years experience working in collaboration with designers and architects to create site-specific installations. His security-mounted wall constructions are made of masonite and/or archival plastics incorporating iridescent and metallic surfaces. They are designed to the client's color and size specifications; commissioned works have ranged from 2 by 2 feet to 10 by 164 feet.

Mr. Wheeler is a versatile artist, able to accept and incorporate the client's suggestions and modifications into his artwork. Such teamwork results in an installation that becomes an integral part of the interior space.

Also see these GUILD publications:
THE GUILD: 4
Designer's Edition: 6, 7, 9

VEGA OVERBY

Interior Designer

Library of Congress interior designer Vega Overby faced many practical constraints when she began working with a daycare center located in the basement of a recently renovated government building in Washington, DC. Nevertheless, her first priority was to bring life and color into a long, blank corridor used daily by very small children.

"Our office, the Facility, Design & Construction arm of the Library of Congress, was assigned to work with the Little Scholars Daycare Center, which serves infants and toddlers," she explains. Overby suspected that custom work would best suit the unusual demands of the space, and so she turned to THE GUILD for inspiration. There, she was immediately drawn to the possibilities fiber art offered. It was bright, it was cheerful, it was textural: The special requirements she had to work with would be well served by such an installation.

"Fiber appealed to me for many reasons, not the least of which was the fact that it could be moved and cleaned. These were elements that needed to be addressed for this job," Overby says. She initially contacted about half a dozen artists from THE GUILD and requested materials, including slides for review. With input from colleagues, she selected fiber artist M.A. Klein of Portola Valley, California.

"I was a little nervous initially about working long distance with an artist," Overby recalls. "But we had a wonderful rapport from the beginning. I sent color swatches, we talked via phone, tossed ideas around, and she sent sketches for the client to review. She obviously had the range of talent we needed, and she was so accommodating about our budget concerns and schedule. Finally, she did a mock-up, which the client approved, and we were able to write up a purchase order."

The piece which resulted from the collaboration is called *A Most Unusual Watering Hole.* Four feet high and nine feet wide, the colorful fabric collage features animals from across the globe. Overby notes that it was extremely simple to install.

"The art is so fresh and so well tailored to the needs of the client," she says. "And best of all, the children really love it!"

Shawn Athari

Shawn Athari's, Inc.
14332 Mulholland Drive
Los Angeles, CA 90077
FAX 818-787-MASK
TEL 310-476-0066
E-Mail: Glassmaker@aol.com

The lightheartedness of these panels is accomplished in major part because of the large palette from which Shawn Athari works. Shawn creates many colors and shapes unique to her work by color mixing and pouring molten glass into desired shapes. This gives the illusion of images dancing across the palette, and creates a fluidity to her glass sculptures that would not be apparent on an otherwise stagnate object.

The various glass techniques displayed here are the culmination of her glass-making experience, which began in 1975.

Galleries include:
The Art of Disney, Walt Disney World, FL
Little Switzerland, Alaska and the Caribbean
Neiman Marcus, various cities
Symmetry, Saratoga Springs, NY
Mindscape, Evanston, IL

Love Me Tender, 14" x 48 "

Dance with Me Baby, 14" x 48"

Eagleton Glass Studio

Char and Kevin Eagleton
118 West Market Street
Mount Carroll, IL 61053
FAX 815-244-3554 (Call first)
TEL 815-244-3554

Accomplished in the field of glass for over 20 years, the Eagletons produce unique and dynamic graphic wall sculptures. Their work employs diverse applications of hand-blown and kiln-fired glass processes.

Each sculptural graphic is a distinct work of art, carefully constructed and engineered with full attention to detail.

The Eagletons' work is featured in many prominent corporate and private collections, both domestic and abroad, including Alcoa, Sunbeam, and Ed Hoy's International.

They welcome working with architects and designers for site-specific commissions. Free-standing sculptures are also available.

Information regarding commissions and prices is available on request.

A *Gaia* (detail), 16" x 16" x 1"

B *Gaia II,* 18" x 24" x 2"

C *Presence of the Heart,* 18" x 24" x 2"

A

B

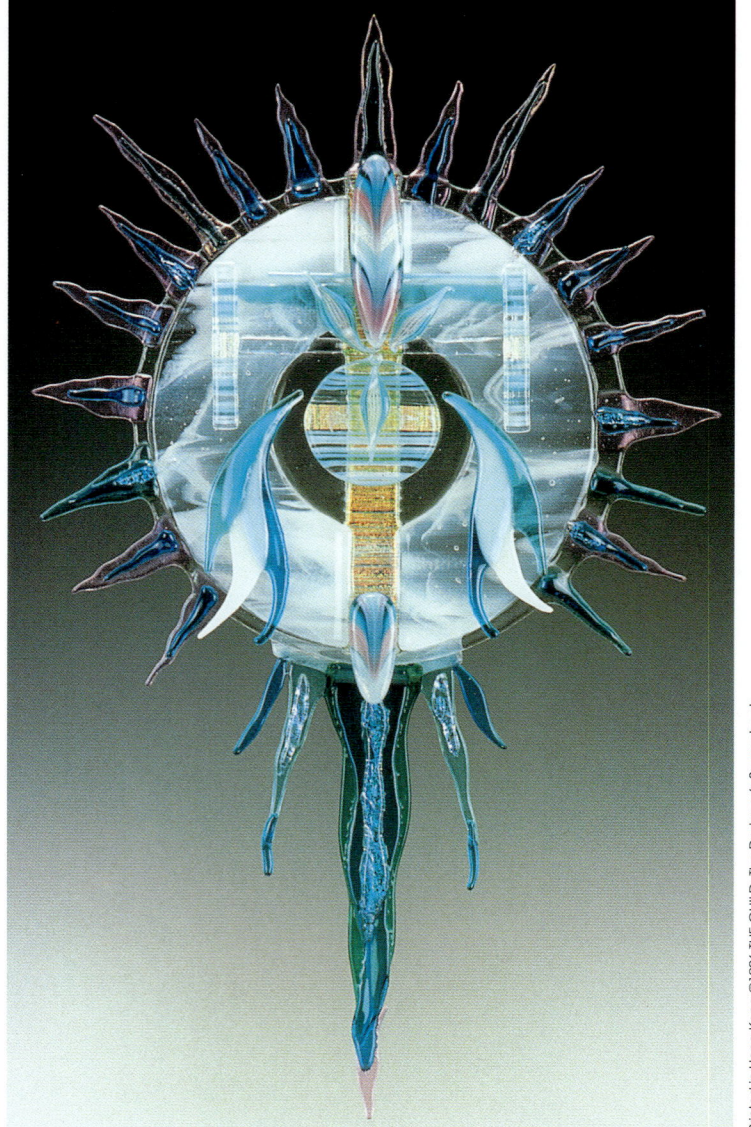

C

Photos: Jerry Anthony

Marvin Lipofsky

Marvin Lipofsky Studios
1012 Pardee Street
Berkeley, CA 94710
FAX 510-843-7594
TEL 510-843-7593

Lipofsky has been using glass for over 30 years. His blown forms, initially conceived in studios and factories in various countries, are transformed into unique sculptures in his Berkeley studio. He incorporates his feelings and impressions of the factory environment, the country, and its culture into his creative process with unique combinations of colors and shapes. His works capture the illusive yet flexible material of glass.

His sculptures are in private and permanent museum collections throughout the world.

A *Group Dieulefit*, 1990-95, wall pieces, France, left: 13^1/$_2$" x 10^1/$_2$" x 7"; right: 13^1/$_2$" x 10^1/$_2$" x 6"

B *"Violetta" Series*, 1992-95, wall piece, Poland, 6^1/$_2$" x 17^1/$_2$"

A

B

Photos: M. Lee Fatherree

THE GUILD REGISTER®
of Glass Art for the Wall

A.R.T. GLASS BY VICTORIA STREET
VICTORIA STREET
5701 ANDREWS RD
MEDFORD, OR 97501
FAX 541-770-2030
TEL 541-770-1141
Established: 1980
Products: murals, lighting, wall reliefs
Techniques: leaded or copper-foiled, painted or enameled, bent, fused or kiln-formed
Size Range: no size limit
Price Range: $100 to $150/sq. ft.
Price Range: $500 to $5,000 for 2D, 3D stained, fused glass art pieces

ACACIA ART GLASS STUDIOS
LUCINDA SHAW
3000 CHESTNUT AVE #336
BALTIMORE, MD 21211-2751
FAX 410-366-6472
TEL 410-467-4038
Established: 1980
Products: tiles, panels or screens, murals
Techniques: leaded or copper-foiled, sandcarved or etched, beveled, painted or enameled, bent, fused or kiln-formed
Size Range: 4" × 3" to 2' × 12.6'
Price Range: $150 to $3,000 for murals, panels

★ ALEXANDER STUDIO
ALEXANDER V. MANDRADJIEV
12756 MOORPARK ST #204
STUDIO CITY, CA 91604
FAX 818-762-5598
TEL 818-762-5598
Established: 1978
Products: mosaics, murals, wall reliefs
Techniques: painted or enameled, hand-cut smalti and glass
Size Range: 12" × 16" to 3' × 21'
Price Range: $150 to $500/sq. ft.
Price Range: $340 and up for panels, etc.

See page 97 for photographs and additional information.

ARTISTIC GLASS WORKS
JACQUELINE GARDNER
313 1100 MEMORIAL AVE
THUNDER BAY, ON P7B 4A3
CANADA
FAX 807-623-5122
TEL 807-344-1863
Established: 1993
Products: glass, mirrored surfaces
Techniques: sandcarved or etched, carved, airbrushed
Size Range: 1" × 1" to 8' × 6'
Price Range: $200 to $500/sq. ft.
Price Range: $500 to $2,000 for panels

★ SHAWN ATHARI
SHAWN ATHARI'S INC.
14332 MULHOLLAND DR
LOS ANGELES, CA 90077
FAX 818-787-MASK
TEL 213-476-0066
Established: 1975
Products: murals, platters, sculpture, masks, totems
Techniques: sandcarved or etched, painted or enameled, bent, fused or kiln-formed, cast, blown
Size Range: 9" × 9" to 55" × 19"
Price Range: $200 to $7,000 for 2D or 3D sculpture

See pages 38 and 105 for photographs and additional information.

JOHN BASSETT
26 SEARLE AVE
BROOKLINE, MA 02146
FAX 617-739-1119
TEL 617-739-1160
Established: 1985
Products: panels or screens, mixed media
Techniques: leaded or copper-foiled, leaded or copper-foiled, painted or enameled, bent, fused or kiln-formed, slumped
Size Range: 12" × 9" to 7' × 3'
Price Range: $300 to $3,000 for panels

★ SANDRA C.Q. BERGÉR
QUINTAL UNLIMITED
100 EL CAMINO REAL #202
BURLINGAME, CA 94010-5225
FAX 415-340-0198
TEL 415-348-0310
Established: 1980
Products: panels or screens, lighting, wall reliefs
Techniques: leaded or copper-foiled, sandcarved or etched, laminated, cast, neon
Size Range: 40" × 20"
Price Range: $150 to $400/sq. ft.

See photograph below.

LAURIE BIEZE
BIEZE'S CITY CENTER
  GALLERY & STUDIO
216 S BARSTOW
EAU CLAIRE, WI 54701
TEL 715-833-0007
Established: 1963
Products: panels or screens, wall reliefs, sculpture
Techniques: leaded or copper-foiled, sandcarved or etched, beveled
Size Range: 30" × 23" to 13' × 25'
Price Range: $120 to $240/sq. ft.

JAY BLAZEK
WESTERN NEON INC.
2700 1ST AVE S
SEATTLE, WA 98134
FAX 206-682-8159
TEL 206-682-7738
Established: 1989
Products: lighting, wall reliefs, free-standing sculpture
Techniques: sandcarved or etched, painted or enameled, engraved, bent, fused or kiln-formed, neon
Size Range: 6" × 3" to 20' × 10'
Price Range: $20 to $200/sq. ft.
Price Range: $400 to $250,000 for free-standing or wall sculpture

Sandra C.Q. Bergér, *Crystal Sheer*, glass with hidden neon, 4'W × 3'H × 9"D, photo: William A. Porter

★ ANNA CABO

2003 6TH ST
SANTA MONICA, CA 90405
FAX 310-450-1011
TEL 310-450-1011
Established: 1990
Products: tiles, panels or screens, murals
Techniques: painted or enameled, bent, fused or kiln-formed
Size Range: 2" × 2" to 20" × 40" per tile
Price Range: $90 to $360/sq. ft.
Price Range: $300 and up for platters, panels, murals

See photograph below.

JILL CASTY

JCD
494 ALVARADO ST
MONTEREY, CA 93940
FAX 408-649-0713
TEL 408-649-0923
Established: 1971
Products: murals, lighting, wall reliefs
Techniques: sandcarved or etched, painted or enameled, bent, fused or kiln-formed, laminated, cast
Size Range: 3' × 4' to 8' × 6'
Price Range: $2,500 to $10,000 for wall reliefs

CELESTIAL STAINED GLASS AND DAGAZ STUDIO

CYNTHIA BOOKER-BINGLER
 AND ROGER BINGLER
PO BOX 43
SARGENTVILLE, ME 04673
FAX 207-359-2558
TEL 207-359-2558
Products: tiles, panels or screens, wall/furniture combo
Techniques: leaded or copper-foiled, sandcarved or etched, beveled, bent, fused or kiln-formed, painted or enameled
Size Range: 2' × 3' to 20' × 40'
Price Range: $800 to $30,000 for murals

CLASSICAL GLASS

DAVID DUFF
1333 MAIN ST
CINCINNATI, OH 45210
TEL 513-381-4334
Established: 1972
Products: panels or screens, lighting, clocks
Techniques: leaded or copper-foiled, beveled, painted or enameled
Size Range: 12" × 12" to 12' × 12'
Price Range: $20 to $200/sq. ft.

CRISTTLE GLASS

RICHARD CRISP
RT 3 BOX 178
SPRUCE PINE, NC 28777
TEL 704-765-5301
Established: 1989
Products: ornaments
Techniques: blown
Size Range: 3" to 18"Dia
Price Range: $8.50 to $100 for ornaments, flowers

CULTUS BAG GLASS

MEREDITH MACLEOD
7712 HELLMAN RD
CLINTON, WA 98236
FAX 360-579-1060
TEL 360-579-3079
Established: 1980
Products: tiles, mosaics, murals
Techniques: painted or enameled, bent, fused or kiln-formed
Size Range: 1" × 1" to 8" × 8" tiles
Price Range: $28 to $432/sq. ft.
Price Range: $2 to $38 per individual tile

★ CHAR AND KEVIN EAGLETON

118 W MARKET ST
MOUNT CARROLL, IL 61053
TEL 815-244-3554
Established: 1978
Products: tiles, lighting, wall reliefs, sculptures
Techniques: sandcarved or etched, painted or enameled, bent, fused or kiln-formed, laminated, cast
Size Range: 10" × 8" × 8' × 4'
Price Range: $500 to $700 for 24" × 24" wall relief

See page 106 for photographs and additional information.

THOMAS H. EMERSON

SANDMAN
166 S BROAD ST
MERIDEN, CT 06450
FAX 203-237-3216
TEL 203-237-3216
Established: 1978
Products: panels or screens, mirrors, windows
Techniques: sandcarved or etched, painted or enameled, glue chip
Size Range: 8" × 10" to 6' × 10'
Price Range: $40 to $350/sq. ft.

LONNIE FEATHER

1528 SE HOLGATE
PORTLAND, OR 97202
TEL 503-234-6642
Established: 1980
Products: panels or screens, murals
Techniques: sandcarved or etched, painted or enameled, mixed media, collage
Size Range: 16" × 12" to 10' × 10'
Price Range: $100 to $300/sq. ft.
Price Range: $1,000 to $30,000 for murals, panels

KEVIN FULTON

KEVIN FULTON GLASS SCULPTOR
PO BOX 7033
BEND, OR 97708
FAX 541-389-2031
TEL 541-382-8636
Established: 1974
Products: murals, platters, wall reliefs
Techniques: bent, fused or kiln-formed, cast, blown, lampwork
Size Range: 12" × 12" to 5' × 15'
Price Range: $100 to $500/sq. ft.
Price Range: $250 to $15,000 for platters to large murals

Anna Cabo, glass tiles, 2'' × 2'', 2'' × 4'', 4'' × 4'' etc. up to 20'' × 40'', photo: Cydney Conger

★ DEBORAH GOLDHAFT

FIRE & ICE GLASS STUDIO
11933 SW COVE RD, PO BOX 2292
VASHON ISLAND, WA 98070
TEL 206-463-3601
E-Mail: fireice@wolfenet.com
Established: 1991
Products: panels or screens, platters, mirrors
Techniques: sandcarved or etched, double-sided deep carving
Size Range: 8" × 10" to unlimited
Price Range: $150 to $200/sq. ft.

See page 40 for photographs and additional information.

NANCY GONG

GONG GLASS WORKS
42 PARKVIEW DR
ROCHESTER, NY 14625-1034
FAX 716-288-2503
TEL 716-288-5520
Established: 1979
Products: panels or screen, murals, tiles
Techniques: leaded or copper-foiled, sandcarved or etched, painted or enameled, laminated
Size Range: no limit
Price Range: $100 and up/sq. ft.
Price Range: $255 and up for large-scale architectural art

RICHARD HARNED

ABSTRACT GLASS
2723 BRANDON RD
UPPER ARLINGTON, OH 43221-3336
TEL 614-488-3688
Established: 1973
Products: panels or screens, lighting, wall reliefs
Techniques: leaded or copper-foiled, sandcarved or etched, cast, blown, neon
Size Range: 2' × 3' to 10' × 10'
Price Range: $3,500 to $14,000 for sculpture relief, panels

HAWKSTEAD STUDIOS

JOHN K. AND CYNTHIA RAY HAWK
4902 LONGFORD DR
RICHMOND, VA 23228
FAX 804-747-5305
TEL 804-747-5305
Products: panels or screens, clocks, mirrors
Techniques: leaded or copper-foiled, beveled
Size Range: 8" × 10" tp 4' × 8'
Price Range: $80 to $200/sq. ft.
Price Range: $225 to $3,000 for clocks, mirrors to panels and windows

SIDNEY R. HUTTER

HUTTER GLASS & LIGHT
PO BOX 1168
WALTHAM, MA 02254-1168
FAX 617-891-8375
TEL 617-647-1923
Established: 1979
Products: panels or screens, lighting, wall reliefs
Techniques: sandcarved or etched, beveled, bent, fused or kiln-formed, laminated, cast
Size Range: 12" × 12" to 6' × 6'
Price Range: $3,000 to $20,000

MARY LADAKH IEMOTO

MU STUDIOS
10208 148TH AVE SE
RENTON, WA 98059
TEL 206-277-9397
Established: 1980
Products: wall reliefs
Techniques: bent, fused or kiln-formed, cast, pate de verre
Size Range: 4" × 4" to 2' × 2'
Price Range: $400 to $1,200 for wall reliefs

KESSLER STUDIOS

BOB AND CINDY KESSLER
273 E BROADWAY
LOVELAND, OH 45140-3121
FAX 513-683-7512
TEL 513-683-7500
Established: 1980
Products: mosaics, stained glass
Techniques: leaded or copper-foiled, sandcarved or etched, painted or enameled, bent, fused or kiln-formed, glass smalti, stone
Size Range: 4' × 3' to 7' × 30'
Price Range: $250 to $500/sq. ft.
Price Range: $100 to $200 for stained glass

LILI LAKICH

LAKICH STUDIO
704 TRACTION AVE
LOS ANGELES, CA 90013-1814
FAX 213-620-8904
TEL 213-620-8641
Established: 1965
Products: neon bas-relief sculpture
Techniques: neon
Size Range: 24" × 24" to 25' × 85'
Price Range: $2,750 to $125,000 for neon bas-relief sculpture

LARANGER STUDIO

RAY AND KATHARYN LARANGER
299 SMADBECK AVE
CARMEL, NY 10512
FAX 914-225-6956
TEL 914-225-6956
Established: 1978
Products: panels or screens, mosaics, textural glass reliefs
Techniques: leaded or copper-foiled, sandcarved or etched, beveled, painted or enameled, dalle de verre
Size Range: 1' × 1' to 6' × 18' and up
Price Range: $75 to $175/sq. ft.

LINDA LICHTMAN

LICHTMAN STAINED GLASS
17 TUDOR ST
CAMBRIDGE, MA 02139
FAX 617-354-1119
TEL 617-876-4660
Established: 1976
Products: panels or screens, murals, glass paintings
Techniques: painted or enameled, engraved, laminated, acid-etched
Size Range: 6" × 2" to 12' × 4'
Price Range: $150 to $450/sq. ft.
Price Range: $250 to $3,200 for panels

R. MERCEDES LINDENOAK

PO BOX 18501
BOULDER, CO 80308-1501
TEL 303-545-8798
Established: 1984
Products: miniature tapestries
Techniques: woven glass beads
Size Range: 6" × 6" to 24" × 30"
Price Range: $600 to $4,000 for miniature wall-hung works

★ MARVIN LIPOFSKY

MARVIN LIPOFSKY STUDIOS
1012 PARDEE ST
BERKELEY, CA 94710-2628
FAX 510-843-7594
TEL 510-843-7593
Established: 1962
Products: sculpture
Techniques: blown
Price Range: $6,000 to $25,000 for sculpture

See page 107 for photographs and additional information.

LONGHOUSE WORKS — CUSTOM DESIGN GLASS

RICHARD PORTER
1417 OCTOBER WAY
MODESTO, CA 95358
TEL 209-544-2527
Established: 1985
Products: tiles, panels or screens, murals, columns, window overlays
Techniques: sandcarved or etched, painted or enameled, engraved
Size Range: 12" × 12" to 8' × 4'
Price Range: $100 to $300/sq. ft.
Price Range: $100 to $800 for panels, partitions, overlays

M.B.C. GLASS STUDIO INC.

HOWARD BOWEN
289A STONE SCHOOL HOUSE RD
BLOOMINGBURG, NY 12721
FAX 914-733-4502
TEL 914-733-4501
Established: 1980
Products: tiles, panels or screens, murals
Techniques: leaded or copper-foiled, sandcarved or etched, laminated, cast, "lifetile" kinetic murals
Size Range: 4" × 4" to 8' × 20'
Price Range: $75 to $350/sq. ft.
Price Range: $500 to $50,000 for murals/panels

BARBARA MALINOSKI

STAINED GLASS ARTWORKS
8634 BERTHA CT
MANASSAS, VA 22110-7008
FAX 800-278-9757
TEL 703-330-5119
Established: 1976
Products: tiles, panels or screens, lighting
Techniques: leaded or copper-foiled, sandcarved or etched, painted or enameled, bent, fused or kiln-formed, lamp working
Size Range: 4" × 4" to 48" × 64"
Price Range: $55 to $145/sq. ft.

CISSY MCCAA

MCCAA GLASS
PO BOX 5391
FULLERTON, CA 92635
FAX 714-671-0608
TEL 714-256-1955
Established: 1977
Products: tiles, wall reliefs
Techniques: sandcarved or etched, beveled, painted or enameled, bent, fused or kiln-formed, laminated
Size Range: 15" × 18" to unlimited
Price Range: $100 to $300/sq. ft.
Price Range: $500 to $25,000 for wall reliefs

TOM MCQUAID

TOM MCQUAID GLASS
2005 ALAMEDA PADRE SERRA
SANTA BARBARA, CA 93103
TEL 805-569-2385
Established: 1977
Products: tiles, platters
Techniques: bent, fused or kiln-formed
Size Range: 4" × 4" to 11" × 17"
Price Range: $150 to $300 for platters

MELTDOWN DESIGN INC.

MIES GRYBAITIS AND B.J. KATZ
15 E JACKSON
PHOENIX, AZ 85004
FAX 602-949-9809
TEL 602-941-4686
Established: 1991
Products: lighting, platters, windows
Techniques: painted or enameled, bent, fused or kiln-formed, cast
Size Range: 12" × 12" to 10' × 5'
Price Range: $150 to $450/sq. ft.
Price Range: $45 to $175 for platters

THE NEON COMPANY

GREGG BRENNER
858 DEKALB AVE NE
ATLANTA, GA 30307
FAX 404-584-6366
TEL 404-873-6366
Products: lighting, signs
Techniques: painted or enameled, bent, fused or kiln-formed, blown, neon, vinyl application
Size Range: 12" × 12" and up
Price Range: $200 to $30,000 for project

WILLIAM COREY PAISLEY

PAISLEY NEON GLASSWORK
650 W COOLIDGE ST
PHOENIX, AZ 85013
FAX 602-230-7857
TEL 602-230-7857
Established: 1987
Products: lighting
Techniques: blown, neon
Size Range: 16" × 20" and up
Price Range: $30 to $60/sq. ft.
Price Range: $625 to $50,000

QUILTS IN GLASS

BRINA B. MELEMED
15 MECHANIC ST #3
PROVINCETOWN, MA 02657
FAX 508-487-5815
TEL 508-487-5810
Established: 1986
Products: panels or screens
Techniques: leaded or copper-foiled, beveled
Size Range: 12" × 12" to 48" × 48"
Price Range: $200 to $10,000 for panels or screens

★ MAYA RADOCZY

CONTEMPORARY ART GLASS
PO BOX 31422
SEATTLE, WA 98103
FAX 206-524-9226
TEL 206-527-5022
Established: 1982
Products: panels or screens, wall reliefs
Techniques: leaded or copper-foiled, bent, fused or kiln-formed, cast
Size Range: 2' × 4' to 7' × 60'
Price Range: $7,000 for wall piece, 3' × 6'

See photograph below.

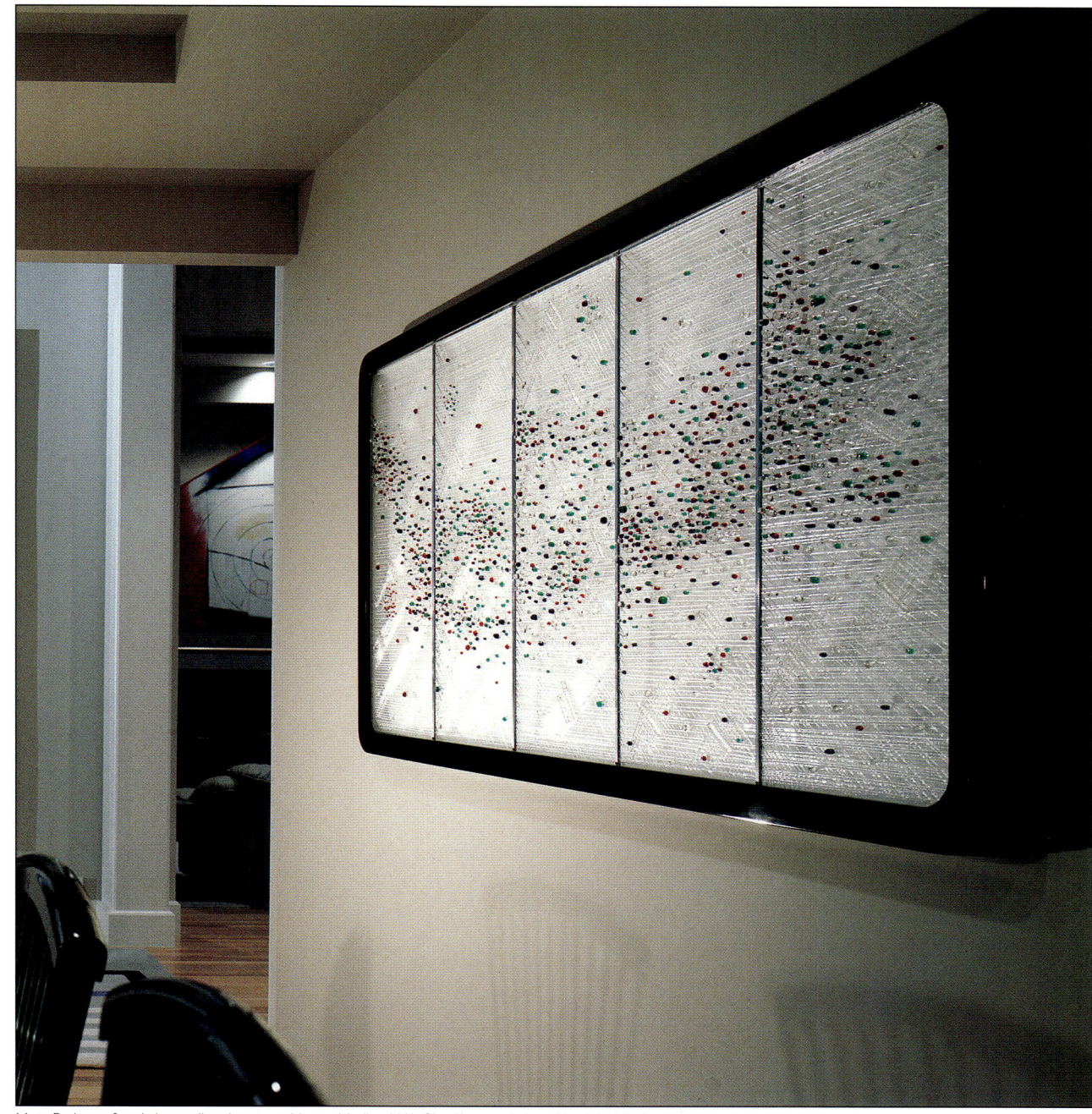

Maya Radoczy, fused glass wall sculpture, residence, Medina, WA, 3' × 6', commissioned by Art Link, Seattle, WA, photo: Dick Springgate

GLASS ART FOR THE WALL

REFLECTIONS

DIANE TOOROIAN
7225 E SYLVANE DR
TUCSON, AZ 85710-5526
TEL 520-886-4063
Established: 1985
Products: panels or screens, mosaics, lighting
Techniques: leaded or copper-foiled, sand-carved or etched, painted or enameled
Size Range: 18" x 12" to 8' x 4'
Price Range: $25 to $150/sq. ft.
Price Range: $80 to $250 for 3D work

RHONDA'S STAINED GLASS WORKSHOP

RHONDA GEE
1825 BOWNESS RD NW
CALGARY, AB T2N 3K5
CANADA
TEL 403-283-1862
Products: panels or screens, murals, lighting
Techniques: leaded or copper-foiled, beveled
Size Range: custom
Price Range: $75 to $500/sq. ft.

SUSAN RUSSELL

KRAATZ & RUSSELL
UPPER GRAFTON RD
 RFD #1 BOX 320C
CANAAN, NH 03741
TEL 603-523-4289
Established: 1976
Products: panels or screens, murals, framed-glass plaques
Techniques: leaded or copper-foiled, blown, decorated blown glass
Size Range: 12" x 12" to 6' x 3'
Price Range: $100 to $400/sq. ft.
Price Range: $200 to $1,800 for panels

SGO DESIGNER GLASS

DANIELA DIESEL AND GARY PARKS
2268 EL CAMINO REAL
MOUNTAIN VIEW, CA 94040
FAX 415-964-4032
TEL 415-964-4333
Established: 1987
Products: panels or screens, windows, door inserts
Techniques: leaded or copper-foiled, sandcarved or etched, beveled, laminated, overlay
Size Range: 1' x 1' to unlimited
Price Range: $40 to $90/sq. ft.

SCHAAK'S GLASS & ENGRAVING INC.

KURT J. SCHAAK
207 N MAIN ST
HARTFORD, WI 53027
TEL 800-950-7301
Established: 1986
Products: tiles, murals, wall reliefs
Techniques: sandcarved or etched, engraved, laminated, cast, blown in 1996
Size Range: 6" x 6" to 7.5' x 22'
Price Range: $35 to $300/sq. ft.
Price Range: $100 to $50,000 for sculpture

JUDE SCHLOTZHAUER

GLASS WORKS
8370 DUSTY LN
MECHANICSVILLE, VA 23111
TEL 804-559-2582
Established: 1973
Products: panels or screens, murals, lighting
Techniques: leaded or copper-foiled, painted or enameled, bent, fused or kiln-formed, pate de verre
Size Range: 18" x 14" to 20' x 60'
Price Range: $120 to $300/sq. ft.
Price Range: $300 to $60,000 for mirrors, murals, lighting

MARY SHAFFER

SHAFFER STUDIOS
10001 PRATT PL
SILVER SPRING, MD 20910
TEL 301-588-4388
Established: 1970
Products: columns, lighting, free-standing work
Techniques: bent, fused or kiln-formed, laminated, cast, fiber optics
Size Range: 3" x 3" to 50' x 30'
Price Range: $400 to $1,000/sq. ft.
Price Range: $2,000 to $240,000 for site-specific sculpture

WAYNE STRATTMAN

STRATTMAN DESIGN
791 TREMONT ST #E517
BOSTON, MA 02118
FAX 617-266-6263
TEL 617-266-8821
Established: 1983
Products: lighting
Techniques: bent, fused or kiln-formed, neon
Size Range: 12" to 12" to 10' x 50'
Price Range: $100 to $300/sq. ft.
Price Range: $200 to $5,000 for fused glass, neon panels

THE 3 OF SWORDS

J.C. HOMOLA
RT 1 BOX 395
AVA, MO 65608
FAX 800-282-4818
TEL 417-683-3460
Established: 1976
Products: murals, platters, wall reliefs
Techniques: sandcarved or etched, engraved, bent, fused or kiln-formed, laminated, lampworked
Size Range: 13" Dia to 6' x 20'
Price Range: $6 to $15/sq. ft.
Price Range: $180 to $575 for platters, disks

WAWRYTKO STUDIOS

MARY FRANCES WAWRYTKO
1945 COLUMBUS RD
CLEVELAND, OH 44113-3540
TEL 216-696-4258
Established: 1975
Products: tiles, panels or screens, wall reliefs
Techniques: painted or enameled, laminated, cast, pate de verre, cameo glass
Size Range: 6" x 6" to 6' x 8'
Price Range: $250 to $750 for glass panels

HELEN WEBBER

HELEN WEBBER DESIGNS
555 PACIFIC AVE
SAN FRANCISCO, CA 94133-4609
FAX 415-989-5746
TEL 415-989-5521
Established: 1972
Products: panels or screens, murals, stained, mirror glass
Techniques: sandcarved, enameled, leaded, painted, etched
Size Range: 36" x 18" to 7.5' x 16'
Price Range: $100 to $200 and up/sq. ft.

MARY B. WHITE

2327 5TH ST
BERKELEY, CA 94710
FAX 510-848-3932
TEL 510-848-3932
Established: 1975
Products: tiles, panels or screens, murals, wall reliefs
Techniques: painted or enameled, bent, fused or kiln-formed
Size Range: 11" x 9" to 8' x 20'
Price Range: $100 to $800/sq. ft.
Price Range: $350 to $20,000 for murals

WINTER GLAS

JOHN WINTER
5924 NW 30TH TERR
GAINESVILLE, FL 32653
FAX 904-335-7327
TEL 904-335-7327
Established: 1972
Products: tiles, lighting, wall reliefs
Techniques: leaded or copper-foiled, sandcarved or etched, bent, fused or kiln-formed, pate de verre
Size Range: 1' x 1' to unlimited
Price Range: $45 to $225/sq. ft.
Price Range: $100 to $50,000 for sculptural reliefs

BARBARA ELLIOTT

Interior Designer

With 25 years of international interior design experience, Barbara Elliott of Concord, California, was no stranger to large-scale, complex projects when she began working on a John Q. Hammond hotel down the coast at Seaside. Elliott, who often uses original art in her award-winning projects, designed a dramatic focal point in the hotel's central foyer by using colorful ceramic floor tile commissioned from a firm in Mexico. Unfortunately, as the construction deadline approached, a problem became evident.

"I knew that the construction schedule couldn't be altered, and it was clear that the supplier was simply not going to get the tile to us as promised. I was as disappointed as I was frustrated," Elliott explains.

"The very day we realized that we couldn't use our original plan, my copy of THE GUILD arrived. I was leafing through the pages, and saw George Fishman's ceramic work pictured. It was beautiful, and looked just like what I had in mind."

Elliott called the Florida artist, explained her predicament, and noted that the deadline was impossible and the budget uncompromising. Fishman agreed to take on the challenge. He prepared the mosaic, premounted the tiles for easy installation, and meticulously packed the work for shipment. Then, en route to California, disaster nearly struck again.

"Somehow, the shipper dropped the package," Elliott recalls. Instead of a premounted mosaic, the designer had many beautiful fragments. Again she called Fishman, who got on a plane, set up a temporary studio in the hotel's construction zone and went to work.

Remarkably, the tile work was in place on time, and a terrific success with the client. "George is so talented and energetic," Elliott says, "and he was such a wonderful team player. I'd highly, highly recommend working with him."

Elliott's positive experiences with GUILD artists didn't end with Fishman.

"I have also been delighted to work with Christina Spann. Her lighting designs add a wonderful, imaginative touch. Like George, she's flexible, accommodating and comes through beautifully on a tight schedule. Both of these artists provide the kind of exciting, high-quality work that elevates a design project into the realm of the memorable."

Photo by Russ Fischella

113

Penelope Fleming

7740 Washington Lane
Elkins Park, PA 19027
TEL 215-576-6830

Penelope Fleming designs wall pieces for public spaces, corporate collections and residential environments. The primary material is slate incorporated with modulated black, white and colored clay. Scale and color are unlimited. Pieces are lightweight, easily shipped and installed.

Fleming has worked with many designers, art consultants and galleries for the last 20 years to meet the criteria of design integrity, budget and completion deadlines. Commissioned wall pieces have been installed for many corporations, including Smithe Kline Beckman, Reichhold Chemical Inc., and Ragu Food Inc., as well as private individuals across the U.S. and Europe. Call or write for a catalog, prices and the availability of already completed pieces.

A *Between Leysin*, 66" x 44" x 4"

B *Diablerets*, 54" x 44" x 8"

A

B

Fox Tile Studio Inc.

Catherine and Garry Fox
5665 South Valley View, Suite 3
Las Vegas, NV 89118
FAX 702-798-6925
TEL 702-454-5776
TEL 702-798-1003

Fox Tile, doing business for over 17 years, has a reputation for creating the highest quality ceramics, while meeting the production and delivery needs of the design and construction communities.

Their range of capability includes mastery of virtually all ceramic techniques, three-dimensional murals of any size and style, sculpted tiles, specialty moldings, heavy-relief terra cotta, stoneware and porcelain for exterior and interior settings, carvings, handmade floral friezes, fountains, columns and many other custom shapes and designs using various methods, and a working palette of 3,500-plus glaze colors.

The scope of projects is limited only by the imagination. Commissions are welcomed.

A Cactus, desert bunnies, high relief, residence

B Figs and grapes, high relief, residence

C Rousseau-style mural, white tiger habitat, Mirage Hotel, Las Vegas, NV

D Cow mural, exterior

E Stoneware bar and armrest, mural and jewel tiles, restaurant

A

C

D

B

E

Beverlee Lehr

RR2, Box 112
Palmyra, PA 17078-9711
FAX 717-838-6428
TEL 717-838-4937

Beverlee Lehr produces sculptural painting in glazed stoneware for specific public, corporate and residential sites. Hand building with clay slabs, she draws inspiration from landscapes, plants, and human anatomy for her abstract, three-dimensional constructions.

Deep sculptural relief is created by the hollow construction of each tile-like module. Because each section is hollow, the overall weight is low for ceramic wall sculpture, averaging just 70 pounds for an installed piece. The beautiful surfaces must be seen to be appreciated.

Lehr's wall sculptures are durable and easily cleaned. Shipping via UPS is economical and installation on the plywood back-plate supplied with each work is a simple follow-the-numbers procedure. Prices start at $2,000.

Cleveland (shown) was exhibited in the 1994 Fletcher Challenge, an annual international ceramic competition held in Auckland, New Zealand. Ms. Lehr's sculpture is represented in the art collection of Monarch Tile, and in civic and private collections.

Also see these GUILD publications:
Designer's Edition: 9, 10

SHOWN: *Cleveland*, 1993, hand-built stoneware, 36" x 36" x 3", $3,000

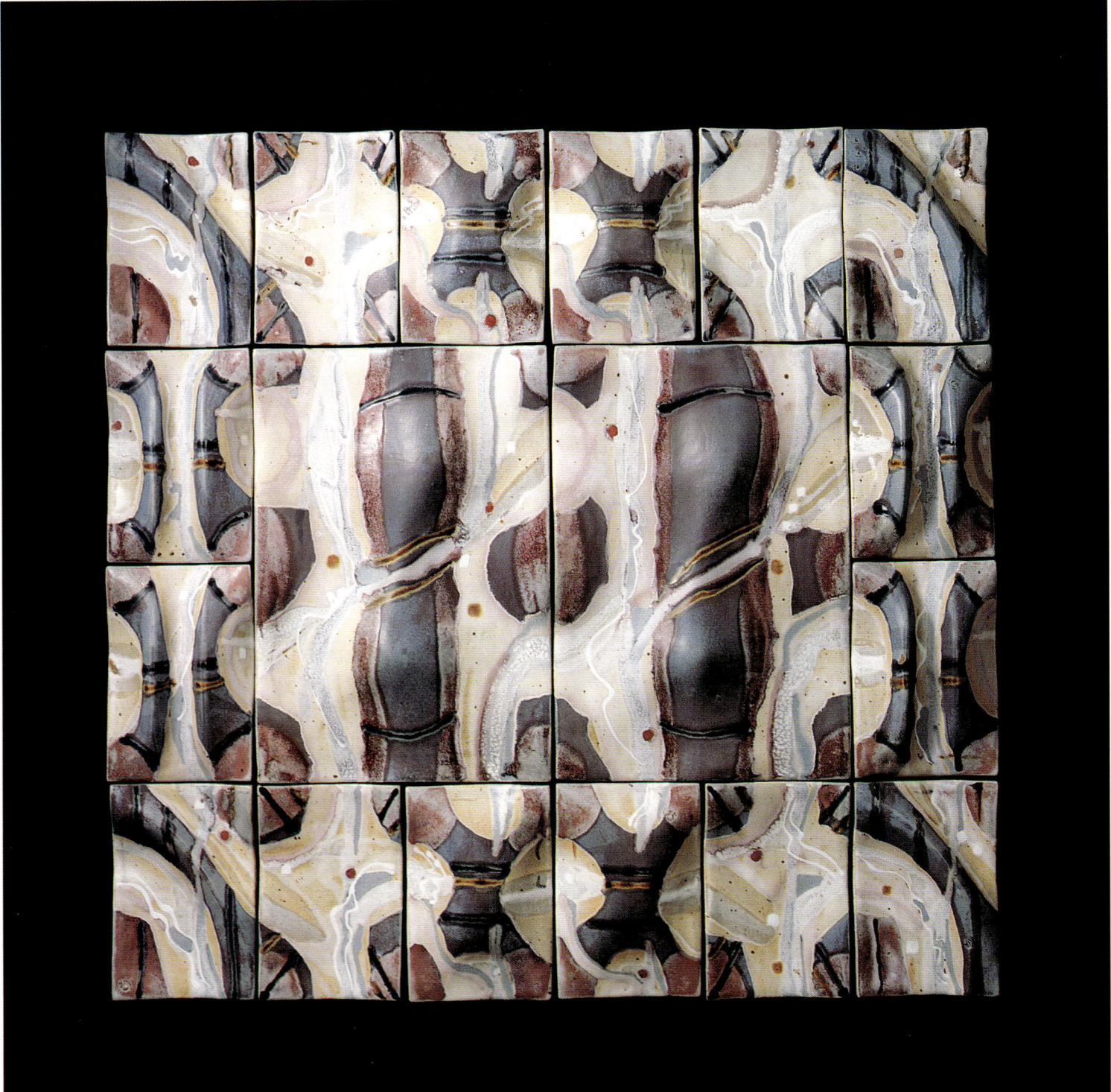

Socolow Photography

Thomas W. Lollar

132 West 65th Street
New York, NY 10023
TEL 212-864-7973
TEL 914-964-0812

Tom Lollar hand builds clay murals which depict architectural and geographical themes. Subjects include landmarks in both frontal bas-relief and aerial views. The unique surface color results from applying copper, bronze and platinum metallic paints and glazes. Each rectangular clay construction is approximately 20" x 20" x 4" and may be placed in combinations of unlimited numbers suitable to wall size.

Lollar has a Master's Degree in ceramic sculpture from Western Michigan University and has been creating clay murals professionally for ten years.

His murals are in the collections of Hyctt Hotels, Revlon, and Steelcase. His work has also been featured in the store windows of Tiffany and Co., Fifth Avenue, New York City.

Also see these GUILD publications:
THE GUILD: 4
Designer's Edition: 7, 8

A & B *Manhattan*, installation view, Loeb & Loeb,
 Park Avenue, New York, NY, 6' x 14' x 3"

C *Manhattan*, detail of rectangular section,
 22" x 20" x 3"

A

B

C

Photos: D. James Dee

THE GUILD REGISTER®
of Ceramic Art for the Wall

PAT ABI-SAAB

SAAB CERAMICS
257 VAN DUYER ST PO BOX 40070
STATEN ISLAND, NY 10304-0002
TEL 718-448-7980
Established: 1989
Products: tiles, platters, wall reliefs
Media: stoneware, earthenware, inlaid
colored clays, metal
Techniques: cast, constructed, wheel
thrown, metal
Size Range: 8" × 8" to 15" × 24"
Price Range: $55 to $280/sq. ft.
Price Range: $350 to $5,000 for
platters, disks

ALFREDO RATINOFF STUDIO

ALFREDO RATINOFF
11908 WINTERTHUR LN #106
RESTON, VA 22091-1956
TEL 703-716-2931
Established: 1984
Products: tiles, murals, one-of-a-kind
pottery
Media: stoneware, porcelain, earthenware
Techniques: constructed, wheel thrown,
raku fired
Size Range: 5" × 5" to 10' × 30'
Price Range: $40 to $100/sq. ft.
Price Range: $50 to $3,000 for
one-of-a-kind pottery

ANTICHITÀ MODERNA

BARBARA PETRARCA
655 UTICA AVE
BOULDER, CO 80304
FAX 303-449-8870
TEL 303-444-3626
Established: 1993
Products: columns, wall reliefs,
entryway surrounds
Media: stoneware, glass, terra cotta
Techniques: cast, salt or sodium fired,
hand-sculpted
Size Range: 4" × 4" to 20" × 15"
Price Range: $150 to $400/sq. ft.

★ ANTIOCH TILE CO.

DEBORAH S. ZIMMER
1410 DEWITT HENRY PO BOX 118
BEEBE, AR 72012
FAX 501-882-3952
TEL 501-882-2024
Established: 1983
Products: tiles, murals
Media: stoneware, earthenware
Techniques: constructed, impressed
Size Range: 4" × 4" to 12" × 12"
Price Range: $24 to $48/sq. ft.

See photograph on page 133.

ARCHITECTURAL CERAMICS

ELIZABETH GRAJALES
667 CARROLL ST
BROOKLYN, NY 11215
FAX 718-857-0729
TEL 718-857-0729
Established: 1978
Products: tiles, mosaics, wall reliefs
Media: stoneware, earthenware, brick
Techniques: cast, constructed, molded
Size Range: 8" × 8" to 15' × 13'
Price Range: $250 to $400/sq. ft.
Price Range: $250 to $400 for tiles

ART ON TILES

RITA PAUL
32 WASHINGTON SQ W
NEW YORK, NY 10011-9194
FAX 212-979-8373
TEL 212-674-6388
Established: 1965
Products: tiles, panels or screens, murals
Media: stoneware, glazed, low-medium
fired
Techniques: constructed
Size Range: 18' × 12" to 6' × 5'
Price Range: $70 to $100/sq. ft.
Price Range: $500 to $10,000 for murals

ARTISTIC LICENSE

GINIA CLEEVES AND
 ANNE SANGUINETTI
1551 16 ST
SANTA MONICA, CA 90404-3308
FAX 310-453-0804
TEL 310-453-0932
Established: 1980
Products: tiles, murals
Price Range: $50 to $150/sq. ft.
Price Range: $7 to $15 for 6" × 6"
or 8" × 8" tiles

MELINDA ASHLEY

MELINA ASHLEY STUDIOS
144 MOODY ST BLDG 18
WALTHAM, MA 02154
FAX 617-891-8811
TEL 617-891-8811
Established: 1976
Products: tiles, murals, platters
Media: stoneware, porcelain, earthenware,
stained glass
Techniques: cast, molded, wheel thrown
Size Range: 2' × 2' to unlimited
Price Range: $100 to $300/sq. ft.
Price Range: $600 to unlimited for murals

AUCIELLO STONE

SHLOMIT AND JOE AUCIELLO
1032 WOTTON MILL RD
WARREN, ME 04864
TEL 207-273-3065
Established: 1083
Products: tiles, wall reliefs
Media: stone
Techniques: carving, sandblasting
Size Range: 12" × 12" to unlimited
Price Range: $85/sq. ft.
Price Range: $85 for 12" × 12" tile

SALLY BARBIER

ALBERTA COLLEGE OF ART & DESIGN
1407 14TH AVE NW
CALGARY, AB T2N 1M4
CANADA
FAX 403-289-6682
TEL 403-277-4580
Established: 1975
Products: wall reliefs
Media: earthenware
Techniques: constructed, glazed,
sawdust fired
Size Range: 20" × 20" to 35" × 35"
Price Range: $400 to $800 for wall
sculptures

Susan O. Bliss, *Woman with Cup*, 1995, terra cotta, 18"W × 27"H,
photo: Charley Freiberg

MARVIN BARTEL

1708 LINCOLNWAY E
GOSHEN, IN 46526-5022
FAX 219-535-7660
TEL 219-533-0171
Established: 1965
Products: tiles, wall reliefs, fireplace surfaces
Media: stoneware, porcelain
Techniques: constructed, wheel thrown, unique tile shapes
Size Range: 6" × 6" to 8' × 12'
Price Range: $50 to $150/sq. ft.
Price Range: $1,000 to $15,000 for tile murals

MARLO BARTELS ARCHITECTURAL CERAMICS

MARLO BARTELS
2307 #7 LAGUNA CANYON RD
LAGUNA BEACH, CA 92651
FAX 714-497-0400
TEL 714-494-4408
Established: 1979
Products: tiles, mosaics, murals
Media: stoneware, earthenware, ceramic/ferro cement
Techniques: constucted, wheel thrown, custom installation
Size Range: any size
Price Range: $40 to $140/sq. ft.
Price Range: $40 to $140 for architectural installation

★ BATIK TILE

JOANNE M. GIGLIOTTI
69 BRALAN CT
GAITHERSBURG, MD 20877
FAX 301-590-3050
TEL 301-590-3050
Established: 1967
Products: tiles
Media: stoneware, porcelain, earthenware
Techniques: cast, constructed, molded
Size Range: 4.25" × 4.25" to unlimited
Price Range: $20 to $180/sq. ft.
Price Range: $50 to $280 for individual art pieces

See photograph on page 133.

CHRISTOPHER BECKSTROM

103 READE ST FL 4
NEW YORK, NY 10013
TEL 212-732-0134
Products: tiles, lighted panels, 3-D constrctions
Media: glass, wood, clay
Techniques: cast, constructed, hand carved
Size Range: 4" × 4" to unlimited
Price Range: $50 to $500/sq. ft.

BARBARA BEDESSEM

NORTHVIEW DESIGNS
544 STORLE AVE
BURLINGTON, WI 53105
TEL 414-763-6545
Established: 1970
Products: tiles, murals
Media: commercial tile
Techniques: custom painting
Size Range: 4" × 4" to 4' × 4'
Price Range: $30 to $75/sq. ft.
Price Range: $3 to $20 for single tiles

SIMI BERMAN

PO BOX 58
CHESTERFIELD, NH 03443-0058
FAX 802-257-5119
TEL 603-256-8477
Established: 1982
Products: wall reliefs
Media: earthenware
Techniques: constructed
Size Range: 12" × 10" to 22" × 18"
Price Range: $110 to $400 for wall sculpture

BILL CART TILES, INC.

BILL CART
31 W 21ST ST
NEW YORK, NY 10010
FAX 212-727-8566
TEL 212-724-7717
Products: tiles, wall reliefs, trivets
Media: earthenware
Techniques: pressed, hand-glazed
Size Range: 6" × 6" and up
Price Range: $16 to $19 for trivets, tiles

★ SUSAN O. BLISS

JOPPA CLAYWORKS
114 JOPPA RD E
WARNER, NH 03278
TEL 603-456-3276
Established: 1975
Products: tiles, wall reliefs, mirrors, doorways
Media: earthenware, terra cotta
Techniques: burnished rolled clay
Size Range: 2" × 2" to 60" × 30"
Price Range: $100 to $300/sq. ft.
Price Range: $300 to $900 for portrait wall tile

See photograph on page 118.

★ BLUE MOON CERAMIC TILE STUDIO

KATRINA WOLF
PO BOX 22-0964
HOLLYWOOD, FL 33022-0964
TEL 954-927-7900
Established: 1985
Products: tiles, murals
Media: stoneware, porcelain, inlaid colored clays
Techniques: constructed, molded
Size Range: 2" × 2" to 10' × 10'
Price Range: $22 to $44/sq. ft.
Price Range: $7 to $25 for feature tiles and accessories

See photograph on page 133.

SUSAN BOOMHOUWER

24035 CORMORANT LN
LAGUNA NIGUEL, CA 92677
TEL 714-362-3595
Established: 1978
Products: tiles, panels or screens, murals
Media: stoneware, porcelain, earthenware
Techniques: cast, constructed, molded
Size Range: 18" × 18" to 15' × 25'
Price Range: $75 to $200/sq. ft.

LINDA BRENDLER

LINDA BRENDLER STUIOS
428 HACKBERRY AVE
MODESTO, CA 95354
TEL 209-522-3534
Established: 1979
Products: murals, platters, wall reliefs
Media: stoneware, porcelain
Techniques: constructed, varied techniques
Size Range: 10" × 30" to 4' × 6'
Price Range: $150 to $5,000 for platters, wall reliefs

CYNTHIA BRINGLE

BRINGLE POTTERY STUDIO
PENLAND SCHOOL RD
PENLAND, NC 28765-9999
FAX 704-765-0240
TEL 704-765-0240
Established: 1965
Products: murals, platters, wall reliefs
Media: stoneware, raku fired
Techniques: constructed, wheel thrown
Size Range: 1' × 3' to 8' × 10'
Price Range: $250 to $600/sq. ft.
Price Range: $500 to $1,000 for platters

Four Corners Tile Designs, *Irises*, 1993, handmade tile mural, 30" × 18", photo: John Langford

CERAMIC ART FOR THE WALL

HARRIET E. BRISSON

BRISSON STUDIO
31 POND ST PO BOX 85
REHOBOTH, MA 02769
TEL 508-252-3024
Established: 1955
Products: tiles, lighted panels
Media: earthenware, stoneware
Techniques: cast, constructed, raku fired
Size Range: 6" × 6" to 32' × 32'
Price Range: $100 to $5,000 for murals

MAUREEN BURNS-BOWIE

MAUREEN BURNS-BOWIE INC.
9124 W BUSH LAKE RD
BLOOMINGTON, MN 55438
TEL 612-828-6078
Established: 1975
Products: platters, wall reliefs, wall sculptures
Media: porcelain, glass
Techniques: constructed, molded, g lass slump
Size Range: 12"' × 7" to 10' × 20'
Price Range: $500 to $10,000 for wall sculptures

★ ANNA CABO

2003 6TH ST
SANTA MONICA, CA 90405
FAX 310-450-1011
TEL 310-450-1011
Established: 1990
Products: tiles, panels or screens, murals
Media: glass
Size Range: 2" × 2" to 40" × 20"
Price Range: $90 to $360/sq. ft.
Price Range: $330 and up for platters, panels, murals

See photograph on page 109.

ROBERT CARLSON
MARILEE HALL

PRIMUS STUDIO
2350 BROWN'S MILL RD
COOKEVILLE, TN 38506
TEL 615-526-6649
Established: 1971
Products: platters, wall reliefs, vessels, sculpture
Media: stoneware, earthenware, raku, pit fire
Techniques: cast, constructed, wheel thrown
Size Range: 10" × 10" to 20' × 30'
Price Range: $250/sq. ft.
Price Range: $450 for platters (23" to 24"Dia)

NANCY CARMAN

NANCY CARMAN STUDIO
330 EMILY ST
PHILADELPHIA, PA 19148
TEL 215-389-7160
Established: 1974
Products: tiles, wall reliefs, wall sculptures
Media: earthenware
Techniques: constructed, molded, glazed
Size Range: 12" × 12" to 9' × 30'
Price Range: $5,000 to $20,000 for wall sculpture

MARY CARROLL

MARY CARROLL CERAMICS
3904 UPTON AVE S
MINNEAPOLIS, MN 55410
TEL 612-922-3914
Established: 1992
Products: tiles, mosaics, murals, mirrors
Media: earthenware
Techniques: cast, molded, hand built
Size Range: 10" × 10" to 5' × 8'
Price Range: $50 to $250/sq. ft.
Price Range: $2,500 to $4,000 for commissioned mirrors, murals

CASCADE DESIGN, INC.

DY WITT
1136 NITTANY CREST AVE
BELLEFONTE, PA 16823
TEL 814-383-2011
Established: 1984
Products: tiles, murals, framed tile paintings
Media: stoneware, porcelain, earthenware
Techniques: constructed, molded, handmade
Size Range: 4" × 4" to unlimited
Price Range: $20 to $100/sq. ft.
Price Range: $10 to $30 for tiles

LYLAMAE T. CHEDSEY

2661 BAHAMAS WAY
GRAND JUNCTION, CO 81506
TEL 303-241-4579
Established: 1980
Products: mosaics, table or counter tops
Media: glass, white clay
Techniques: constructed hand-cut, fused-glass glaze
Size Range: 7" × 5" to 3' × 3'
Price Range: $75 to $1,000 for framed wall hung, table tops

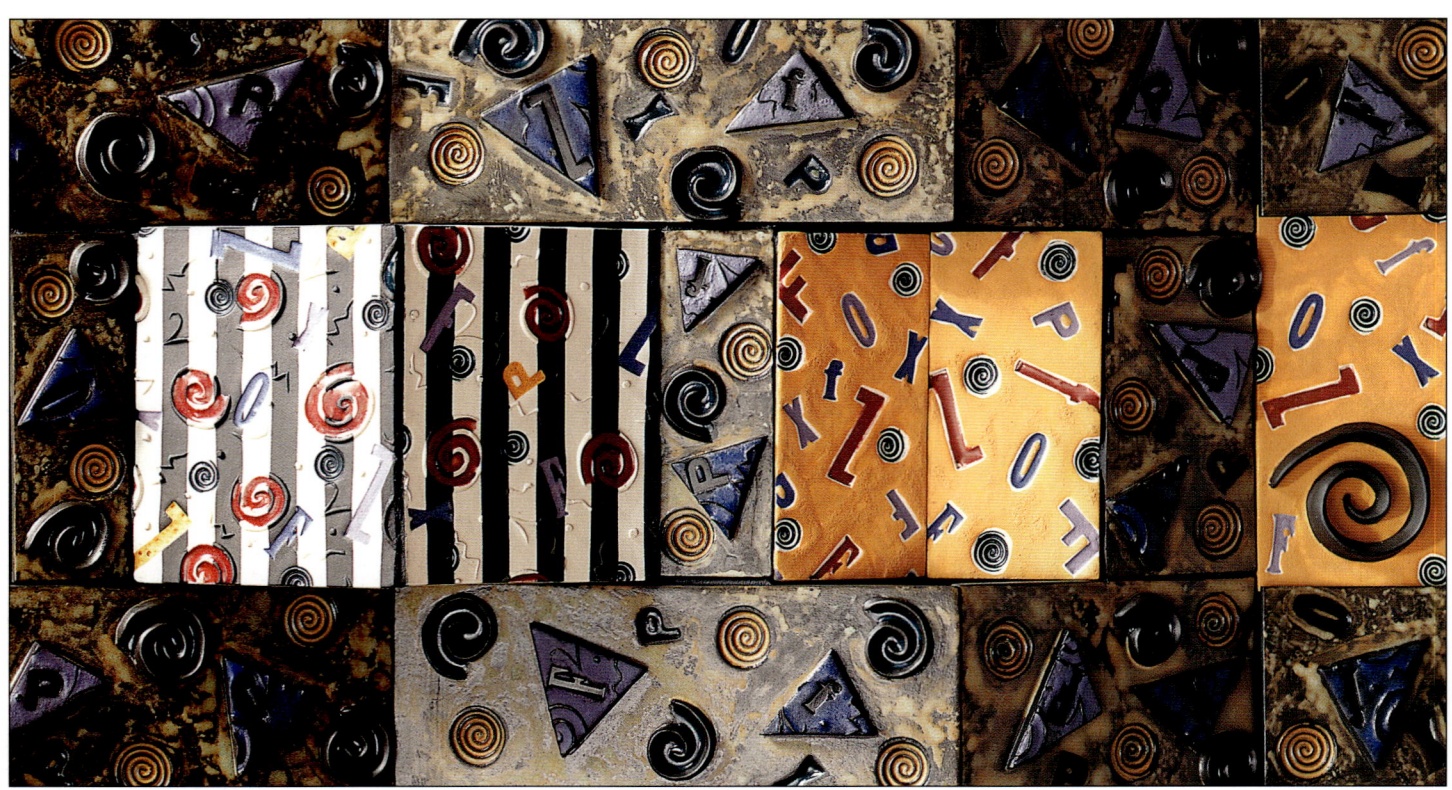

Claudia Hollister, untitled, 1996, colored porcelain, commissioned by Fineman Associates, San Francisco, CA, 1'H × 9'L × 5"D

COELHO STUDIOS

JACK M. NEULIST-COELHO
PO BOX 620
6135 W EVANS CREEK RD
ROGUE RIVER, OR 97537
FAX 541-432-5109
TEL 541-582-0216

Established: 1974
Products: murals, columns, wall reliefs, tiles, entryway surrounds
Media: stoneware, porcelain, earthenware, mixed media
Techniques: constructed, molded, wheel thrown, sculpted
Size Range: 18" × 16" to unlimited scale
Price Range: $500 to $10,000 for large, complex pieces

FRANK COLSON

COLSON STUDIO/COLSON
  SCHOOL OF ART, INC.
1666 HILLVIEW ST
SARASOTA, FL 34239
FAX 941-953-5892
TEL 941-953-5892

Established: 1960
Products: tiles, wall reliefs
Media: stoneware, earthenware
Techniques: constructed, molded, wheel thrown
Size Range: 10" × 10" to 18' × 12'
Price Range: $35 to $60/sq. ft.
Price Range: $25 to $60 for mural composits

★ COUNTRY FLOORS

15 E 16TH ST
NEW YORK, NY 10003
FAX 212-627-7742
TEL 212-627-8300
Products: tiles, panels or screens, mosaics
Media: earthenware, inlaid colored clays, etc.
Techniques: molded, hand painted

See photographs on page 131.

DIANA CRAIN

DIANA CRAIN PORCELAINS
173 LIVE OAK DR
PETALUMA, CA 94952-1016
FAX 707-795-2451
TEL 707-795-2451
Products: wall reliefs wall vases and tables
Media: porcelain, terra cotta, colored painted porcelain
Techniques: constructed
Size Range: 10" × 5" to 22" × 10"
Price Range: $30 to $410 for wall vase

LYNDA CURTIS

L. CURTIS DESIGNS
145 HUDSON ST
NEW YORK, NY 10013-2103
FAX 212-966-1720
TEL 212-966-1720
Established: 1989
Products: tiles, murals, wall reliefs
Media: stoneware, earthenware
Techniques: cast, constructed, molded
Size Range: 4" × 4" to 7' × 15'
Price Range: $15 to $300/sq. ft.
Price Range: $8 to $20,000 for individual tiles, furniture, murals

DABBERT STUDIO

DAVE & PAT DABBERT
3009 MAYFIELD WY
MICHIGAN CITY, IN 46360
TEL 219-879-7201
TEL 813-925-9929

Established: 1970
Products: tiles wall sculptures
Media: porcelain
Techniques: constructed, wheel thrown
Size Range: 3.5" × 10" to unlimited
Price Range: $200 to $300/sq. ft.

PHILLIP ! DANZIG

GET CRACKIN'!
70 E 10TH ST
NEW YORK, NY 10003
TEL 212-674-3721
Established: 1970
Products: mosaics, murals, tiles
Media: porcelain, stoneware, hand-cracked tile
Techniques: constructed, shaped
Size Range: 2' × 2' to 20' × 40'
Price Range: $75 to $150/sq. ft.

Margie Hughto Studio, *Golden Threads,* 1995, ceramic triptych, each tile 44"H × 19"W, photo: Anthony Potter

CERAMIC ART FOR THE WALL

LYNN BLACKWELL DENTON

607 S 9TH ST
PHILADELPHIA, PA 19147
TEL 215-923-6192
Established: 1968
Products: tiles, mosaics, murals
Media: stoneware, porcelain, earthenware
Techniques: constructed
Size Range: 3' × 4' to 10' × 30'
Price Range: $2,000 to $25,000 for murals

DESIGN TILES OF MIFFLINBURG

JOANNAH SKUCEK
508 CHESTNUT ST
MIFFINBURG, PA 17844
FAX 717-966-3128
TEL 717-966-3373
Established: 1983
Products: tiles, murals
Media: earthenware
Techniques: molded
Size Range: 3' × 3" to 12' × 12'
Price Range: $22 to $100/sq. ft.
Price Range: $50 to $2,000 for ceramic
tile murals

NELL DEVITT

NELL DEVITT POTTERY
RR3 BOX 84
BLOOMFIELD, IN 47424
TEL 812-384-3012
Established: 1985
Products: tiles, murals, wall reliefs
Media: earthenware
Techniques: constructed
Size Range: 8" × 8" to 7' × 9'
Price Range: $200 to $6,000 for clay
tiles, murals

ERIC DOCTORS

CERAMIC TILES,
 VESSELS AND SCULPTURE
123 KEDZIE AVE
EVANSTON, IL 60202
FAX 312-609-9839
TEL 708-864-4288
Established: 1983
Products: panels or screens, tiles, murals
Media: stoneware
Techniques: slab built, scored
Size Range: 4" × 4" to 6' × 10'
Price Range: $40 to $120/sq. ft.

STEVEN DONEGAN

915 SPRING GARDEN ST
PHILADELPHIA, PA 19123-2605
FAX 215-232-5664
TEL 215-232-5459
Established: 1976
Products: tiles, murals
Media: earthenware
Techniques: constructed
Size Range: 31" × 22" to 11' × 12'
Price Range: $250/sq. ft.

MAUREEN ELLIS

ELLIS CERAMICS
3070 KERNER BLVD #N
SAN RAFAEL, CA 94901-5419
FAX 415-485-4305
TEL 415-453-2116
Established: 1980
Products: tiles, murals, platters
Media: earthenware
Techniques: constructed, molded
Size Range: 4" × 4" to 30' × 500'
Price Range: $5 to $500/sq. ft.

MELANIE ENDERLE

ART TILES
8048 10TH AVE NW
SEATTLE, WA 98117
FAX 206-782-5982
TEL 206-782-5982
Established: 1979
Products: tiles, panels or screens, murals
Media: ceramic tile
Techniques: painted, glazed tiles
Size Range: 6" × 6" to 10' × 20'
Price Range: $100 to $250/sq. ft.
Price Range: $10 to $500 for tiles and
tile murals

RANDY FEIN

MOUNTAIN STUDIO
4163 YOUNGSTOWN RD
LINCOLNVILLE, ME 04849
TEL 207-763-3433
Established: 1975
Products: murals, columns, house
portraits
Media: clay, colored glass
Techniques: constructed one-of-a-kind
constructions
Size Range: 24" × 24" to unlimited
Price Range: $1,000 to $50,000 for relief
sculpture installations

JEROME FERRETTI

CUSTOM MASONRY
2000 BROOKLYN
DETROIT, MI 48226-1010
TEL 313-965-3697
Established: 1952
Products: panels or screens, murals,
columns, fireplaces
Media: brick
Techniques: cast, constructed
Size Range: 12" × 12" to 12' × 12'
Price Range: $200 to $500/sq. ft.

FIRECLAY TILE

PAUL BURNS
495 W JULIAN ST
SAN JOSE, CA 95110-2337
FAX 408-275-1187
TEL 408-275-1182
Established: 1986
Products: tiles
Media: stoneware, porcelain, earthenware
Techniques: molded
Size Range: 1" × 1" to 12" × 12"
Price Range: $9 to $16/sq. ft.
Price Range: $6 to $20 for relief
decorative tiles

GEORGE F. FISHMAN

103 NE 99TH ST
MIAMI SHORES, FL 33138
FAX 305-751-1770
TEL 305-758-1141
Established: 1986
Products: mosaics, murals, columns
Media: porcelain, glass, glazed tile and
stone
Techniques: cast, constructed
Size Range: 18" × 24" to 10' × 20'
Price Range: $50 to $250/sq. ft.
Price Range: $150 to $1,000 for cast
mosaic plaques

★ PENELOPE FLEMING

7740 WASHINGTON LN
ELKINS PARK, PA 19027
TEL 215-576-6830
Established: 1972
Products: wall reliefs, tiles
Media: earthenware, stoneware, slate
Techniques: constructed, raku fired
Size Range: 12" × 12" to 96" × 170"
Price Range: $400 to $20,000 for
wall reliefs

**See page 114 for photographs
and additional information.**

E. Joseph McCarthy, *Abstract Palm Tree* (detail), 5" × 5" terra cotta tiles, 6'3"W × 4'2"H overall,
photo: André Banville

DIANE E. FOULDS

PO BOX 117
BURLINGTON, VT 05402-0117
FAX 802-658-0900
TEL 802-658-0900
Established: 1991
Products: wall hangings
Media: painted or enameled
Size Range: 10" × 12" to 30" × 40"
Price Range: $250 to $300/sq. ft.
Price Range: $300 to $2,500 for wall
hangings

★ FOUR CORNERS TILE DESIGNS/HOME OF VOLATILE™

ELENA EIDELBERG
1215 W 5TH
AUSTIN, TX 78702
FAX 512-320-0705
TEL 512-320-0705
Established: 1991
Products: tiles, mosaics, murals
Media: earthenware
Techniques: cast, molded
Size Range: 6" × 6" to 15' × 15'
Price Range: $65 to $85/sq. ft.
Price Range: $10 to $30 for ceramic-cast tiles

See photograph on page 119.

★ FOX TILE STUDIO INC.

CATHERINE AND GARY FOX
5665 S VALLEY VIEW VISTA
SUITE 3
LAS VEGAS, NV 89118
TEL 702-454-5776
Products: tiles, panels or screens, murals,
columns, wall reliefs
Media: stoneware, porcelain, earthenware
Techniques: constructed, molded,
raku fired
Size Range: variable
Price Range: $12 and up/sq. ft.

**See page 115 for photographs
and additional information.**

FULPER TILE

ANNE FULPER
BOX 373
YARDLEY, PA 19067
TEL 215-736-8512
Established: 1987
Products: tiles
Media: stoneware
Techniques: molded, extruded
Size Range: 1" × 1" to 12" × 12"
Price Range: $60 to $93/sq. ft.

FRANK GIORGINI

GIORGINI DESIGN - UDU INC.
RT 67 BOX 126
FREEHOLD, NY 12431
FAX 518-634-2488
TEL 518-634-2559
Established: 1971
Products: tiles, murals, wall reliefs
Media: stoneware, earthenware
Techniques: constructed, salt or sodium
fired, molded
Size Range: 2" × 1" to 8' × 34'
Price Range: $100 to $400/sq. ft.
Price Range: $1,000 to $20,000 for wall
plaques, murals

GOOSENECK DESIGNS

JACKIE & CHRIS SMITH
2020 HUGHES SHOP RD
WESTMINSTER, MD 21158-2963
TEL 410-848-5663
Products: tiles, murals, columns,
wall reliefs
Media: stoneware, porcelain, earthenware
Techniques: constructed, molded,
wheel thrown
Size Range: 32" × 40" to 8' × 24'
Price Range: $45 to $110/sq. ft.
Price Range: $2,200 to $5,600 for
fireplace surrounds, fountains, murals

ELISE GRAY

ELISE GRAY STUDIO
1483 OGLETHORPE ST
MACON, GA 31201
TEL 912-738-0438
Established: 1972
Products: wall reliefs, murals, platters
Media: stoneware cement
Techniques: constructed, molded, cast
Size Range: 16" × 12" to 9'10" × 12'
Price Range: $200 to $400/sq. ft.
Price Range: $250 to $595 for platters

MICHELLE GREGOR

812 E 24TH ST
OAKLAND, CA 94606
TEL 510-834-1324
Established: 1985
Products: wall reliefs, fireplace surrounds
Media: stoneware
Techniques: constructed, colored slips
Size Range: 2' × 2' to 9' × 3'
Price Range: $200 to $350/sq. ft.
Price Range: $500 to $10,000 for sculpted
wall reliefs, mostly figurative

KAREN M. GUNDERMAN

11618 N COUNTRY LN
MEQUON, WI 53092
FAX 414-229-6154
TEL 414-229-6351
Established: 1975
Products: mosaics, murals, wall reliefs
Media: earthenware, glass
Techniques: constructed
Size Range: 30" × 48" to 9' × 15'
Price Range: $2,800 to $18,000 for murals

LARRY HALVORSEN

LARRY HALVORSEN/CERAMICS
335 NW 51
SEATTLE, WA 98107
TEL 206-781-1434
Established: 1981
Products: tiles, platters, wall reliefs
Media: stoneware
Techniques: constructed
Size Range: 14" × 14" to unlimited
Price Range: $75 to $125/sq. ft.

DEBORAH HECHT

CUSTOM DESIGN ON TILE
1865 HARVEST LN
BLOOMFIELD HILLS, MI 48302
TEL 810-333-2168
Products: tiles, murals, wall reliefs
Media: stoneware, earthenware,
overglaze painting
Techniques: constructed, molded,
opus sectile
Size Range: 5" × 8" to 4' × 10'
Price Range: $100 to $400/sq. ft.

★ GRETCHEN HEUGES MARGARET HEUGES

HEUGES TILES
RR 1 BOX 1020
SUGARLOAF, PA 18249
TEL 717-788-0628
Products: tiles, mosaics, wall reliefs
Media: earthenware
Techniques: constructed, molded
Size Range: 4" × 4" to unlimited
Price Range: $75 and up/sq. ft.
Price Range: $25 for hand-cast relief tile,
4" × 4"

See photograph on page 133.

HILLTOP STUDIO

BEVERLY LEVINER AND
NANCY SARANGOULIS
RD 1 BOX 1211
LEESPORT, PA 19533
TEL 610-779-0708
Products: tiles, mosaics, wall reliefs
Media: earthenware, terra cotta
w/out glaze
Techniques: molded, hand-cut mosaics
Size Range: 1" × 1" to unlimited
Price Range: $150/sq. ft.
Price Range: $4 and up for tiles

★ CLAUDIA HOLLISTER

1314 NW IRVING ST #206
PORTLAND, OR 97209-2722
FAX 503-226-0429
TEL 503-636-6684
Established: 1980
Products: tiles, murals, wall reliefs
Media: porcelain, inlaid colored clays
Techniques: constructed, molded
Size Range: 12" × 12" to 8' × 10'
Price Range: $50 to $300/sq. ft.
Price Range: $500 to $25,000 for wall
constructions

See photograph on page 120.

JERI HOLLISTER

801 AMHERST AVE
ANN ARBOR, MI 48105-1652
FAX 313-747-4121
TEL 313-761-1971
Established: 1987
Products: panels or screens, wall reliefs
Media: earthenware
Techniques: constructed
Size Range: 18" × 12" to 60" × 72"
Price Range: $500 to $5,000 for
wall reliefs and free-standing panels

RICHARD HOUSTON

PO BOX 1356
ASHLAND, OR 97520-0046
TEL 541-482-7323
Established: 1986
Products: panels or screens, murals
Media: drywall
Techniques: constructed
Size Range: 12" × 12" to 32' × 160'
Price Range: $1,200 to $50,000 for murals

SYLVIA HYMAN

OBJECTS IN CLAY
1112 PARK RIDGE DR
NASHVILLE, TN 32515
TEL 615-665-1143
Established: 1938
Products: tiles, panels or screens,
wall reliefs
Media: porcelain
Techniques: constructed
Size Range: 17" × 19" to 42" × 62"
Price Range: $1,000 to $4,500 for
irregularly shaped wall relief

CERAMIC ART FOR THE WALL

MARY LADAKH IEMOTO

MU STUDIOS
10208 148TH AVE SE
RENTON, WA 98059
TEL 206-277-0755
Products: murals, wall reliefs, sculpture
Media: stoneware, earthenware, glass
Techniques: cast, constructed, wood fired
Size Range: 5" × 5" to 24" × 24"
Price Range: $1,000 to $1,500 for wall reliefs

★ ILLAHE TILEWORKS

SUE SPRINGER WERSCHKUL
695 MISTLETOE RD #E
ASHLAND, OR 97520
FAX 541-488-2741
TEL 541-488-5072
Established: 1974
Products: tiles, murals, signs
Media: stoneware, porcelain, inlaid colored clays
Techniques: constructed, molded, pressed
Size Range: 4" × 4" to 20' × 100' murals
Price Range: $15 to $100/sq. ft.
Price Range: $5 to $500 for framed tile pieces

See photographs on page 133.

JEFF IRWIN

JEFF IRWIN CERAMIC ART
(STUDIO 1)
3594 3 AVE
SAN DIEGO, CA 92103
TEL 619-544-6420
Established: 1982
Products: tiles, platters, wall reliefs
Media: stoneware, porcelain, earthenware
Techniques: constructed, molded
Size Range: 1' × 1' to 8' × 10'
Price Range: $200 to $300/sq. ft.
Price Range: $400 to $600 for 22" platter, hand drawn tiles

J.E. JASEN

JUNE JASEN
36 E 10TH ST
NEW YORK, NY 10003-6219
FAX 212-777-6375
TEL 212-674-6113
Established: 1979
Products: tiles, murals, custom design
Media: enamel
Techniques: glass on metal
Size Range: 4" × 4" to unlimited
Price Range: $175 to $450/sq. ft.

SHELLIE JACOBSON

RD2 GRANDVIEW RD
SKILLMAN, NJ 08558
TEL 609-466-3612
Established: 1978
Products: tiles, platters, wall reliefs
Media: porcelain
Techniques: constructed, hand built
Size Range: 15.5 × 12.75 to 4'2" × 4'2"
Price Range: $150 to $1,500 for wall reliefs, wall platters

ANTHONY J. JEROSKI

A.J. DESIGNS INC.
PO BOX 576
MUNCIE, IN 47308-0576
TEL 317-287-1647
Established: 1988
Products: tiles, panels or screens, murals
Media: stoneware, porcelain, mixed media
Techniques: constructed, molded
Size Range: 18" × 10" to 10' × 18'
Price Range: $150 to $25,000 for sculptural forms/murals

JOCELYN STUDIO

JOCELYN GOLDMAN
39 OLD TOWN ST
EAST HADDAM, CT 06423
TEL 860-526-1581
Established: 1988
Products: tiles, platters, wall relief
Media: stoneware, earthenware, inlaid colored clays
Techniques: constructed, molded, raku fired
Size Range: 4" × 4" to 4' × 4'
Price Range: $8 to $50/sq. ft.

TOVE B. JOHANSEN

6613 BRAWNER ST
MCLEAN, VA 22101
TEL 703-893-6728
Established: 1952
Products: tiles, panels or screens, mosaics, requests from architects
Media: brick, refractory clay, marble
Techniques: cast, constructed, molded
Size Range: 2' × 3' to 12' × 54'

Carolyn Payne, *Spanish Plaza, Seville, Spain,* 1992, tile clock for Country Club Plaza, Kansas City, MO, commissioned by Miller Nichols/J.C. Nichols Co., 5'Dia

JULIE MATTHEWS STUDIO

JULIE MATTHEWS
131 W KLATT RD
ANCHORAGE, AK 99515
FAX 907-344-2529
TEL 907-344-2529
Established: 1978
Products: tiles, murals, columns
Media: porcelain, earthenware
Techniques: constructed
Size Range: 4" × 4" to 9' × 40'
Price Range: $150 to $25,000 for
wall installations

TERRY KAPLAN

TERRY TILES
10240 SW 133RD ST
MIAMI, FL 33176
FAX 305-253-6407
TEL 305-253-6407
Established: 1975
Products: tiles, mosaics, murals
Media: earthenware, mixed media,
stone, metal
Techniques: constructed
Size Range: 12" × 12" to unlimited
Price Range: $50 to $100/sq. ft.
Price Range: $100 to $300 for mosaic

SHERRY KARVER

4333 HOLDEN ST #54
EMERYVILLE, CA 94608
FAX 510-428-2660
TEL 510-653-2524
Established: 1980
Products: mosaics, murals, wall reliefs
Media: ceramic, mixed media
Techniques: constructed, painted,
smoke fired
Size Range: 2' × 2' to 10' to unlimited
Price Range: $2,000 to $25,000 for wall
reliefs, installation

STEVEN AND SUSAN KEMENYFFY

SWIFT CREEK POTTERY & PRESS
4570 OLD STATE RD
MCKEAN, PA 16426-2239
FAX 814-734-4736
TEL 814-734-4421
Established: 1967
Products: tiles, murals, wall reliefs
Media: raku
Techniques: constructed raku fired
Size Range: 7" × 7" to 11' × 12'
Price Range: $1,500 to $9,000 for wall
reliefs, sculpture

SHELBY KENNEDY

TILE AND MOSAIC WORKSHOP
474 VALENCIA #125
SAN FRANCISCO, CA 94103
FAX 415-864-0378
TEL 415-695-9816
Established: 1985
Products: tiles, mosaics, ceramic signage
Media: stoneware, earthenware, glass
Techniques: cast, molded
Size Range: 3" × 5" to 1, 050 sq.ft.
Price Range: $40 to $200/sq. ft.

KEPPERS POTTERY

KEN KEPPERS
235 US HWY 8
TURTLE LAKE, WI 54889-9110
TEL 715-986-4322
Established: 1976
Products: tiles, platters
Media: stoneware, porcelain
Techniques: wheel thrown, wood fired
Size Range: 3" × 3" to 32' × 36'
Price Range: $2 to $5/sq. ft.
Price Range: $12 to $300 for platters,
ceramic prints

STEPHEN KNAPP

74 COMMODORE RD
WORCESTER, MA 01602-2727
FAX 508-797-3228
TEL 508-757-2507
Established: 1972
Products: mosaics, murals, wall reliefs
Media: glass, inlaid colored clays
Techniques: mosaics, over-glazed tile
Size Range: 4' × 8' to 9' × 38'
Price Range: $200 to $700/sq. ft.

KRISTENSEN STUDIO

GAIL KRISTENSEN
360 CATHEDRAL ROCK TR
SEDONA, AZ 86336
TEL 520-282-2448
Established: 1960
Products: wall reliefs
Media: stoneware, porcelain, glass
Techniques: constructed, hand construction
Size Range: 12" × 12" to 6' × 40'
Price Range: variable/sq. ft.

KRYSIA

KRYSIA STRONSKI
1360 LUCERNE
MONTREAL, QB H3R 2H9
CANADA
TEL 514-731-0234
Established: 1985
Products: panels or screens, murals,
wall reliefs
Media: stoneware, earthenware,
paper clay
Techniques: cast, constructed,
wheel thrown
Size Range: 1' × 1' to 8'x 1'
Price Range: $30 to $100/sq. ft.
Price Range: $150 to $1,500 for panel

PETER LADOCHY

PETER LADOCHY MOSAICS
17 OCEAN FRONT AVE
CAYUCOS, CA 93430-1642
FAX 805-995-0118
TEL 805-995-3579
Established: 1977
Products: mosaics, murals, panels or
screens, relief, sculpture
Media: porcelain, glass, inlaid colored
clays, hardwood inlays
Techniques: constructed
Size Range: 2' × 3' to unlimited
Price Range: $60 to $600 for murals/sq. ft.

LA LUZ CANYON STUDIO

JERRY WELLMAN &
  NINA MASTRANGELO
PO 10627
ALAMEDA, MN 87184
FAX 505-898-8819
TEL 505-899-9977
Established: 1982
Products: tiles, murals, full-room design
Media: stoneware, porcelain, earthen-
ware
Techniques: handpainted, glazed
Size Range: 4.25" × 4.25" to unlimited
Price Range: $30 to $270/sq. ft.
Price Range: $3.50 to $30 for individual
tiles

Will Richards, ceramic panels, 6'W × 3'H overall

LATKA STUDIOS

TOM & JEAN LATKA
229 MIDWAY AVE
PUEBLO, CO 81004-1912
TEL 710-543-0720

Established: 1965
Products: tiles, mosaics, murals, custom extruded clay
Media: stoneware, earthenware, brick, bronze
Techniques: constructed, molded, wheel thrown, extruded molding
Size Range: 1' x 1' to 8' x 8'
Price Range: $100 to $300 for murals/sq. ft.
Price Range: $100 to $300, for wall work

PATRICIA LAY

77 GRAND ST
JERSEY CITY, NJ 07302-4521
TEL 201-333-5437

Established: 1968
Products: tiles, murals, wall reliefs
Media: stoneware, earthenware
Techniques: cast, constructed, molded
Size Range: 12" x 12" to 12' x 40'
Price Range: $300 to $800/sq. ft.

DEIRDRE LEE

URBAN JUNGLE ART AND DESIGN
244 W BROOKES AVE
SAN DIEGO, CA 92103-4810
FAX 619-296-1570
TEL 619-299-1644

Established: 1971
Products: tiles, murals
Media: ceramic
Techniques: constructed, molded, reduction fired, hand painted
Size Range: 6" x 18" and up
Price Range: $50 to $80/sq. ft.
Price Range: $100 and up for murals and borders

★ BEVERLEE LEHR

RR 2 BOX 112
PALMYRA, PA 17078
FAX 717-838-6428
TEL 717-838-4937

Established: 1973
Products: panels or screens, wall reliefs, hollow 3D tiles
Media: stoneware
Techniques: constructed, press molded
Size Range: 24" x 36" to 8' x 10'
Price Range: $300 to $350/sq. ft.

See page 116 for photographs and additional information.

EUTHOLD CERAMICS

MARC LEUTHOLD
355 CENTRAL PARK WEST
NEW YORK, NY 10025
TEL 212-222-0923

Established: 1988
Products: tiles, murals, wall reliefs, sculptures
Media: stoneware, porcelain, glass
Techniques: molded, carved ceramics
Size Range: 2" x 2" to 100" x 200"
Price Range: $200 to $1,000/sq. ft.
Price Range: $500 to $5,000 for sculptures, one-of-a-kind

VERA LIGHTSTONE

347 W 39TH ST
NEW YORK, NY 10018
Established: 1960
Products: wall reliefs, platters
Media: stoneware
Techniques: constructed, glazed, unglazed
Size Range: 2' x 1' to 10' x 14'
Price Range: $300 to $600 for platters

★ THOMAS W. LOLLAR

50 W 106TH ST #2A
NEW YORK, NY 10025-3888
TEL 212-864-7973

Established: 1979
Products: tiles, panels or screens, murals
Media: stoneware, earthenware
Techniques: constructed, slab, bas relief
Size Range: 24" x 22" to 10' x 10'
Price Range: $300 to $500/sq. ft.
Price Range: $10,000 to $15,000 for 5' x 12' murals

See page 117 for photographs and additional information.

LORA SUMMERVILLE CERAMICS

LORA SUMMERVILLE
RT3 BOX 249
CASEY, IL 62420-9219
TEL 217-923-5594

Established: 1990
Products: wall reliefs
Media: stoneware
Techniques: constructed, hand built
Size Range: 4" x 3" to 23" x 23"
Price Range: Up to $200 for wall reliefs

★ LUTZ CUSTOM TILE

TERRI LUTZ
12715 133RD AVE E
PUYALLUP, WA 98374
FAX 206-840-8545
TEL 206-840-5011

Established: 1987
Products: tiles, murals, wall reliefs
Media: porcelain, earthenware
Techniques: cast, molded, press molded
Size Range: 2" x 2" to 8" x 16"
Price Range: $24 to $100/sq. ft.
Price Range: $3 to $70 for relief tiles

See photograph on page 133.

★ ELIZABETH MACDONALD

BOX 186
BRIDGEWATER, CT 06752
FAX 860-350-4052
TEL 860-354-0594

Established: 1972
Products: tiles, murals, wall reliefs
Media: stoneware
Techniques: constructed
Size Range: 8" x 8" to 14' x 72'
Price Range: $200 to $250/sq. ft.

See photographs on page 132.

★ MARGIE HUGHTO STUDIO

MARGIE HUGHTO
6970 HENDERSON RD
JAMESVILLE, NY 13078
TEL 315-469-8775

Established: 1971
Products: tiles, murals
Media: stoneware, earthenware, inlaid colored clays
Techniques: constructed, molded
Size Range: 12" x 12" to 32' x 40'
Price Range: $300 to $500/sq. ft.
Price Range: $3,000 to $100,000 for ceramic tile murals

See photograph on page 121.

★ E. JOSEPH MCCARTHY

CUSTOM TILE STUDIO
39 ELEVENTH ST
TURNERS FALLS, MA 01376
FAX 413-863-4913
TEL 413-863-3121

Established: 1980
Products: tiles, murals
Media: ceramic tile
Techniques: hand painted
Size Range: single tile to large-scale murals
Price Range: $50 to $200/sq. ft.

See photograph on page 122.

Jamie Santaniello, installation, basket of fruit with grape leaves and borders, 1996, majolica underglaze on handmade tile, 38"W x 26"H

DONNA MCGEE
47 EAST ST
HADLEY, MA 01035
TEL 413-584-0508
Established: 1978
Products: tiles, murals, platters
Media: earthenware
Techniques: constructed
Size Range: 19" × 12" to unlimited
Price Range: $85 and up for plaques, platters, murals

MERRYWOMAN STUDIOS
CHRISTINE MERRIMAN
PO BOX 18
BRIDGEWATER, VT 05034
TEL 802-672-5141
Established: 1970
Products: tiles, panels or screens, murals
Media: raku fired, low fired
Techniques: salt or sodium fired raku fired, hand-welded metal frames
Size Range: 2" × 2" to 24" × 24"
Price Range: $50 to $200/sq. ft.
Price Range: $125 to $500 for welded frames, tiles

BRENDA MINISCI
STUDIO DEL PINETO
PANTRY RD BOX 85
N HATFIELD, MA 01066
TEL 413-247-5262
Established: 1961
Products: panels or screens, murals, wall reliefs
Media: stoneware, porcelain, earthenware, cold-cast porcelain
Techniques: cast, constructed, molded, hand formed
Size Range: no limits
Price Range: $150 to $500/sq. ft.
Price Range: $350 and up for panels, etc.

JUDY MOONELIS
JUDY MOONELIS STUDIO
63 ORCHARD ST FL 5
NEW YORK, NY 10002
TEL 212-925-7667
Established: 1980
Products: wall installations
Media: earthenware, mixed media
Techniques: constructed, hand formed
Size Range: 3" × 4" to 12' × 20'
Price Range: $2,500 to $25,000 for wall installations

LAUREL NEFF
3180 23RD ST
SAN FRANCISCO, CA 94110
TEL 415-206-1394
Established: 1991
Products: mosaics
Media: glass, mirror, ceramic tile
Techniques: constructed
Size Range: 1' × 1' to 12' × 12' or larger
Price Range: $15 and up/sq. ft.
Price Range: $100 and up for portable pieces

LEON NIGROSH
LEON NIGROSH/CERAMIC DESIGNER
11 CHATANIKA AVE
WORCESTER, MA 01602-1109
TEL 508-757-0401
Established: 1963
Products: murals, wall reliefs custom designs
Media: stoneware, porcelain, earthenware
Techniques: constructed, molded, hand built
Size Range: 4" × 6" to 5' × 20'
Price Range: $100 to $300/sq. ft.

SUSAN NOWOGRODZKI
TOUCHSTONE CERAMICS
261 ELLIOT RD
EAST GREENBUSH, NY 12061
TEL 518-477-7780
Established: 1974
Products: tiles, murals
Media: stoneware, porcelain, earthenware
Techniques: constructed
Size Range: 8" × 12" to 4' × 6'
Price Range: $125 to $2,500 per piece for tile mural

RUTH O'DAY
FIREWORKS
1234 E 12TH ST
OAKLAND, CA 94606
TEL 510-536-5235
Established: 1982
Products: tiles, mosaics, murals
Media: stoneware, earthenware, inlaid colored clays
Techniques: constructed, hand carved
Size Range: 1' × 1' to 2' × 1,000'
Price Range: $20 to $60/sq. ft.

ONE OFF STUDIO
CAROL SMERALDO
35 LAKEMIST CT
EAST PRESTON, NS B2Z 1G4
CANADA
FAX 902-434-1336
TEL 902-434-1336
Established: 1972
Products: murals, platters, wall reliefs
Media: stoneware, porcelain
Techniques: constructed, molded, wheel thrown
Size Range: 12" × 30" to 5' × 10'
Price Range: $150 to $6,000 for platters, murals, wall reliefs

PHYLLIS PACIN
PHYLLIS PACIN CERAMIC DESIGN
4097 39TH AVE
OAKLAND, CA 94619
TEL 510-530-7059
Established: 1973
Products: tiles, murals, wall reliefs
Media: stoneware, porcelain, earthenware
Techniques: constructed, raku fired
Size Range: 4" × 4" to 9.5' × 27'
Price Range: $40 to $46 for free-hanging sculptures

★ CAROLYN PAYNE
PAYNE CREATIONS TILE
4829 N ANTIOCH
KANSAS CITY, MO 64119
FAX 816-452-0070
TEL 816-452-8660
Established: 1972
Products: tiles, murals
Media: hand-painted tile
Techniques: re-glaze manufactured tiles
Size Range: 6" × 6" to 10' × 26'
Price Range: $75 to $250/sq. ft.
Price Range: $10 to $25 for individual tiles

**See photographs on pages
124 and 133.**

PEACE VALLEY TILE
64 BEULAH RD
NEW BRITAIN, PA 18901
FAX 215-340-1536
TEL 215-340-0888
Established: 1985
Products: tiles, mosaics, murals
Media: stoneware, earthenware
Techniques: constructed, molded, wheel thrown
Size Range: 1" × 1" to unlimited
Price Range: $8 to $50/sq. ft.
Price Range: $100 and up for murals

DONALD C. PENNY
DON'S POTTERY
2005 BAYTREE RD
VALDOSTA, GA 31602-3503
FAX 912-244-1443
TEL 912-247-0289
Established: 1960
Products: tiles, murals, waterfalls with pools
Media: stoneware, porcelain, earthenware
Techniques: constructed, molded, carved
Size Range: 4" × 4" to 68" × 212"
Price Range: $65 to $100/sq. ft.

PEOPLES HOUSING
COMMUNITY ARTS
KAY HAUCK
7510 N ASHLAND AVE
CHICAGO, IL 60626
FAX 312-262-7033
TEL 312-262-5900
Products: tiles, murals, wall reliefs
Media: stoneware, earthenware
Techniques: constructed, molded, tile/mosaic combinations
Size Range: 4.25" × 4.25" × 24" × 24"
Price Range: $50 to $200/sq. ft.
Price Range: $10 to $30 for trivets

POWNING DESIGNS LTD.
PETER W. POWNING
R.R. #5
SUSSEX, NB
CANADA
FAX 506-433-6979
TEL 506-433-1188
Established: 1972
Products: tiles, murals, fireplace surrounds
Media: glass, raku
Techniques: constructed, molded, wheel thrown
Size Range: 18" × 24" to 10' × 20'
Price Range: $150 to $250/sq. ft.

PROJECTILE
DAVID ALAN CATRAMBONE
4630 SALOMA AVE
SHERMAN OAKS, CA 91403
FAX 818-501-3614
TEL 818-501-3614
Established: 1988
Products: tiles, mosaics, murals
Media: glass, tile, marble
Techniques: constructed, cut-broken
Size Range: 8" × 8" to 4' × 12'
Price Range: $30 to $150/sq. ft.
Price Range: $1,500 to $3,000 for murals

CERAMIC ART FOR THE WALL

JUD RANDALL
IMPRESSIONS IN CLAY
8705 GARDNER RD #14
TAMPA, FL 33625-3714
TEL 813-920-2410
Established: 1981
Products: tiles, wall reliefs
Media: stoneware, earthenware, raku-fired
Techniques: constructed, wheel thrown, raku fired
Size Range: 2" × 1" to 10' × 10'
Price Range: $20 to $45/sq. ft.
Price Range: $100 and up for platters, tiles, wall reliefs

MISSY REHFUSS
THE PAINTED REEF
53 STEINER AVE
NEPTUNE CITY, NJ 07753
TEL 908-776-7292
Established: 1985
Products: tiles, murals, sinks
Media: porcelain, ceramic tiles/ware
Techniques: detailed paintings
Size Range: 4" × 4" to 4' × 18'
Price Range: $500 to $5,000 for custom murals, matching accessories

★ WILL RICHARDS
WILL RICHARDS
PO BOX 361
UNDERWOOD, WA 98651
FAX 509-493-2732
TEL 509-493-3928
Established: 1980
Products: platters, wall reliefs, lighting
Media: stoneware
Techniques: constructed
Size Range: 11" × 11" to 3' × 12'
Price Range: $120 to $2,500 for plates and panels

See photograph on page 125.

EILEEN PENDERGAST RICHARDSON
409 E SOLA ST
SANTA BARBARA, CA 93101
TEL 805-899-4241
Established: 1959
Products: tiles, platters
Media: porcelain
Techniques: constructed, wheel thrown, underglaze paintings
Size Range: 2" × 10" to 2" × 15"
Price Range: $250 to $350/sq. ft.
Price Range: $500 to $1,500 for platters

★ JAMIE SANTANIELLO
WAVERLY TILES
FAX 619-438-2456
TEL 619-722-6199
Established: 1975
Products: tiles, murals, borders; custom work
Media: earthenware, handmade tile
Techniques: majolica underglaze
Size Range: 13" × 13" to unlimited
Price Range: $200 to $750/sq. ft.
Price Range: $5 to $45 for borders, tics, decos

See photograph on page 126.

LOIS S. SATTLER
LOIS SATTLER CERAMICS
3620 PACIFIC AVE
VENICE, CA 90292-5724
TEL 310-821-7055
Established: 1974
Products: platters, wall reliefs
Media: stoneware, porcelain
Techniques: constructed, molded low-fired
Size Range: 14" × 16" to 3' × 6'
Price Range: $220 to $2,000 from platters to wall pieces

LOREN SCHERBAK
5718 WAINWRIGHT AVE
ROCKVILLE, MD 20851
TEL 301-468-0159
Established: 1985
Products: tiles, platters, wall reliefs
Media: stoneware, earthenware
Techniques: cast, constructed, molded
Size Range: 6" × 6" to 16" × 35"
Price Range: $75 for 12" × 12" platters; $300 for triptych wall reliefs

SEBASTIAN STUDIOS
BARBARA SEBASTIAN
1777 YOSEMITE AVE #4B-1
SAN FRANCISCO, CA 94124
TEL 415-822-3243
Established: 1975
Products: panels or screens, murals, wall reliefs
Media: low fired clay and canvas
Techniques: constructed
Size Range: 12" × 12" to 20' × 100'
Price Range: $75 to $150/sq. ft.

ERICKA CLARK SHAW
451 EUREKA ST
SAN FRANCISCO, CA 94114-2714
TEL 800-484-9955 X 8271
Established: 1974
Products: wall reliefs
Media: earthenware
Techniques: constructed, molded, airbrushed
Size Range: 12" × 12" to 60' to 40'
Price Range: $180 to $250/sq. ft.

MICHAEL SHEBA
140 EVELYN AVE
TORONTO, ON M6P 2Z7
CANADA
TEL 416-766-9411
Established: 1974
Products: murals, platters, wall reliefs
Media: earthenware, raku
Techniques: constructed, molded, wheel thrown
Size Range: 14" × 14" to 6' × 10'
Price Range: $150 to $250/sq. ft.
Price Range: $250 to $750 for platters, wall reliefs

SHEL NEYMARK ARCHITECTURAL CERAMICS
SHEL NEYMARK
PO BOX 25
EMBUDO, NM 87531
FAX 505-579-4432
TEL 505-579-4432
Established: 1974
Products: murals, wall reliefs, installations
Media: frost free or raku clay
Techniques: constructed, raku fired
Size Range: 16" × 12" to 10' × 60'
Price Range: $50 to $100,000 for custom installations

CHRISTINE SIBLEY
CHRISTINE SIBLEY POTTERY
  AT URBAN NIRVANA
15 WADDELL ST NE
ATLANTA, GA 30307
FAX 404-688-0665
TEL 404-688-3329
Established: 1973
Products: tiles, murals, columns
Media: stoneware, earthenware, cement, gypsom
Techniques: cast, constructed, molded, slab construction
Size Range: 6" × 8" to 4' × 6'
Price Range: $50 to $200/sq. ft.
Price Range: $5 to $450 for wall reliefs

J. PAUL SIRES
CENTER OF THE EARTH
3204 N DAVIDSON ST
CHARLOTTE, NC 28205-1034
FAX 704-375-5756
TEL 704-375-5756
Established: 1983
Products: murals, platters, wall reliefs
Media: stoneware, earthenware, brick
Techniques: constructed, molded, carved
Size Range: 19" × 19" to 24' × 24'
Price Range: $25 to $150/sq. ft.
Price Range: $450 for large platters

Susanne G. Stephenson, *Dusk II*, 1995, slips plus vitreous engobes on terra cotta, 27"W × 29"H × 10"D, photo: Suzanne Coles

NAN SMITH

NAN SMITH STUDIO
2310 NW 142ND AVE
GAINESVILLE, FL 32609
FAX 904-329-8453
TEL 904-485-2942
Established: 1977
Products: tiles, murals, wall reliefs, commissioned works
Media: earthenware, mounted on plexiglass
Techniques: constructed, molded, airbrushed, glazed
Size Range: 24" x 18" to 8' x 20'
Price Range: $2,500 to $25,000 for airbrushed tile installations

PAT SMITH

90 GREENE ST
NEW YORK, NY 10012-3855
TEL 212-219-8519
Established: 1975
Products: murals, wall reliefs
Media: porcelain, slate, copper, steel
Techniques: cast, constructed
Size Range: 12" x 12" to 8' x 6'
Price Range: $250 to $300/sq. ft.
Price Range: $400 to $1,800 for wall works or sculpture

STARBUCK GOLDNER TILE

BETH STARBUCK &
  STEVEN GOLDNER
315 W FOURTH ST
BETHLEHEM, PA 18015
FAX 610-866-5279
TEL 610-866-6321
Established: 1980
Products: tiles, mosaics, wall reliefs
Media: porcelain, earthenware, inlaid colored clays
Techniques: constructed, molded
Size Range: 6" x 6" to full walls
Price Range: $10 to $300/sq. ft.
Price Range: $1,000 and up for wall installations

ALAN STEINBERG

BRATTLEBORO CLAYWORKS
RD 5 BOX 250 PUTNEY RD
BRATTLEBORO, VT 05301-9190
TEL 802-254-9174
Established: 1976
Products: murals, wall reliefs wall reliefs
Media: stoneware, porcelain, inlaid colored clays
Techniques: constructed
Size Range: 4" x 4" to 4' x 8'
Price Range: $100 to $200/sq. ft.
Price Range: $18 to $7,000 for murals

★ SUSANNE G. STEPHENSON

STEPHENSON CERAMICS
4380 WATERS RD
ANN ARBOR, MI 48103
TEL 313-663-2679
Established: 1960
Products: platters, wall reliefs
Media: earthenware
Techniques: constructed, molded, wheel thrown, various finishes
Size Range: 12" x 12" to 27" x 30"
Price Range: $300 to $2,000 for platters, wall reliefs

See photograph on page 128.

STEWART SPECIALITY TILES

DIANNE STEWART
1777 KIRTS BLVD
TROY, MI 48084
TEL 810-637-3184
Established: 1992
Products: tiles, mosaics, murals, interlocking cobblestones
Media: stoneware, hand-painted tiles
Techniques: hand-shaped tiles
Size Range: 4" x 4" to unlimted
Price Range: $50 to $300/sq. ft.

SUMMITVILLE TILES, INC.

PETER C. JOHNSON, JR.
PO BOX 73
SUMMITVILLE, OH 43962
FAX 216-223-1414
TEL 216-223-1511
Products: tiles, murals, wall reliefs
Media: porcelain, ceramic tiles
Techniques: constructed, molded
Size Range: 2" x 2" to unlimited
Price Range: $25 to $180 for 6" x 6" murals

★ SURVING STUDIOS

NATALIE AND RICHARD SURVING
RD4 BOX 44
MIDDLETOWN, NY 10940
FAX 914-355-1517
TEL 914-355-1430
TEL 800-768-4954
Established: 1970
Products: tiles, murals, wall reliefs
Techniques: molded
Size Range: 2" x 2" to 5' x 10'
Price Range: $54 to $324/sq. ft.
Price Range: $6 to $72 for tile

See photograph on page 134.

DENISE S. TENNEN

CLAY CONSTRUCTIONS
895 FRONT AVE
ST PAUL, MN 55103
FAX 612-489-4374
TEL 612-489-4374
Established: 1988
Products: wall reliefs
Media: sculpture clay
Techniques: coil and slab built
Size Range: 12" x 12" and up
Price Range: $500 to $6,000 for wall sculpture, relief

TERRA DESIGNS

ANNA SALIBELLO
241 E BLACKWELL ST
DOVER, NJ 07801-4140
FAX 201-328-3624
TEL 201-539-2999
Established: 1969
Products: tiles, mosaics, ceramic murals
Media: stoneware, porcelain, earthenware
Techniques: constructed, molded, extruded
Size Range: 1/2" x 1/2" to 12' x 35'
Price Range: $14 to $500/sq. ft.

TETKOWSKI STUDIO

NEIL TETKOWSKI
432 W 19TH ST
NEW YORK, NY 10011
FAX 212-255-2608
TEL 212-255-1850
Established: 1987
Products: wall reliefs, murals, sculpture
Media: earthenware
Techniques: constructed, wheel thrown, salt or sodium fired
Size Range: 18" x 18" to 10' x 24'
Price Range: $300 to $400/sq. ft.
Price Range: $5,000 for 36" disk

VINCENT AND CAROLYN LEE TOLPO

SHAWNEE MOUNTAIN POTTERY
55918 US HWY 285 PO BOX 134
SHAWNEE, CO 80475
TEL 303-670-1733
Established: 1975
Products: murals, platters, wall reliefs
Media: stoneware
Techniques: constructed, wheel thrown press mold
Size Range: 4" x 5" to 8' x 16'
Price Range: $50 to $150/sq. ft.
Price Range: $260 to $600 for platters

TRIKEENAN TILEWORKS

KRISTIN & STEPHEN POWERS
9 FOREST RD
HANCOCK, NH 03449
FAX 603-525-4245
TEL 603-525-4245
Established: 1984
Products: tiles, mosaics, murals
Media: stoneware, earthenware
Techniques: constructed, molded, carved
Size Range: 4" x 6" to 10' x 25'
Price Range: $100 to $500/sq. ft.
Price Range: $25 to $4,000 for individual tiles, murals

KATHY TRIPLETT

175 MCDARIS COVE RD
WEAVERVILLE, NC 28787
TEL 704-658-3207
Established: 1972
Products: tiles, lighted panels, wall reliefs
Media: earthenware, glass
Techniques: constucted
Size Range: 6" x 6" to 10' x 12'
Price Range: $150 to $500/sq. ft.

C. Keen Zero, *Mandala #9*, 1995, stoneware, 39"Dia, photo: Matthew Grasse

SUSAN TUNICK

771 WEST END AVE #10E
NEW YORK, NY 10025
TEL 212-962-1750
TEL 212-962-1864
Established: 1968
Products: mosaics, murals, wall reliefs
Media: stoneware, porcelain, earthenware
Techniques: constructed, ceramic mosaic
Size Range: 7" x 7" to 16'l x 1'w
Price Range: $600 to $18,000 for murals, wall reliefs

GAYLE L. TUSTIN

3842 EDGEWOOD RD
WILMINGTON, NC 28403
TEL 910-392-4408
Established: 1982
Products: tiles, murals, wall reliefs
Media: stoneware, earthenware, brick
Techniques: cast, constructed, molded
Size Range: 1" x 1" to 22' x 13'
Price Range: $100 to $400/sq. ft.
Price Range: $400 to $3,000 for original wall relief panels

VACCARO STUDIO

LOUIS VACCARO
531 SPRINGTOWN RD
NEW PALTZ, NY 12561-3028
TEL 914-658-9859
Products: wall reliefs
Media: earthenware
Techniques: constructed
Size Range: 2' x 2' to 4' x 5'
Price Range: $800 to $2,000 for wall reliefs

★ SHERYL VANDERPOL

UNTAPPED RESOURCE
4020 PILGRIM LN
MINNEAPOLIS, MN 55441
FAX 612-542-1119
TEL 612-542-1116
Established: 1990
Products: tiles, murals
Media: porcelain, commercial ceramic tile
Techniques: kiln-fired on commercial tile
Size Range: 4" x 4" to unlimited
Price Range: $50 to $500/sq. ft.
Price Range: $200 to $5,000 for murals and sinks

See photographs on page 134.

WATSON STUDIOS

3404 UPPER TUG FORK
ALEXANDRIA, KY 41001
TEL 606-635-5599
Established: 1989
Products: tiles, panels or screens, murals, installations
Media: stoneware, porcelain, earthenware
Techniques: constructed, hand sculpted
Size Range: 16" x 12" to 42" x 54"
Price Range: $75 to $200/sq. ft.

HELEN WEBBER

HELEN WEBBER DESIGNS
555 PACIFIC AVE
SAN FRANCISCO, CA 94133-4609
FAX 415-989-5746
TEL 415-989-5521
Established: 1972
Products: mosaics, murals, wall reliefs
Media: fired sculpted clay tile
Techniques: cast kiln-fired sculpted clay
Size Range: 15" x 18" to 9' x 27'
Price Range: $100 to $200 and up/sq. ft.

MAUREEN R. WEISS

MAUREEN R. WEISS, ARTIST
PO BOX 8615
RANCHO SANTA FE, CA 92067-8615
TEL 619-792-9206
Established: 1980
Products: tiles, wall reliefs, platters
Media: glass, earthenware, inlaid colored clays
Techniques: constructed, molded, hand built
Size Range: 3" x 3" to 10' x 10'
Price Range: $10 to $10,000 for ceramic wall sculptures

JOAN WEISSMAN

3710 SILVER SE
ALBUQUERQUE, NM 87108
FAX 505-268-9665
TEL 505-265-0144
Established: 1970
Products: tiles, murals, platters
Media: porcelain, earthenware, inlaid colored clays
Techniques: constructed
Size Range: 12" x 12" to 10' x 50'
Price Range: $100 to $200/sq. ft.
Price Range: $300 to $500 for sconces, platters

HELEN WEISZ

ARCHITECTURAL CERAMICS
1775 HILLSIDE RD
SOUTHAMPTON, PA 18966
TEL 215-322-5128
Established: 1972
Products: tiles, panels or screens, wall reliefs
Media: stoneware, earthenware, inlaid colored clays
Techniques: unglazed, colored
Size Range: 12" x 12" to 6' x 20'
Price Range: $250 to $300 for tile panels

SUSAN AND JIM WHALEN

PARADOX POTTERY
2004 BAY ST
CHARLOTTE, NC 28205
TEL 704-372-9394
Established: 1975
Products: platters, sculpture, fish, plants
Media: stoneware, earthenware
Techniques: constructed, wheel thrown, raku fired
Size Range: 4" x 3" to 36" x 9"
Price Range: $20 to $500 for small fish to organic sculpture

FRED WIESENER

231 W MAIN ST
DANVILLE, KY 40422
FAX 606-236-0304
TEL 606-236-3079
Established: 1970
Products: panels or screens, murals, wall reliefs
Media: stoneware, cast bronze, fiber
Techniques: cast, constructed
Size Range: 60" x 18" to 9' x 7'
Price Range: $150 to $250/sq. ft.
Price Range: $950 to $9,500 for wall hangings

★ WISEMAN•SPAULDING DESIGNS

BRADLEY WISEMAN
  AND PAUL SPAULDING
12 SHAWHILL RD
HAMDEN, ME 04444
FAX 207-862-4513
TEL 207-862-3513
Established: 1980
Products: tiles, wall reliefs
Media: stoneware, porcelain
Techniques: constructed, molded, wood fired
Size Range: 1" x 6" to 3' x 3'
Price Range: $22 to $200/sq. ft.
Price Range: $2 to $150 for field tiles, handsculpted relief

See photograph on page 134.

★ DY WITT

REMODELER'S WORKSHOP
PLEASANT GAP, PA 16823
TEL 814-359-3072
Established: 1983
Products: tiles, murals, wall reliefs
Media: stoneware, porcelain, earthenware
Techniques: handmade tile
Size Range: 4" x 4" to 8" x 8"
Price Range: $45 to $135/sq. ft.
Price Range: $5 to $20 for each tile

See photographs on page 134.

HOGAN YOUNG

PO BOX 1314
IDYLLWILD, CA 92549-1314
FAX 909-659-3224
TEL 909-659-3224
Established: 1970
Products: tiles, murals, wall reliefs
Media: stoneware, porcelain, earthenware
Techniques: constructed, molded
Size Range: 11" x 11" to 10' x 70'
Price Range: $50 to $125/sq. ft.
Price Range: $90 to $250 for wall hangings

★ C. KEEN ZERO

GONZO MOJO ENTERPRISES
128 ODD ST
ATHENS, GA 30601
TEL 706-613-6270
Established: 1991
Products: tiles, mosaics, wall reliefs
Media: stoneware, mixed media
Techniques: constructed, molded
Size Range: 16" Dia to 48" Dia
Price Range: $500 to $2,500 for relief mosaic mandalas

See photograph on page 129.

DALE ZHEUTLIN

55 WEBSTER AVE
NEW ROCHELLE, NY 10801
FAX 914-738-8373
TEL 914-576-0082
Products: tiles, murals, wall reliefs
Media: porcelain
Techniques: constructed
Size Range: 13" x 13" to 20' x 20'
Price Range: $250 to $350/sq. ft.

ARNOLD ZIMMERMAN

76 AINSLIE ST
BROOKLYN, NY 11211
FAX 212-242-3703
TEL 718-388-4914
Established: 1979
Products: tiles, platters, wall reliefs
Media: stoneware, glass cast metal
Techniques: cast, constructed, molded
Size Range: 4.5" x 4.5" to 120" x 240"
Price Range: $20 to $150/sq. ft.
Price Range: $500 to $25,000 for platters, tiles, murals

Country Floors

See page 121.

HELENE AND DAVID ELLISON

WEL Sun Plaque, 15" x 13", architectural terra cotta

KAREN PATTERSON, MEDIEVAL TILERY

WKP Hampshire, 6" x 6", inlaid terra cotta, a full series of medieval tiles

PRATT AND LARSON TILE

WT Andy Balmer Relief Series, AR6, 6" x 6", glaze: CG16

JENSEN/MARINEAU

WBJ Sea Life, 6" x 6", hand-painted tiles, *Flotsam and Jetsam Blanc*, 6" x 6"

PRATT AND LARSON TILE

WT Craftsman Series: Bear, 4" x 8", botanical moldings

PRATT AND LARSON TILE

WT Seashore Series, 4" x 4", borders: 4" x 8" and 1" x 8", color way 3, field glaze: C4

ZLATKA PANEVA

WSN Sofia, handmade wall tiles, *Hunter*, 4" x 4", barock border

PRATT AND LARSON TILE

WT LJ Heron Panels, Grass Panel, 6" x 6", glaze: C200

DIANA AND TOM WATSON

WND Peacock Plaque, 6" x 18", traditional California tiles

Elizabeth MacDonald

See page 126.

Landscape, 45" x 42½", layered pigment

Woven Work, 3' x 3', relief: 2"

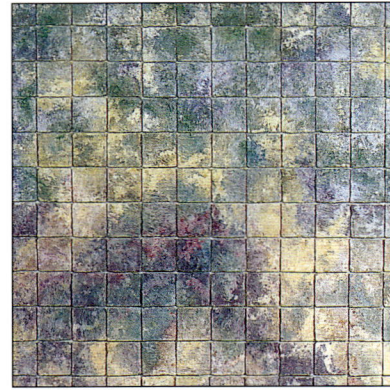

Dance, 45" x 42", tile size: 3"

Detail

Detail

Detail

Patterned Relief, silver mica surface

Pyramid, from 8" to 18"

Spiral Relief, 34"

ANTIOCH TILE CO.
See page 118.

Rose, 6" x 6", custom patterns and colors available, send for more information

GRETCHEN AND MARGARET HEUGES
See page 123.

Wildflowers, 4" x 4", low relief, custom colors available

ILLAHE TILEWORKS
See page 124.

Rogue Valley Harvest Series: Pears, 6" x 6", relief designs, custom colors

BATIK TILE
See page 119.

Splash of Vegetables (detail), 6" x 66", versatile, vibrant, hand-painted

ILLAHE TILEWORKS
See page 124.

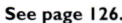

Gresham Series: Oak Leaf Relief, 8"L, traditional styles, custom colors

LUTZ CUSTOM TILE
See page 126.

Old World Grapes, 6" x 8", rope border ¹/₂" x 8", dramatically sculpted relief tiles

BLUE MOON CERAMIC TILE STUDIO
See page 119.

Mothership Gammara, custom mosaic tile, versatile line also available

ILLAHE TILEWORKS
See page 124.

Grapevine Lines, period style, 3" x 6", twelve tile designs, custom colors

CAROLYN PAYNE
See page 127.

BT-3, BTC-3 (corner), custom designs available, no more boring borders!

CERAMIC ART FOR THE WALL

SURVING STUDIOS
See page 129.

Chameleon tile, 4" x 4", bas-relief, free tile catalog, call 800-768-4954

SHERYL VANDERPOL
See page 130.

Pansies in Your Bath, hand-painted tiles and sink to match border

DY WITT
See page 130.

Iris, mural of 4" handmade tile installed in bathroom wall

SHERYL VANDERPOL
See page 130.

Vegetable Basket, mural, hand-painted on textured tile

WISEMAN·SPAULDING DESIGN
See page 130.

Woodnymph, 10" x 10", many designs available: relief, Deco, accent, borders, etc.

SHERYL VANDERPOL
See page 130.

Contemporary Fruits, hand-painted to match wallcovering

DY WITT
See page 130.

Example of relief-carved tile, 4" x 6", obtain multiples by cast molding

JUDITH LEPOW
ELAINE GALMAN

Corporate Art Advisors

With almost 20 years of experience as corporate-art advisers based in the Philadelphia area, Judith Lepow and Elaine Galman have had the pleasure of seeing many of the collections they helped build grow in value and stature with the passing years.

Galman Lepow Associates (GLA) provides a complete art service for its clients, with a great many contacts among both established and emerging artists. "THE GUILD is a wonderful resource for us," says Judith Lepow. "It's like having an exhibit in our office! It gives us a very successful way to find fine new artists throughout the country and the world."

Fiber artist Janet Kuemmerlein, who helped GLA solve an especially complex design challenge, is a case in point. When Dupont built a new world headquarters for its Textile Fibers Division, Galman Lepow Associates managed the project, including one highly unusual commission. For the focal area of an atrium space, the client wanted to use a work of art that would incorporate over 50 types of fiber, all created by Dupont.

"We found Janet through THE GUILD, and were intrigued with her bundling and stitching

technique worked on the surface of the fabric," says Judith Lepow. "She flew into Philadelphia from Kansas, met with everyone and contacted all of the divisions she needed to work with to obtain fibers for the project. The finished work exceeded expectations and she was there for the installation, which went extremely well. Janet was someone we would never have found without THE GUILD."

GLA has worked successfully with other GUILD artists as well. Bruce Bleach, for one, brought terrific drama and dynamic energy to a recent GLA lobby-design project with his innovative, sculptural metal relief paintings.

Lepow and Galman note that they have found three distinct ways to use GUILD sourcebooks. Elaine Galman explains: "We often use THE GUILD to stimulate the client's imagination; it offers such a range of visual imagery and this is very helpful. We also use it, of course, to find artists. But we put it to work in a third way, too. When we travel to other parts of the country, we sometimes need to get in touch with people in our field. Then we turn to the informational listings in the back of the book. Over the years, we've developed some very good relationships through this network."

Photo of Elaine Galman (left) and
Judith Lepow by Norman Levinson

Beth Cassidy

2416 NW 60th Street
Seattle, WA 98107
FAX 206-706-0406
TEL 206-783-6226

Beth Cassidy's fiber works stimulate a multi-dimensional sensory feast. Subtle in her use of color and bold in her construction technique, Cassidy creates work that holds the eye with the tenacity of a significant event half remembered.

Found objects, natural and constructed, embellish these pieces, evoking a sense of landscape, both external and internal.

Extensive resume, portfolio, price list, samples, and contract information always available.

Also see this GUILD publication:
Designer's Edition: 10

A *Aerial Archipelago,* 52" x 84"

B *Icarus Carpet/Feathered Diamonds,*
    48" x 56"

Photos: Roy Mullin

Robin Cowley

2451 Potomac Street
Oakland, CA 94602-3032
FAX 510 482-9465
TEL 510 530-1134

Robin Cowley's contemporary studio art quilts are of a graphic nature, with strong colors and always an upbeat, happy look. She works intuitively with fabric and thread, combining colors and textures with a sure hand and a keen understanding of the interaction between elements.

Robin has numerous works in private and corporate collections. Commissions are welcomed; slides and pricing are available upon request.

A *Winter Dreams,* 26"W x 38"H

B *Mars Multiples,* 30"W x 51"H

C *Chinese Coin,* 24"W x 56"H

A

B

C

Photos: Don Tuttle Photography

Marilyn Henrion

505 Laguardia Place #23D
New York, NY 10012-2005
TEL 212-982-8949
TEL 717-775-6471 (Studio)

Celebrating the quilt as a canvas for artistic expression, Marilyn Henrion transforms geometric elements into abstract metaphorical images with strong graphic impact. Frequently referred to as cloth poems, her work uses color, line and form much as a poet employs words to convey a particular emotion or idea.

Marilyn is a graduate of Cooper Union. Her art quilts have been exhibited and acclaimed internationally, and are included in museum, corporate and private collections. All are finely crafted and hand quilted by the artist.

Completed works are available. Commissions and exhibition opportunities are welcomed. Slides and prices upon request.

Also see this GUILD publication:
Designer's Edition: 9

A *Andalusian Odyssey*, © 1995, silk, cotton and reflective fabrics, machine pieced, hand appliquéd, hand quilted, 64" x 57"

B *Dark Matter*, © 1993, cotton fabrics, machine pieced, hand quilted, 42" x 42"

C *Eclipse*, © 1994, silk, cotton and metallic fabrics, machine pieced, hand appliquéd, hand quilted, 61" x 61"

A

B

C

Photos: Karen Bell

Printed in Hong Kong ©1996 THE GUILD: The Designer's Sourcebook

Wendy C. Huhn

Art Quilts
81763 Lost Creek Road
Dexter, OR 97431
TEL 541-937-3147

Imagery is crucial in Wendy C. Huhn's work, as it is the force that motivates her. Wendy's expertise in the image-transfer processes allows her to break all the rules. Inspiration comes from everyday situations. These occurrences, coupled with humor, allow the quilts to practically make themselves.

Wendy's work is represented in both public and private collections. Commissions are welcome and additional information is available upon request. Wendy is a serious artist with a sense of humor.

A *Joy of Ironing*, 1995, mixed-media quilt, 48" x 48" x ¹/₂"

B *Housework*, 1994, photo-copy fabric, stencils, paint, 38" x 38" x ¹/₂"

A

B

Photos: David Loveall & Associates

M.A. Klein

M.A. Klein Design
2443 Fair Oaks Blvd. #344
Sacramento, CA 95825
TEL 800-700-7815

M.A. Klein's current work can be called contemporary narrative mixed-media collage incorporating fabrics, papers and threads. Techniques include painting, dyeing, gluing, sewing, fabric manipulation and stitchery.

A professional artist for 30 years, M.A. is noted for her active groupings of people (children and adults), animals, birds and fish. She creates individual pieces and groupings of related works in a wide variety of sizes.

Prices for her unique, highly textured designs vary according to complexity and size of work. Contact artist for information regarding commissions and cvailable work.

Also see these GUILD publications:
Designer's Edition: 8, 9, 10
Gallery Edition: 1

A Most Unusual Watering Hole, 42" x 108", commission for the Library of Congress, Washington, DC, 1994

A Most Unusual Watering Hole (detail)

Verena Levine

Verena Levine Pictorial and Narrative Quilts
4305 37th Street NW
Washington DC 20008
TEL   202-537-0916

Verena Levine's quilts depict scenes of contemporary urban and rural American life. For 15 years she has produced original works of all sizes for corporate and residential spaces in the U.S. and abroad.

Machine-pieced and appliquéd from many different fabrics, her quilts are sturdy and easy to install. The time from contract to the completed work averages 6 to 12 weeks.

Slides, pricing and scheduling upon request.

Completed works also available.

A *Tuba Christmas,* 41" x 29"

B *Springtime in Washington, DC,*
   39" x 62"

A

B

Photos: Mark Gulezian

Therese May

651 North 4th Street
San Jose, CA 95112
TEL 408-292-3247

Therese May's quilts are made up of playful fantasy animal and plant imagery and are machine appliquéd using straight stitch and satin stitch. Threads are left uncut to form a network of texture across the surface. Acrylic paint is added as a finishing touch. Her work is widely published and exhibited throughout the U.S., Europe and Japan.

Prices for finished pieces range from $1,000 to $40,000. Commissions accepted; May will work with clients via drawings and samples.

More information available upon request.

Also see these GUILD publications:
Designer's Edition: 6, 7, 8, 10

K-Quilt, 1994, embellished quilt, 60" x 62"   Superior Color

Rats 'n Tats 'n Tea-Eye-O, 1995, 52" x 52"   Pat Kirk

Karen Perrine

512 North K Street
Tacoma, WA 98403-1621
TEL   206-627-0449

Inspired by nature, Karen Perrine's distinctive fiber landscapes are included in numerous private and corporate collections in the U.S. and Japan. A nationally recognized surface designer, she dyes and paints cotton, linen, rayon and silk fabrics with layers of color, then creates evocative scenes from the unique yardage.

Slides and information on prices and commissions are available upon request.

Also see these GUILD publications:
Designer's Edition: 8, 10

A *Red Rocks,* 1995, 17"H x 54"W

B *Pool,* 1995, 31"H x 54"W

B

JAN THOMPSON

Interior Designer

Houston interior designer Jan Thompson often works together with the architect, builder, client and artist from the very beginning of a project. This approach not only wins awards for the high-end residential projects that are her specialty, but also creates a close rapport between Jan and her clients. With this ideal in mind, Thompson, who is currently secretary of the Texas Association for Interior Design, has logged many miles traveling to galleries and showrooms with her clients to get a feel for what appeals to them.

"I have to say that the great advantage of THE GUILD for me is that it's such a great time saver. I can show clients an exceptional assortment of extremely high-quality work and ask what speaks to them. Furthermore, it's a real inspiration for me as a designer. It suggests creative ideas and combinations of materials I may not have seen before, or thought to use."

"GUILD artists are serious, professional, and in general just great to work with," she explains. "You don't need to worry about working over distance, because they're so capable of handling details from beginning to end."

One of Thompson's favorite recent projects included the work of GUILD artist Elizabeth MacDonald of Bridgewater, Connecticut,

whose sophisticated, haunting tile murals suggest nature's erosion, the patinas of age and use, or the shifting patterns of clouds or smoke.

"We were working with one of my long-term clients, creating a study

in textures in her dining room. She wanted something for the walls with subtle, but vibrant, earth tones, something different from the oil paintings she had chosen for adjoining rooms."

Thompson sent MacDonald photographs of the space, along with dimensions and fabric samples.

"Elizabeth sent sample tiles and color renditions. It all went very smoothly. Within just a few weeks we had a design, and soon after, the tiles were shipped and installed. Her management of all the business details was just excellent. And most important, the work is beautiful, the client is very happy and I look forward to working with the artist again."

Photo by Gittings

144

Karen Adachi

702 Monarch Way
Santa Cruz, CA 95060
TEL   408-429-6192

Karen Adachi creates her three-dimensional handmade paper wall sculptures by using layers of irregularly shaped vacuum-cast paper. She makes free-standing, two-sided sculptures and wall pieces for corporate, private and residential interiors. Her works are shown nationally through major galleries and representatives.

The pieces are richly-textured and embellished with dyes, acrylics, metallics and pearlescents. Painted bamboo and wood sticks are used to create a dramatic statement of pattern and line.

Prices range from $250 - $4,000 depending on size.

Selected collections: Marriott Hotel, Bally's Hotel, AT&T, International Paper, Bloomingdale's, Saks Fifth Avenue, Varian Corporation, 3-COmm, Cadence, American Airlines, Bank of Reno, Vision Systems, Almaden Athletics, Royal Courts Athletic Club, Metro Plaza, Indianapolis Hospital, Stanford Hospital, Quantum Corporation, and Synopsis.

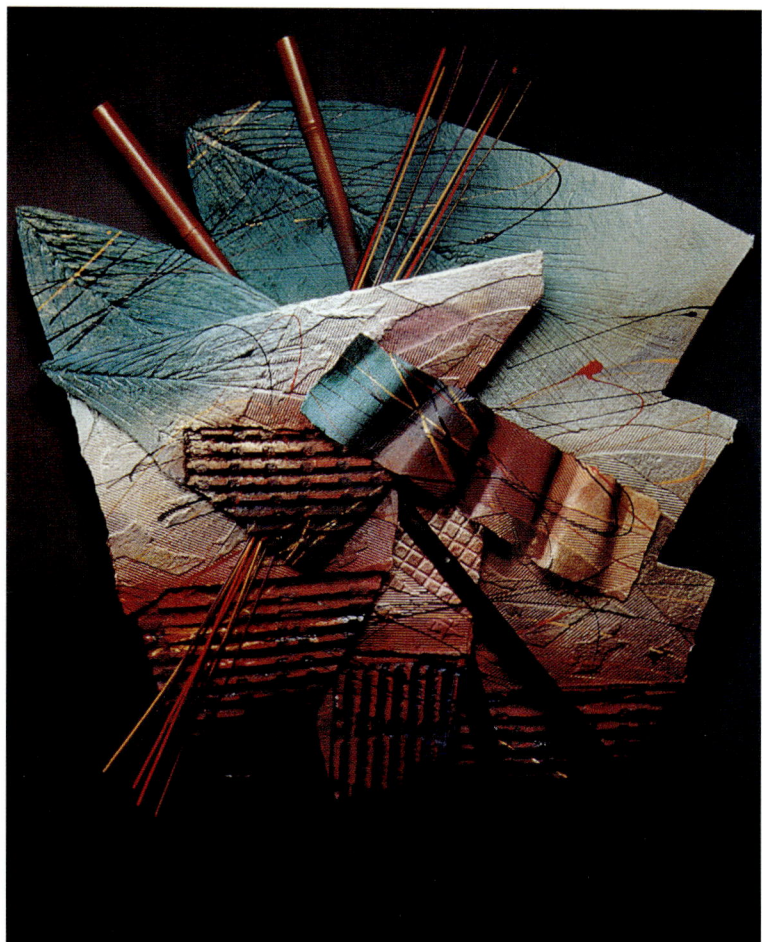

AZO Inc.

Susan Singleton
1101 East Pike Street
Seattle, WA 98122
FAX 206-322-5062
TEL 206-322-0390
TEL 800-344-0390

Singleton's *Ziggurat* works have been placed around the world, from the Tobu Sapporo Hotel in Japan to the U.S. Embassy in South Africa. The work ranges in size from 17 inches x 17 inches to 12 feet x 12 feet. Commissions, as well as available current work, can be further explained by calling the AZO studio.

These pieces reference ancient walls and objects from ancestral cultures. The tactile quality simulates leather or transparent skins. This work is made by stitching Asian papers together, forming a grid that is repeated in the patterns of metallic leafing on the artwork surface. As this style of work has developed, it is clear that it springs from a place that has nothing to do with language or politics, but rather reflects the search for balance and spirit.

Six Ziggurats, each 12' x 12'

Rick Semple

Ralph Irwin Studio

Ralph C. Irwin
627 Main Street
PO Box 1305
Van Buren, AR 72956
TEL 501-474-4114

Ralph Irwin's artistic contributions span a career of 30 years and are represented nationally and internationally in museums, corporate offices, hospitals, restaurants, churches and private collections. Working in approximately 25 different mediums, including glass, exotic woods, copper, oil, acrylic, watercolor and fabric, he has unrivaled skill and versatility. This diversification has made him a creative source for major architectural and interior design firms.

The works pictured below express the sensitivity Irwin has for color and form. Coupling this with his interest in archeological and natural history themes opens an unlimited realm of possibilities for your clients. These durable works are easily mounted and, when properly framed, are 'stand-out' works of art.

Early involvement of the artist allows flexibility in design and insures timely execution.

Also see this GUILD publication:
Architect's Edition: 11

A *Aegean Argonaut*, 1996, diptych,
enamel paint on paper, 23"H x 72"W

B *Dusk*, 1996, triptych, enamel paint
on paper, 35"H x 72"W

A

B

Photos: Martin Duckworth, Van Buren, AR

Juno Sky Studio

Betty Fulmer
844 South Main Street
Findlay, OH 45840
FAX 419-423-9907
TEL 419-423-9591

An understanding of the interpretive possibilities of a variety of materials, along with two decades of technical innovation, has enabled the artist to create unique paperworks of rich color, sensual texture, and emotive content. Opulent and engaging, the works incorporate handmade paper, iridescent acrylics, gold leaf, wood, and brass wire. They are protection-treated for durability.

The artist's works are included in public and private collections in the U.S. and Europe. Recent commissions include: the Marathon Oil Co., the Toledo Museum of Art, U.S. Gypsum, Hyatt Regency Hotels, the Thermos Corp., and the U.S. Customs Service.

Commissions and site specific projects are welcome.

Works shown are from the *Juno Sky Precious Earth Collection.*

A *Spirit Vessels,* tallest: 8" x 24"; wall piece, 18" x 34", handmade paper, gold leaf, acrylic

B *New Millennium: Voices,* 40" x 60", handmade paper, acrylic

A

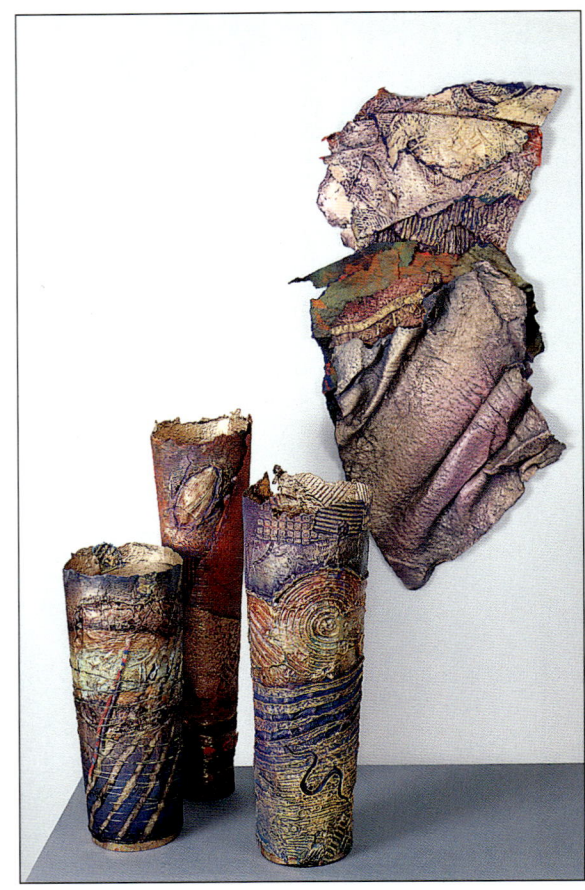

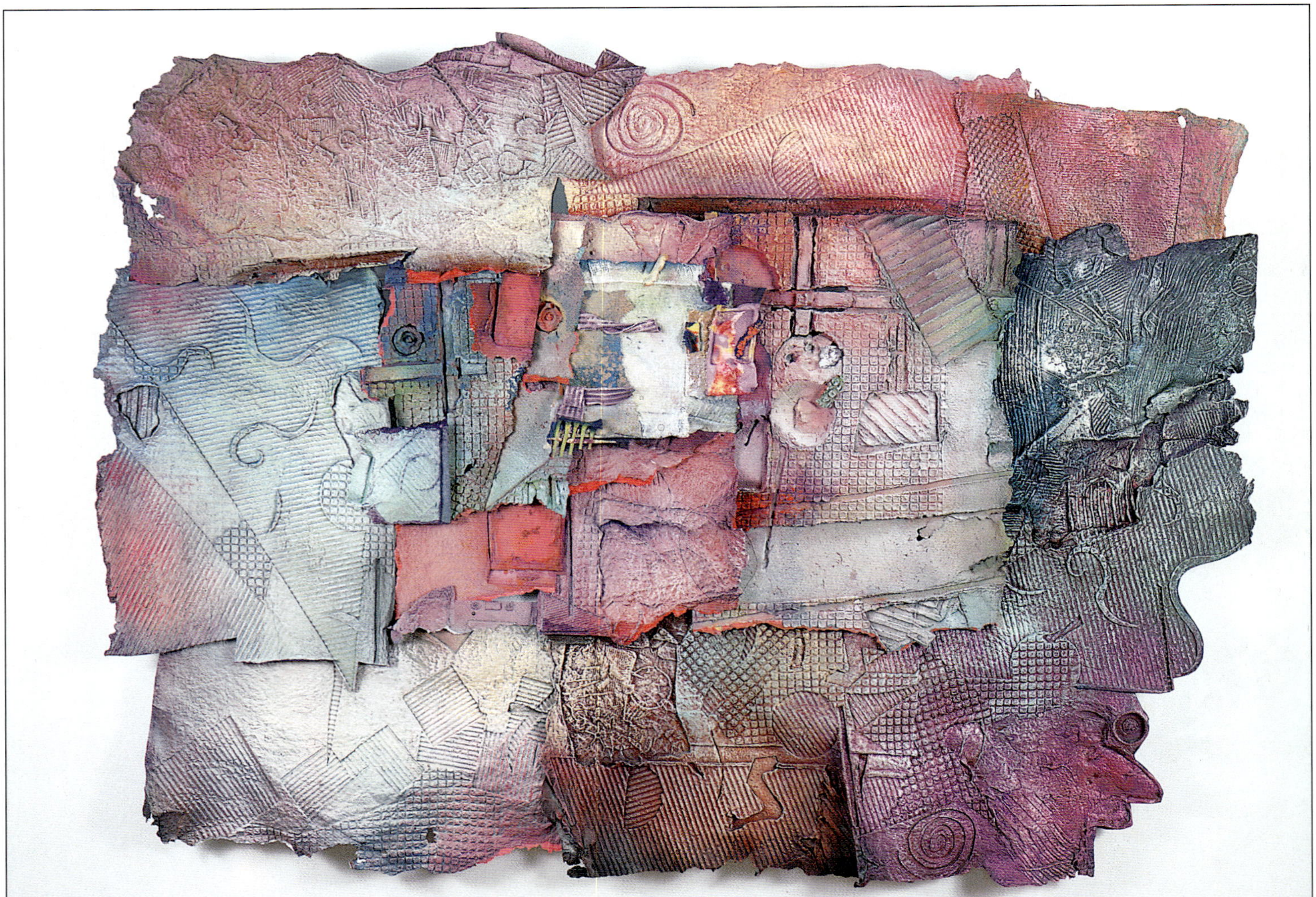

B

Photos: Douglas Cameron

Gloria Zmolek Smith

Zpapersmith
PO Box 1294
Cedar Rapids, IA 52406-1294
FAX 319-365-9611
TEL 319-365-9611
E-Mail: zpaper@cedarnet.com

Gloria Zmolek Smith's work crosses boundaries by using handmade paper tiles within a traditional quilt structure. Origami gives the work an additional dimension.

Her art is largely influenced by her children and concern for their world. The *Only a Thousand Lives* series is an international plea for pecce. The *Safe Haven* series is inspired by her daughter's love for all living creatures. Works by Zmolek Smith are exhibited and collected nationally.

Slides, resume and prices are available upon request.

Only a Thousand Lives: Chechnya, 1995, handmade paper, 30" x 51" x 2"

Mike Schlotterback

Safe Haven: Water Creatures, 1995, handmade paper, 40" x 24" x 2"

French Studios

Nancy J. Young
Allen Young

11416 Brussels NE
Albuquerque, NM 87111
FAX 505-299-2238
TEL 505-299-6108

The Youngs create two- and three-dimensional free-standing sculptures and mixed media wall art. Color preferences and commissions accepted. Prices range from $200 - $3,000, depending on size and complexity.

Photos, pricing and scheduling upon request.

Selected commissions include: the U.S. State Department for embassies in Port Moresby, New Guinea, and Caracas, Venezuela; IBM; AT&T; and American Express.

Also see these GUILD publications:
THE GUILD: 1, 2, 3, 4, 5
Designer's Edition: 6, 7, 8, 9, 10

A *Abushanti, Rupikela,* patinated mixed media, each 34"H x 8"W x ⅝"D

B Bronze patinated hand-cast paper vessels, top 38"Dia x 8½"D; bottom: 13"H x 18"Dia, on steel stand

A

B

Photos: Pat Berrett

Ellen Zahorec

Island Ford Studio
396 Amazon Avenue
Cincinnati, OH 45220
FAX 513-861-4419
TEL   513-861-7419

Artist Ellen Zahorec creates one-of-a-kind mixed-media collages which are inspired by the ancient tradition of icons. Zahorec's influence is based on her personal experience as a second-generation Slovak-American Byzantine Catholic.

The incongruity of images examines historic doctrine in a desire to explore an internal vision of spirituality. The collages literally glow in the dark and consist of hundreds of meticulously cut, sewn and embellished images on a thick ground of acrylic paint, handmade paper, and cotton linters. New myths rise from the richly textured surface in response to the merging of the sacred and the secular.

Zahorec's artwork is found worldwide in numerous corporate and private collections. Each unique piece can also be designed to meet specific color ranges and dimensions.

Prices range from $100 to $2,000.

Also see these GUILD publications:
THE GUILD: 5
Designer's Edition: 8

Guardians of the Many Madonnas, 1994, 40" x 32"

Communion of Saints and Forgiveness of Sinners, 1994, 40" x 32

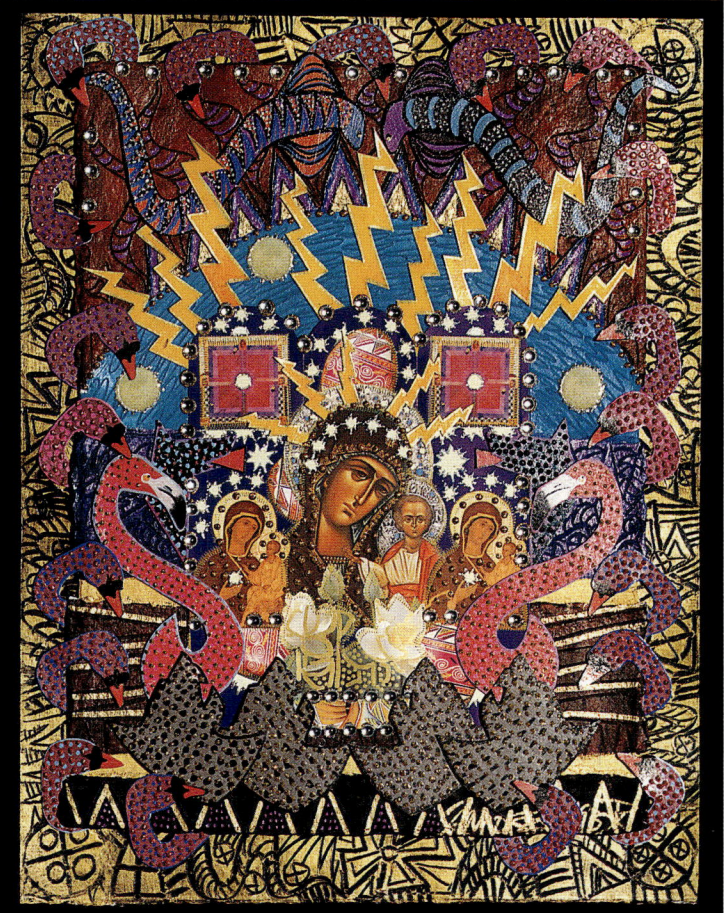

Madonna of the Heavenly Dome, 1994, 40" x 32"

Photos: Alex Hughes

ANATOMY OF A COMPETITION
The Story of the ACC-Hines Project

By Ellen Kochansky

Some ideas seem to arrive fully formed and mature, like Athena. This one may have had its roots in a number of unrecognized or forgotten fragments scattered through the 15 years I had already been in the commission business, but it presented itself nearly unbidden in the fall of 1992. On these pages you see some of the fruits of the tree. Here is how it germinated and grew.

people, I had a hunch (and hunches have a way of turning into missions) that the ACC could be more things to more people. At our last meeting, my graduating class was enjoined to go out and continue to be, as Carol Edelman put it, "ambassadors for the craft movement." I'm not sure how great a board member I was, but I can be a zinger of an ambassador! I love this field and the people in it. Compared to the fashion business, where I cut my professional teeth, it is heaven.

Winning design by Sheila O'Hara, Oakland, CA

I had just left the board of the American Craft Council (ACC). Board membership has its frustrations, especially for entrepreneurial types — as craft artists tend (need) to be. Things take a while, and if — as a board member — you have some projects you'd like to see done, you need a good measure of patience: Your projects are likely to be diluted or swamped by other priorities.

Though no organization, no matter how national, can be all things to all

Still, the industry is not without problems, and one of my major concerns has been the lack of markets for artists whose work does not fit comfortably into the existing craft show format. Some of my own most satisfying and profitable work has been done for architectural commissions, on a scale that won't fit a craft show booth. The most convincing promotional tool in this arena, as THE GUILD has gone a long way to prove, is a good photograph of a completed work, installed in the location for which it was designed. Unfortunately, this kind of photo is even harder to come by than a good commission, since artists are rarely in a position to hire good photographic services in the commission location, which may well be half a continent away.

In the mid-80s, I had participated in an

As stated in the call for entries, the goals of the ACC-Hines 'Art in Architecture' project were:

1. To provide an opportunity for craft artists whose work is or might be suitable for architectural scale, and to foster the vision, experience, and presentation skills to develop future such works.

2. To generate interest and awareness in the business community for the humanizing and softening effect that architectural-scale craft art can have on the corporate environment.

3. To produce photographs that will broaden public awareness of the artists, the organizations, and the concept of this competition.

Ellen Kochansky, fiber artist and advocate for the decorative arts, lives in South Carolina.

intriguing program sponsored by the Wool Bureau, in New York. Through this program, a number of fiber artists produced work for display in the Bureau's headquarters in exchange for a very fair rent over a three-month period. The works were then returned to the artists.

Winning design by Ardyth Davis, Leesburg, VA

This opportunity expanded my horizons, and nudged me into finding invaluable solutions to problems of scale and transportation for my own work. Now, ten years later, I wanted to adapt this idea to a new site, with two additions: first, a competition format, which would generate publicity and train applicants in presentation skills; and second, awards, including an installation shot for each of the winners, and purchase of one of the works for permanent display at the site.

In 1991, I had been awarded a commission for a large work in the lobby of a Cincinnati office complex by the international development firm Hines Interests Limited Partnership. Hines'

corporate standards of architecture and management are exceptional: travertine by the acre . . . lobby space like artists see in their dreams. Two years later, when Hines contacted me about artwork for another wall, I suggested my competition idea. They liked it. Hunter Kariher, newly on board as director of the American Craft Council, liked it too, and the ACC signed on to co-sponsor the project.

Though the format of the competition presumed that emerging artists would respond, many applicants were nationally prominent. Everybody loves a chance to get their name in lights.

In September, a panel composed of Michael Monroe (former curator-in-charge of the Smithsonian's Renwick Gallery), Toni Sikes (publisher of THE GUILD) and myself viewed slides and chose 20 finalists. One short month later, 20 incredibly professional and varied maquettes (scale models), in an astounding assortment of materials and techniques, were ready to ship to a judging location.

Winning design by Susan Sargent, Pawlet, VT

Photos used in this article were taken by Jay Bachemin

Winning design by William Baran-Mickle, Rochester, NY

losers, and each of my hopes for the idea were realized, save two. First is my vision of all these remarkable scale models and finished works being brought together as a formal show, documented for the enlightenment of future potential commission artists. And second is my hope that the competition will be repeated; after all, the American Craft Council saw this as a 'pilot project.'

There are plenty of corporate walls out there that need the warmth American craft artists can provide. Here is a way for them to find each other.

Organizations interested in sponsoring an art-in-architecture competition may contact:

Hunter Kariher, Executive Director
American Craft Council
72 Spring Street
New York City, NY 10012
FAX 212-274-0650
TEL 212-274-0630

Fortunately the timing for the final judging coincided with a conference sponsored by the Southeastern regional division of the ACC at Arrowmont school in Gatlinburg, Tennessee. Hundreds of attendees had the chance to see — and learn from — the models.

Ultimately, four winners were selected. Each completed the proposed piece and received rent for a three-month display. After consecutively viewing the four winning pieces, tenants of the building voted to select one work to be purchased for permanent installation. William Baran-Mickle's work in metal was chosen.

According to Hines' facility manager, Gary Beck, this project pleased the building's tenants in several ways. They liked the fact that the scenery changed in an exciting way every few months, and appreciated their role in choosing the winner.

The ACC-Hines competition was that rare project in which there were no

1993 ACC-HINES ART IN ARCHITECTURE COMPETITION

Completed projects of the four competition winners are shown on these pages.
Other participants include:

WINNERS
William Baran-Mickle
Ardyth Davis
Shelia O'Hara
Susan Sargent

RUNNERS-UP
Susan Dunshee
Jamie Fine

FINALISTS
George-Ann Bowers	Laura Militzer Bryant	Jane Burch Cochran	Peter Grimord
Joan M. Hall	Gail Kristensen	Thomas Mann	Jean Neblett
Ellen Oppenheimer	Nanilee S. Robarge	Susan Singleton	
Alice Van Leunen	Bhakti Ziek	Susan Venable	

B.J. Adams

Art in Fiber
2821 Arizona Terrace NW
Washington, DC 20016
FAX 202-686-1042
TEL 202-364-8404

B.J. Adams designs mixed-media wall hangings for commercial and residential interiors. Commissioned artwork can be colorful or subdued, textured or flat, illustrative or abstract, large or small.

Work has been commissioned by collectors as well as business, banking, medical, government, and hotel facilities.

A   *Trust* (detail), 15" x 15"

B   *Too Brief* (detail), machine embroidery over
    painted canvas

C   *Too Brief*, 57" x 69", created for memorial
    exhibit, dedicated to the 19 children killed
    in Oklahoma City bombing, April 19, 1995

A

B

C

Photos: Breger and Associates, Kensington, MD

Doris Bally

420 North Craig Street
Pittsburgh, PA 15213
FAX 412-621-9030
TEL 412-621-3709

Commissioned for numerous private, civic and
corporate spaces, Bally's designs range from
abstract landscapes to natural forms, focusing
on color in its myriad combinations. Her tapestries
enhance any environment with their soft, colorful
texture, and they absorb sound. They are easy
to install, with only two fasteners per panel.

Typical sizes are 4 feet by 14 feet, and 6 feet by
9 feet. Larger installations can be assembled from
multiple panels. Slides upon request.

Also see these GUILD publications:
THE GUILD: 1, 3
Designer's Edition: 7, 9

A *Turmoil,* 39" x 61"

B *Catalpa,* 75" x 110"

A

B

Printed in Hong Kong ©1996 THE GUILD: The Designer's Sourcebook

Laura Militzer Bryant

2595 30th Avenue North
St. Petersburg, FL 33713
FAX 813-321-1905
TEL 813-327-3100

Laura Militzer Bryant has been producing award-winning artworks for 18 years. She is a recipient of both National Endowment for the Arts and Florida State individual fellowships, and her works are in major collections including the City of St. Petersburg, Mobil Oil, Eli Lilly, Xerox Corporation and Seton Hall University.

Laura works in wool, rayon and nylon; each layer of her double-weave tapestries is dyed and painted separately. Her artwork has been featured in both *American Craft* and *Fiberarts* magazines, and has generated numerous commissions throughout the country. She recently had a one-person retrospective in the State Capitol Gallery in Tallahassee, Florida.

Also see this GUILD publication:
Designer's Edition: 10

A *Edifice Constructed*, 1993. 58 1/2" x 48"

B *Genesis*, 1995, Hines competition semi-finalist, 52" x 79"

A

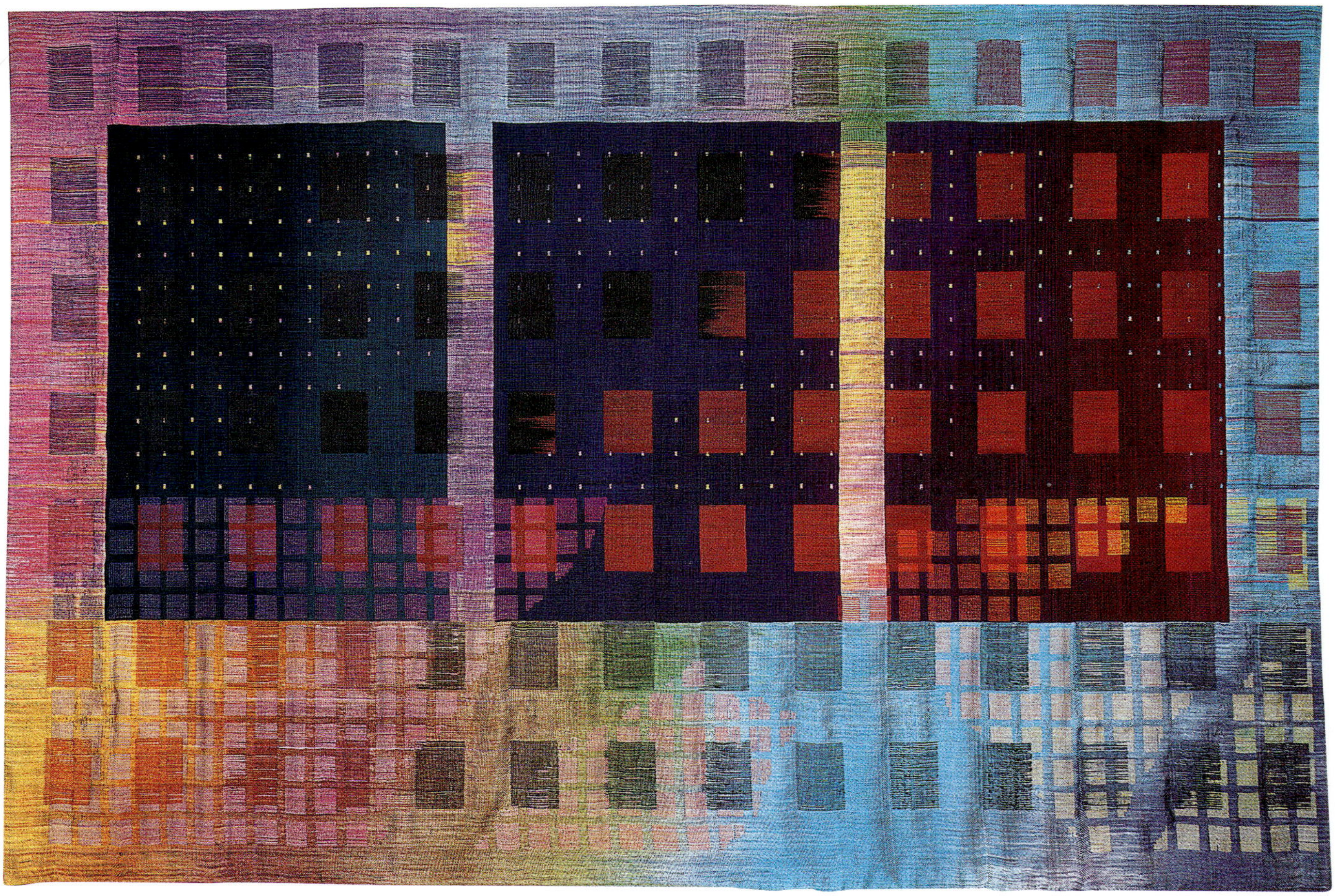

B

Photos: Thomas Bruce

Barbara Cade

262 Hideaway Hills Drive
Hot Springs, AR 71901
TEL 501-262-4065

Luscious vegetation.

One flower or one whole bouquet.

For people who are not afraid of getting back to nature.

For people who like making dramatic statements.

For people who like being different.

Working in age-old primitive methods, Barbara Cade creates one-of-a-kind, hand-felted wool flowers and other natural forms. Her work has been exhibited in museum juried shows for 25 years, is represented in many corporation collections and is part of the permanent collection of the Tacoma Art Museum.

Easy to install. Arrangeable.

Care: dust with hose-type spray vacuum; use insect spray labeled for fabrics, only if necessary. No weeding required.

For slides of other species and varieties, send $20 (refundable). Commissions welcome.

Also see these GUILD publications:
Designer's Edition: 8, 9, 10

SHOWN: *Sparaxis*, 1995, felt, 27"H x 32"W x 7"D

Cindy Momchilov

Susan Dunshee

986 Acequia Madre
Santa Fe, NM 87501
TEL   505-982-0988

Susan Dunshee's layered fiber constructions evoke a sense of metamorphosis, conveying both strength and vulnerability. She draws her inspiration from time-worn objects — old quilts, vintage clothing, weathered bark, striated rock formations.

Using an original technique of machine-stitching dyed yarns and fabric shreds between layers of nylon netting, Dunshee is able to create work of rich texture, complex color and great depth.

Receiving an M.F.A. from California College of Arts and Crafts over 15 years ago, Dunshee has subsequently been awarded NEA funding and other honors, and has exhibited nationally and internationally. Her work is in private and corporate collections, including Hyatt, GTE, American Express and HBO.

A *Furrow,* 56" x 73"

B *Prelude,* 72" x 62"

A

B

Carl Erikson

35 Morningside Commons
Brattleboro, VT 05301
TEL 802-254-9176

Carl Erikson's textile constructions glow with color and unique design. The textiles in many are stretched over frameworks, building up bas-relief dimensions. In others, the textiles float freely from supporting rods. His designs range from pure abstractions to evocations of specific ideas and experiences.

Although much of Erikson's work is in the form of wall pieces, he has also created ceiling-mounted pieces (kites, magic carpets, and totem poles), bedcovers, window treatments, and wall-substi-tutes. Site-specific work and work incorporating the customer's fabric or design elements are particularly enticing to him.

Erikson has exhibited in galleries, public libraries, corporate spaces, and restaurants.

A *Etude #21,* textile construction, mixed fabrics, 30" x 60"

B *Caribbean,* textile construction, mixed fabrics, 44" x 51"

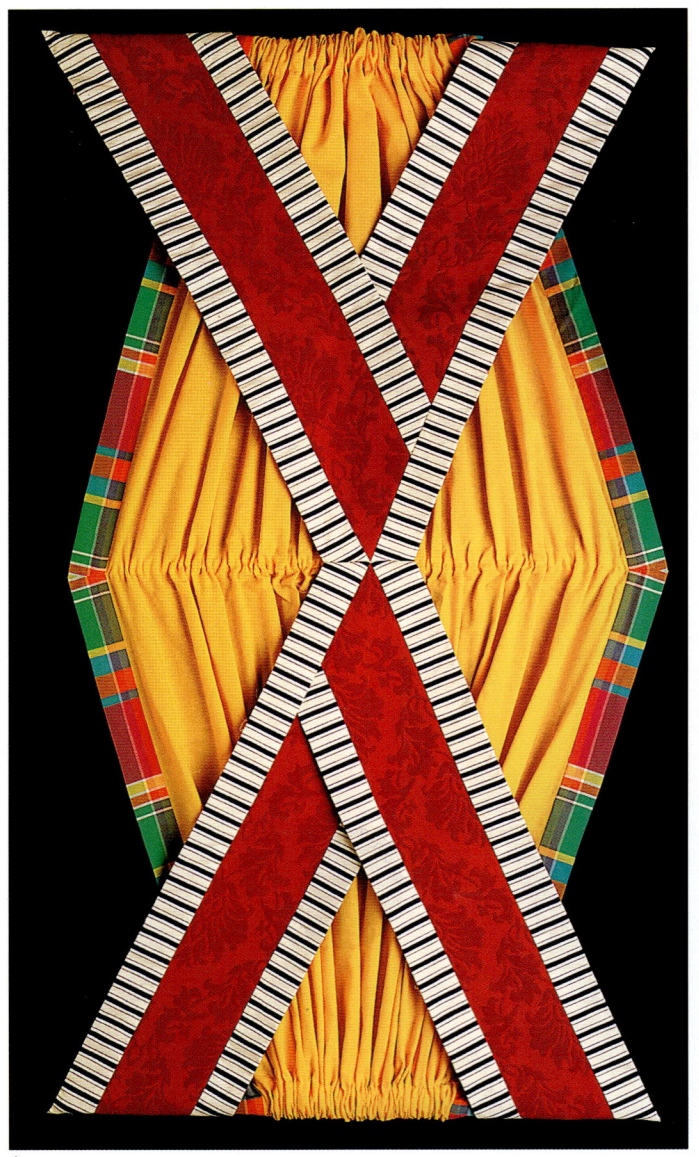

A

B

Phyllis Ceratto Evans

6969 Island Center Road NE
Bainbridge Island, WA 98110
TEL   206-842-5042

By fusing aged Japanese kimono fabric to canvas, Phyllis Ceratto Evans creates her compelling images. Each piece is beautifully crafted and retains the natural iridescence of the silk. Protective coating ensures easy maintenance and longevity without compromising the tactile quality of the fabric.

Phyllis' creativity with textiles spans many years. Her award-winning work resides in an American embassy, in addition to corporate and private collections.

Also see these GUILD publications:
Designer's Edition: 9, 10

A *poling down the avenue—*
   alla Venezia, 19" x 29"

B *Comogli—andremo insieme*
   (we go together), 39" x 24"

A

B

Photos: Wally Hampton, Photography

Marilyn Forth

416 David Drive
North Syracuse, NY 13212
FAX 315-458-0913
TEL 315-458-3786

Marilyn Forth's majestic batik floral paintings add grace and style. Each painting has a fresh, immediate quality to it. Marilyn paints with a brush loaded with fiber-reactive dye. The dyes give her paintings a vibrant look unmatched by other art media. The paintings are steamed to set the dyes, and then stretched on half-inch foam-core board. Lucite is used instead of glass for easy shipping.

Batik paintings by Marilyn Forth are being shown in many galleries throughout the United States. They can be seen in Sun Vail Condominiums, Vail, CO; Kaiser Permanente Center, Anaheim, CA; Saginaw Gold & Diamond Center, Saginaw, MI; and Ann's Gifts Plus, Decatur, IL.

Also see these GUILD publications:
Designer's Edition: 6, 7, 8, 10

A *Southwest Flowers*, batik, 45" x 72"

B *Flower Arrangements*, batik, 45" x 45"

A

B

Photos: Anthony Potter

Barbara Grenell

1132 Hall's Chapel Road
Burnsville, NC 28714
FAX 704-675-4073
TEL 704-675-4073

Barbara Grenell's unique partial wrap-faced technique and rich fiber palette create a more painterly control of line and composition than traditional tapestry. Her multiple-panel tapestries and dimensional constructions are internationally collected and commissioned for corporate private and public sites. Awarded an N.E.A. fellowship, Barbara Grenell creates landscapes which are widely exhibited and unlimited in size and format.

Clients include: Association of American Medical Colleges, Washington, DC; Bankers Trust, New York, NY; Duke University, Durham, NC; Ernst & Young, Washington, DC; Merck & Co., Rahway, NJ; Nations Bank, Charlotte, NC; Sheraton Hotel, Burlingame, CA; Southern Bell, Atlanta, GA; and West Allis Memorial Hospital, Milwaukee, WI.

Highland Autumn, 60"H x 48"W

Zenith, 36"H x 72"W

Carole Harris

667 West Bethune
Detroit, MI 48202
TEL   313-871-4155

Carole Harris's rhythmically constructed, non-traditional tapestries are composed of hundreds of richly colored fabrics which are cut, overlaid, appliquéd, pieced and quilted. A professional interior designer and fiber artist, she creates one-of-a-kind, improvisational works that provide warmth and texture to enhance commercial and residential interiors.

Harris's work has been exhibited nationally in museums and galleries.

A slide portfolio and price list of works are available upon request. Commissioned work will be considered.

A *Do You Feel Like Dancing?*, 1995, cotton, silk, wool, lurex, 55$\frac{1}{2}$"W x 75$\frac{1}{2}$"H

B *Something Like a Jitterbug*, 1994, quilted cottons, 44$\frac{1}{4}$"W x 65$\frac{1}{2}$"H

A

B

Photos: Bill Saunders

M. Helsenrott Hochhauser

Marilyn H. Hochhauser
1409 Las Canoas Lane
Santa Barbara, CA 93105
TEL 805-966-2921

The artist's flexibility in various media reveals the versatility of her artistic expression.

The drama created in the unique process of manipulating handmade paper and canvas into three-dimensional non-objective sculptural forms is powerful in its impact.

The use of strong gestural drawing and painting strokes combined with found objects create the artist's style. Rich blacks and reds pay tribute to her interest in Oriental art.

Ms. Hochhauser is a former professor of art whose work is in corporate offices, private collections and museums in the United States and abroad.

More information upon request.

Commissions accepted.

Mortimaniacal Fourteen, 1993, handmade paper, mixed media, 30" x 24"

#152 Eleven X (detail), 1991, acrylic painting, mixed media, 40" x 84"

Photos: Timothy Hearsum

Marie-Laure Ilie

Marilor Art Studio
106 Via Sevilla
Redondo Beach, CA 90277
FAX 310-375-4977
TEL 310-375-4977

Ilie creates large, abstract compositions by combining layers of organza and hand-painted silk. Her unusual appliqué technique enhances the inherent sophistication of silk with rich, painterly effects. These paintings come ready to hang like tapestries. They can also be framed. Colors are fade proof.

For the past 20 years, Ilie has exhibited extensively in the United States and Europe. She has created innumerable successful commissions. Patrons include both residential and corporate collections.

Call for prices, photos, slides, samples or proposal designs.

Also see these GUILD publications:
THE GUILD: 4, 5
Designer's Edition: 7, 8, 9, 10

A   *Morning Frolic,* 84" x 60"

B   *Twin City Rhapsody,* 120" x 54"

A

B

Ulrika Leander

Contemporary Tapestry Weaving
107 Westoverlook Drive
Oak Ridge, TN 37830
FAX 423-483-7911
TEL   423-482-6849

Ulrika Leander has established a reputation for superb craftsmanship and a remarkable range of creative and imaginative designs. With 25 years of experience in this field, Leander has installed more than 150 tapestries commissioned for public, private and commercial settings in the United States and in her native Scandinavia.

Using 100 percent natural fibers, she produces single pieces measuring up to 12' x 30'.

Resume and slides are available upon request.

Also see these GUILD publications:
Designer's Edition: 8, 9, 10
Architect's Edition: 11

A   *Healig Flight,* 1994, tapestry, St. Michael Hospital,
    Texarkana, TX, 5' x 12'

B   *After the Rain,* 1995, private collection, 8' x 3'

A

B

Photos: J.W. Nave

Joyce P. Lopez

Joyce Lopez Studio
1147 West Ohio Street #304
Chicago, IL 60622-5874
FAX 312-243-5033
TEL 312-243-5033

Joyce Lopez meticulously creates her sculpture out of metal poles and silk-like colored thread. With over 300 exquisite colors to choose from, color specifications are always met. These stunning works enrich corporate, public and private interiors.

Collections include the Sony Corporation, Bank of America, City of Chicago, State of Washington, Michael Reese Hospital, and private residences.

Easily maintained, commissioned sculptures take two to four months to complete. Prices from $2,500 to $80,000. Call, fax or write for a brochure.

Also see these GUILD publications:
THE GUILD: 2, 3, 4, 5
Designer's Edition: 6, 7, 8, 9, 10
Architect's Edition: 8

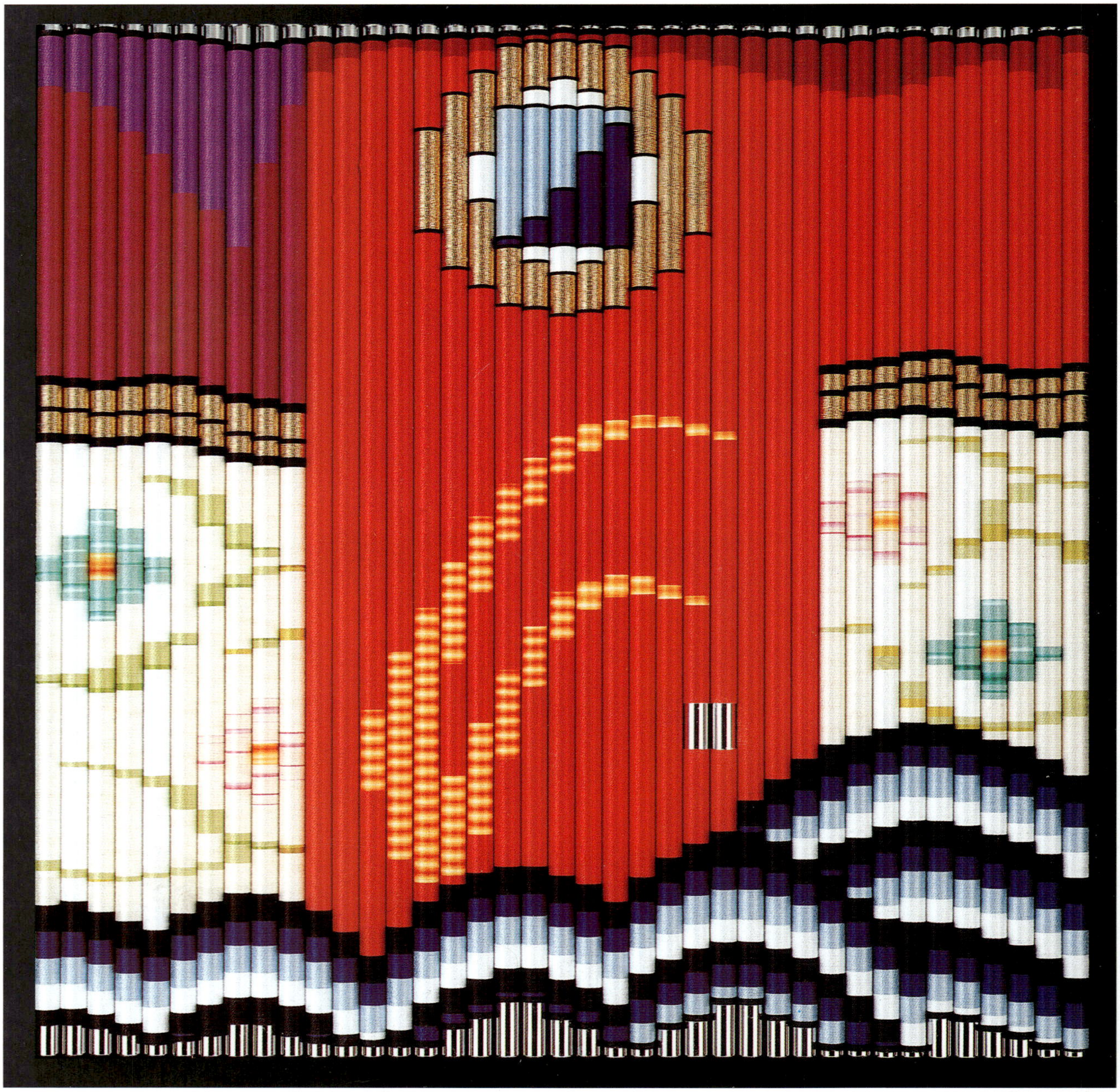

Quiet in Red, sculpture, chromed steel and thread, 32" x 32" x 2"

Photos: Mark Belter

Patti Mitchem

28 Witchtrot Road
South Berwick, ME 03908
FAX 207-384-1938
TEL 207-384-2195

The vibrant colors and imagery of Patti Mitchem's woven hangings have led to numerous corporate, public and residential commissions during her 15-year career.

Some of Patti's best and most original work has been done as a result of commissions. The pieces harmonize with their settings and subtly reflect the interests of the clients. Recent work includes detailed architectural images of community landmarks.

The warp-face weave results in a heavy, sturdy fabric. Works are completely reversible, ideal for banners, and easily maintained.

Price range: $90 to $180 per square foot.

A Keyport Insurance, Boston, 36"H x 144"W

B *Manchester, New Hampshire,* area of detail: 36"H x 27"W

C Burndy commission, suppliers to the power industry, 14'H x 6$^{1/2}$'W

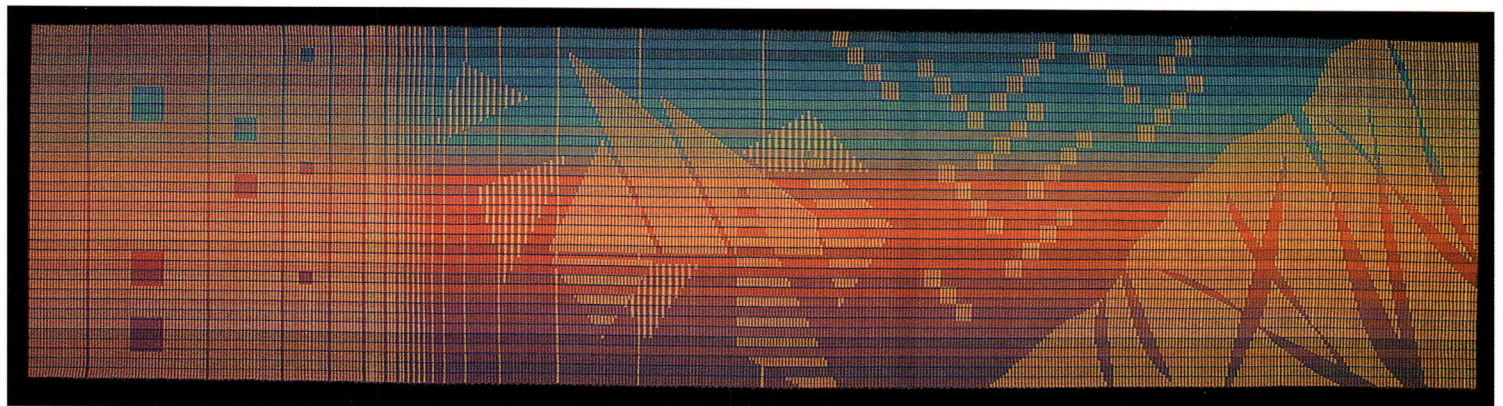

A

B

C

Photos: Sandy Agrafiotis

Sharron Parker

5823 Mapleridge Road
Raleigh, NC 27609
TEL 919-828-4533
TEL 919-872-2227

Sharron Parker has been creating wall hangings from handmade felt for 16 years. Her pieces are known for their rich colors, unique textures and varied forms, which can fit curved walls, fill niches and even drape across corners.

The pieces are made of wool, with silk, mohair, etc. yarns on the surface. They are lightweight, moth-proofed, and cleanable by gentle vacuuming. Completed pieces are available, and commissions are welcome.

Clients include Duke Divinity School, Kaiser Permanente, North Orlando Hilton, Northern Telecom, and Wachovia Bank.

A, B, D *Raku Flight*, (triptych),
68" x 190" x 16" overall

C *Raku Cloak*, 48" x 55" x 5"

A

Mike Back

Mike Back

C

Seth Tice-Lewis

Mike Back

A.R.T. TAPESTRIES BY VICTORIA STREET

VICTORIA STREET
5701 ANDREWS RD
MEDFORD, OR 97501
FAX 541-770-2030
TEL 541-770-1141
Established: 1980
Products: tapestries
Techniques: weaving, beading, unique fiber combinations
Size Range: no size limit
Price Range: $150 to $350/sq. ft.

SOPHIE ASHESON

ACHESON STUDIOS
6 POST OFFICE LN PO BOX 372
GREENS FARMS, CT 06436
TEL 203-255-1349
Established: 1978
Products: paper
Techniques: painting, appliqué, embossing
Size Range: 5" x 5" to 40" x 50"
Price Range: $300 to $3,000/sq. ft.

★ KAREN ADACHI

702 MONARCH WAY
SANTA CRUZ, CA 95060-3091
TEL 408-429-6192
Established: 1972
Products: paper
Techniques: painting, dyeing, airbrush
Size Range: 2' x 2' to 7' x 10'
Price Range: $500 to $4,000/piece

See page 145 for photographs and additional information.

SANDY ADAIR

FIBRE DESIGN
RR 3 BOX 912
BOONE, NC 28607-9544
TEL 704-264-0259
Established: 1978
Products: tapestries, macramé
Techniques: weaving, embroidery, off-loom weaving
Size Range: 1' x 3' to 6' x 10'
Price Range: $100 to $125/sq. ft.

★ B.J. ADAMS

ART IN FIBER
2821 ARIZONA TER NW
WASHINGTON, DC 20016-2642
FAX 202-686-1042
TEL 202-364-8404
Established: 1970
Products: fabric constructions
Techniques: painting, appliqué, machine embroidery
Size Range: 12" x 12" to unlimited (modular)
Price Range: $100 to $400/sq. ft.

See page 155 for photographs and additional information.

ADELA AKERS

16200 RIO NIDO RD
GUERNEVILLE, CA 95446
TEL 707-869-9753
Established: 1963
Products: tapestries
Techniques: weaving, dyeing
Size Range: 3' x 3' to 8' x 30'
Price Range: $300 to $600/sq. ft. (trade discount available)

LEONORE ALANIZ

519 E 82ND ST #58
NEW YORK, NY 10028-7171
TEL 212-737-4416
Products: fabric constructions, transparent banners, hand printed
Techniques: tree leaves imprinted on fabric, with text
Size Range: any size
Price Range: $80 and up/sq. ft.

DONNA ALBERT

DONNA ALBERT STUDIO
15 OAK HILL DR
PARADISE, PA 17562
FAX 717-687-5115
TEL 717-687-5114
Established: 1969
Products: art quilts, pictorial quilts
Techniques: embroidery, quilting, heat-fusion appliqué
Size Range: 12" x 18" to 10' x 10'
Price Range: $400 to $8,000/piece

MARTA AMUNDSON

HC36-85 GOOSE KNOB DR
RIVERTON, WY 82501
FAX 307-856-5176
TEL 307-856-3373
Established: 1976
Products: art quilts
Techniques: appliqué, embroidery, quilting
Size Range: 2' x 2' to 12' x 12'
Price Range: $500 to $18,000/piece

★ ANANSA-PURUO DESIGNS

ROBYN DAUGHTRY
8 FILBERT COURT
GAITHERSBURG, MD 20879
FAX 301-258-8920
TEL 301-258-8313
Established: 1980
Products: paper
Techniques: painting, dyeing, collage
Size Range: 8" x 14" to 6' x 8'
Price Range: $150 to $225/sq. ft.

See photograph below.

CAROL ARMSTRONG

CAROL ARMSTRONG QUILTS
STAR SIDING RD HC 01 BOX 125
SHINGLETON, MI 49884
TEL 906-452-6469
Established: 1980
Products: art quilts
Techniques: appliqué, embroidery, quilting
Size Range: 8" x 8" to 100" x 100"
Price Range: $50 to $5,000/piece

ART IN QUILTS

KAY KOEPER SORENSEN
24920 73RD ST
SALEM, WI 53168
TEL 414-843-2348
Established: 1977
Products: art quilts
Techniques: dyeing, quilting, piecing
Size Range: 12" x 12" to 120" x 120"
Price Range: $100 to $200/sq. ft.

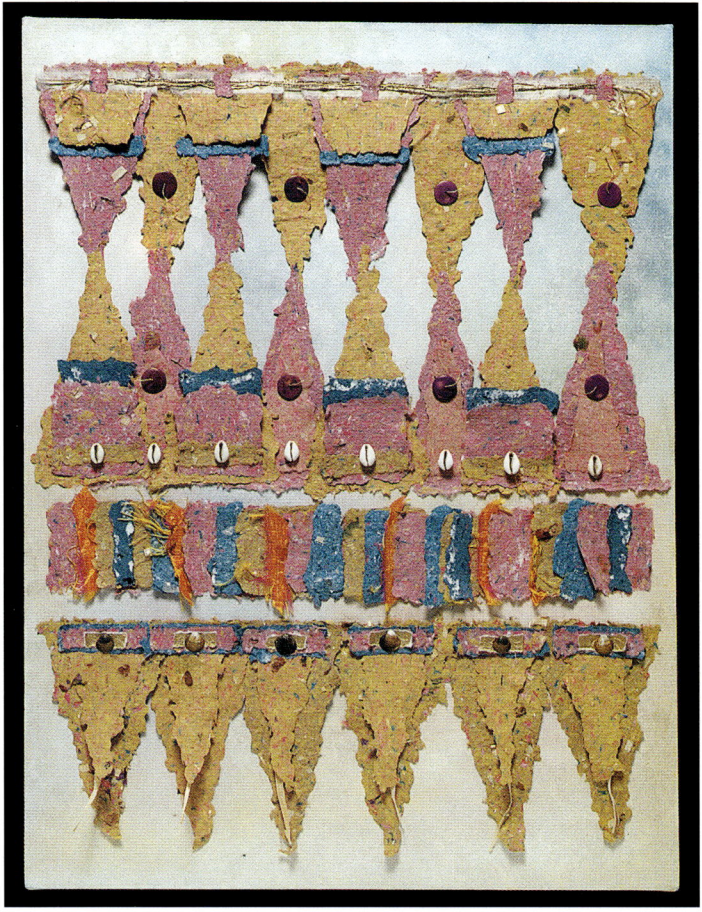

Anansa-Puruo Designs. *Indian Summer*, 1995, handmade paper with natural inclusions of flowers, grasses, metallics on painted canvas, 33"H x 25"W, photo: Mark Gulezian/QuickSilver

FIBER ART FOR THE WALL

SANDY ASKEW

50951 EXPRESSWAY
BELLEVILLE, MI 48111
TEL 313-483-5529
Established: 1975
Products: fiber installations
Techniques: contemporary coil weaving
Size Range: 12" x 36" to 6' x 12'
Price Range: $100 to $5,000/piece

CATHY PHILLIPS ATEN

CATHY ATEN TEXTILES
RR 2 BOX 154
SANTA FE, NM 87505-8659
TEL 505-983-7753
Established: 1978
Products: painted wool tapestries
Techniques: painting, stamping or printing
Size Range: 4' x 6' to 10' x 20'
Price Range: $1,800 to $8,000/piece

ELLEN ATHENS

PO BOX 1386
MENDOCINO, CA 95460-1386
TEL 707-937-2642
Established: 1982
Products: tapestries
Techniques: weaving
Size Range: 2' x 2' to 5' x 15'
Price Range: $400 to $18,000/piece

CAROL ATLESON

FIBER ART STUDIO
465 RUSKIN RD
AMHERST, NY 14226-4235
TEL 716-834-9384
Established: 1979
Products: tapestries
Techniques: weaving
Size Range: 2' x 3' to 7' x 7'
Price Range: $1,200 to $10,000/piece

BAAS STUDIO

BARB MACLEOD
RR1
THORNBURY, ON N0H 2P0
CANADA
TEL 519-599-2963
Established: 1974
Products: 2D, 3D fiber installations
Techniques: weaving, airbrush, padde fabric construcions
Size Range: 3' x 4' to unlimited
Price Range: $50 to $250/sq. ft.

JOHN BABCOCK

4780 SOQUEL CREEK RD
SOQUEL, CA 95073
FAX 408-462-5949
TEL 408-476-6302
Established: 1966
Products: hand-formed paper
Techniques: laminating, casting, pouring
Size Range: 3' x 2' to 6' x 15'
Price Range: $500 to $8,000/piece

JOANN BACHELDER

RIVERTOWN TEXTILES
1001 S HENRY ST
BAY CITY, MI 48706-5007
TEL 517-892-3013
Established: 1978
Products: wall hangings
Techniques: dyeing, weaving
Size Range: 20" x 20" to 9' x 12'
Price Range: $350 to $2,500/piece

★ SALLY BAILEY

HOOKED ON ART
PO BOX 60204
SANTA BARBARA, CA 93160-0204
TEL 805-563-0227
Established: 1969
Products: hooked art hangings
Techniques: traditional hooking
Size Range: 12" x 18" to 36" x 72"
Price Range: $75 to $200/sq. ft.

See photograph below.

MARTIN K. BAKER

ARTESANOS
 TIPICOS/COYOTE DESIGNS
715 CLEVELAND ST
MISSOULA, MT 59801-3738
FAX 406-728-3668
TEL 406-728-2789
Established: 1974
Products: tapestries
Techniques: painting, silkscreen, weaving
Size Range: 24" x 24" to 22' x 36'
Price Range: $10 to $100/sq. ft.

★ DORIS BALLY

420 N CRAIG ST
PITTSBURGH, PA 15213-1105
FAX 412-621-9030
TEL 412-621-3709
Established: 1963
Products: tapestries
Techniques: weaving
Size Range: 20" x 20" to 94" x 20'
Price Range: $155/sq. ft.

See page 156 for photographs and additional information

BARBARA FARRELL ARTS

BARBARA FARRELL
PO BOX 2944
SANFORD, FL 32772-2944
FAX 407-321-8666
TEL 407-321-0100
Established: 1973
Products: mixed media installations
Techniques: painting, stitchery, fresco
Size Range: 4' x 5' to 10' x 12'
Price Range: $100 minimum/sq. ft.

BARKER-SCHWARTZ DESIGNS

915 SPRING GARDEN ST #315
PHILADELPHIA, PA 19123-2605
TEL 215-236-0745
Established: 1980
Products: woven floorcloths
Techniques: appliqué, weaving, painting
Size Range: 4' x 3' to 8' x 11'
Price Range: $50 to $125/sq. ft.

TERESA BARKLEY

9 KENSINGTON TERR
MAPLEWOOD, NJ 07040
TEL 201-378-5815
Established: 1978
Products: art quilts
Techniques: appliqué, painting, quilting
Size Range: 16" x 20" to 103" x 110"
Price Range: $500 to $20,000/piece

SONYA LEE BARRINGTON

837 47TH AVE
SAN FRANCISCO, CA 94121-3207
TEL 415-221-6510
Established: 1972
Products: art quilts
Techniques: dyeing, quilting, piecing, appliqué
Size Range: 2' x 2' to 8' x 8'
Price Range: $125 to $225/sq. ft.

BARRON CUSTOM WALLHANGINGS & WINDOW TREATMENTS

BARBARA, STEVE AND
 RUTH BARRON
1943 NEW YORK AVE
HUNTINGTON STATION, NY 11768
FAX 516-549-9122
TEL 516-549-4242
Established: 1973
Products: fiber installations, window treatments
Techniques: embroidery, weaving, wrapping
Size Range: 2' x 1' to 24' x 24'
Price Range: $150 to $175/sq. ft.

CATHY BARTELS

1079 WYKOFF WAY
LAGUNA BEACH, CA 92651-3036
FAX 714-497-0400
TEL 714-494-8942
Established: 1982
Products: mixed media installations 'canvas reconstructions'
Techniques: painting, photo techniques, machine-image transfers
Size Range: 24" x 24" to 10' x 10'
Price Range: $300 to $5,000/piece
Price Range: $50 to $150/sq. ft.

DOREEN BECK DINK SIEGEL

100 W 57TH ST #10G
NEW YORK, NY 10019-3327
TEL 212-246-9757
Established: 1974
Products: art quilts
Techniques: appliqué, quilting
Size Range: 2' x 3' to 4' x 5'
Price Range: $1,500 to $10,000/piece

JUDY BECKER

27 ALBION ST
NEWTON, MA 02159-2119
TEL 617-332-6778
Established: 1981
Products: art quilts
Techniques: appliqué, dyeing, quilting
Size Range: 3' x 3' to 10' x 15'
Price Range: $900 to $8,000/piece
Price Range: $50 to $100/sq. ft.

Sally Bailey, *Grand Canyon Kaleidoscope*, 1995, recycled wool hand-hooked on burlap, 35"H x 70"W, photo: Wayne McCall

PAMELA E. BECKER
5 HENDRICK RD
FLEMINGTON, NJ 08822-7155
TEL 908-806-4911
Established: 1978
Products: painted fabric constructions
Techniques: appliqué, painting, piecing
Size Range: 28" × 32" to 8' × 16'
Price Range: $3,000 and up/piece

NANCY BELFER
1906 DELAWARE AVE
BUFFALO, NY 14216-3514
TEL 716-877-7398
Products: tapestries
Techniques: weaving, painting, embroidery
Size Range: 30" × 72" to 45" × 72"
Price Range: $100 to $150/sq. ft.

SUE BENNER
8517 SAN FERNANDO WAY
DALLAS, TX 75218-4306
TEL 214-324-3550
Established: 1980
Products: art quilts
Techniques: dyeing, painting, quilting
Size Range: 15" × 15" to 12' × 15'
Price Range: $400 to $25,000/piece

ASTRID HILGER BENNETT
909 WEBSTER ST
IOWA CITY, IA 52240-4738
TEL 319-338-9176
Established: 1978
Products: art quilts
Techniques: dyeing, painting, screen printing
Size Range: 18" × 24" to 8' × 10'
Price Range: $250 to $8,000/piece

CHRISTINA BENSON-VOS
15 GRAMERCY PARK
NEW YORK, NY 10003
TEL 212-982-5960
Established: 1986
Products: tapestries
Techniques: weaving
Size Range: 4' × 6' to 6' × 8'
Price Range: $5,000 to $15,000/piece

LYNN BERKOWITZ
PO BOX 121
SLATEDALE, PA 18079-0121
TEL 610-767-8072
Established: 1978
Products: fabric constructions
Techniques: dyeing, weaving
Size Range: 10" × 10" to 8' × 8'
Price Range: $400 to $5,000/piece

JANNA BERNSTEIN
CREATIONS
319 FERNWAY COVE
MEMPHIS, TN 38117-2012
TEL 901-680-0812
Established: 1974
Products: tapestries, fiber installations, rugs
Techniques: weaving, screen printing, wrapping
Size Range: 1' × 1' and up
Price Range: $100 to $400/sq. ft.

LOUISE LEMIEUX BÉRUBÉ
CENTRE DES METIERS D'ART
1751 RUE RICHARDSON, BUREAU 5530
MONTREAL, QC H3K 1G6
CANADA
FAX 514-933-6305
TEL 514-933-3728
Established: 1979
Products: fabric constructions
Techniques: weaving with metal wires
Size Range: 8" × 8" to 6' × 6'
Price Range: $300 to $15,000/piece

BIG SUR HANDWOVENS
LAVERNE MCLEOD
HC67 BOX 1145
BIG SUR, CA 93920
TEL 408-667-2788
Established: 1986
Products: fiber installations
Techniques: weaving, quilting, beading
Size Range: 8.5" × 14" to 5' × 5'
Price Range: $500 to $9,000/piece

ELIZABETH BILLINGS
E.P. BILLINGS, WEAVER
ONE PHILLIPS COVE
CAPE NEDDICK, ME 03902
TEL 207-361-2777
Established: 1987
Products: tapestries
Techniques: weaving, natural-dyed ikat
Size Range: 24" × 24" to 20' × 30'
Price Range: $100 to $350/sq. ft.

BINGO PAJAMA WALLWORKS
SHANNON AND MATTHEW SCHERING
6 WASHINGTON ST #C
PO BOX 165
TRUMANSBURG, NY 14886
TEL 607-387-4924
Established: 1993
Products: fiber/wood wallworks
Techniques: dyeing, airbrushing, wood sculpting
Size Range: 12" × 12" to 40" × 60"
Price Range: $100 to $800/piece

CECILIA BLOMBERG
3613 44TH ST CT NW
GIG HARBOR, WA 98335
FAX 206-858-7447
TEL 206-858-8210
Established: 1976
Products: tapestries
Techniques: weaving
Size Range: 12" × 12" to 8' × 20'
Price Range: $300 to $50,000/piece

REBECCA BLUESTONE
PO BOX 1704
SANTA FE, NM 87504-1704
FAX 505-986-3412
TEL 505-989-9599
Established: 1984
Products: tapestries
Techniques: weaving, dyeing, embroidery
Size Range: 5' × 3' to 20' × 6'
Price Range: $80 to $175/sq. ft.

NANCY BONEY
97 KING ST
FANWOOD, NJ 07023-1517
TEL 908-889-8219
Established: 1973
Products: fabric constructions
Techniques: appliqué, fabric sculpture
Size Range: 24" × 36" to 5' × 8'
Price Range: $73 to $100/sq. ft.

DANA BOUSSARD
2 HEART CREEK RRT #1
ARLEE, MT 59821
FAX 406-726-4136
TEL 406-726-3357
Established: 1966
Products: fiber installations
Techniques: airbush, appliqué, painting
Size Range: 3' × 10' to 10' × 100'
Price Range: $150 to $300/sq. ft.

KAREN BOVARD
SPECTRUM QUILTS
259 FARM HILL RD
MIDDLETOWN, CT 06457-4224
TEL 203-346-1116
Established: 1986
Products: art quilts
Techniques: painting, beading, quilting
Size Range: 2' × 2' to 100" × 120"
Price Range: $80 to $150/sq. ft.

★ GEORGE-ANN BOWERS
1199 CORNELL AVE
BERKELEY, CA 94706-2305
TEL 510-524-3611
Established: 1983
Products: tapestries
Techniques: weaving, painting, dyeing
Size Range: 15" × 15" to 48" × 108"
Price Range: $200 to $300/sq. ft.

See photograph on page 174.

ODETTE BRABEC
1107 GOLF AVE
HIGHLAND PARK, IL 60035-3637
TEL 708-432-2704
Established: 1977
Products: tapestries
Techniques: weaving
Size Range: 24" × 24" to 5' × 10'
Price Range: $1,000 to $13,000/piece

DAVID BRACKETT
404 PENN ST
NEW BETHLEHEM, PA 16242
TEL 814-275-1846
Products: fabric constructions
Techniques: weaving, dyeing, screen printing
Size Range: 73" × 57" to 96" × 120"
Price Range: $2,000 to $6,000/piece

JEANNE BRAEN
14 LEVESQUE LN
MONT VERNON, NH 03057-1420
TEL 603-672-7822
Established: 1975
Products: tapestries
Techniques: weaving
Size Range: 3' × 5' to 9' × 12'
Price Range: $80 to $100/sq. ft.

LAURENCE BRANSCU
ART/DESIGN
6527 N NORTHWEST HWY
CHICAGO, IL 60631
FAX 312-631-1682
TEL 312-631-1682
Established: 1980
Products: hand-painted silk
Techniques: painting, airbrushing, resist dyeing
Size Range: 15" × 15" to 4' × 8'
Price Range: $150 to $4,000/piece

ANN BRAUER
PO BOX 164 282 EMMET RD
ASHFIELD, MA 01330-0164
TEL 413-628-4014
Established: 1981
Products: art quilts
Techniques: quilting, appliqué
Size Range: 4" × 4" to 8' × 12'
Price Range: $200 to $10,000/piece

LYNDA BROTHERS
4255 HITCH BLVD
MOORPARK, CA 93021-9731
TEL 805-523-3101
Established: 1969
Products: tapestries
Techniques: painting, weaving, marbling
Size Range: unlimited
Price Range: $35 to $400/sq. ft.

FIBER ART FOR THE WALL

TAFI BROWN

TY BRYN DESIGN STUDIOS
PO BOX 319
ALSTEAD, NH 03602-0319
TEL 603-756-3412
Established: 1975
Products: art quilts
Techniques: quilting, cyanotype
Size Range: 12" × 12" to 96" × 96"
Price Range: $250 to $18,000/piece

RACHEL BRUMER

1112 HARVARD AVE E
SEATTLE, WA 98102
TEL 206-328-7007
Established: 1990
Products: art quilts
Techniques: dyeing, appliqué, quilting
Size Range: 50" × 40" to 80" × 80"
Price Range: $2,000 to $3,500/piece

LOIS BRYANT

503 S 8TH ST
LINDENHURST, NY 11757-4616
TEL 516-226-7819
Established: 1979
Products: fiber installations
Techniques: weaving
Size Range: 1' × 1' to 8' × 17'
Price Range: $175 to $250/sq. ft.

★ LAURA MILITZER BRYANT

2595 30TH AVE N
SAINT PETERSBURG, FL 33713
FAX 813-321-1905
TEL 813-327-3100
Established: 1978
Products: tapestries
Techniques: weaving, painting, dyeing
Size Range: 18" × 18" to 10' × 4.5'
Price Range: $900 to $10,000/piece
Price Range: $200/sq. ft.

**See page 157 for photographs
and additional information.**

ELIZABETH J. BUCKLEY

HERITAGE TAPESTRIES
13418 MOUNTIAN VIEW AVE NE
ALBUQUERQUE, NM 87123
TEL 505-291-9635
Established: 1982
Products: tapestries
Techniques: weaving
Size Range: 8" × 12" to 30" × 48"
Price Range: $500 to $10,000/piece

PATTI J. BULLARD

SOUTHWEST TAPESTRIES
103 CHAMBERLAIN AVE
COLORADO SPRINGS, CA 80906
FAX 719-576-4196
TEL 719-579-0597
Established: 1990
Products: fabric constructions
Techniques: painting, quilting, machine
embroidery
Size Range: 15" × 36" to 48" × 60"
Price Range: $100 to $1,000/piece

MYRA BURG

2913 3RD ST #201
SANTA MONICA, CA 90405
FAX 310-399-0623
TEL 310-399-5040
Established: 1977
Products: mixed media installations, rare
wood, metals
Techniques: wrapping, assemblies
Size Range: 1' × 1' to 100' × 200'
Price Range: $150 to $100,000/piece
Price Range: $150 to $450/sq. ft.

TRICIA BURLING

WILLOWWEAVE
37 WELLS RD
MONROE, CT 06468
TEL 203-268-4794
Established: 1979
Products: wall hangings
Techniques: dyeing, weaving, wrapping
Size Range: panels up to any size
Price Range: $45 to $50/sq. ft.

SUSAN EILEEN BURNES

6980 MILL RD
BRECKSVILLE, OH 44141-1812
FAX 216-526-0874
TEL 216-838-5955
Established: 1991
Products: fabric constructions
Techniques: embroidery, appliqué,
beading
Size Range: 4" × 4" to 60" × 72"
Price Range: $200 to $4,000/piece

ELIZABETH A. BUSCH

RR 1 BOX 365
BANGOR, ME 04401-9705
FAX 207-942-7820
TEL 207-942-7820
Established: 1987
Products: art quilts
Techniques: airbush, painting, quilting
Size Range: 12" × 12" to 10' × 25'
Price Range: $200 to $12,000/piece
Price Range: $200 to $300/sq. ft.

MARY BALZER BUSKIRK

BUSKIRK STUDIOS
53 VIA VENTURA
MONTEREY, CA 93940-4340
TEL 408-375-6165
Established: 1956
Products: tapestries
Techniques: painting, weaving, gold and
silver leaf
Size Range: 1' × 1' to 20' × 20'
Price Range: $100 to $175/sq. ft.

★ BARBARA CADE

262 HIDEAWAY HILLS DR
HOT SPRINGS, AR 71901-8841
TEL 501-262-4065
Established: 1978
Products: sculpture
Techniques: felting, weaving, wrapping
Size Range: 24" × 24" to 60" × 78"
Price Range: $600 to $8,000/piece

**See page 158 for photographs
and additional information.**

MONECA CALVERT

3858 BALTIC CIR
ROCKLIN, CA 95677
TEL 916-632-3306
Established: 1983
Products: art quilts
Techniques: appliqué, embroidery,
quilting, piecing
Size Range: 2' × 2' to 8' × 8' and larger
Price Range: $1,800 to $20,000/piece

SUSAN CARLSON

FABRIC IMAGES
272 CRANBERRY MEADOW RD
BERWICK, ME 03901
FAX 207-698-5416
TEL 207-698-5358
Established: 1983
Products: art quilts
Techniques: appliqué, quilting, piecing
Size Range: 12" × 12" to 4' × 6'
Price Range: $400 to $6,000/piece

LUCINDA CARLSTROM

LUCINDA CARLSTROM STUDIO
1075 STANDARD DR NE
ATLANTA, GA 30319-3357
TEL 404-231-0227
Established: 1974
Products: mixed media installations
Techniques: quilting, gold leaf piece work
with paper, silk
Size Range: 20" × 20" to 80" × 120"
Price Range: $160 to $250/sq. ft.

George-Ann Bowers, *Madrone*, 1995, multiple-layer weaving, 32" × 42", photo: Dana Davis

ERIKA CARTER

2440 KILLARNEY WAY SE
BELLEVUE, WA 98004-7038
TEL 206-451-9712
Established: 1984
Products: art quilts
Techniques: appliqué, painting, quilting
Size Range: 26" x 36" to 60" x 66"
Price Range: $125 to $175/sq. ft.

★ BETH CASSIDY

2416 NW 60TH ST
SEATTLE, WA 98107
FAX 206-706-0406
TEL 206-783-6226
Established: 1980
Products: fabric constructions
Techniques: quilting, laminating, beading
Size Range: 12" x 12" to any size
Price Range: $300 to $8,000/piece
Price Range: $10 to $75/sq. ft.

**See page 136 for photographs
and additional information.**

MARY ALLEN CHAISSON

ALLEN POINT STUDIO
ALLEN POINT RD RR1 BOX 285
S HARPSWELL, ME 04079
FAX 207-833-6820
TEL 207-833-6842
Established: 1972
Products: art quilts
Techniques: appliqué, painting, quilting
Size Range: 2' x 2' to 7' x 7'
Price Range: $100/sq. ft.

CLAUDIA A. CHASE

MIRRIX TAPESTRY STUDIO
N1465 NORTH RD
GREENVILLE, WI 54942
TEL 414-757-0457
Established: 1990
Products: tapestries
Techniques: weaving
Size Range: 1' x 1' to 5' x 8'
Price Range: $150 to $300/sq. ft.

★ MARTHA CHATELAIN

ARTFOCUS, LTD.
PO BOX 9855
SAN DIEGO, CA 92169-0855
FAX 619-581-6536
TEL 619-581-6410
Established: 1982
Products: paper
Techniques: casting, dyeing, sculpting
Size Range: 10" x 10" to 4' x 14'
Price Range: $300 to $8,500/piece

See photograph this page.

JILL NORDFORS CLARK

JILL NORDFORS CLARK
 FIBER ART & INTERIOR DESIGN
3419 N ADAMS ST
TACOMA, WA 98407-6038
TEL 206-759-6158
Established: 1974
Products: mixed media installations
Techniques: appliqué, embroidery, painting
Size Range: 16" x 20" to 30" x 40"
Price Range: $750 to $1,200/piece

SUSANNE CLAWSON

5093 VELDA DAIRY RD
TALLAHASSEE, FL 32308-6801
TEL 904-893-5656
Established: 1985
Products: paper
Techniques: dyeing, painting, wrapping
Size Range: 12" x 12" to 10' x 10' or larger
Price Range: $250 to $15,000/piece

JANE BURCH COCHRAN

6830 RABBIT HASH HILL RD
RABBIT HASH, KY 41005
TEL 606-586-9169
Established: 1970
Products: art quilts
Techniques: quilting, beading
Size Range: 20" x 20" to 6' x 6'
Price Range: $500 to $10,000/piece

ANTONIO COCILOVO

LIFEFORMS
2600 PINE DR
PRESCOTT, AZ 86301-4098
TEL 602-445-1643
Established: 1974
Products: paint on custom fabrics
Techniques: painting, airbrush
Size Range: 2' x 2' and up
Price Range: $200 to $5,000/piece
Price Range: $30 to $50/sq. ft.

ELAINE ALBERS COHEN

32106 LAKE RD
AVON LAKE, OH 44012-1808
TEL 216-933-5979
Established: 1965
Products: cast paper reliefs
Techniques: casting, dyeing, painting
Size Range: 18" x 24" to 6' x 6'
Price Range: $100 to $150/sq. ft.

LAURA F. COHEN

INDONESIAN CONNECTIONS
431 MARY WATERSFORD RD
BALA CYNWYD, PA 19004
FAX 610-667-7932
TEL 610-667-5071
Established: 1989
Products: batik paintings
Techniques: painting, dyeing,
wax resist (batik)
Size Range: 15" x 12" to 556" x 56"
Price Range: $300 to $2,000/piece

MARY KAY COLLING

MARY KAY COLLING GALLERY
VILLAGE GATE SQ
ROCHESTER, NY 14607
TEL 716-442-8946
E-MAIL: MCOLLING@EZNET.NET
Established: 1988
Products: paper
Techniques: painting, screen printing,
casting, hand sculpting
Size Range: any size
Price Range: $100 to $300/sq. ft.

★ BRIGITTE SEKIRKA COOPER

BSC DESIGN
PO BOX 871840
WASILLA, AK 99687-1840
TEL 907-373-6067
Established: 1979
Products: art quilts
Techniques: painting, appliqué, quilting
Size Range: 24" x 24" to 10' x 10'
Price Range: $70 to $200/sq. ft.

See photograph on page 177.

STEPHANIE RANDALL COOPER

2911 YORK RD
EVERETT, WA 98204-5407
FAX 205-745-2115
TEL 206-745-2115
Established: 1987
Products: art quilts
Techniques: painting, dyeing,
rip and tear assembly
Size Range: 12" x 12" to 108" x 144"
Price Range: $200 to $8,000/piece

BARBARA CORNETT

FIBERSTRUCTIONS
1101 JEFFERSON ST
LYNCHBURG, VA 24504-1709
TEL 804-528-3136
Established: 1976
Products: mixed media installations
Techniques: painting, felting, fiber sculpture
Size Range: 2' x 3' to 12' x 20'
Price Range: $500 to $50,000/piece

COVERINGS BY RIFFI

RIFFI KAUFMAN
RD #2 MOUNTAINVIEW RD
PATTERSON, NY 12563
TEL 914-878-6642
Established: 1980
Products: art quilts
Techniques: quilting
Size Range: 24" x 24" to 64" x 54"
Price Range: $300 to $1,200/piece

★ ROBIN COWLEY

2451 POTOMAC ST
OAKLAND, CA 94602-3032
FAX 510-482-1007
TEL 510-530-1134
Established: 1990
Products: art quilts
Techniques: dyeing, appliqué, quilting
Size Range: 16" x 16" to 72" x 84"
Price Range: $200 to $3,000/piece

**See page 137 for photographs
and additional information.**

Martha Chatelain, *Tierra Bonita*, ©1995, handmade paper, sculpture with copper, 30" x 66" x 5"

JOYCE CRAIN
2901 BENTON BLVD
MINNEAPOLIS, MN 55416-4328
TEL 612-920-1704
Established: 1970
Products: mixed media installations
Techniques: interlacing
Size Range: 12" × 12" to 9' × 15'
Price Range: $500 to $40,000/piece

BARBARA LYDECKER CRANE
18 HILL ST
LEXINGTON, MA 02173-4318
TEL 617-862-1579
Established: 1985
Products: art quilts
Techniques: dyeing, painting, quilting
Size Range: 2' × 2' to 6' × 6'
Price Range: $200 to $8,000/piece

CREATIVE VISIONS
NANCY M. EHA
3898 DELLVIEW AVE
SAINT PAUL, MN 55112
FAX 612-633-2107
TEL 612-633-3668
Established: 1990
Products: contemporary beadwork
Techniques: embroidery, appliqué, beading
Size Range: 2" × 2" to 3' × 2'
Price Range: $50 to $5,000/piece

GLORIA E. CROUSE
FIBER ART
4325 JOHN LUHR RD NE
OLYMPIA, WA 98516-2320
TEL 206-491-1980
Established: 1970
Products: fabric installations
Techniques: beading, embroidery, rug hooking
Size Range: 5" × 5" to 20' × 20'
Price Range: $50 to $150/sq. ft.

MELODY CRUST
26530 LK FENWICK RD S
KENT, WA 98032
TEL 206-859-0446
Established: 1991
Products: art quilts
Techniques: quilting, embroidery, beading
Size Range: 10" × 10" to 60" × 80"
Price Range: $125 to $250/sq. ft.

★ BETH CUNNINGHAM
32 SWEETCAKE MOUNTAIN RD
NEW FAIRFIELD, CT 06812-4107
TEL 203-746-5160
Established: 1976
Products: mixed media installations
Techniques: airbush, painting, layering
Size Range: 1' × 1' to 6' × 12'
Price Range: $100 to $150/sq. ft.

See page 91 for photographs
and additional information.

MARGARET CUSACK
124 HOYT ST
BROOKLYN, NY 11217-2215
FAX 718-237-2430
TEL 718-237-0145
Established: 1972
Products: fiber installations, wall hangings
Techniques: appliqué, airbrush, dyeing
Size Range: 18" × 24" to 72" × 144"
Price Range: $180 to $500/sq. ft.

JUDY B. DALES
JUDY DALES, QUILTMAKER
129 HOLLY LN
BOONTON, NJ 07005-1624
TEL 201-334-1563
Established: 1980
Products: art quilts
Techniques: quilting, curved piecing
Size Range: 30" × 40" to 90" × 90"
Price Range: $500 to $10,000/piece

SUZANNE DALTON
DALTON & FOLES DESIGN
12387 SCOTT RD
ELLSWORTH, MI 49729
FAX 616-599-2496
TEL 616-599-2496
E-MAIL: SUZDALTON@AOL.COM
Established: 1977
Products: fiber installations
Techniques: weaving
Size Range: 2' × 6' to 30' × 40'
Price Range: $1,200 to $40,000/piece

KAY HENNING DANLEY
MULTNOMAH STUDIO
8675 SW ALYSSA LN
PORTLAND, OR 97225
TEL 503-297-7404
Established: 1978
Products: paintings on silk
Techniques: dyeing, painting, stamping
Size Range: 24" × 15" to 72" × 36"
Price Range: $150 to $2,500/piece

NATALIE DARMOHRAJ
NATALKA DESIGNS
PO BOX 40309
PROVIDENCE, RI 02940-0309
FAX 401-351-2685
TEL 401-351-8841
Products: woven wall pieces
Techniques: dyeing, weaving
Size Range: 40" × 40" to 60" × 90"
Price Range: $500 to $5,000/piece

HEIDI DARR-HOPE
3718 TOMAKA RD
COLUMBIA, SC 29205-1558
FAX 803-771-4140
TEL 803-782-5341
Established: 1982
Products: one-of-a-kind accent pillows
Techniques: embroidery, painting, collage
Size Range: 10" × 14" to 6' × 12'
Price Range: $300 to $8,000/piece

KAREN DAVIDSON
PO BOX 637
HANA, HI 96713-0637
TEL 808-248-7094
Established: 1980
Products: paper
Techniques: casting, dyeing, painting
Size Range: 24" × 24" to 8' × 15'
Price Range: $300 to $10,000/piece

D. JOYCE DAVIES
185 ROBINSON ST PH2
OAKVILLE, ON L6J 7N9
CANADA
FAX 905-845-6823
TEL 905-845-6823
Established: 1980
Products: art quilts
Techniques: appliqué, quilting, embellishments
Size Range: 36" × 36" to 70" × 70"
Price Range: $800 to $3,500/piece

★ ALONZO DAVIS
PO BOX 12248
MEMPHIS, TN 38182-0248
FAX 901-276-0660
TEL 901-276-9070
Established: 1973
Products: paper
Techniques: painting, weaving
Size Range: 30" × 22" to 8' × 10'
Price Range: $1,500 to $15,000/piece

See page 48 for photographs
and additional information.

ARDYTH DAVIS
11436 HOLLOW TIMBER CT
RESTON, VA 22094-1980
TEL 703-904-8027
Established: 1975
Products: fabric constructions
Techniques: dyeing, painting, pleating
Size Range: 12" × 12" to 80" × 80"
Price Range: $150 to $10,000/piece

★ JAMIE DAVIS
JAMIE DAVIS SCULPTURE
1239 MILE CREEK RD
PICKENS, SC 29671
FAX 864-868-4250
TEL 864-868-3302
Established: 1973
Products: mixed media installations, fiber, metal collage
Techniques: painting, embossing, cutting metal
Size Range: 22" × 24" to 48" × 6' and up
Price Range: $175/sq. ft.

See page 92 for photographs
and additional information.

NANCY STANFORD DAVIS
26 AUSTIN RD
WILMINGTON, DE 19810-2203
TEL 302-478-7529
Established: 1992
Products: art quilts
Techniques: dyeing, quilting, weaving
Size Range: 2' × 2' to 8' × 8'
Price Range: $75 to $125/sq. ft.

NANETTE DAVIS-SHAKLHO
1289 E GRAND AVE #318
ESCONDIDO, CA 92027-3063
TEL 619-745-6091
Established: 1986
Products: mixed media installations
Techniques: dyeing, painting, laminating, pleating
Size Range: 2' × 2' to 6' × 12'
Price Range: $1,100 to $21,600/piece
Price Range: $185 to $300/sq. ft.

BERTHA DAY
BOX 304
SAINT ANDREWS, NB E0G 2X0
CANADA
FAX 506-529-3375
TEL 506-529-8837
Established: 1994
Products: fabric constructions
Techniques: painting, embroidery, appliqué
Size Range: 15" × 15" to 72" × 72"
Price Range: $200 to $7,000/piece

JEAN DEEMER
1537 BRIARWOOD CIR
CUYAHOGA FALLS, OH 44221-3623
TEL 216-929-1995
Established: 1975
Products: paper constructions
Techniques: painting, collage
Size Range: 18" × 24" to 5' × 6'
Price Range: $375 to $3,500/piece

ANDREA DEIMEL
82 E HILLCREST AVE
CHALFONT, PA 18914
TEL 215-997-7964
Established: 1977
Products: mixed media installations
Techniques: embroidery, sculptural wood frames
Size Range: 12" × 10" to 24" × 30"
Price Range: $400 to $1,000/piece

E. DELZOPPO
GREY SEAL WEAVING STUDIO
#3886 POINT MICHAUD
CAPE BRETON ISLAND, NS B0E 1W0
CANADA
TEL 902-587-2494
Established: 1984
Products: damask compositions
Techniques: weaving, drawloom damask
Size Range: 6" × 6" to 45" × 72"
Price Range: $150 to $3,000/piece

LINDA DENIER
DENIER TAPESTRY STUDIO
745 EDENWOOD DR
ROSELLE, IL 60172-2824
TEL 708-893-5854
Established: 1990
Products: tapestries
Techniques: weaving
Size Range: 3" × 5" to 5' × 6'
Price Range: $150 to $175/sq. ft.

LAURA DILL-KOCHER

70 LAFAYETTE PKWY
ROCHESTER, NY 14625
TEL 716-381-0669
Established: 1979
Products: tapestries
Techniques: weaving, dyeing, felting
Size Range: 12" × 12" to 30' × 8'
Price Range: $55 to $150/sq. ft.

SALLY DILLON

7123 DALEWOOD LN
DALLAS, TX 75214-1812
TEL 214-821-1018
Established: 1970
Products: art quilts
Techniques: dyeing, painting, quilting
Size Range: 12" × 12" to 72" × 96"
Price Range: $100 to $10,000/piece
Price Range: $75 to $200/sq. ft.

JUDITH DINGLE

JUDITH DINGLE DESIGN
140 EVELYN AVE
TORONTO, ON M6P 2Z7
CANADA
TEL 416-766-9411
Established: 1978
Products: fabric constructions, textile, mixed media constructions
Techniques: laminating, quilting, pieced and constructed
Size Range: 48" × 48" to 20' × 40'
Price Range: $125 to $250/sq. ft.

JUDY DIOSZEGI

JUDY DIOSZEGI, DESIGNER
2628 ROSLYN CIR
HIGHLAND PARK, IL 60035-1910
TEL 708-433-2585
Established: 1976
Products: tapestries
Techniques: appliqué, embroidery, quilting
Size Range: 18" × 36" to 12' × 24'
Price Range: $200 to $30,000/piece

SEENA DONNESON

SEENA DONNESON STUDIO
4349 10TH ST
LONG ISLAND CITY, NY 11101-6926
TEL 718-706-1342
Established: 1968
Products: tapestries, mixed media installations, paper
Techniques: painting, molding
Size Range: 20" × 20" to 60" × 60"
Price Range: $1,000 to $15,000/piece

MORRIS DAVID DORENFELD

PO BOX 126 ISLAND AVE
SPRUCE HEAD, ME 14859
TEL 207-594-5142
Established: 1979
Products: tapestries
Techniques: weaving
Size Range: 60" × 36" to 72" × 46"
Price Range: $1,200 to $3,000/piece

ARNELLE A. DOW

THE BATIK LADY
448 MILTON ST
CINCINNATI, OH 45210-1428
TEL 606-261-4523
Established: 1973
Products: fiber installations
Techniques: appliqué, painting, batik, oriental rug restoration
Size Range: 2" × 2" to 10' × 65'
Price Range: $65 to $15,000/piece

PAT DOZIER

PO BOX 76
MEDANALES, NM 87548-0076
TEL 505-685-4776
Established: 1992
Products: tapestries
Techniques: weaving
Size Range: 24" × 24" to 80" × 32"
Price Range: $95 to $125/sq. ft.

★ SUSAN DUNSHEE

986 ACEQUIA MADRE ST
SANTA FE, NM 87501-2819
TEL 505-982-0988
Products: fiber constructions
Techniques: dyeing, laminating, machine stitching
Size Range: 10" × 18" to 12' × 12'
Price Range: $95 to $210/sq. ft.

See page 159 for photographs and additional information.

DONNA DURBIN

4034 WOODCRAFT ST
HOUSTON, TX 77025-5709
TEL 713-664-4764
Established: 1987
Products: mixed media tapestries
Techniques: weaving, painting, collage
Size Range: 8" × 8" to 8' × 20'
Price Range: $150 to $200/sq. ft.

MARGIT ECHOLS

ROWHOUSE PRESS
PO BOX 20531
NEW YORK, NY 10025-1514
FAX 212-662-7828
TEL 212-662-9604
Established: 1972
Products: art and traditional quilts
Techniques: appliqué, quilting, piecing
Size Range: 24" × 24" to 12' × 12'
Price Range: $1,000 to $10,000/piece

ELLEN ANNE EDDY

THREAD MAGIC
6257 N LAKEWOOD AVE #2
CHICAGO, IL 60660
TEL 312-262-2751
Established: 1988
Products: art quilts
Techniques: dyeing, embroidery, appliqué
Size Range: 18" × 18" to 52" × 71"
Price Range: $150 to $4,000/piece

LORE EDZARD

815 RUNNING DEER
NASHVILLE, TN 37221-2234
TEL 615-662-2583
Established: 1967
Products: tapestries
Techniques: dyeing, embroidery, weaving, knotting
Size Range: 2' × 3' to 8' × 10'
Price Range: $100 to $150/sq. ft.

EFREM WEITZMAN ART WORKS

EFREM WEITZMAN
PO BOX 1092
SOUTH FALLSBURG, NY 12779-1092
FAX 914-434-2408
TEL 914-434-2408
Established: 1960
Products: tapestries
Techniques: appliqué, weaving, quilting, arraiolos, hand-tufting
Size Range: 4' × 7' to 90' × 20'
Price Range: $175 to $400/sq. ft.

SU EGEN

SU EGEN, HANDWEAVER/DESIGNER
2233 E HAWTHORNE ST
TUCSON, AZ 85719-4941
FAX 520-325-0009
TEL 520-325-0009
Established: 1970
Products: tapestries
Techniques: weaving
Size Range: unlimited
Price Range: $125 to $300/sq. ft.

Brigitte Sekirka Cooper, *Passage*, art quilt, cotton, metallics, private collection, Honolulu, HI, 48"W × 58"H

SYLVIA H. EINSTEIN
11 OAK AVE
BELMONT, MA 02178-2751
TEL   617-484-9541
Established: 1980
Products: art quilts
Techniques: quilting
Size Range: 8" x 8" to 60" x 90"
Price Range: $150 to $6,000/piece

NANCY N. ERICKSON
DANCING RABBIT STUDIOS
3250 PATTEE CANYON RD
MISSOULA, MT 59803-1703
TEL   406-549-4671
Established: 1963
Products: art quilts, oil paintstick works
Techniques: appliqué, painting, quilting
Size Range: 16" x 24" to 9' x 10'
Price Range: $400 to $8,200/piece

★ CARL ERIKSON
35 MORNINGSIDE COMMONS
BRATTLEBORO, VT 05301
TEL   802-254-9176
Established: 1992
Products: fabric constructions, stretched-fabric shapes
Techniques: appliqué, stitching, piecing
Size Range: 18" x 18" to 60" x 60"
Price Range: $400 to $2,000/piece

See page 160 for photographs and additional information.

JOHANNA ERICKSON
GLAD RAGS
48 CHESTER ST
WATERTOWN, MA 02172
TEL   617-926-1737
Established: 1970
Products: tapestries, fiber installations
Techniques: weaving
Size Range: 3' x 2' to 10' x 5'
Price Range: $50 to $500/piece

KAREN EUBEL
150 1ST AVE #404
NEW YORK, NY 10009-5704
TEL   212-995-9624
Established: 1970
Products: paper
Techniques: painting, weaving, stenciling
Size Range: 1' x 1' to 4' x 5'
Price Range: $400 to $2,200/piece

EURO ARTS
BEATA PIES
543 PACIFIC ST
BROOKLYN, NY 11217-1902
FAX   212-229-2854
TEL   212-229-2854
Established: 1983
Products: mixed media installations
Techniques: weaving, painting, stamping
Size Range: 18" x 18" to 72" x 96"
Price Range: $1,000 to $10,000/sq. ft.

★ PHYLLIS 'CERATTO' EVANS
6969 ISLAND CENTER RD NE
BAINBRIDGE ISLAND,
WA 98110-1681
TEL   206-842-5042
Established: 1987
Products: fiber collage
Techniques: laminating
Size Range: unlimited
Price Range: $400 to $10,000/piece

See page 161 for photographs and additional information.

JUDITH POXSON FAWKES
LAURA RUSSO GALLERY
805 NW 21ST AVE
PORTLAND, OR 97209-1408
TEL   503-226-2754
Established: 1970
Products: tapestries
Techniques: weaving
Size Range: 3' x 3' to 8' x 20'
Price Range: $150 minimum/sq. ft.

MARTHA FERRIS
9433 FISHER FERRY RD
VICKSBURG, MS 39180
FAX   601-634-1007
TEL   601-636-4066
Established: 1990
Products: mixed media installations
Techniques: painting, dyeing, stamping
Size Range: 16" x 20" to 6' x 12'
Price Range: $400 to $7,000/piece

FIBER ART STUDIO
KAIJA RAUTIAINEN
1610 JOHNSTON ST
GRANVILLE ISLAND
VANCOUVER, BC V6H 3LS2
CANADA
FAX   604-528-9978
TEL   604-688-3047
Established: 1974
Products: tapestries
Techniques: weaving
Size Range: 16" x 16" to 7' x 5'
Price Range: $300 to $350/sq. ft.

★ DORIS FINCH
DORIS FINCH FABRIC ART
2144 CRESCENT DR
ALTADENA, CA 91001-2112
TEL   818-797-6172
Established: 1987
Products: fabric constructions
Techniques: dyeing, appliqué, stuffing
Size Range: 30" x 20" to 90" x 48"
Price Range: $1,000 to $7,000/piece

See photograph on page 179.

FIRST WEAVERS OF THE AMERICAS
MARTINA MASAQUIZA
825 LOCUST ST
LAWRENCE, KS 66044
FAX   913-838-4486
TEL   800-571-0156
Established: 1986
Products: tapestries
Techniques: weaving
Size Range: 20" x 20" to 46" x 27"
Price Range: $75 to $500/piece
Price Range: $27 to $50/sq. ft.

PAMELA FLANDERS
FLANDERS FINE ART
6820 ROYALWOOD WAY
SAN JOSE, CA 95120-2228
TEL   408-997-8438
Established: 1983
Products: paper
Techniques: laminating, painting, collage
Size Range: 8" x 8" to 40" x 60"
Price Range: $200 to $500/piece

MARTI FLEISCHER
128 MONTICELLO RD
OAK RIDGE, TN 37830-8258
TEL   423-483-0772
Established: 1990
Products: tapestries
Techniques: weaving
Size Range: 4" x 3" to 4' x 7'
Price Range: $200 to $2,000/piece
Price Range: $60 to $100/sq. ft.

★ MARI MARKS FLEMING
1431 GLENDALE AVE
BERKELEY, CA 94708-2027
FAX 510-548-3121
TEL 510-548-3121
Established: 1989
Products: mixed media installations
Techniques: laminating, painting, fiber constructions
Size Range: 18" x 12" to 10' x 15'
Price Range: $500 to $15,000/piece

See page 49 for photographs and additional information.

BARBARA FLETCHER
88 BEALS ST
BROOKLINE, MA 02146-3011
TEL   617-277-3019
Established: 1987
Products: paper
Techniques: airbush, casting, dyeing
Size Range: 3" x 4" to 30" x 40"
Price Range: $25 to $1,000/piece

THE FOOTHILLS COMPANY
PAMELA JOHNSON-BRICKELL
PO BOX 962
APEX, NC 27502
FAX   919-363-0334
TEL   919-363-0334
Established: 1985
Products: mixed media installations
Techniques: weaving, painting, elements from nature
Size Range: 18" x 25" to 45" x 50"
Price Range: $450 to $4,000/piece

ROBERT FORMAN
412 GRAND ST
HOBOKEN, NJ 07030-2703
TEL   201-659-7069
Established: 1975
Products: yarn painting
Techniques: yarn glued to board
Size Range: 24" x 30" to 60" x 96"
Price Range: $1,500 and up/piece

★ MARILYN FORTH
416 DAVID DR
N SYRACUSE, NY 13212-1929
FAX 315-458-0913
TEL 315-458-3786
Established: 1974
Products: framed batiks
Techniques: painting, wax drawn line
Size Range: 1' x 1' to 4' x 6'
Price Range: $180 to $2,500/piece

See page 162 for photographs and additional information.

FOWLER AND THELEN STUDIO
201 FAIRBROOK ST
NORTHVILLE, MI 48167-1503
TEL   313-348-6654
Established: 1972
Products: mixed media installations
Techniques: weaving
Size Range: 2' x 3' to 50' x 50'
Price Range: $500 to $5,000/piece

MARY EDNA FRASER
PO BOX 12250
CHARLESTON, SC 29422
TEL   803-762-2594
Established: 1974
Products: fiber installations
Techniques: dyeing, batik on silk
Size Range: 5" x 3" to 3' x 74 yds.
Price Range: $150 to $125/sq. ft.

CHRISTINE FRENCH
101 SEMINARY STREET
BEREZ, OH 44017
TEL   216-826-0169
Established: 1986
Products: mixed media installations
Techniques: painting, casting, paper making
Size Range: 8" x 10" to 36" x 40"
Price Range: $50 to $560/piece
Price Range: $8 to $10/sq. ft.

LIZ FREY
LIZ FREY HANDWOVENS
W 2390 SATSOP-CLOQUALLUM RD
ELMA, WA 98541
TEL   360-482-1291
Established: 1986
Products: fiber installations, fiber constructions
Techniques: dyeing, painting, weaving, warp painting
Size Range: 1' x 1' to no limit
Price Range: $40 to $400/sq. ft.

SUZAN FRIEDLAND

718 19TH AVE
SAN FRANCISCO, CA 94121
TEL 415-750-9463
Established: 1990
Products: fiber installations
Techniques: painting, dyeing, quilting
Size Range: variable
Price Range: $500 and up/piece
Price Range: $180/sq. ft.

ALEXANDRA FRIEDMAN

56 ARBOR ST
HARTFORD, CT 06106-1203
TEL 860-236-3311
Established: 1972
Products: tapestries
Techniques: weaving, embroidery
Size Range: open and flexible
Price Range: $150 to $250/sq. ft.

JAN FRIEDMAN

1409 E DAVENPORT ST
IOWA CITY, IA 52245-3021
TEL 319-338-1934
Established: 1979
Products: tapestries
Techniques: weaving, dyeing, collage
Size Range: 24" x 20" to 15' x 10'
Price Range: $90 to $100/sq. ft.

JUDITH GEIGER

JUDITH GEIGER GALLERY
1921 DE LA VINA ST #B
SANTA BARBARA, CA 93101-2816
FAX 805-687-8868
TEL 805-687-8868
Established: 1982
Products: hand-painted silk
Techniques: dyeing, painting, gutta resist
Size Range: 4" x 6" to 33" x 44"
Price Range: $20 to $450/piece

CAROL H. GERSEN

STUDIO ART QUILTS
18839 MANOR CHURCH RD
BOONSBORO, MD 21713-2511
TEL 301-432-6484
Established: 1981
Products: art quilts
Techniques: dyeing, quilting
Size Range: 3' x 3' to 5' x 8'
Price Range: $900 to $6,000/piece

JAMES R. GILBERT

WOVEN STRUCTURES
PO BOX 474
BLOOMFIELD HILLS, MI 48303-0474
TEL 810-772-7087
Established: 1970
Products: fiber installations
Techniques: weaving, screen printing, color dyeing
Size Range: 3' x 3' to 6' x 90'
Price Range: $350 to $7,000/piece

DEANNA GLAD

PO BOX 1962
SAN PEDRO, CA 90733
TEL 310-831-6274
Established: 1970
Products: fabric constructions, bas-relief wall hangings
Techniques: embroidery, appliqué, quilting, stamping
Size Range: 24" x 30" to 7' x 5.5'
Price Range: $1,100 to $8,000/piece

ROBERTA GLIDDEN

TEXTILE ARTS STUDIO
1009 23RD ST
OGDEN, UT 84401
TEL 801-394-5688
Established: 1980
Products: painting on silk
Techniques: painting, dyeing
Size Range: 20" x 20" to 36" x 48"
Price Range: $150 to $1,000/piece

SANDRA GOLBERT

PO BOX 193
PIERMONT, NY 10968
FAX 914-356-6093
TEL 914-365-6093
Established: 1980
Products: fiber installations
Techniques: dyeing, wrapping, paper making
Size Range: 10" x 10" to 6' x 20'
Price Range: $200 to $50,000/piece

JON GOLDMAN

GOLDMAN ARTS
107 SOUTH ST #403
BOSTON, MA 02111-2811
FAX 617-423-6601
TEL 617-423-6606
E-Mail: zoozles@aol.com
Established: 1980
Products: inflatable sculptures
Techniques: airbrush, appliqué, quilting
Size Range: 1' x 1' to 100' x 100'
Price Range: $5 to $40,000/piece

LAYNE GOLDSMITH

PO BOX 563
SNOHOMISH, WA 98291-0563
FAX 206-334-5569
TEL 206-334-5569
Established: 1972
Products: felted wall constructions
Techniques: dyeing, felting, mixed textile media
Size Range: 4' x 5' to 12' x 60'
Price Range: $500 to $45,000/piece
Price Range: $100 to $300/sq. ft.

INA GOLUB

366 ROLLING ROCK RD
MOUNTAINSIDE, NJ 07092-2120
FAX 908-232-7981
TEL 908-232-5376
Established: 1963
Products: tapestries
Techniques: appliqué, beading, weaving
Size Range: 2' x 2' to 10' x 12'
Price Range: $2,000 to $25,000/piece

Doris Finch, *Wings of the Phoenix*, 1995, machine appliqué, new and old fabric, artist-dyed ground, 34" x 84"

RUTH GOWELL

7010 ARONOW DR
FALLS CHURCH, VA 22042-1805
TEL 703-532-8645
Established: 1978
Products: wall hangings
Techniques: dyeing, weaving
Size Range: 16" x 16" to 5' x 10'
Price Range: $250 to $4,000/piece

CHARLES GRAY

14425 N 42ND PL
PHOENIX, AZ 85032
FAX 602-966-2319
TEL 602-996-2319
Established: 1973
Products: Kinetic Canvas™
Techniques: weaving
Size Range: 1' x 1' to 40' x 60'
Price Range: $147 to $278/sq. ft.

LAURA ELIZABETH GREEN

5523 HIGHLAND ST S
ST PETERSBURG, FL 33705-5135
TEL 813-867-1204
Established: 1973
Products: art quilts
Techniques: appliqué, dyeing, quilting
Size Range: 4" x 4" to 8' x 8'
Price Range: $250 to $2,500/piece

★ BARBARA GRENELL

1132 HALLS CHAPPEL RD
BURNSVILLE, NC 28714-9760
TEL 704-675-4073
Established: 1972
Products: fiber installations
Techniques: dyeing, weaving
Size Range: all sizes
Price Range: $100 to $175/sq. ft.

See page 163 for photographs
and additional information.

DON GRIFFIN

3306 KENJAC RD
BALTIMORE, MD 21244-1322
TEL 410-655-8755
Established: 1973
Products: mixed media installations
Techniques: painting, collage
Size Range: 36" x 30" to 6' x 10'
Price Range: $500 to $3,500/piece

JOAN GRIFFIN

FIBER DESIGN STUDIO
1800 YORKTOWN DR
CHARLOTTESVILLE, VA 22901-3037
FAX 804-979-4402
TEL 804-979-4402
Established: 1980
Products: tapestries
Techniques: weaving
Size Range: 12" x 12" to 5' x 10'
Price Range: $180 to $9,500/piece

MARILYN GRISHAM

315 POST RD
EL DORADO, KS 67042-4059
Established: 1970
Products: tapestries
Techniques: weaving, embroidery,
weft-face brocade
Size Range: 3' x 5' to 12' x 24'
Price Range: $2,500 to $55,000/piece

ISAELLE GUENAT

641 HOWARD AVE #310
MONTEBELLO, CA 90640
TEL 213-724-9544
Products: tapestries
Techniques: weaving
Size Range: 15" x 15" to 50" x 50"
Price Range: $300 to $3,00/piece

CLAIRE FAY HABERFELD

QUILTVISION
10751 W 107TH CIR
WESTMINSTER, CO 80021
TEL 303-469-1403
Established: 1981
Products: art quilts
Techniques: appliqué, beading, quilting
Size Range: 1' x 1' to 10' x 10'
Price Range: $85 to $100/sq. ft.

HARRIET HANSON

THE STUDIOSPACE
1732 W HUBBARD ST
CHICAGO, IL 60622-6271
TEL 312-243-4144
Established: 1970
Products: handmade paper
Techniques: dimensional sculpture
Size Range: 18" x 24" to 36" to 48"
Price Range: $600 to $3,000/piece

TIM HARDING

HARDING DESIGN STUDIO
402 N MAIN ST
STILLWATER, MN 55082-5051
TEL 612-351-0383
Established: 1974
Products: fiber installations
Techniques: dyeing, quilting, slashing
and fraying
Size Range: 50" x 70" to 10' x 18'
Price Range: $75 to $175/sq. ft.

★ CAROLE HARRIS

667 W BETHUNE
DETROIT, MI 48202
FAX 313-964-0170
TEL 313-871-4155
Established: 1976
Products: art quilts
Techniques: quilting, mixed media
Size Range: 37" x 16" to 75" x 60"
Price Range: $900 to $6,000/piece

See page 164 for photographs
and additional information.

PETER HARRIS

TAPESTRY AND DESIGN
RR 2
AYTON, ON N0G 1C0
CANADA
TEL 519-665-2245
Established: 1973
Products: tapestries
Techniques: weaving
Size Range: 36" x 48" to 60" x 96"
Price Range: $2,500 to $10,000/piece

RENEE HARRIS

RENEE HARRIS STUDIO
642 CLEMMER AVE
CINCINNATI, OH 45219-1038
TEL 513-241-5909
Established: 1985
Products: fiber installations
Techniques: embroidery, felting
Size Range: 16" x 20" to 3' x 4'
Price Range: $300 to $1,200/piece

ANN L. HARTLEY

TREE HOUSE STUDIO
13515 SEA ISLAND DR
HOUSTON, TX 77069-2436
TEL 713-444-1118
Established: 1975
Products: mixed media collage
Techniques: painting, stamping/printing,
wrapping
Price Range: $300 to $1,500/piece

SHARON HEIDINGSFELDER

8010 DAN THOMAS RD
LITTLE ROCK, AR 72206-4148
FAX 501-671-2251
TEL 501-490-0405
Established: 1973
Products: art quilts
Techniques: dyeing, quilting,
screen printing
Size Range: 72" x 72" to 78" x 84"
Price Range: $2,000 to $6,500/piece

MARTHA HEINE

7 HAGGIS CT
DURHAM, NC 27705-2166
TEL 919-479-3270
Established: 1980
Products: tapestries
Techniques: weaving
Size Range: 48" x 36" to 60" x 72"
Price Range: $2,200 to $7,600/piece
Price Range: $175 to $250/sq. ft.

SHEILA A. HELD

2762 MAYFAIR CT
WAUWATOSA, WI 53222-4105
TEL 414-475-6479
Established: 1975
Products: tapestries
Techniques: weaving
Size Range: 36" x 36" to 80" x 50"
Price Range: $1,000 to $6,000/piece
Price Range: $200 to $300/sq. ft.

HELIO GRAPHICS

DAWN WILKINS
PO BOX 6213
KEY WEST, FL 33041-6213
TEL 305-294-7901
Established: 1980
Products: mixed media installations,
painted canvas and nature prints
Techniques: painting, screen printing,
pressed images
Size Range: 20" x 20" to 50" x 60"
Price Range: $100 to $2,000/piece

BARBARA HELLER

FIBRE ARTS STUDIO
4796 W SEVENTH AVE
VANCOUVER, BC V6T 1C6
CANADA
TEL 604-224-3047
Established: 1975
Products: tapestries
Techniques: weaving
Size Range: 12" x 12" to 4' x 6'
Price Range: $350 to $10,000/piece
Price Range: $350 to $450/sq. ft.

SUSAN HART HENEGAR

5449 BELLEVUE AVE
LA JOLLA, CA 92037-7625
FAX 619-459-5693
TEL 619-459-5681
Established: 1978
Products: tapestries
Techniques: weaving, Aubusson tapestry
Size Range: 8" x 8" to 8' x 24'
Price Range: $150 to $400/sq. ft.

★ MARILYN HENRION

505 LAGUARDIA PL #23D
NEW YORK, NY 10012-2005
TEL 212-982-8949
Established: 1978
Products: art quilts
Techniques: hand quilting
Size Range: 24" x 24" to 80" x 80"
Price Range: $500 to $7,500/piece

See page 138 for photographs
and additional information.

HELENA HERNMARCK

HELENA HERNMARCK TAPESTRIES, INC.
879 N SALEM RD
RIDGEFIELD, CT 06877-1714
FAX 203-431-9570
TEL 203-438-9220
Established: 1964
Products: tapestries
Techniques: weaving
Size Range: 10 sq. ft. to 400 sq. ft.
Price Range: $600 to $1,200/sq. ft.

JANE HERRICK

4219 MEADOW LN
EAU CLAIRE, WI 54701-7487
TEL 715-833-9745
Established: 1982
Products: fabric constructions
Techniques: laminating, painting, drawing,
heat transfer
Size Range: 18" x 24" to 6' x 8'
Price Range: $600 to $4,000/piece

SUSAN HERSEY

105 DANVERS ST
SAN FRANCISCO, CA 94114
FAX 415-436-9871
TEL 415-621-4125
Established: 1960
Products: paper
Techniques: painting, dyeing, spraying
Size Range: 17" × 13" to 6' × 10'
Price Range: $200 to $5,000/piece

PAMELA HILL

PO BOX 800 8500 LAFAYETTE
MOKELUMNE HILL, CA 95245-0800
FAX 209-286-1001
TEL 209-286-1217
Established: 1975
Products: art quilts
Techniques: quilting, piecing
Size Range: 40" × 40" to 10' × 24'
Price Range: $600 to $5,000/piece

BILL HIO

34 CYPRESS DR
SCOTIA, NY 12302-4325
TEL 518-399-7404
Established: 1990
Products: tapestries
Techniques: needle stitch
Size Range: 32" × 32" to 64" × 128"
Price Range: $400 to $4,000/piece

MIDGE HOFFMAN

PO BOX 1239/91239 N HARRISON ST
COBURG, OR 97408
TEL 541-485-0047
Established: 1981
Products: art quilts
Techniques: painting, appliqué, fusing
Size Range: 2'6" to 2' to 11' × 28'
Price Range: $100 to $150/sq. ft.

DOROTHY HOLDEN

301 KENT RD
CHARLOTTESVILLE, VA 22903-2409
TEL 804-971-5803
Established: 1977
Products: art quilts
Techniques: quilting
Size Range: 2' × 2' to 6' × 7'
Price Range: $850 to $6,500/piece

ELIZABETH HOLSTER

PAPER BY HOLSTER
727 E A ST
IRON MOUNTAIN, MI 49801-3505
TEL 906-779-2592
Established: 1974
Products: paper
Techniques: casting, painting,
drawing/collagraph
Size Range: 24" × 24" to 60" × 60"
Price Range: $500 to $5,000/piece

MELISSA HOLZINGER

30516 SR 530 NE
ARLINGTON, WA 98223
TEL 360-435-5060
Established: 1983
Products: art quilts
Techniques: painting, dyeing, airbrushing
Size Range: 24" × 24" to 60" × 60"
Price Range: $100 to $150/sq. ft.

KATHERINE HOLZKNECHT

22828 57TH AVE SE
WOODINVILLE, WA 98072-8660
TEL 206-481-7788
Established: 1976
Products: mixed media installations
Techniques: dyeing, laminating, lashing
Size Range: 2' × 2' to 20' × 60'
Price Range: $150 to $300/sq. ft.

DORA HSIUNG

HSIUNG DESIGN
95 WARREN ST
NEWTON, MA 02159-2334
TEL 617-969-4630
Established: 1978
Products: wall hangings
Techniques: wrapping, original off-loom
weaving
Size Range: 12" × 12" to 16' × 21'
Price Range: $200 to $30,000/piece

JOHN D. HUBBARD

1420 W LITTLE SHAG RD
GWINN, MI 49841
TEL 906-227-2194
Established: 1968
Products: paper
Techniques: casting, airbrush, paper
assemblage
Size Range: 18" × 20" to 48" × 60"
Price Range: $500 to $4,500/piece

DOROTHY HUGHES

DOROTHY HUGHES STUDIO
850 N MILWAUKEE AVE
CHICAGO, IL 60622-4143
FAX 312-563-1456
TEL 312-421-7045
Established: 1970
Products: fiber sculpture
Techniques: dyeing, weaving
Size Range: 12" × 12" to 22' × 33'
Price Range: $300 to $90,000/piece
Price Range: $150 to $500/sq. ft.

★ WENDY C. HUHN

81763 LOST CREEK RD
DEXTER, OR 97431-9735
FAX 541-937-1740
TEL 541-937-3147
Established: 1982
Products: art quilts
Techniques: screen printing, quilting,
beading, transfers
Size Range: 38" × 38" to 72" × 72"
Price Range: $1,200 to $4,000/piece
Price Range: $150/sq. ft.

See page 139 for photographs
and additional information.

CONSTANCE HUNT

1270 SANCHEZ ST
SAN FRANCISCO, CA 94114-3833
TEL 415-282-5170
Established: 1980
Products: tapestries
Techniques: weaving
Size Range: 6" × 9" to 72" × 80"
Price Range: $400 to $20,000/piece

JANET M. HUTCHINSON

ISLAND SILK
LAUREL RUN FARM
HC-82 BOX 253A
MARLINTON, WV 24954
FAX 304-799-7158
TEL 304-799-7158
Established: 1986
Products: fiber installations
Techniques: painting, dyeing
Size Range: 30" × 20" to 8' × 4'
Price Range: $250 to $3,000/piece

★ MARIE-LAURE ILIE

MARILOR ART STUDIO
106 VIA SEVILLA
REDONDO BEACH, CA 90277-6749
FAX 310-375-4977
TEL 310-375-4977
Established: 1975
Products: fiber wall hangings
Techniques: painting, airbrush, layering
Size Range: 2' × 3' to 8' × 15'
Price Range: $60 to $120/sq. ft.

See below and page 166 for photographs and additional information.

IRA ONO DESIGNS

PO BOX 112
VOLCANO, HI 96785
TEL 808-967-7261
Products: fabric constructions, Japanese-
paste paper screens
Techniques: painting, Japanese-paste
paper
Size Range: 16" × 24" to 7' × 15'
Price Range: $400 to $4,000/piece

Marie-Laure Ilie, *Medieval Scene*, hand-painted silk, 68"H × 48"W

FIBER ART FOR THE WALL

ELAINE IRELAND
711 HAMPSHIRE ST
SAN FRANCISCO, CA 94110-2129
TEL 415-648-8813
Established: 1972
Products: tapestries
Techniques: weaving combined w/mixed mediums
Size Range: miniatures to unlimited
Price Range: $500 to $1,000/sq. ft.

PEG IRISH
114 METOXIT RD
WAQUOIT, MA 02536-7723
TEL 508-548-3230
Established: 1988
Products: fiber installations
Techniques: dyeing, embroidery, rug hooking
Size Range: 8" × 8" to 4' × 8'
Price Range: $150 to $300/sq. ft.

CAROL KASMER IRVING
THE WEAVER'S WEB
1204 8TH AVE S
ESCANABA, MI 49829-3217
TEL 906-786-0331
Established: 1977
Products: wall or floor rugs
Techniques: weaving
Size Range: 2' × 3' to 6' × 12'
Price Range: $35 to $50/sq. ft.

SUSAN IVERSON
SUSAN IVERSON - TAPESTRIES
904 BUFORD OAKS CIR
RICHMOND, VA 23235-4680
TEL 804-272-0225
Established: 1975
Products: tapestries
Techniques: dyeing, weaving
Size Range: 3' × 7' to 8' × 12'
Price Range: $125 to $200/sq. ft.

JK DESIGN
JOYCE KLIMAN
34 LASALLE PKWY
VICTOR, NY 14564
TEL 716-381-3259
Established: 1980
Products: art quilts
Techniques: stamping, painting, quilting, appliqué, photo transfer
Size Range: 2' × 2' to 10' × 10'
Price Range: $125 to $4,000/piece

NANCY JACKSON
TIMSHEL TAPESTRY STUDIO
10 BUENA VISTA AVE
VALLEJO, CA 94590
TEL 707-554-4128
Established: 1983
Products: tapestries
Techniques: weaving, dyeing, painting
Size Range: 2' × 3' to 8' × 10'
Price Range: $1,200 to $16,000/piece
Price Range: $200 to $350/sq. ft.

★ CARRIE JACOBSON-MAY
504 PACHECO AVE
SANTA CRUZ, CA 95062
TEL 408-459-9559
Established: 1974
Products: tufted wall hangings
Techniques: dyeing, wrapping, tufting
Size Range: 30" × 30" to 10' × 12'
Price Range: $65 to $100/sq. ft.

See photograph below.

VICTOR JACOBY
1086 17TH ST
EUREKA, CA 95501-2623
TEL 707-442-3809
Established: 1975
Products: tapestries
Techniques: weaving
Size Range: 2' × 2' to 8' × 24'
Price Range: $400 to $48,000/piece

Carrie Jacobson-May, *Walpi*, tufted wall hanging, wool, 39" × 57"

MARY E. JAEGER

MARY E. JAEGER LTD.
404 E 55TH ST #4D
NEW YORK, NY 10022
FAX 212-755-3814
TEL 212-755-3814
Established: 1980
Products: fabric constructions
Techniques: dyeing, painting, appliqué
Size Range: 10" x 10" to 15' x 4'
Price Range: $50 to $75/sq. ft.

LUCY A. JAHNS

1702 BELMONT DR
GREEN OAKS, IL 60048
TEL 847-362-2144
Established: 1982
Products: fabric constructions
Techniques: appliqué, embroidery, painting
Size Range: 24" x 36" to 6' x 10'
Price Range: $600 to $5,800/piece

MICHAEL JAMES

STUDIO QUILTS
258 OLD COLONY AVE
SOMERSET, MA 02726-5930
FAX 508-672-1370
TEL 508-672-1370
Established: 1973
Products: art quilts
Techniques: quilting, piecing
Size Range: 39" x 39" to 72" x 144"
Price Range: $3,500 to $16,000/piece

JANICE JANAS

PO BOX 461
ARVADA, CO 80001-0461
TEL 303-467-2007
Established: 1980
Products: mixed media constructions
Techniques: painting, dyeing, stamping
Size Range: 18" x 24" to 2.5' x 3.5'
Price Range: $400 to $8,000/piece

CATHERINE JANSEN

152 HEACOCK LN
WYNCOTE, PA 19095-1517
TEL 215-884-3174
Established: 1976
Products: art quilts
Techniques: photo process on cloth
Size Range: 8" x 10" to room sized
Price Range: $225 to $20,000/piece

JOCELYN STUDIO

JOCELYN GOLDMAN
39 OLD TOWN RD
EAST HADDAM, CT 06423-1453
FAX 203-526-2205
TEL 203-526-1581
Established: 1988
Products: art quilts
Techniques: weaving, appliqué, embroidery
Size Range: 12" x 12" to 36" x 48"
Price Range: $200 to $1,000/piece

JOELL MILEO—PAPERMAKER

JOELL MILEO
PO BOX 8
MENDON, NY 14506-0008
TEL 716-624-9152
Established: 1988
Products: paper
Techniques: airbush, casting, dyeing
Size Range: 11" x 14" to 2' x 3'
Price Range: $125 to $1,500/piece

ROSITA JOHANSON

657 WOODBINE AVE
TORONTO, ON M4E 2J3
CANADA
TEL 416-699-4881
Established: 1984
Products: miniature fiber art
Techniques: appliqué, embroidery
Size Range: 6" x 6" to 8" x 9"
Price Range: $900 to $10,000/piece

★ MARCIA HEWITT JOHNSON

71 LLANFAIR CIR
ARMORE, PA 19003
TEL 610-649-7282
Established: 1988
Products: art quilts
Techniques: painting, dyeing, quilting
Size Range: 3' x 3' to 6' x 6'
Price Range: $500 to $5,000/piece

See photograph below.

VICKI L. JOHNSON

V & T GRAPHICS
225 MUIR DR
SOQUEL, CA 95073-9523
FAX 408-476-7567
TEL 408-476-7567
Established: 1970
Products: art quilts
Techniques: appliqué, painting, quilting
Size Range: 2' x 2' to 6' x 8'
Price Range: $400 to $10,000/piece

ANN JOHNSTON

910 YORK RD
LAKE OSWEGO, OR 97034-1742
TEL 503-635-1173
Established: 1981
Products: art quilts
Techniques: dyeing, quilting, painting
Size Range: 8" x 8" to 9' x 9'
Price Range: $400 to $10,000/piece

JOYCE HULBERT TAPESTRY & TEXTILE RESTORATION

JOYCE HULBERT
2339 3RD ST STE 31
SAN FRANCISCO, CA 94107-3137
TEL 415-255-4560
Established: 1988
Products: textile restorations
Techniques: dyeing, weaving, sewing
Size Range: miniature to 10' x 12'
Price Range: project estimate based on hourly fee/piece

★ JUNO SKY STUDIO

BETTY FULMER
844 S MAIN ST
FINDLAY, OH 45840
FAX 419-423-9907
TEL 419-423-9591
Established: 1971
Products: paper
Techniques: painting, dyeing, casting
Size Range: 10" x 14" to 68" x 160"
Price Range: $300 to $10,000/piece

See page 148 for photographs and additional information.

DEBRA KAM

136 DRINKWATER RD
HAMPTON FALLS, NH 03844
TEL 603-772-8580
Established: 1993
Products: art quilts
Techniques: painting, quilting, piecing
Size Range: 1' x 1' to 6' x 4'
Price Range: $500 to $3,000/piece

HENDRIKA KAMSTRA

GINKGO STUDIO
1825 W COTTAGE ST
STEVENS POINT, WI 54481-3414
TEL 715-341-3599
Established: 1984
Products: mixed media installations paper
Techniques: dyeing, casting, airbrushing
Size Range: 15" x 12" to 30" x 40"
Price Range: $195 to $1,350/piece

★ JANIS KANTER

1923 W DICKENS AVE
CHICAGO, IL 60614-3935
FAX 312-862-0440
TEL 312-252-2119
Established: 1988
Products: tapestries with neon
Techniques: weaving
Size Range: 4' x 4' to 5' x 8'
Price Range: $5,000 to $10,000/piece

See photograph on page 184.

ANNA KARESH

ART STUDIO WEST
PO BOX 900528
SAN DIEGO, CA 92190-0528
FAX 619-565-1161
TEL 619-258-0766
Established: 1970
Products: mixed media installations
Techniques: casting, painting
Size Range: 2' x 3' to 8' x 12'
Price Range: $60 to $120/sq. ft.

MARCIA KARLIN

45 KINGS CROSS DR
LINCOLNSHIRE, IL 60069-3342
TEL 708-940-4930
Established: 1985
Products: art quilts
Techniques: dyeing, painting, embroidery
Size Range: 15" x 20" to 7' x 8'
Price Range: $500 to $10,000/piece

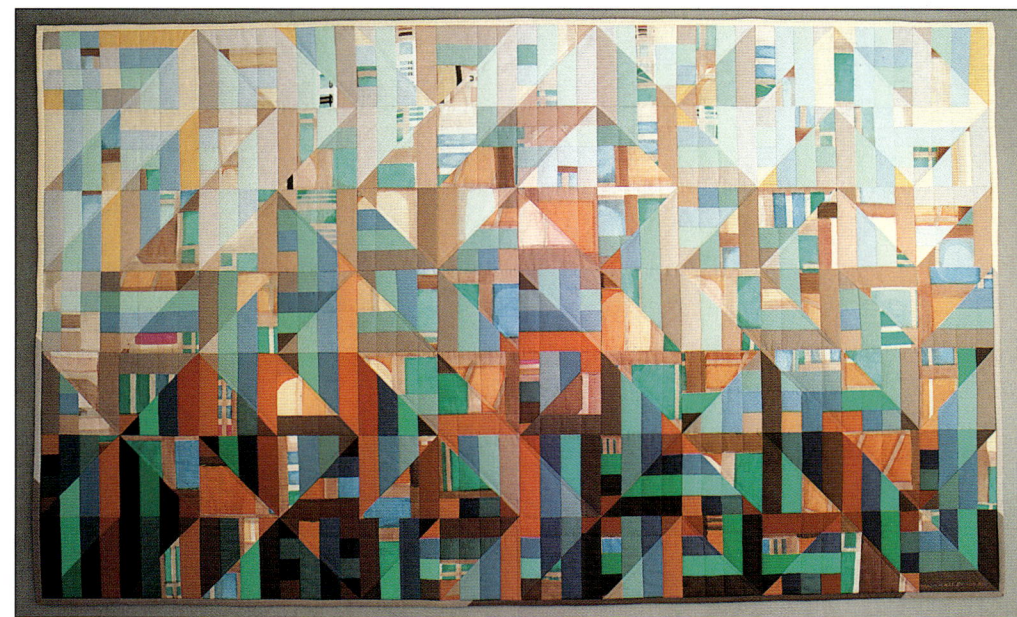

Marcia Hewitt Johnson, *Mediterranean Possibilities*, ©1995, art quilt, painted and hand dyed, 42" x 72"

KATHLEEN O'CONNOR—QUILTS

KATHLEEN O'CONNOR
RR3 BOX 735
PUTNEY, VT 05346
TEL 802-387-4172

Established: 1988
Products: art quilts
Techniques: painting, dyeing, quilting
Size Range: 42" × 42" to 13' × 27'
Price Range: $500 to $6,000/piece

★ DENISE KATZ

ART FRAMES
2336 14TH ST
BOULDER, CO 80304
TEL 303-444-8046

Established: 1975
Products: paper
Techniques: painting, dyeing, casting
Size Range: 24" × 30" to 40" × 40"
Price Range: $250 to $600/piece

See photograph on page 185.

ANNE MARIE KENNY

INDUSTRIAL QUILT STUDIO
1465 HOOKSETT RD #109
HOOKSETT, NH 03106-1862
TEL 603-268-0336

Established: 1982
Products: industrial quilts
Techniques: painting, stitching, wire-cloth
Size Range: 3' × 3' to 12' × 12'
Price Range: $1,500 to $25,000/piece

BETTY KERSHNER

PO BOX 3266
SEWANEE, TN 37375-3266
TEL 615-598-5723

Established: 1970
Products: fiber installations
Techniques: painting, dyeing, stamping
Size Range: 4' × 2' to 20' × 6'
Price Range: $30 to $100/sq. ft.

SUSAN KIMBER

61 WARREN ST
NEW YORK, NY 10007-1016
TEL 212-766-3714

Established: 1973
Products: mixed media tapestries
Techniques: weaving, painting, photography
Size Range: 12" × 12" to 4' × 16'
Price Range: $350 to $20,000/piece

CHRIS KING

RR 1
BADDECK, NS B0E 1B0
CANADA
FAX 902-295-3141
TEL 902-295-3141

Established: 1989
Products: art quilts
Techniques: dyeing, piecing ("dyed and pieced")
Size Range: 9" × 12" to 10' × 10'
Price Range: $150 to $2,000/piece

SARA NEWBERG KING

KING'S KREATIONS
6950 100TH ST NW
PINE ISLAND, MN 55963-9659
TEL 507-356-8839

Established: 1984
Products: art quilts
Techniques: quilting, embroidery, discharge shibori
Size Range: 6" × 6" to 9' × 12'
Price Range: $50 to $2,500/piece

KIMBERLY HALDEMAN KLEIN

K.H. KLEIN
925 GRANDVIEW BLVD
LANCASTER, PA 17601-5105
TEL 717-293-9453

Established: 1976
Products: art quilts
Techniques: quilting, piecing
Size Range: 40" × 40" to 60" × 60"
Price Range: $400 to $1,200/piece

Janis Kanter, *Le Voyeur*, 1995, tapestry with neon, 61"H × 61"W, photo: Michael Tropea

★ **M.A. KLEIN**

M.A. KLEIN DESIGN
2443 FAIR OAKS BLVD #344
SACRAMENTO, CA 95825
TEL 800-700-7815

Established: 1962
Products: mixed media installations
Techniques: painting, embroidery, collage
Size Range: 10" × 12" to 9' × 12'
Price Range: $225 to $25,000/piece

See pages 140 and 186 for photographs and additional information.

NANCY SMITH KLOS

KLOS STUDIOS
2407 NE 9TH
PORTLAND, OR 97212
FAX 503-282-7028
TEL 503-282-7028

Established: 1985
Products: tapestries
Techniques: weaving, painting, dyeing
Size Range: 12" × 12" and up
Price Range: $100 to $10,000/piece
Price Range: $300 to $350/sq. ft.

★ **ELLEN KOCHANSKY**

EKO
1237 MILE CREEK RD
PICKENS, SC 29671-8703
FAX 864-868-4250
TEL 864-868-9749

Established: 1978
Products: fiber installations
Techniques: quilting, wrapping
Size Range: 6" × 6" to 6' × 20'
Price Range: $150 to $400/sq. ft.

See photograph on page 187.

ANNA KOCHEROVSKI

6154 QUAKER HILL DR
WEST BLOOMFIELD, MI 48322
TEL 810-661-0560

Established: 1987
Products: tapestries
Techniques: weaving
Size Range: 18" × 18" to 40" × 60"
Price Range: $250 to $3,000/piece

★ **JEREMY KOEHLER**

KOEHLER STUDIO
PO BOX 279
SANTA FE, NM 87504-0279
FAX 505-989-9810
TEL 505-422-2201

Established: 1977
Products: tapestries
Techniques: weaving, dyeing
Size Range: 36" × 36" to 120" × 96"
Price Range: $125 to $200/sq. ft.

See photograph on page 188.

★ **NANCY KOENIGSBERG**

435 E 57TH ST
NEW YORK, NY 10022
FAX 212-980-6642
TEL 212-644-2398

Established: 1970
Products: fabric installations, woven-wire constructions
Techniques: weaving, knotting
Size Range: 1" × 1" to 8' × 16' and up
Price Range: $100 to $250/sq. ft.

See photograph on page 189.

★ **JOAN KOPCHIK**

1335 STEPHEN WAY
SOUTHAMPTON, PA 18966-4349
TEL 215-322-1862

Established: 1976
Products: paper
Techniques: casting, painting, weaving
Size Range: all sizes
Price Range: $125 to $200/sq. ft.

See photograph on page 190.

LIBBY KOWALSKI

32 UNION SQUARE E #216
NEW YORK, NY 10003
FAX 212-254-7434
TEL 212-254-7551

Established: 1981
Products: tapestries
Techniques: weaving
Size Range: 14" × 27" to 96" × 120"
Price Range: $500 to $6,000/piece

GRACE KRAFT

STONE SCHOOL HOUSE
MADRID, NM 87010
TEL 505-471-8062

Established: 1970
Products: fabric installations
Techniques: screen printing screened on silk, engraved aluminum frames
Size Range: 32" × 32" to 45' × 45'
Price Range: $600 to $36,000/piece

DOROTHY SIMPSON KRAUSE

32 NATHANIEL WAY
PO BOX 421
MARSHFIELD HILLS, MA 02051
TEL 617-837-1682

Established: 1968
Products: mixed media installations
Techniques: painting, laminating, digital imaging on fabric
Size Range: 24" × 36" to 10' × 30'
Price Range: $66 to $110/sq. ft.

CANDACE KREITLOW

PO BOX 113
MAZOMANIE, WI 53560-0113
TEL 608-795-4680

Established: 1976
Products: woven wall constructions
Techniques: weaving, painting, sculpted over frame
Size Range: 36" × 24" to 48" × 76" and larger
Price Range: $600 to $6,000/piece

TRACY KRUMM

12011 RED OAK CT N
BURNSVILLE, MN 55337
TEL 612-890-2605

Established: 1987
Products: paper
Techniques: weaving, drawing, crochetimg
Size Range: 7" × 7" to 60" × 60"
Price Range: $300 to $5,000/piece

LIALIA KUCHMA

2423 W SUPERIOR ST
CHICAGO, IL 60612-1213
TEL 312-227-5445

Established: 1973
Products: tapestries
Techniques: weaving
Size Range: 36" × 48" to 96" × 240"
Price Range: $2,000 to $32,000/piece
Price Range: $150 to $350/sq. ft.

★ **SILJA (TALIKKA) LAHTINEN**

SILJA'S FINE ART STUDIO
5220 SUNSET TRL
MARIETTA, GA 30068-4740
FAX 770-992-0350
TEL 770-992-8380

Established: 1978
Products: prints on chamois
Techniques: beading, painting, screen printing, photo etching
Size Range: 19" × 23" to 72" × 65"
Price Range: $250 to $29,000 per group/piece
Price Range: $3.03 to $292.50/sq. ft.

See page 95 for photographs and additional information.

COLETTE LAICO

968C HERITAGE HILLS DR
SOMERS, NY 10589-1913
TEL 914-276-2591

Established: 1976
Products: mixed media installations
Techniques: painting
Size Range: 9" × 12" to 4' × 6'
Price Range: $300 to $2,000/piece

Denise Katz, *Madness*, 1995, handmade paper with acrylic, collection of Dr. Joel Goldstein, 24" × 37", photo: Azad

MARY LANE

703 N FOOTE ST
OLYMPIA, WA 98502
TEL 360-754-1105
Established: 1982
Products: tapestries
Techniques: weaving
Size Range: 4" × 4" to 5' × 10'
Price Range: $100 to $5,000/piece

RAGNHILD LANGLET

PO BOX 508
SAUSALITO, CA 94966-0508
TEL 415-332-5007
Established: 1965
Products: mixed media
Techniques: painting, dyeing, embroidery
Size Range: 18" × 24" to 4'x 8' or 8' × 4'
Price Range: $1,500 to $10,000/piece
Price Range: $350 to $500/sq. ft.

ITALA LANGMAR

604 EXMOOR RD
KENILWORTH, IL 60043-1021
TEL 708-251-0427
Established: 1984
Products: fiber installations, papier maché vessels
Techniques: painting, casting, crocheting
Size Range: 15" × 25" to 5' × 7'
Price Range: $150 to $4,000/piece
Price Range: $15 to $45/sq. ft.

GAIL LARNED

LARNED MARLOW STUDIOS
144 S MONROE AVE
COLUMBUS, OH 43205-1084
TEL 614-258-7239
Established: 1974
Products: fiber installations
Techniques: dyeing, wrapping, knotting
Size Range: 2' × 4' to 5' × 15'
Price Range: $1,000 to $45,000/piece
Price Range: $35 to $200/sq. ft.

KAREN LARSEN

CACOPHONY
7 AUSTIN PARK
CAMBRIDGE, MA 02139-2509
TEL 617-491-4025
Established: 1975
Products: art quilts
Techniques: appliqué, quilting, weaving
Size Range: 22" × 22" to 10' × 15'
Price Range: $60 to $100/sq. ft.

JUDITH LARZELERE

CORPORATE FIBER ART
226 BEECH ST
BELMONT, MA 02178-1945
TEL 617-484-6091
Established: 1974
Products: art quilts
Techniques: quilting, strip piecing
Size Range: 20" × 20" to 112" × 144"
Price Range: $125 to $375/sq. ft.

★ ULRIKA LEANDER

**CONTEMPORARY TAPESTRY
 WEAVING**
107 WESTOVERLOOK DR
OAK RIDGE, TN 37830-3825
FAX 423-483-7911
TEL 423-482-6849
Established: 1971
Products: tapestries
Techniques: weaving
Size Range: 4' × 4' to 12' × 30'
Price Range: $150 to $500/sq. ft.

**See page 167 for photographs
and additional information.**

SUSAN WEBB LEE

963 WOODS LOOP
WEDDINGTON, NC 28173-9376
TEL 704-843-1323
Established: 1979
Products: art quilts
Techniques: appliqué, painting, dyeing
Size Range: 25" × 25" to 6' × 8'
Price Range: $300 to $8,000/piece

LENKER FINE ARTS

MARLENE LENKER
28 NORTHVIEW TER
CEDAR GROVE, NJ 07009
FAX 201-239-8671
TEL 201-239-8671
TEL 203-767-2098
Established: 1966
Products: mixed media
Techniques: painting, collage
Size Range: 10" × 10" to 60" × 90"
Price Range: $200 to $10,000/piece

MICHELLE LESTER

MICHELLE LESTER STUDIO
15 W 17TH ST FL 9
NEW YORK, NY 10011-5506
FAX 212-627-8553
TEL 212-989-1411
Established: 1967
Products: tapestries, children's rugs
Techniques: weaving
Size Range: unlimited
Price Range: $250 to $550/sq. ft.

ARLENE LEVEY

336 S HARDING RD
COLUMBUS, OH 43209-1946
TEL 614-231-8601
Established: 1982
Products: mixed media installations
Techniques: dyeing, embroidery, laminating
Size Range: 24" × 24" to 144" × 144"
Price Range: $250 to $10,000/piece
Price Range: $25 to $100/sq. ft.

JUDY ZOELZER LEVINE

9415 N FAIRWAY DR
MILWAUKEE, WI 53217-1322
TEL 414-351-2631
Established: 1991
Products: art quilts
Techniques: appliqué, beading, quilting
Size Range: 15" × 15" to 60" × 80"
Price Range: $200 to $4,000/piece

M.A. Klein, *Fish Gotta Swim, Birds Gotta Fly*, for Art Quilt International 1994, 39"H × 56" W

★ VERENA LEVINE

**VERENA LEVINE PICTORIAL
AND NARRATIVE QUILTS
4305 37TH ST NW
WASHINGTON, DC 20008
TEL 202-537-0916**

Established: 1978
Products: art quilts
Techniques: appliqué, quilting, piecing
Size Range: 20" × 20" to 5' × 20'
Price Range: $150 minimum/sq. ft.

**See page 141 for photographs
and additional information.**

BONNY LHOTKA

5658 CASCADE PL
BOULDER, CO 80303-2950
FAX 303-494-3472
TEL 303-494-5631

Established: 1972
Products: tapestries
Techniques: laminating, painting, stamping/printing digital imaging on fabric
Size Range: 24" × 36" to 10' × 30'
Price Range: $66 to $110/sq. ft.

WENDY LILIENTHAL

740 BUTTERFIELD RD
SAN ANSELMO, CA 94960-1105
TEL 415-453-1019

Established: 1978
Products: hand-cast paper
Techniques: dyeing, casting, collage
Size Range: 18" × 24" to 4' × 9'
Price Range: $500 to $5,000/piece

LIN LACY LIMITED EDITIONS

LIN LACY
1021 FAIRMOUNT
SAINT PAUL, MN 55105
TEL 612-291-0587

Established: 1990
Products: art quilts
Techniques: embroidery, appliqué, beading
Size Range: 1' × 1' to 8' × 8'
Price Range: $100 to $10,000/piece
$100 to $150/sq. ft.

RACHEL LINDSTROM

24231 N 41ST AVE
GLENDALE, AZ 85310-3235
TEL 602-780-0861

Products: mixed fiber collages
Techniques: painting, dyeing, laminating
Size Range: 20" × 20" to 72" × 72"
Price Range: $200 to $500/sq. ft.

CAL LING

CAL LING PAPERWORKS
441 CHERRY ST
CHICO, CA 95928-5114
FAX 916-893-1319
TEL 916-893-0882

Established: 1983
Products: paper
Techniques: painting, dyeing, casting
Size Range: 11.5" × 16" to 20' × 20'
Price Range: $300 to $40,000/piece
$100 to $250/sq. ft.

M. JOAN LINTAULT

306 N SPRINGER ST
CARBONDALE, IL 62901-1428
TEL 618-457-7815

Established: 1965
Products: art quilts
Techniques: dyeing, quilting, silkscreen
Size Range: 14" × 15" to 12' × 24'
Price Range: $200/sq. ft.

ROSLYN LOGSDON

MONTPELIER CULT ART CEN
12826 LAUREL BOWIE RD
LAUREL, MD 20708
TEL 301-490-1136

Established: 1970
Products: hooked wall hangings
Techniques: rug hooking
Size Range: 18" × 12" to 48" × 60"
Price Range: $350 to $6,000/piece

KIT LONEY

PO BOX 857
FOLLY BEACH, SC 29439
TEL 803-588-6222

Established: 1980
Products: tapestries
Techniques: weaving, dyeing, painting
Size Range: 8" × 5" to 84" × 25"
Price Range: $175 to $2,000/piece

★ PHYLLIS HARPER LONEY

**10 GRASSHOPPER LN
ACTON, MA 01720
TEL 508-263-3715**

Established: 1975
Products: dye-painted fabric
Techniques: painting, quilting, sewn construction
Size Range: 12" × 9" to 90" × 45"
Price Range: $150 to $2,500/piece

See photograph on page 191.

★ JOYCE P. LOPEZ

**JOYCE LOPEZ STUDIO
1147 W OHIO ST #304
CHICAGO, IL 60622-5874
FAX 312-243-5033
TEL 312-243-5033**

Established: 1979
Products: sculpture/fiber
Techniques: wrapping
Size Range: 24" × 24" to 20' × 30'
Price Range: $2,800 to $75,000/piece

**See page 168 for photographs
and additional information.**

ANTONIA LOWDEN

ANTONIA LOWDEN DESIGN
155 S ARLINGTON AVE
RENO, NV 89501-1701
TEL 702-826-3655

Established: 1970
Products: tapestries
Techniques: weaving, mixed media
Size Range: 2' × 2' to 6' × 12'
Price Range: $500 to $20,000/piece

PEGGY CLARK LUMPKINS

RR 1 BOX 4650
BROWNVILLE, ME 04414-9720
TEL 207-965-8526

Established: 1979
Products: transparent tapestry
Techniques: weaving
Size Range: 2' × 1'6" to 8' × 14'
Price Range: $90 to $250/sq. ft.

YAEL LURIE
JEAN PIERRE LAROCHETTE

LURIE-LAROCHETTE
2216 GRANT ST
BERKELEY, CA 94703-1714
TEL 510-548-5744

Established: 1960
Products: tapestries
Techniques: weaving
Size Range: 8" × 12" to 6' × 16'
Price Range: $600 to $35,000/piece

NANCY LYON

102 SHAKER RD
NEW LONDON, NH 03257-5014
TEL 603-526-6754

Established: 1971
Products: hand-painted wall pieces
Techniques: painting, stamping or printing
Size Range: 24" × 24" to unlimited
Price Range: $30 to $50/sq. ft.

MARGO MACDONALD

5814 CRESCENT BEACH RD
VAUGHN, WA 98394
TEL 206-884-2955

Established: 1980
Products: tapestries
Techniques: weaving
Size Range: 13" × 20" to 4'6" to 4'6"
Price Range: $500 to $2,000/piece

Ellen Kochansky, *Soft Bricks*, 1995, recycled textiles, wire, modular wall sculpture, detail shown: 7" × 12" (bricks: 2" cube)

FIBER ART FOR THE WALL

ANN MACEACHERN

MACEACHERN
  HANDWEAVING & BASKETRY
PO BOX 80
ACTON, ME 04001-0080
TEL 207-636-2539
Established: 1970
Products: fiber installations
Techniques: embroidery, weaving,
wrapping, knotting, twining
Size Range: 8" × 12" to 2' × 8'
Price Range: $50 to $500/piece

JACKIE MACKAY

HANDWOVEN COUNTRY INTERIORS
RR 5
BERWICK, NS B0P 1E0
CANADA
TEL 902-538-3315
Established: 1984
Products: tapestries
Techniques: dyeing, weaving
Size Range: 3' × 5' to 5' × 5'
Price Range: $300 to $2,000/piece

IRENE MAGINNISS

770 ANDOVER RD S
MANSFIELD, OH 44907-1511
TEL 419-756-2841
Established: 1970
Products: mixed media installations
Techniques: collage, embedding
Size Range: 12" × 12" to 6' × 8'
Price Range: $125 to $175/sq. ft.

JULIANNA S. MAHLEY

404 COUNCIL DR NE
VIENNA, VA 22180-4740
FAX 703-281-0368
TEL 703-281-9106
Established: 1989
Products: fiber installations
Techniques: painting, embroidery, dyeing
Size Range: 5" × 5" to 25" × 25"
Price Range: $400 to $2,000/piece

PATRICIA MALARCHER

93 IVY LN
ENGLEWOOD, NJ 07631
FAX 201-567-3709
TEL 201-568-1084
Established: 1963
Products: fabric constructions
Techniques: appliqué, painting, stamping
or printing
Size Range: 6" × 6" and up
Price Range: $200 to $400/sq. ft.

RUTH MANNING

177 ROGERS PKY
ROCHESTER, NY 14617-4205
TEL 716-467-6250
Established: 1980
Products: tapestries
Techniques: dyeing, weaving
Size Range: 1' × 1' to 4' × 6'
Price Range: $100 to $200/sq. ft.

CAMILLE MANSFIELD

MANSFIELD STUDIOS
507 MODOC AVE
RENO, NV 89509-3339
TEL 702-333-5282
Established: 1994
Products: art quilts
Techniques: appliqué, embroidery,
quilting, piecing, hand dyeing
Size Range: 40" × 40" to 120" × 120"
Price Range: $1,000 to $10,000/piece

SHARON MARCUS

TAPESTRY
4145 SW CORBETT AVE
PORTLAND, OR 97201-4201
FAX 503-796-1234
TEL 503-796-1234
Established: 1975
Products: tapestries
Techniques: weaving
Size Range: 3' × 3' to 9'6" × 15'
Price Range: $350/sq. ft.

JANE GOLDING MARIE

620 CHICAGO AVE
HASTINGS, NE 68901-5831
TEL 402-463-2669
Established: 1973
Products: fabric constructions
Techniques: painting, embroidery,
wrapping
Size Range: 12" × 12" to 8' × 12'
Price Range: $100 to $150/sq. ft.

MARY KAY COLLING CONTEMPORARY PAPER ART

COLLING, MARY KAY
VILLAGE GATE SQ
274 N GOODMAN ST
ROCHESTER, NY 14607
TEL 716-442-8946
Established: 1988
Products: paper
Techniques: appliqué, casting, painting
Size Range: no size limit
Price Range: $100 to $300/sq. ft.

MARTHA MATTHEWS

7200 TERRACE DR
CHARLOTTE, NC 28211-6143
TEL 704-364-3435
Established: 1973
Products: tapestries
Techniques: weaving
Size Range: 2' × 3' to 8' × 20'
Price Range: $1,200 to $48,000/piece
Price Range: $240 to $300/sq. ft.

★ THERESE MAY

651 N 4TH ST
SAN JOSE, CA 95112-5143
TEL 408-292-3247
Established: 1965
Products: art quilts
Techniques: appliqué, embroidery,
painting
Size Range: 1' × 1' to 14' × 14'
Price Range: $500 to $41,000/piece

See page 142 for photographs
and additional information.

PHOEBE MCAFEE

6 MONTEZUMA ST
SAN FRANCISCO, CA 94110-5109
TEL 415-282-3448
Established: 1967
Products: tapestries
Techniques: weaving, appliqué,
embroidery
Size Range: 1' × 2' to 8' × 24'
Price Range: $200 to $50,000/piece

SUSAN MCGEHEE

METALLIC STRANDS
540 23RD ST
MANHATTAN BEACH, CA 90266
TEL 310-545-4112
Established: 1989
Products: woven-metal sculptures
Techniques: weaving
Size Range: 2" × 24" to 5' × 38'
Price Range: $140 to $180/sq. ft.

JULIE MCGINNIS

515 E ROCK ST
FAYETTEVILLE, AR 72701-4323
TEL 501-582-3707
Established: 1988
Products: art quilts
Techniques: dyeing, quilting, piecing
Size Range: 30" × 40" to 120" × 120"
Price Range: $300 to $4,000/piece

Jeremy Koehler, *Koshare Window IV*, 1994, hand-dyed wool tapestry, 53¹⁄₂" × 58¹⁄₂", photo: Bob Wartell

★ SALLY MCKENNA

SALLY MCKENNA SCULPTURE
7050 E DIXILETA DR
CAVE CREEK, AZ 85331
FAX 602-585-5290
TEL 602-585-7034
Established: 1978
Products: mixed media installations
Techniques: weaving, painting
Size Range: 2'6" × 1'6" to 20' × 12'
Price Range: $1,200 to $95,000/piece

**See page 98 for photographs
and additional information.**

DIANNE MCKENZIE

COMET STUDIOS
PO BOX 337
THE SEA RANCH, CA 95497-0337
FAX 707-785-2567
TEL 707-785-2567
E-Mail: comet@mcn.org
Established: 1974
Products: tapestries
Techniques: dyeing, weaving
Size Range: 6' × 8' to 12' × 20' and up
Price Range: $250 to $500/sq. ft.

BETH MINEAR

171 MONUMENT RD
ORLEANS, MA 02653-3507
TEL 508-255-3430
Established: 1978
Products: rugs, floor or wall
Techniques: weaving
Size Range: 3' × 5' and up
Price Range: $70 to $80/sq. ft.

NORMA MINKOWITZ

25 BROADVIEW RD
WESTPORT, CT 06880-2303
TEL 203-227-4497
Established: 1960
Products: mixed media installations
Techniques: painting, fiber construction
Size Range: 12" × 23" to 50" × 63"
Price Range: $3,000 to $10,000/piece

★ PATTI MITCHEM

28 WITCHTROT RD
SOUTH BERWICK, ME 03908-2170
FAX 207-384-1938
TEL 207-384-2195
Established: 1976
Products: fiber installations
Techniques: weaving
Size Range: 2' × 3' to unlimited
Price Range: $90 to $180/sq. ft.

**See page 169 for photographs
and additional information.**

KATHLEEN MOLLOHAN

524 S ROBERTS ST
HELENA, MT 59601-5435
TEL 406-442-9028
Established: 1983
Products: tapestries
Techniques: beading, painting, weaving
Size Range: 4' × 5' to 6' × 9'
Price Range: $130 to $150/sq. ft.

DOTTIE MOORE

1134 CHARLOTTE AVE
ROCK HILL, SC 29732-2452
TEL 803-327-5088
Established: 1976
Products: art quilts
Techniques: appliqué, embroidery, quilting
Size Range: 24" × 24" to 72" × 72"
Price Range: $800 to $9,000/piece
Price Range: $200 to $300/sq. ft.

EDWARD MORDAK

801 SUTTER ST #305
SAN FRANCISCO, CA 94109-6108
TEL 415-673-8046
Established: 1985
Products: mixed media installations, paper
Techniques: beading, painting, weaving, knotting
Size Range: 30" × 20" to 5' × 10'
Price Range: $600 to $12,000/piece

ROSLYN MORESH

PO BOX 294
HOOLEHUA, HI 96729
TEL 806-567-6766
Established: 1979
Products: paper
Techniques: dyeing, painting, casting
Size Range: 2" × 3" to 38" × 48"
Price Range: $40 to $6,000/piece

★ LORETTA MOSSMAN

LM TAPESTRIES
2524 BROWN ST
PHILADELPHIA, PA 19130
FAX 215-483-4864
TEL 215-763-4060
Established: 1980
Products: tapestries
Techniques: painting, appliqué, embroidery
Size Range: unlimited
Price Range: $900 to $10,000/piece
Price Range: $200 to $300/sq. ft.

See photograph on page 192.

STEPHANIE NADOLSKI

NADOLSKI FINE ART & DESIGN
25287 BARSUMIAN DR
BARRINGTON, IL 60010-1118
FAX 847-526-5208
TEL 847-526-5208
Established: 1975
Products: mixed media installations, handmade paper
Techniques: painting, casting, stamping or printing
Size Range: 20" × 20" to 60" × 84"
Price Range: $250 to $6,000/piece

NAN GOSS INC.

NAN GOSS-BILODEAU
18801 SE 263RD ST
KENT, WA 98042
FAX 206-639-4898
TEL 206-572-5930
Established: 1984
Products: mixed media assemblages
Techniques: painting, embroidery, beading
Size Range: 5" × 7" to 36" × 96"
Price Range: $.75 to $3.00/sq. ft.

DOMINIE NASH

8612 RAYBURN RD
BETHESDA, MD 20817-3630
TEL 202-722-1407
Established: 1972
Products: art quilts
Techniques: dyeing, quilting, silkscreen
Size Range: 18" × 14" to 84" × 72"
Price Range: $400 to $4,000/piece
Price Range: $150 to $200/sq. ft.

MIRIAM NATHAN-ROBERTS

1351 ACTON ST
BERKELEY, CA 94706-2501
TEL 510-525-5432
Established: 1982
Products: art quilts
Techniques: airbush, appliqué, quilting
Size Range: 30" × 30" to 96" × 108"
Price Range: $100 to $200/sq. ft.

★ JEAN NEBLETT

628 RHODE ISLAND ST
SAN FRANCISCO, CA 94107-2628
FAX 415-821-2772
TEL 415-550-2613
Established: 1977
Products: art quilts
Techniques: appliqué, painting, quilting
Size Range: 4" × 5" to 5' × 6'
Price Range: $200 to $9,600/piece

See photograph on page 193.

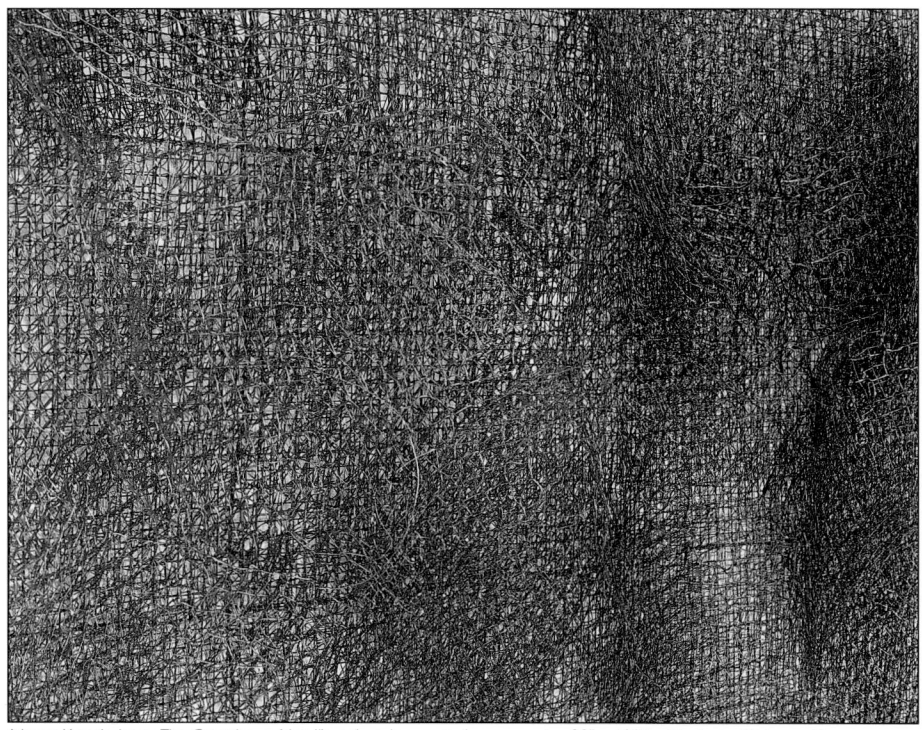

Nancy Koenigsberg, *The Great Lawn* (detail), poly-nylon-coated copper wire, 39" × 132" × 6", photo: D. James Dee

FIBER ART FOR THE WALL

DANA H. NELSON
155 FAIRVIEW RD
STOCKBRIDGE, GA 30281-1045
FAX 770-507-6583
TEL 770-389-8562
Established: 1980
Products: tapestries
Techniques: dyeing, embroidery, weaving
Size Range: 18" × 18" to 12'6" × 14'
Price Range: $50 to $10,000/piece

KEIKO NELSON
KEIKO NELSON ART STUDIO
2604 3RD ST
SAN FRANCISCO, CA 94107
FAX 510-527-4822
TEL 415-824-1545
Established: 1976
Products: mixed media installations.
paper
Techniques: painting, screen printing,
casting
Size Range: 5" × 5" to 200' × 200'
Price Range: $500 to $50,000/piece

ANNA NESBITT
ROSE CREATIONS
3310 PIPER'S GLEN DR
LAFAYETTE, IN 47905
TEL 317-474-5229
Established: 1985
Products: 'home portraits' on canvas
panels
Techniques: painting
Size Range: 11" × 14" to customer request
Price Range: $200 to $3,000/piece

ROCHELLE NEWMAN
PYTHAGOREAN PRESS
PO BOX 5162
BRADFORD, MA 01835-0162
TEL 508-372-3129
Established: 1963
Products: tapestries
Techniques: weaving, wrapping,
crocheting
Size Range: 2' × 3' to 8' × 8'
Price Range: $100 to $150/sq. ft.

ANNE MCKENZIE NICKOLSON
5020 N ILLINOIS ST
INDIANAPOLIS, IN 46208-2612
FAX 317-257-8929
TEL 317-257-8929
Established: 1978
Products: fabric constructions
Techniques: embroidery, airbrush,
appliqué
Size Range: 10" × 10" to 14' × 14'
Price Range: $200 to $250/sq. ft.

CYNTHIA NIXON
CYNTHIA NIXON STUDIO
427 S NIXON RD
STATE COLLEGE, PA 16801-2318
TEL 814-238-4811
Established: 1978
Products: art quilts
Techniques: painting, appliqué, quilting
Size Range: 1' × 1' to 10' × 20'
Price Range: $200 to $15,000/piece

ELIZABETH NORDGREN
6 RYAN WAY
DURHAM, NH 03824-2916
TEL 603-868-2873
Established: 1973
Products: fiber installations
Techniques: dyeing, painting, weaving
Size Range: 3" × 5" to 6' × 12'
Price Range: $100 to $5,000/piece

INGE NØRGAARD
907 PIERCE ST
PORT TOWNSEND, WA 98368-8046
TEL 360-385-0637
Established: 1972
Products: tapestries
Techniques: weaving
Size Range: 3" × 3" to 10' × 15'
Price Range: $100 to $50,000/piece

Joan Kopchik, *Sanctuary*, handmade paper, 17"H × 30"W × 7"D

SUSAN M. OAKS

6581 FOX RUN
SAN ANTONIO, TX 78233-4706
TEL 210-656-8440
Established: 1979
Products: framed fiber collage
Techniques: dyeing, painting,
stamping/printing
Size Range: 8" × 10" to 3'6" × 4'6"
Price Range: $200 to $850/piece

SHEILA O'HARA

7101 THORNDALE DR
OAKLAND, CA 94611-1031
TEL 510-339-3014
Established: 1977
Products: tapestries
Techniques: weaving
Size Range: 12" × 20" to 20' × 30'
Price Range: Trade discount
available/piece
Price Range: $250 to $1,000/sq. ft.

IRA ONO

IRA ONO DESIGNS
PO BOX 112
VOLCANO, HI 96785-0112
TEL 808-967-7261
Established: 1968
Products: mixed media installations
paper
Techniques: Japanese-paste paper
Size Range: 8" × 10" to 9' × 14'
Price Range: $140 to $4,000/piece

ELLEN OPPENHEIMER

448 CLIFTON ST
OAKLAND, CA 94618-1163
TEL 510-658-9877
Established: 1970
Products: art quilts
Techniques: dyeing, quilting, printing
Size Range: 34" × 34" to 82" × 82"
Price Range: $100 to $150/sq. ft.

LEAH ORR

LEAH ORR STUDIO
926 N ALABAMA
INDIANAPOLIS, IN 46202-3319
FAX 317-637-9235
TEL 317-637-4532
Established: 1977
Products: wire works: copper, PVC,
telephone
Techniques: weaving, wrapping, knotting
Size Range: 20" × 20" to 20' × 10'
Price Range: $1,000 to $10,000/piece

BARBARA OTTO

8940 15TH ST N
LAKE ELMO, MN 55042
TEL 612-739-3798
Established: 1988
Products: art quilts
Techniques: painting, stamping, printing,
resist, discharge
Size Range: 2' × 3' to 8' × 8'
Price Range: $300 to $2,500/piece

CAROL OWEN

54 FEARRINGTON POST
PITTSBORO, NC 27312-8549
TEL 919-542-0616
Established: 1970
Products: paper
Techniques: laminating, painting,
assemblage
Size Range: 16" × 16" to 4' × 8'
Price Range: $100 to $150/sq. ft.

PAPER PEOPLE

DAVID LECLERC AND
PAMELA HUR
PO BOX 213
CUMMAQUID, MA 02637
TEL 508-362-2414
Established: 1975
Products: paper
Techniques: painting, casting
Size Range: 12" × 18" to 16' × 50'
Price Range: $200 to $20,000/piece

PAPERS OF DISTINCTION BY WENDY

WENDY WHITNEY HARBATH
121 GALENA RD PO BOX 509
FOOTVILLE, WI 53537
TEL 608-876-4139
Products: handmade paper
Techniques: laminating, embossing,
stitching
Size Range: 6" × 6" to 30' × 40'
Price Range: $70 to $1,000/piece

SOYOO HYUNJOO PARK

SOYOO ART STUDIO
193 CLOSTER DOCK RD
CLOSTER, NJ 07624-1907
FAX 201-767-0497
TEL 201-767-8766
Established: 1978
Products: tapestries
Techniques: painting, Gobelin tapestry
weaving
Size Range: 7" × 7" to 10' × 10'
Price Range: $250 to $50,000/piece

★ SHARRON PARKER

ARTSPACE STUDIO 217
201 E DAVIE ST
RALEIGH, NC 27601-1869
TEL 919-828-4533
TEL 919-872-2227
Products: wall hangings
Techniques: felting, stitching
Size Range: 10" × 12" to 5' × 10'
Price Range: $200 to $8,000/piece
**See page 170 for photographs
and additional information.**

DIANN PARROTT

DIANN PARROTT — YARDAGE ART
875 ST CLAIR AVE #4
ST PAUL, MN 55105-3278
FAX 612-222-4149
TEL 612-222-4149
Established: 1984
Products: pieced installations
Techniques: yardage printing, sewing,
hand fringing
Size Range: 3' × 3' to 25' × 25'
Price Range: $150 to $250/sq. ft.

JACQUE PARSLEY

2005 INDIAN CHUTE
LOUISVILLE, KY 40207-1184
TEL 502-893-2092
Established: 1976
Products: fabric constructions
Techniques: appliqué, embroidery,
collage/assemblage
Size Range: 12" × 12" to 4' × 6'
Price Range: $800 to $2,000/piece

PAM PATRIE

PATRIE STUDIO
314 SW 9TH AVE #5
PORTLAND, OR 97205-2803
TEL 503-284-2963
Established: 1974
Products: tapestries
Techniques: weaving, painting,
needlepoint
Size Range: 2' × 5' to 10' × 100'
Price Range: $200 to $500/sq. ft.

EVE S. PEARCE

RR 1 BOX 3880
BENNINGTON, VT 05201-9604
TEL 802-823-5580
Established: 1980
Products: tapestries
Techniques: weaving
Size Range: 2' × 2' to 4' × 8'
Price Range: $200 to $250/sq. ft.

Phyllis Harper Loney, *Solar Fragments*, dye-painted cotton, quilted with glass beads, 38"H × 41"W

FIBER ART FOR THE WALL

KATHRYN ALISON PELLMAN

734 S DETROIT ST #3
LOS ANGELES, CA 90036
TEL 213-936-9692
Established: 1987
Products: art quilts
Techniques: appliqué, quilting
Size Range: 1' x 1' to 12' x 12'
Price Range: $200 to $10,000/piece

★ KAREN PERRINE

512 N K ST
TACOMA, WA 98403-1621
TEL 206-627-0449
Established: 1977
Products: fiber installations
Techniques: dyeing, painting, quilting
Size Range: 8" x 8" to 8' x 16'
Price Range: $100 to $300/sq. ft.

**See page 143 for photographs
and additional information.**

JUDITH H. PERRY

JUDITH H. PERRY DESIGNS
1916 WASHINGTON
WILMETTE, IL 60091
TEL 847-251-9056
Established: 1978
Products: art quilts
Techniques: painting, dyeing, quilting
Size Range: 16" x 20" to 60" x 90"
Price Range: $150 to $7,000/piece

LINDA S. PERRY

ART QUILTS
96 BURLINGTON ST
LEXINGTON, MA 02173-1708
TEL 617-863-1107
Established: 1972
Products: art quilts
Techniques: dyeing, printing, metallic leaf
Size Range: 2' x 3' to 5' x 8'
Price Range: $125/sq. ft.

JEWELL PETERSON

TACTILE IMPRESSIONS
3226 E PATRICIA ST
TUCSON, AZ 85716-4657
TEL 602-324-0327
Established: 1982
Products: fiber installations
Techniques: dyeing, felting, stitching
Size Range: 10" x 15" to 75" x 75"
Price Range: $150 to $7,000/piece
Price Range: $135/sq. ft.

SUE PIERCE

PIERCEWORKS
14414 WOODCREST DR
ROCKVILLE, MD 20853-2335
TEL 301-460-8111
Established: 1978
Products: art quilts
Techniques: appliqué, painting, quilting
Size Range: 15" x 15" to 6' x 12'
Price Range: $200 to $10,000/piece

RAY PIEROTTI

PO BOX 54385
ATLANTA, GA 30308
FAX 404-874-6672
TEL 404-874-6672
Established: 1966
Products: fabric and wood screens
Techniques: painting, dyeing, drawing
Size Range: 12" x 14" to 96" x 144"
Price Range: $300 to $15,000/piece
Price Range: $75 to $250/sq. ft.

PIPSISSEWA

FRANCES PUSCH
HC 68 BOX 46F
CUSHING, ME 04563-9505
TEL 207-354-0148
Established: 1992
Products: pieced-fabric pictures
Techniques: sewing
Size Range: 2.5" x 3.5" (8" x 10" framed)
Price Range: $42/piece

**PLASTIC BUCKET
COMMUNICATIONS/DAES STUDIO**

DAVID A. ELIZONDO
PO BOX 28528
SAN ANTONIO, TX 78228-0528
FAX 210-616-0735
TEL 210-616-0735
Established: 1975
Products: mixed media installations
Techniques: painting, wrapping, tying
Size Range: 1' x 1' to 5' x 3'
Price Range: $100 to $600/piece

JUDITH PLOTNER

JUDITH PLOTNER ART
  QUILTS/L'ATELIER PLOTNER
214 GOAT FARM RD
GLOVERSVILLE, NY 12078-7315
TEL 518-725-3222
TEL 718-548-0581
Established: 1962
Products: art quilts
Techniques: painting, quilting, piecing
Size Range: 15" x 15" to 6' x 7'
Price Range: $400 to $6,000/piece

BEVERLY PLUMMER

2720 WHITE OAK LEFT
BURNSVILLE, NC 28714
TEL 704-675-5208
Established: 1978
Products: paper
Techniques: painting
Size Range: 20" x 22" to 8' x 40'
Price Range: $120 to $800/piece
Price Range: $100 to $150/sq. ft.

JASON POLLEN

4348 LOCUST ST
KANSAS CITY, MO 64110-1531
FAX 816-561-6404
TEL 816-561-6261
Products: fused-silk works
Techniques: painting, dyeing, screen
printing fusing
Size Range: 15" x 20" to 4' x 7'
Price Range: $4,000 to $10,000/piece

DEE FORD POTTER

DEE FORD POTTER ART STUDIO
45 NW GREELEY AVE
BEND, OR 97701-2911
TEL 541-382-4797
Established: 1972
Products: woven sculpture
Techniques: weaving, painting, resin
forming, assemblage
Size Range: 1' x 1' to full wall
Price Range: $100 to $14,000/piece

SUZANNE PRETTY

SUZANNE PRETTY TAPESTRY STUDIO
4 ELM ST
FARMINGTON, NH 03835-1508
TEL 603-755-3964
Established: 1969
Products: tapestries
Techniques: weaving
Size Range: 30" x 30" to 5' x 15'
Price Range: $250 to $450/sq. ft.

NANCY PRICHARD

2604 W CHUBB LAKE AVE
VIRGINIA BEACH, VA 23455-1322
TEL 804-363-9272
Established: 1980
Products: paper
Techniques: collage
Size Range: 16" x 18" to 36" x 36"
Price Range: $275 to $450/piece

Loretta Mossman, *Vestido en Magica*, 1992, wool tapestry with mixed media appliqué, 72" x 47", photo: Robin Miller

GAYLE PRITCHARD

31001 CARLTON DR
BAY VILLAGE, OH 44140-1428
TEL 216-871-1419
Established: 1985
Products: art quilts
Techniques: painting, quilting, collage
Size Range: 24" × 24" to 100" × 80"
Price Range: $150 to $3,500/piece

QUILTS BY DONNA

DONNA SHARP
4214 N PRESTON HWY
SHEPHERDSVILLE, KY 40165-9408
FAX 502-955-6779
TEL 502-955-8673
Established: 1981
Products: art quilts
Techniques: quilting
Size Range: 4' × 4' to 9' × 10'
Price Range: $160 to $4,000/piece
Price Range: $16 to $17/sq. ft.

BILL RAFNEL

THE LOOMINARY
1326 GRANDVIEW RD
VISTA, CA 92084
TEL 619-726-8178
Established: 1985
Products: damask wall hangings
Techniques: weaving
Size Range: 45" × 32" to 8' × 20'
Price Range: $80 to $260/sq. ft.

MARY CURTIS RATCLIFF

630 NEILSON ST
BERKELEY, CA 94707
TEL 510-526-8472
Established: 1972
Products: mixed media installations
Techniques: painting, weaving, knotting
Size Range: 31" × 38" to 45" × 90"
Price Range: $750 to $3,500/piece

COLLINS REDMAN

PO BOX 5287
WOODLAND PARK, CO 80135
TEL 303-647-2250
Established: 1988
Products: tapestries wall or floor
Techniques: weaving, dyeing
Size Range: 20" × 20" to 80" × 60"
Price Range: $75 to $150/sq. ft.

FRAN REED

FREED FIBERS
2424 SPRUCEWOOD ST
ANCHORAGE, AK 99508-3975
FAX 907-279-8195
TEL 907-276-7717
Established: 1975
Products: fiber installations, fish skin
and gut forms
Techniques: airbush, weaving, surface
design
Size Range: 40" × 40" to 5' × 20'
Price Range: $1,000 to $25,000/piece
Price Range: $100 to $1,000/sq. ft.

MYRA REICHEL

121 E SIXTH ST
MEDIA, PA 19063-2503
TEL 610-565-5028
Established: 1973
Products: tapestries
Techniques: weaving, inlaid weaving,
tapestry
Size Range: 6" × 6" to 30' × 40'
Price Range: $50 to $500/sq. ft.

ROBIN REIDER

WEAVINGS BY ROBIN
PO BOX 687
CHIMAYO, NM 87522-0687
TEL 505-351-4474
Established: 1980
Products: tapestries
Techniques: dyeing, weaving
Size Range: 45" × 16" to 75"× 50"
Price Range: $180 to $3,000/piece

PAULA RENEE

RIVERCREST 103 GEDNEY ST #1H
NYACK, NY 10960
TEL 914-358-3059
Established: 1978
Products: tapestries
Techniques: weaving, painting, appliqué
Size Range: 1' × 1' to 14'x 5'
Price Range: $300 to $20,000/piece

SISTER REMY REVOR

MARIAN STUDIO
2900 N MENOMONEE RIVER PKY
MILWAUKEE, WI 53222-4545
TEL 414-258-4810
Products: screen printed panels
Techniques: dyeing, screen printing,
stamping
Size Range: 36" × 24" to 48" × 96"
Price Range: $200 to $400/piece

AMANDA RICHARDSON

RICHARDSON KIRBY
PO BOX 2147
FRIDAY HARBOR, WA 98250-2147
TEL 360-378-4359
Established: 1978
Products: fiber installations
Techniques: dyeing, laminating, Richardson
Tapestry
Size Range: 3' × 4' to unlimited
Price Range: $500/sq. ft.

★ RIVER WEAVING
AND BATIK COMPANY

MARY TYLER
326 W KALAMAZOO AVE #401
KALAMAZOO, MI 49007
TEL 616-345-3120
Established: 1980
Products: fabric constructions
Techniques: painting, dyeing, hot wax
batik
Size Range: 3' × 2' to 8' × 6'
Price Range: $100 to $200/sq. ft.

See photograph on page 194.

NANILEE S. ROBARGE

1260 HAIGHT ST #4
SAN FRANCISCO, CA 94117-3040
TEL 415-241-9182
Established: 1991
Products: weavings
Techniques: dyeing, silkscreen, weaving
Size Range: 12" × 15" to 6' × 6'
Price Range: $100 to $7,000/piece

ROCOCO STUDIO OF FIBER,
COLOR & DESIGN

CAROL ANN MCCOLLUM
18 HORSESHOE RIDGE
BARNARDSVILLE, NC 28709
TEL 704-626-3777
Established: 1993
Products: fiber installations, kimono floats
Techniques: weaving, dyeing, original
designs
Size Range: 10" × 4" to 5' × 5'
Price Range: $145 to $3,000/piece

GRETCHEN ROMEY-TANZER

TANZER'S FIBERWORK
33 MONUMENT RD
ORLEANS, MA 02653-3511
TEL 508-255-9022
Established: 1987
Products: tapestries
Techniques: dyeing, silkscreen, weaving
Size Range: any size
Price Range: $30 to $50/piece

GLORIA F. ROSS

GLORIA F. ROSS TAPESTRIES
21 E 87 ST
NEW YORK, NY 10128-0506
TEL 212-369-3337
Established: 1965
Products: tapestries
Techniques: weaving
Size Range: 5' × 2.5' to 18' × 45'
Price Range: $2,000 to $200,000/piece
Price Range: $55 to $500/sq. ft.

Jean Neblett, *Abstraction XI: Moody Blues*, 1995, layered, scrunched, scrimmed, appliquéd, quilted,
35"H × 44"W, photo: David Belda

BERNIE ROWELL

BERNIE ROWELL STUDIO
1525 BRANSON AVE
KNOXVILLE, TN 37917-3843
TEL 423-523-5244
Established: 1975
Products: fiber installations
Techniques: appliqué, embroidery, painting
Size Range: 30" × 40" to 6' × 24'
Price Range: $80 to $95/sq. ft.

★ ZUZANA RUDAVSKÁ

GOLDEN SPIRAL PRODUCTIONS
254 WYTHE AVE
BROOKLYN, NY 11211
FAX 718-486-6420
TEL 718-486-6520
Established: 1986
Products: mixed media installations fiber wall hangings
Techniques: dyeing, appliqué, laminating, "own techniques"
Size Range: unlimited
Price Range: $2,000 to $20,000/piece

See photograph on page 195.

JUDE RUSSELL

733 NW EVERETT ST #17
PORTLAND, OR 97209-3517
TEL 503-295-0417
Established: 1979
Products: art quilts
Techniques: airbush, appliqué, painting
Size Range: 2' × 3' to 7' × 24'
Price Range: $1,850 to $24,000/piece

KAREN JENSON RUTHERFORD

KAREN JENSON RUTHERFORD STUDIO
513 S 21ST ST
TERRE HAUTE, IN 47803-2531
TEL 812-234-2928
E-Mail:heruthe@ruby.indstate.edu
Established: 1978
Products: fiber installations
Techniques: weaving, painting, paper making
Size Range: 11" × 8" to 5' × 9'
Price Range: $500 to $5,000/piece

ARTURO ALONZO SANDOVAL

HIGH-TECH ART FORMS
PO BOX 237
LEXINGTON, KY 40584-0237
TEL 606-273-8898
Established: 1969
Products: fabric constructions
Techniques: weaving, machine stitching, interlacing collage
Size Range: 8" × 8" to 30' × 40'
Price Range: $250 to $75,000/piece
Price Range: $150 to $500/sq. ft.

STEPHANIE SANTMYERS

QUILT ART
7 PIPERS GLEN CT
GREENSBORO, NC 27406-5500
TEL 910-852-6439
Established: 1985
Products: art quilts
Techniques: quilting watercolor quilts
Size Range: 36" × 36" to 72" × 72"
Price Range: $225 to $2,200/piece

JOY SAVILLE

244 DODDS LN
PRINCETON, NJ 08540-4108
TEL 609-924-6824
Established: 1976
Products: fabric constructions
Techniques: piecing
Size Range: 28" × 28" to unlimited
Price Range: $2,000 to $30,000/piece

★ SUSAN SAWYER

RR 1 BOX 107
EAST CALAIS, VT 05650-9506
TEL 802-456-8836
Established: 1971
Products: art quilts
Techniques: piecing quilting appliqué
Size Range: 8" × 8" to 84" × 84"
Price Range: $100 to $7,000/piece
Price Range: $125 to $150/sq. ft.

See photograph on page 196.

TOMMYE MCCLURE SCANLIN

403 S PARK ST
DAHLONEGA, GA 30533
TEL 706-864-7288
Established: 1972
Products: tapestries
Techniques: weaving
Size Range: 3" × 3" to 90" × 60"
Price Range: $200 to $400/sq. ft.

DEIDRE SCHERER

PO BOX 156
WILLIAMSVILLE, VT 05362-0156
FAX 802-348-7136
TEL 802-348-7807
Established: 1970
Products: fabric constructions
Techniques: appliqué, machine-stitching, piecing, layering
Size Range: 8" × 6" to 6' × 15'
Price Range: $500 to $25,000/piece

JULIA SCHLOSS

HANDWOVEN ORIGINALS
RR 1 BOX 5053
BAR HARBOR, ME 04609-9748
TEL 207-288-9882
Established: 1976
Products: tapestries
Techniques: weaving
Size Range: 36" × 55" to 56" × 120"
Price Range: $1,000 to $10,000/piece
Price Range: $100 to $150/sq. ft.

JOAN SCHULZE

808 PIPER AVE
SUNNYVALE, CA 94087-1245
FAX 408-736-7833
TEL 408-736-7833
Established: 1970
Products: art quilts
Techniques: laminating, painting, quilting
Size Range: 16" × 20" to 10' × 20'
Price Range: $800 to $30,000/piece

LAURA SCOONOVER

2640 SANDERS DR
SAINT LOUIS, MO 63129-4241
TEL 314-846-0048
Established: 1993
Products: mixed media installations
Techniques: weaving, felting, casting
Size Range: 4" × 6" to 73" × 28"
Price Range: $20 to $350/piece

LIBBY SEABERG

667 10TH ST
BROOKLYN, NY 11215-4501
FAX 718-768-7280
TEL 718-768-7280
TEL 212-431-5321
Established: 1968
Products: mixed media installations
Techniques: painting, laminating, drawing
Size Range: 12" × 13.5" to 90" × 200"
Price Range: $300 to $3,000/piece

AMANDA SEARS

PO BOX 244
SANTA CRUZ, CA 95061-0244
TEL 408-457-1630
Established: 1983
Products: raffia rugs
Techniques: dyeing, tufting
Size Range: 2' × 3' to 9' × 12'
Price Range: $85 to $100/sq. ft.

River Weaving and Batik Company, *Night River I*, 1993, hot-wax batik, 40"W × 48"H, photo: Zolton Cohen

WARREN SEELIG
SHERRIE GIBSON

328 MAIN ST STUDIO 300
ROCKLAND, ME 04841
FAX 207-594-0138
TEL 207-594-0138
Established: 1976
Products: fabric constructions, mixed media installations
Techniques: assemblage
Size Range: 16" × 24" to 14' × 32'
Price Range: $1,200 to $6,000/piece

★ SALLY A. SELLERS

**3919 WAUNA VISTA DR
VANCOUVER, WA 98661-6031
TEL 360-693-4160**
Established: 1989
Products: art quilts
Techniques: appliqué, painting, quilting
Size Range: 2' × 2' to 6' × 6'
Price Range: $450 to $4,000/piece
See photograph on page 197.

SYBIL SHANE

PO BOX 478
NEVADA CITY, CA 95959
FAX 916-265-9086
TEL 916-265-9086
Established: 1994
Products: paper
Techniques: painting, wrapping, 3D construction
Size Range: 7" × 5" to 3.5' × 2.5'
Price Range: $100 to $1,500/piece

VERLA SHANER

4036 N 116TH CIR
OMAHA, NE 68164
TEL 402-492-9366
Established: 1990
Products: art quilts
Techniques: dyeing, screen printing piecing
Size Range: 12" × 12" to 8' × 8'
Price Range: $400 to $1,200/piece

DONNA SHARP

4214 N PRESTON HWY
SHEPHERDSVILLE, KY 40165
Products: quilted wall hangings
Techniques: appliqué, quilting patchwork
Size Range: 20" × 20" to 10' × 10'
Price Range: $60 to $3,000/piece

KATHLEEN SHARP

17360 VALLEY OAK DR
MONTE SERENO, CA 95030-2217
TEL 408-395-3014
Established: 1978
Products: art quilts
Techniques: appliqué, quilting, piecing
Size Range: 14" × 14" to 75" × 100"
Price Range: $300 to $9,000/piece

BARBARA SHAWCROFT

4 ANCHOR DR #243
EMERYVILLE, CA 94608-1564
FAX 510-658-8264
TEL 510-658-6694
Products: mixed media installations, 3D-sculptural wall installations
Techniques: hand constructed, 3D
Size Range: 2" × 2" to 50' × 20'
Price Range: $1,500 to $50,000/piece

SUSAN SHIE
JAMES ACORD

TURTLE MOON STUDIOS
2612 ARMSTRONG DR
WOOSTER, OH 44691-1806
TEL 216-345-5778
Established: 1977
Products: art quilts
Techniques: appliqué, embroidery, painting, airbrush, beading, leather, clay
Size Range: 6" × 8" to 100" × 100"
Price Range: $200 to $25,000/piece

SALLY SHORE

SALLY SHORE/WEAVER
LUDLAM LANE
LOCUST VALLEY, NY 11560
TEL 516-671-7276
Established: 1971
Products: fiber installations
Techniques: weaving
Size Range: 9" × 9" to 7' × 15'
Price Range: $150 to $10,000/piece

Zuzana Rudavská, *Red Fields*, fiber wall hanging, 101" × 68"

DIANE SHULLENBERGER
RR1 BOX 259
JERICHO, VT 05465
TEL 802-899-4993
Established: 1978
Products: fabric constructions
Techniques: layering, stitching
Size Range: 21" × 23" to 32" × 36"
Price Range: $1,000 to $2,000/piece

ANE SHUSTA
PO BOX 18
SNOQUALMIE PASS, WA 98068-0018
TEL 206-434-6115
Established: 1983
Products: tapestries
Techniques: weaving
Size Range: 3' × 5' to 5' × 8'
Price Range: $1,000 to $10,000/piece

LAURA LAZAR SIEGEL
10 CROSSWAY
SCARSDALE, NY 10583-7118
FAX 212-808-0406
TEL 914-723-9392
Established: 1960
Products: fiber installations
Techniques: painting, dyeing
Size Range: 22" × 28" to 5' × 7'
Price Range: $800 to $2,500/piece

ELANA SIEGAL
1825 W 14TH AVE
VANCOUVER, BC V6J 2J3
CANADA
TEL 604-736-2774
Established: 1990
Products: fiber installations
Techniques: felting
Size Range: 10" × 8" to 8' × 6'
Price Range: $150 to $5,000/piece

LOUISE SILK
CITY QUILT
210 CONOVER RD
PITTSBURGH, PA 15208-2604
TEL 412-361-1158
Established: 1978
Products: art quilts
Techniques: appliqué, quilting, stamping/printing
Size Range: 8" × 8" to 18' × 18'
Price Range: $50 to $5,500/piece

ELLY SIMMONS
ELLY SIMMONS FINE ART
BOX 463-36 SPRING AVE
LAGUNITAS, CA 94938
TEL 415-488-4177
Established: 1981
Products: tapestries
Techniques: weaving
Size Range: 18" × 27" to 80" × 60"
Price Range: $850 to $5,000/sq. ft.

MARY JO SINCLAIR
SINCLAIR STUDIO
10 MILTON ST
SAINT AUGUSTINE, FL 32095-2114
FAX 904-824-1441
TEL 904-824-1441
Established: 1978
Products: mixed media installations
Techniques: weaving, painting, laminating
Size Range: 3' × 4' to unlimited
Price Range: $2,000 to $25,000/piece

★ SUSAN SINGLETON
AZO INC.
1101 E PIKE ST
SEATTLE, WA 98122-3915
FAX 206-322-5062
TEL 206-322-0390
Established: 1971
Products: paper
Techniques: painting, dyeing, gold leafing
Size Range: 15 × 15" to 12' × 12'
Price Range: $100 to $150/sq. ft.
See page 146 for photographs and additional information.

DELDA SKINNER
8111 DOE MEADOW DR
AUSTIN, TX 78749
TEL 512-288-1116
Established: 1979
Products: mixed media paper
Techniques: painting, stamping, handmade paper
Size Range: 12" × 12" to 48" × 72"
Price Range: $300 to $2,000/piece

LOUISE SLOBODAN
COASTAL TEXTURES STUDIO
135 HOLLAND RD
NANAIMO, BC V9R 6V9
CANADA
TEL 604-753-7359
Established: 1980
Products: art quilts
Techniques: quilting, screen printing, laser printing, photo screen
Size Range: 2' × 2' to 8' × 7'
Price Range: $50 to $100/sq. ft.

MARY E. SLY
SAN JUAN SILK
PO BOX 1925
FRIDAY HARBOR, WA 98250-1925
TEL 206-378-7110
Established: 1980
Products: silk, floral wall hangings
Techniques: resist, hand painted with dyes
Size Range: 15" × 65" to 60" × 60"
Price Range: $95 to $2,500/piece

C. ELIZABETH SMATHERS
3002 SIMMONS AVE
NASHVILLE, TN 37211-2425
TEL 615-331-4619
Established: 1985
Products: tapestries
Techniques: weaving
Size Range: 18" × 18" to unlimited
Price Range: $100 to $225/sq. ft.

ELLY SMITH
PO BOX 523
MEDINA, WA 98039-0523
TEL 206-720-1247
Established: 1974
Products: framed stitcheries, family samplers
Techniques: embroidery
Size Range: 9" × 8" to 74" × 74"
Price Range: $250 to $300/sq. ft.

★ GLORIA ZMOLEK SMITH
ZPAPERSMITH
PO BOX 1294
CEDAR RAPIDS, IA 52406-1294
FAX 319-365-9611
TEL 319-365-9611
Established: 1983
Products: handmade paper quilts
Techniques: embroidery, wrapping, origami
Size Range: unlimited
Price Range: $100 to $200/sq. ft.
See page 149 for photographs and additional information.

PATTY CARMODY SMITH
4309 TONKAWOOD RD
MINNETONKA, MN 55345
TEL 612-933-7230
Established: 1995
Products: hand-hooked fiber art
Techniques: hand hooking
Size Range: 26" × 24" to 72" × 96"
Price Range: $80 to $110/sq. ft.

KAREN N. SOMA
1134 N 81ST ST
SEATTLE, WA 98103
TEL 206-522-8541
Established: 1975
Products: art quilts
Techniques: dyeing, quilting, screen printing
Size Range: 24" × 24" to 60" × 72"
Price Range: $800 to $2,000/piece

LYN SOUTHWORTH
821 14TH ST #4
SANTA MONICA, CA 90403
FAX 310-395-2537
TEL 310-395-2537
Established: 1985
Products: mixed media installations
Techniques: painting, dyeing
Size Range: 12" × 12" to 60" × 48"
Price Range: $200 to $4,000/piece

HOLLY M. SOWLES
HOLLY SOWLES FINE ARTS
1230 MANITOU
BOISE, ID 83706
TEL 208-345-9458
Established: 1991
Products: mixed media installations, paper
Techniques: painting, dyeing, wrapping, stamping
Size Range: 17" × 12" to 60" × 48"
Price Range: $8 to $2,000/piece

Susan Sawyer, *August Offering* (detail), pieced and hand-quilted cotton, this view: 32"H × 21"W, photo: Ken Burris

KATHY SPOERING

KATHY SPOERING, TAPESTRIES
2306 DOGWOOD CT
GRAND JUNCTION, CO 81506-8473
TEL 970-242-9081

Established: 1989
Products: tapestries
Techniques: weaving
Size Range: 18" x 18" to 48" x 48"
Price Range: $1,100 to $6,000/piece

SPRINGFLOWER

PO BOX 54
GAYS MILLS, WI 54631-0054
TEL 608-735-4941

Established: 1986
Products: belts to hang on wall
Techniques: embroidery, weaving
Size Range: 4" x 1" to 6' x 2"
Price Range: $10 to $30/piece

KAREN STAHLECKER

PO BOX 201566
ANCHORAGE, AK 99520-1566
TEL 907-566-0039

Established: 1976
Products: paper
Techniques: handmade papers
Size Range: 12" x 12" to 8' x 8'
Price Range: $300 to $8,000/piece

CARE STANDLEY

1040 TALBOT AVE
ALBANY, CA 94706-2332
TEL 510-525-8609

Established: 1982
Products: tapestries
Techniques: weaving
Size Range: 1' x 1' to 4' x 6'
Price Range: $650 to $10,000/piece

HILLARY STEEL

HILLARY L. STEEL — HANDWEAVER
1502 SHARON DR
SILVER SPRING, MD 20901
TEL 301-587-8373

Established: 1981
Products: resist dyed, woven wall pieces
Techniques: weaving, dyeing, resist dyeing
Size Range: 14" x 14" to 10' x 10'
Price Range: $250 to $15,000/piece

ELINOR STEELE

61 WEYBRIDGE ST
MIDDLEBURY, VT 05753-1024
TEL 802-388-6546

Established: 1974
Products: tapestries
Techniques: weaving
Size Range: 2' x 3' to 8' x 12'
Price Range: $200 to $400/sq. ft.

LEORA KLAYMER STEWART

LLAMA STUDIOS
203 PARK PL #2F
BROOKLYN, NY 11238-4375
TEL 718-783-0379

Established: 1970
Products: textile restoration
Techniques: weaving, embroidery, wrapping
Size Range: 6" x 6" to 20' x 24'
Price Range: $100 to $2,000/piece
Price Range: $50 to $100/sq. ft.

JOY STOCKSDALE

2145 OREGON ST
BERKELEY, CA 94705-1004
FAX 707-829-3285
TEL 510-841-2008

Established: 1981
Products: fiber installations
Techniques: painting, quilting, silkscreen
Size Range: 3' x 4' to 8' x 10'
Price Range: $250 to $1,000/piece

GLENNE STOLL

900 S GENEVA
AURORA, CO 80231
FAX 303-355-2401
TEL 303-364-3927

Established: 1970
Products: art quilts
Techniques: quilting, piecing
Size Range: 2' x 2' to 12' x 12'
Price Range: $200 to $10,000/piece
Price Range: $50 to $150/sq. ft.

Sally A. Sellers, *The Greenhouse Effect*, 1994, appliqué on canvas, 69" x 46¹/₂", photo: Bill Bachhuber

NANCY TAYLOR STONINGTON

22735 CAREY RD SW
VASHON, WA 98070-6809
FAX 206-463-6598
TEL 206-463-2860
Established: 1970
Products: fiber installations
Techniques: construction
Size Range: 4' × 9' to 20' × 20'
Price Range: $10,000 to $60,000/piece

SUSAN STOVER

1080 23RD AVE #301
OAKLAND, CA 94606
TEL 510-533-8404
Established: 1991
Products: mixed media installations
Techniques: weaving, painting, mixed media
Size Range: 12" × 12" to 96" × 60"
Price Range: $500 to $7,500/piece
Price Range: $100 to $500/sq. ft.

★ MEREDITH STRAUSS

2621 KENNINGTON DR
GLENDALE, CA 91206-1826
TEL 818-246-2600
Established: 1983
Products: cotton cord
Techniques: dyeing, painting, interlacing
Size Range: 2' × 2' to unlimited
Price Range: $1,000 to $50,000/piece
Price Range: $150 to $180/sq. ft.

See photograph on page 199.

JOAN STUBBINS

2616 S MAHONING AVE
ALLIANCE, OH 44601-8212
TEL 216-823-7328
Established: 1988
Products: tapestries
Techniques: dyeing, embroidery, weaving
Size Range: 20" × 30" × 40" × 55"
Price Range: $100/sq. ft.

JANICE M. SULLIVAN

4166A 20TH ST
SAN FRANCISCO, CA 94114-2850
TEL 415-431-6835
Established: 1984
Products: fabric constructions
Techniques: weaving, painting, airbrush
Size Range: 20" × 20" to 96" × 108"
Price Range: $200 to $300/sq. ft.

LYNNE SWARD

625 BISHOP DR
VIRGINIA BEACH, VA 23455-6543
TEL 804-497-7917
Established: 1974
Products: art quilts
Techniques: appliqué, beading, embellishment
Size Range: 8" × 8" to 36" × 80"
Price Range: $200 to $4,000/piece

SUZANNE TAHENY

SUZANNE TAHENY SILKS
30932 SHERWOOD RD
FORT BRAGG, CA 95437
TEL 707-964-0054
Established: 1985
Products: art quilts
Techniques: painting, dyeing, quilting
Size Range: 30" × 26" to 45" × 64"
Price Range: $450 to $1,400/piece

TERRY TAUBE

73-1100 ALIHILANI DR
KAILUA-KONA, HI 96740
TEL 808-325-5496
Established: 1985
Products: paper
Techniques: casting, dyeing, weaving
Size Range: all sizes
Price Range: $100 to $200/sq. ft.

★ CAMERON TAYLOR-BROWN

418 S MANSFIELD AVE
LOS ANGELES, CA 90036-3516
FAX 213-938-0088
TEL 213-938-0088
Established: 1982
Products: mixed media installations
Techniques: weaving, embroidery, painting
Size Range: 24" × 24" and up
Price Range: $100 to $175/sq. ft.

See photograph on page 200.

RENA THOMPSON

705 ALMSHOUSE RD
CHALFONT, PA 18914-3803
TEL 215-345-8185
Established: 1980
Products: tapestries
Techniques: weaving, double-weave pickup
Size Range: 50" × 50" to 50" × 100"
Price Range: $1,500 to $3,800/piece
Price Range: $85 to $140/sq. ft.

LYNN THOR

CONTEMPORARY FIBER DESIGNS
PO BOX 70 632 TUNNEL RD
TUNNEL, NY 13848-0070
TEL 607-693-1572
Established: 1975
Products: fiber installations
Techniques: weaving, inlay, painted warp
Size Range: 12" × 14" to 30" × 45"
Price Range: $125 to $850/piece

DANIELE TODARO

TODARO & ASSOCIATES
4920 W 63RD ST
LOS ANGELES, CA 90056
FAX 213-299-9394
TEL 213-299-9393
Established: 1974
Products: textile collage
Techniques: appliqué, quilting, stamping, printing, collage
Size Range: 1' × 1' to 6' × 9'
Price Range: $100 to $150/sq. ft.

CAROLYN & VINCENT TOLPO

PO BOX 134
SHAWNEE, CO 80475-0134
TEL 303-670-1733
Established: 1979
Products: fiber installations
Techniques: painting, wrapping
Size Range: 30" × 36" to 10' × 30'
Price Range: $600 to $12,000/piece

RAYMOND D. TOMASSO

INTER-OCEAN CURIOSITY STUDIO
2998 S BANNOCK ST
ENGLEWOOD, CO 80110-1519
TEL 303-789-0282
Established: 1978
Products: paper
Techniques: airbush, casting, painting
Size Range: 9" × 11" to 8' × 8'
Price Range: $500 to $10,000/piece
Price Range: $160 to $300/sq. ft.

MARJORIE TOMCHUK

44 HORTON LN
NEW CANAAN, CT 06840-6824
FAX 203-972-3182
TEL 203-972-0137
Established: 1965
Products: paper
Techniques: airbush, casting, painting, embossings
Size Range: 10" × 13" to 4' × 6'
Price Range: $175 to $3,000/piece

PAMELA TOPHAM

LANDSCAPE TAPESTRIES
PO BOX 1057
WAINSCOTT, NY 11975-1057
TEL 516-537-2871
Established: 1976
Products: tapestries, landscape tapestries
Techniques: weaving
Size Range: 12" × 14" to 9' × 18' and up
Price Range: $1,200 and up/piece
Price Range: $450/sq. ft.

JUDITH TOMLINSON TRAGER

TRAGER STUDIO QUILTS
2132 KINCAID PL
BOULDER, CO 80304-1900
FAX 303-492-0969
TEL 303-443-5976
Established: 1973
Products: art quilts
Techniques: embroidery appliqué quilting
Size Range: 20" × 30" to 96" × 96"
Price Range: $800 to $3,000/piece

ANNE TRIGUBA

HOUSE OF TRIBUGA, INC.
1463 RAINBOW DR NE
LANCASTER, OH 43130
TEL 614-687-1338
Established: 1986
Products: art quilts
Techniques: painting, appliqué, quilting
Size Range: 24" × 20" to 70" × 70"
Price Range: $800 to $5,000/piece

MICHELE TUEGEL

MICHELE TUEGEL PAPERWORKS
433 MONTE CRISTO BLVD
TIERRA VERDE, FL 33715-1840
TEL 813-821-7391
Established: 1977
Products: paper
Techniques: casting, laminating
Size Range: 8" × 10" to 40" × 60"
Price Range: $75 to $1,500/piece

TUMBLEWEED FABRIC & DESIGNS

ANNE WINTON
260 NORTHWOOD WAY #3
PO BOX 777
KETCHUM, ID 83340
FAX 208-788-9098
TEL 208-726-2580
Established: 1991
Products: baby quilts
Techniques: painting, quilting
Size Range: 16" × 16" to 76" × 82"
Price Range: $50 to $550/piece

JUDITH UEHLING

152 WOOSTER ST
NEW YORK, NY 10012-5331
FAX 212-254-2075
TEL 212-254-2075
Established: 1970
Products: paper
Techniques: painting, casting, bronze
Size Range: 23" × 28" to 8'4" × 44"
Price Range: $750 to $5,000/piece

CONNIE UTTERBACK

3641 MIDVALE AVE #204
LOS ANGELES, CA 90034-6600
TEL 310-841-6675
Established: 1981
Products: fabric constructions
Techniques: construction technique
Size Range: 2' × 3' to 7' × 12'
Price Range: $700 to $9,500/piece

FRANCES VALESCO

135 JERSEY ST
SAN FRANCISCO, CA 94114
TEL 415-648-3814
Established: 1969
Products: mixed media installations
Techniques: dyeing, painting, printing
Size Range: 11" × 14" to mural size
Price Range: $150 to $10,000/piece

LYDIA VAN GELDER

FIBER ARTS
758 SUCHER LN
SANTA ROSA, CA 95401-3623
TEL 707-546-4139
Established: 1950
Products: fiber installations
Techniques: weaving, dyeing, ikat
Size Range: 12" × 12" to 5' × 9'
Price Range: $1,000 to $2,000/piece

VANGRODWORKS/ART BY DESIGN

JOHN AND PHYLLIS VAN GROD
8420 ULMERTON RD #477
LARGO, FL 34641-3882
FAX 813-530-0864
TEL 813-530-0864
Established: 1970
Products: art quilts
Techniques: dyeing, embroidery, quilting
Size Range: 30" x 15" to 5' x 3'
Price Range: $300 to $2,100/piece

ALICE VAN LEUNEN

PO BOX 408
LAKE OSWEGO, OR 97034-0408
FAX 503-636-0787
TEL 503-636-0787
Established: 1968
Products: mixed media installations
Techniques: painting, weaving, metallic
foil work
Size Range: 24" x 30" to 10' x 12'
Price Range: $500 to $30,000/piece

★ SUSAN VENABLE

VENABLE STUDIO
214 S VENICE BLVD
VENICE, CA 90291-4537
FAX 310-822-0050
TEL 310-827-7233
Established: 1975
Products: mixed media installations
Techniques: painting, copper wire
constructions
Size Range: 24" to 48" minimum, no
upper limit
Price Range: $2,000 to $75,000/piece

**See page 102 for photographs
and additional information.**

BETTY VERA

41 UNION SQUARE W #521
NEW YORK, NY 10003-3208
TEL 212-924-2478
Products: tapestries
Techniques: weaving, warp painting,
embroidery
Size Range: 1' x 1' to 8' x 10'
Price Range: $500 to $30,000/piece

PAULINE VERBEEK-COWART

3924 STETSON DR
LAWRENCE, KS 66049-4160
TEL 913-865-5805
Established: 1992
Products: tapestries
Techniques: weaving, dyeing, screen
printing
Size Range: 30" x 40" to 8' x 12'
Price Range: $125 to $175/sq. ft.

MEINY VERMAAS-VAN DER HEIDE

MEINY VERMAAS-VAN DER HEIDE
  STUDIO ART QUILTS
1219 E LA JOLLA DR
TEMPE, AZ 85282-5513
TEL 602-838-5262
Established: 1989
Products: art quilts
Techniques: quilting, patchwork
Size Range: 24" x 24" to 6' x 9'
Price Range: $500 to $6,000/piece
Price Range: $90 to &125/sq. ft.

JUDITH VEROSTKA-PETREE

JUDITH VEROSTKA-PETREE,
  TAPESTRIES
2903 PARKWOOD AVE
RICHMOND, VA 23221
TEL 804-358-7659
Established: 1987
Products: tapestries
Techniques: weaving
Size Range: 1' x 2' to 4' x 8'
Price Range: $50 to $200/sq. ft.

JUDITH VIEROW

803 GILBERT ST
COLUMBUS, OH 43206-1518
TEL 614-444-4568
Established: 1974
Products: art quilts
Techniques: appliqué, painting, quilting,
piecing, stitching
Size Range: 16" x 20" to 96" x 96"
Price Range: $500 to $10,000/piece

BETSY WADSWORTH-MANDELL

7405 E KERR CREEK RD
BLOOMINGTON, IN 47408
TEL 812-334-0567
Established: 1985
Products: art quilts
Techniques: dyeing, stamping, beading
Size Range: 24" x 36" to 60" x 48"
Price Range: $500 to $5,000/piece

BARBARA ALLEN WAGNER

THE CROW'S NEST
7 SKYLINE PL
ASTORIA, OR, 97103-6439
TEL 503-325-5548
Established: 1955
Products: tapestries
Techniques: embroidery, weaving,
needlepoint
Size Range: 1'6" x 3' to 5' x 8'
Price Range: $200 to $400/sq. ft.

DAVID WALKER

2905 PROBASCO CT
CINCINNATI, OH 45220-2712
TEL 513-961-9065
Established: 1987
Products: art quilts
Techniques: appliqué, quilting,
embellishment
Size Range: 12" x 12" to 8' x 8'
Price Range: $300 to $5,000/piece

ALISON WAMPLER

CONTEMPORARY
  HANDHOOKED RUGS
RT 1 BOX 1850 MORGAN BAY RD
SURRY, ME 04684
TEL 207-667-6031
Established: 1992
Products: tapetas (wall rugs)
Techniques: hooked fabrics
Size Range: 24" x 24" to 56" x 10'
Price Range: $100 to $200/sq. ft.

LAURA WASILOWSKI

324 VINCENT PL
ELGIN, IL 60123
TEL 708-931-7684
Established: 1986
Products: art quilts
Techniques: dyeing, quilting,
stamping or printing
Size Range: 1' x 1' to 5' x 6'
Price Range: $100 to $200/sq. ft.

MONA WATERHOUSE

102 DELBANK PT
PEACHTREE CITY, GA 30269-1184
TEL 770-487-2881
Established: 1978
Products: mixed media installations
Techniques: painting, printing, paper and
encaustic
Size Range: 37" x 37" to 6' x 10'
Price Range: $1,200 to $2,700/piece

WEAVING/SOUTHWEST

RACHEL BROWN
216 B PUEBLO NORTE
TAOS, NM 87571
TEL 505-758-0433
Established: 1962
Products: tapestries
Techniques: weaving
Size Range: 24" x 24" to 96" x 60"
Price Range: $21 to $300/sq. ft.

HELEN WEBBER

HELEN WEBBER DESIGNS
555 PACIFIC AVE
SAN FRANCISCO, CA 94133-4609
FAX 415-989-5746
TEL 415-989-5521
Established: 1973
Products: tapestries
Techniques: painting, casting, collage
Size Range: 3' x 4' to 10' x 65'
Price Range: $150 to $300/sq. ft.

LEANNE WEISSLER

28 LINCOLN CIR
CRESTWOOD, NY 10707
TEL 914-337-6952
Established: 1975
Products: mixed media installations
Techniques: painting, airbrush, drawing
Size Range: 12" x 12" to 40" x 50"
Price Range: $150 to $1,500/piece

Meredith Strauss, *Shaft Switch*, 1994, cotton cord and wire mesh, 4'H x 8'W x 3"D

JOAN WEISSMAN

JOAN WEISSMAN CUSTOM RUGS
AND TAPESTRIES
3710 SILVER SE
ALBUQUERQUE, NM 87108
FAX 505-268-9665
TEL 505-265-0144
Established: 1071
Products: tapestries
Techniques: weaving hand-tufted wool
Size Range: 4' x 4' to 30' x any length
Price Range: $65 to $95/sq. ft.

CAROL D. WESTFALL

162 WHITFORD AVE
NUTLEY, NJ 07110
FAX 201-235-0218
TEL 201-235-0813
Established: 1972
Products: fiber art
Techniques: weaving, quilting,
computer collage
Size Range: 2" x 2" to 3' x 2'
Price Range: $350 to $3,000/piece

JUDI MAUREEN WHITE

RENAISSANCE FIBRES
2062 E MALIBU DR
TEMPE, AZ 85282-5966
TEL 602-320-7557
TEL 602-838-0416
Established: 1970
Products: mixed media installations
Techniques: painting, weaving, sculpting
Size Range: 12" x 24" to 96" x 240"
Price Range: $200 to $500/sq. ft.

NANCY WHITTINGTON

105 WATTERS RD
CARRBORO, NC 27510
FAX 919-933-0631
TEL 919-933-0624
Established: 1975
Products: art quilts
Techniques: appliqué, dyeing, painting
Size Range: 32" x 22" to 56" x 60"
Price Range: $150/sq. ft.

ELIZABETH WILEY

EW WEAVES
1481 BUCKHORN RD PO BOX 1181
WILLITS, CA 95490-1181
TEL 707-459-9293
Established: 1982
Products: woven wall pieces
Techniques: weaving, dyeing, embroidery
Size Range: 18" x 18" to 108" x 108"
Price Range: $20 to $200/sq. ft.

JODY WILLIAMS

FLYING PAPER
3953 16TH AVE S
MINNEAPOLIS, MN 55407-2828
TEL 612-721-2891
Established: 1982
Products: handmade paper
Techniques: casting, stamping/printing,
collage
Size Range: 6" x 8" to 36" x 60"
Price Range: $250 to $3,000/piece

JEANNE WILLIAMSON

18 ERLANDSON RD
NATICK, MA 01760-2333
FAX 508-651-1696
TEL 508-655-4560
Established: 1985
Products: art quilts
Techniques: appliqué, quilting, stamping
Size Range: 24" x 24" to 45" x 45"
Price Range: $80/sq. ft.

JAY WILSON

WILSON & YAMADA ART STUDIO
3155 NAHENAHE PL
KIHEI, HI 96753-9314
TEL 808-874-3597
Established: 1976
Products: tapestries
Techniques: dyeing, weaving
Size Range: 6' x 4' to 8' x 12'
Price Range: $15,000 to $75,000/piece

NANCY WINES-DEWAN

CONTEMPORARY MAINE TEXTILES
PO BOX 861
YARMOUTH, ME 04096-0861
TEL 207-846-6058
Established: 1970
Products: tapestries
Techniques: weaving
Size Range: 10" x 10" to 120" x 144"
Price Range: $200 to $250/sq. ft.

YARDSTICKS

ROSEMARIE HOHOL AND
ROGER HAUGE
1129 MAPLE AVE
EVANSTON, IL 60202
TEL 847-864-8131
Established: 1992
Products: woven twig frame baskets
Techniques: weaving, dyeing, beading
Size Range: 5" x 7" to 40" x 40"
Price Range: $70 to $500/piece

★ ELLEN ZAHOREC

ISLAND FORD STUDIO
396 AMAZON AVE
CINCINNATI, OH 45220-1139
TEL 513-861-7419
Products: mixed media, collaged
wall pieces
Techniques: painting
Size Range: 8" x 10" to unlimited
Price Range: $100 to $5,000/piece
Price Range: $100/sq. ft.

**See page 151 for photographs
and additional information.**

MAUREEN ZALE

PO BOX 117
UNION LAKE, MI 48387-0117
TEL 810-698-1748
Established: 1993
Products: mixed media installations
Techniques: painting, wrapping, fabric
manipulation
Size Range: 20" x 16" to 40" x 60"
Price Range: $175 to $1,000/piece

MARY ZICAFOOSE

4371 SW TERWILLIGER BLVD
PORTLAND, OR 97201-2874
TEL 503-241-0202
Established: 1979
Products: tapestries
Techniques: dyeing, weaving,
weft-faced ikat
Size Range: 2' x 2' to 20' x 15'
Price Range: $85 to $300/sq. ft.

BHAKTI ZIEK

5225 GREENE ST
PHILADELPHIA, PA 19144-2927
TEL 215-844-4402
Established: 1980
Products: tapestries
Techniques: dyeing, painting, weaving
Size Range: 4" x 8" to 9' x 20'
Price Range: $100 to $300/sq. ft.

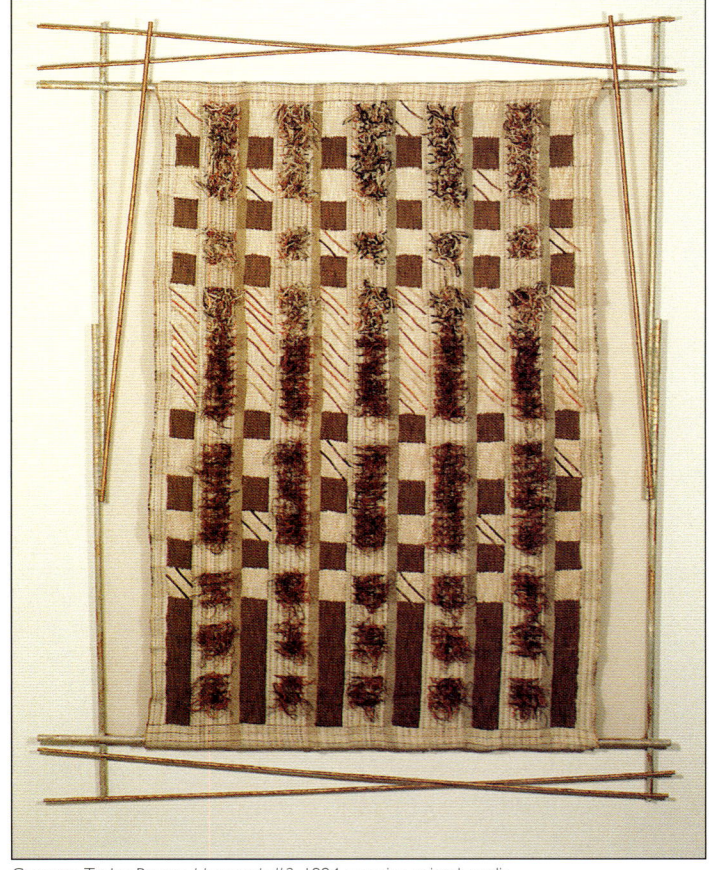

Cameron Taylor-Brown, *Hopscotch #2*, 1994, weaving, mixed media

COMMISSIONED ARTWORK IN THE MID-1990s

A Survey of GUILD Users

THE GUILD's second in-depth survey on the commissioning process sheds new light on the people, steps and goals involved in commissioned artwork. One hundred and sixty-one surveys were distributed to design professionals who actively commission artwork through THE GUILD. A response rate of 32 percent included twenty-four interior designers, fifteen architects, eight art consultants, three developers and two art brokers.

Survey questions focused on two areas. Part one involved specific projects generated through use of GUILD sourcebooks; part two asked about characteristics of the respondent's firm, including its overall history of commissioning artwork and the various ways it uses THE GUILD. Responses to both sections are summarized on the following pages. In addition, descriptions of GUILD-generated projects can be found throughout this book in a series of interviews with survey respondents.

For us, it was particularly heartening to read —over and over again—about successful collaborations between design professionals and GUILD artists. Almost without exception, respondents reported both a positive working relationship and an exceptional aesthetic outcome. "The artist was extremely responsive and intuitive as to the needs of the client and the space," said one respondent. "A wonderful team experience," wrote another.

A grateful thanks to all who participated in the survey.

The first part of the survey focused on commissions involving GUILD artists. Respondents described over 66 distinct projects.

SURVEY RESULTS

What were the goals of including artwork in the project?

Create a more beautiful environment	52%
Enhance company image	27%
Public relations	5%
Increase property value	5%
Enhance employee morale	5%
Build client's art collection	5%
Reach a broader audience	1%

Who initiated including artwork in the project?

Interior designer	55%
Architect	21%
Art consultant	18%
Developer	3%
Client	3%

What were the most important factors in selecting the artist?

Quality of the artist's portfolio	43%
Artist's track record with similar jobs	16%
Strength of proposal for this project	13%
Personal chemistry with the artist	11%
Artist's prominence	10%
Artist's unique style	4%
Low cost of proposal	2%
Artist's location	1%

Overall, was this project a positive experience for you and your client?

Yes	97%
No	3%

FINDING: Increased property value is seldom the top goal of site-specific commissions.

To our surprise, only 5 percent of respondents ranked increased property value as the priority outcome for the project described. The variety of goals listed reflect a wide range of opinions about the value of art. But over half of respondents chose 'creating a more beautiful environment' as the primary goal for including artwork, clearly emphasizing the aesthetic and spiritual qualities of art much more than its financial worth.

FINDING: The client is seldom the first to suggest incorporating artwork in a project.

Real or perceived obstacles—including cost, time, and difficulty in accomplishing the task—may lead a client to believe that artwork is not feasible within a given budget or schedule. As a result, the design professional must often persuade the client that including artwork is both possible and desirable. Many respondents reported that the completed projects shown in GUILD sourcebooks were motivating to clients. And of course the pride of ownership, once all is said and done, is shared by all; 97 percent of respondents reported that the art component of the project was ultimately rewarding, both for themselves and their client.

FINDING: Low cost alone is not a significant factor in the choice of artist for a project.

Survey respondents indicate that previous work, as evidenced by a portfolio and track record with similar projects, is most helpful in selecting an artist. They also want a clear idea of what working with the artist will be like, based on the proposal and the initial collaborative chemistry. Interestingly, for the projects described, location and cost were not determining factors in the choice of artist.

CHARACTERISTICS OF SURVEY RESPONDENTS

The second part of the survey focused on general information about the respondent's firm and its history of commissioning artwork.

SURVEY RESULTS

FINDING: Firms of every size, budget and focus commission artwork.

Firms working in every area of the design industry use THE GUILD to commission artwork. Surveys were returned by professionals specializing in areas as diverse as luxury hotels, landscape construction, liturgical design, and homes.

Almost 70 percent of survey responses were from firms employing just one to five design professionals, a range consistent with the average size of North American design and architecture firms. However, despite the small size of most firms, three of every four report annual income over $400,000; one in four have revenue over $3 million.

What is your firm's primary design focus?

Commercial/office	29%
Residential	22%
Interior architecture	11%
Medical/health care	9%
Renovation/restoration	7%
Retail	6%
Hospitality/recreational	5%
Liturgical	4%
Educational	3%
Municipal/government	3%
Industrial/warehouse	1%

How many design professionals are employed by your firm?

1 - 5	69%
6 - 10	4%
11 - 20	10%
21 - 50	4%
51 - 99	8%
100+	4%

What is your firm's annual dollar volume?

Under $200,000	6%
$200,000 - $399,000	19%
$400,000 - $999,999	21%
$1,000,000 - $2,999,999	27%
$3,000,000 - $4,999,999	10%
Over $5,000,000	17%

SURVEY RESULTS

How are GUILD sourcebooks used by your firm?

Generate ideas and see what's available	96%
Identify artists for projects, using color pages	88%
Motivate clients to include artwork in a project	63%
Identify artists for projects, using B&W listings	29%
Loan to clients, for calling artists directly	25%
Display in the reception area	21%

What types of artwork have you or your firm commissioned?

Architectural glass	75%
Furniture	67%
Work for the wall	65%
Painted finishes/murals	65%
Architectural metal	63%
Textiles/floor coverings	58%
Architectural wood	58%
Sculpture (large standing)	52%
Architectural ceramics	50%
Sculptural objects	50%
Sculpture (atrium)	40%
Accessories	42%

Do you expect to increase the amount of artwork you commission in the coming years?

Yes	67%
No	6%
Unsure	27%

FINDING: Design professionals use THE GUILD in many ways to include a broad range of artworks in their projects.

Surveys confirmed that professionals use THE GUILD in all the ways we intend—and highlighted some additional benefits. Interior designer Carol Kodis likes GUILD sourcebooks because, "They show installations and give us a context. They help us think early on about how to include the artist's work in a project."

Across the board, respondents reported commissioning several types of artwork. Architectural glass and furniture lead the way with 75 and 67 percent respectively. But over half also commission work for the wall; painted finishes or murals; architectural metal, wood, or ceramics; textiles or floor coverings; and sculpture.

FINDING: Professionals predict continued good health for the architectural arts.

Our survey indicates that companies will commission more artwork in the coming years, with only 6 percent of respondents forecasting a decrease. This optimism might be explained by the observation of one respondent, an interior designer, who stated, "In my own community, people are becoming more aware of—and interested in—the arts each day."

GALLERY LISTINGS
A State-by-State Directory

Nearly 1,800 galleries are included in this year's listing. All carry the work of craft artists. Some specialize in media, others have a regional or thematic focus, and many can facilitate special orders and projects. The listing is a great travel companion and may reveal some unfamiliar galleries in your own backyard.

ALABAMA

HOLLAND SMITH GALLERY
301 JEFFERSON ST N
HUNTSVILLE, AL 35801-4853
TEL 205-534-1982

JEFFERSON STREET GALLERY
313 E JEFFERSON ST
MONTGOMERY, AL 36104-3645
TEL 205-263-5703

KENTUCK MUSEUM
3500 MCFARLAND BLVD
NORTHPORT, AL 35476-3183
TEL 205-333-1252

L. FREUD TITANIUM
2825 2ND AVE SOUTH #K
BIRMINGHAM, AL 35233
TEL 205-320-0980

MARALYN WILSON GALLERY
2010 CAHABA RD
BIRMINGHAM, AL 35223-1110
TEL 205-879-0582

WOLFF GALLERY
32 SO SECTION
FAIRHOPE, AL 36533
TEL 205-928-8338

ALASKA

BUNNELL ST. GALLERY
106 BUNNELL ST
HOMER, AK 99603
TEL 907-235-2662

GALLERY OF THE LAKES
PO BOX 520994
BIG LAKE, AK 99652
TEL 907-892-8579

KIKO B FIBERARTS
108 CARLYLE WAY
FAIRBANKS, AK 99709-2930
TEL 907-456-2202

OBJECTS OF BRIGHT PRIDE
165 S FRANKLIN ST
JUNEAU, AK 99801-1321
TEL 907-586-4969

STONINGTON GALLERY
415 F ST
ANCHORAGE, AK 99501-2218
TEL 907-272-1489

ARIZONA

AGUAJITO DEL SOL
TLAQUEPAQUE 103A
PO BOX 1607
SEDONA, AZ 86336
TEL 602-282-5258

ART OF THE TOY
4151 N MARSHALL WAY #4
SCOTTSDALE, AZ 85251
TEL 602-423-2911

ARTAMERICA GALLERY OF ART
9301 E SHEA BLVD
SCOTTSDALE, AZ 85260-6733
TEL 602-661-8772

ARTISTIC GALLERIES
7077 E MAIN ST
SCOTTSDALE, AZ 85251-4325
TEL 602-945-6766

AUSI GALLERY
38 CAMINO OTERO
TUBAC, AZ 85646
TEL 602-398-3193

BENTLEY TOMLINSON GALLERY
4161 N MARSHALL WAY
SCOTTSDALE, AZ 85251-3809
TEL 602-941-0078

BERTA WRIGHT GALLERY
260 E CONGRESS ST
TUCSON, AZ 85701-1829
TEL 602-742-4134

CLAY PIGEON
71 BREWER SPUR
SEDONA, AZ 86336
TEL 520-282-2845

DESERT MOON
2785 WEST 89A
SEDONA, AZ 86336
TEL 602-204-1195

EL PRADO GALLERIES, INC
PO BOX 1849
SEDONA, AZ 86339-1849
TEL 602-282-7390

ES POSIBLE GALLERY
34505 N SCOTTSDALE RD
SCOTTSDALE, AZ 85262-1202
TEL 602-488-3770

EVERY BLOOMING THING, INC
2010 E UNIVERSITY DR
TEMPE, AZ 85281-4681
TEL 602-921-1196

FERRARAS
5027 N 44TH ST
PHOENIX, AZ 85018
TEL 602-840-1591

GALERIA MESA
155 N CENTER
MESA, AZ 85201-6626
TEL 602-644-2242

GALLERY FOREST
251 HWY 179
PO BOX 1234
SEDONA, AZ 86339
TEL 520-282-2744

GALLERY TEN
7045 E 3RD AVE
SCOTTSDALE, AZ 85251-3801
TEL 602-994-0405

GALLERY THREE
3819 N 3RD ST
PHOENIX, AZ 85012-2074
TEL 602-277-9540

GIFTED HANDS
PO BOX 1388
SEDONA, AZ 86339-1388
TEL 602-282-4822

HORWITCH NEWMAN GALLERY
4211 N MARSHALL
WAY, AZ 85251

GALLERY LISTINGS

IMAGINE GALLERY
CONRAD LEATHER BOUTIQUE
34505 N SCOTTSDALE RD #E8
SCOTTSDALE, AZ 85262
TEL 602-488-2190

JOANNE RAPP GALLERY
THE HAND AND THE SPIRIT
4222 N MARSHALL WAY
SCOTTSDALE, AZ 85251
TEL 602-949-1262

LA FUENTE GALLERY
B123 TLAQUEPAUE
P O BOX 2169
SEDONA, AZ 86339-2169
TEL 602-282-5276

LEKAE GALLERIES
7100 E MAIN ST
SCOTTSDALE, AZ 85251

MIND'S EYE CRAFT GALLERY
4200 N MARSHALL WAY
SCOTTSDALE, AZ 85251-3204
TEL 602-941-2494

NELLIE BLY
136 MAIN ST
JEROME, AZ 86331
TEL 602-634-0255

OBSIDIAN GALLERY
4340 N CAMPBELL AVE #90
TUCSON, AZ 85718-6582
TEL 602-577-3598

OLD TOWN GALLERY
2 W SANTA FE AVE
FLAGSTAFF, AZ 86001
TEL 602-774-7770

PEARSON & COMPANY
7022 E MAIN ST
SCOTTSDALE, AZ 85251-4314
TEL 602-840-6447

PHILABAUM GLASS STUDIO
711 S 6TH AVE
TUCSON, AZ 85705
TEL 602-884-7604

PINK ADOBE GALLERY
222 E CONGRESS ST
TUCSON, AZ 85701-1810
TEL 602-623-2828

RAKU GALLERY
GENERAL DELIVERY
PO BOX 965
JEROME, AZ 86331-9999
TEL 602-639-0239

SUN WEST GALLERY
152 S MONTEZUMA ST
PRESCOTT, AZ 86303-4718
TEL 602-778-1204

SUZANNE BROWN GALLERIES
7160 E MAIN ST
SCOTTSDALE, AZ 85251-4316
TEL 602-945-8475

TOTALLY SOUTHWESTERN GALLERY
5575 E RIVER RD #131
TUCSON, AZ 85715-6737
TEL 602-577-2295

ARKANSAS

ARKANSAS CRAFT GALLERY
33 SPRING ST
EUREKA SPRINGS, AR 72632
TEL 501-253-7072

ARKANSAS CRAFT GALLERY
231-8 CENTRAL AVE
HOT SPRINGS, AR 71901
TEL 501-321-1640

ARKANSAS CRAFT GALLERY
518 W. DICKSON
FAYETTEVILLE, AR 72701
TEL 501-521-2016

CONTEMPORANEA GALLERY
516 CENTRAL AVE
HOT SPRINGS, AR 71901-3556
TEL 501-624-0516

CRAZY BONE GALLERY
37 SPRING ST
EUREKA SPRINGS, AR 72632-3147
TEL 501-253-6600

FORT SMITH ARTS CENTER GALLERY
423 N 6TH ST
FORT SMITH, AR 72901
TEL 520-784-2787

GALLERY AT TERRA STUDIOS INC.
12103 HAZEL VALLEY RD
FAYETTEVILLE, AR 72701
TEL 501-643-3314

CALIFORNIA

A GALLERY OF FINE ART
73580 EL PASEO
PALM DESERT, CA 92260-4306
TEL 619-346-8885

A NEW LEAF GALLERY
1286 GILMAN ST
BERKELEY, CA 94706-2353
TEL 510-525-7621

A PASSING GLIMPSE
9219 W PICO BLVD
LOS ANGELES, CA 90035-1318

ACCI
1652 SHATTUCK AVE
BERKELEY, CA 94709

AGNES BOURNE, INC
2 HENRY ADAMS ST #220
SAN FRANCISCO, CA 94103-5024
TEL 415-626-6883

ALLEN FINE ART GALLERY
37656 BANKSIDE DR
CATHEDRAL CITY, CA 92234-7827
TEL 619-341-8655

AMBIANCE GALLERY
405 2ND ST
EUREKA, CA 95501-0405
TEL 707-445-8950

AMERICAN MUSEUM OF QUILTS, TEX
776 S 2ND ST
SAN JOSE, CA 95112-5859
TEL 408-971-0323

AMERICAN PANACHE
31430 BROADBEACH RD
MALIBU, CA 90265-2669

ANGIE & COMPANY
360 TITLEIST CT
SAN JOSE, CA 95127-5439

ARCHITECT'S INTERIOR
1300 N SANTA CRUZ AVE
LOS GATOS, CA 95030
TEL 408-354-1020

ART COLLECTOR'S GALLERY
4151 TAYLOR ST
SAN DIEGO, CA 92110-2740
TEL 619-299-3232

ART OPTIONS
319 S ROBERTSON BLVD
LOS ANGELES, CA 90048-3805
TEL 310-392-9099

ART OPTIONS
372 HAYES ST
SAN FRANCISCO, CA 94102-4420
TEL 415-567-8535

ART WORKS
340 WESTBOURNE ST
LA JOLLA, CA 92037-5345
TEL 619-459-7688

ARTFUL EYE
1333A LINCOLN AVE
CALISTOGA, CA 94515-1701
TEL 707-942-4743

ARTIFACT
17 STOCKTON ST
SAN FRANCISCO, CA 94108-5805
TEL 415-788-9375

ARTIFAX INT'L GALLERY & GIFTS
450 1ST ST E #C
SONOMA, CA 95476-6760
TEL 707-996-9494

ARTISANCE
278 BEACH ST
LAGUNA BEACH, CA 92651-2105
TEL 714-494-0687

ARTISTS COLLABORATIVE GALLERY
1007 SECOND ST, OLD TOWN
SACRAMENTO, CA 95814
TEL 916-444-3764

BANAKER GALLERY
251 POST ST
SAN FRANCISCO, CA 94108
TEL 415-397-1397

BAY ARTS
1847 INDIAN VALLEY RD
NOVATO, CA 94947-4226
TEL 415-399-9925

BAYSIDE GALLERY
4555 N PERSHING AVE #33153
STOCKTON, CA 95207-6740
TEL 619-233-4350

BAZAR DEL MUNDO
2754 CALHOUN ST
SAN DIEGO, CA 92110-2706

BELL'OCCHIO
8 BRADY ST
SAN FRANCISCO, CA 94103-1211
TEL 415-864-4048

BENDICE GALLERY
380 1ST ST W
SONOMA, CA 95476-5631
TEL 707-938-2775

BETH CHRISTENSEN FINE ART
538 SILVERADO DR
TIBURON, CA 94920-1321
TEL 415-435-2314

BOB LEONARD, INC
2727 MAIN ST
SANTA MONICA, CA 90405-4052
TEL 310-399-3251

BRAUNSTEIN QUAY GALLERY
250 SUTTER ST
SAN FRANCISCO, CA 94108-4403
TEL 415-392-5532

BRAVO GALLERY
3433 GRIM AVE
SAN DIEGO, CA 92104-4224
TEL 619-283-3886

BRENDAN WALTER GALLERY
1001 COLORADO AVE
SANTA MONICA, CA 90401-2809
TEL 310-395-1155

BRONZE PLUS, INC
6790 DEPOT ST
SEBASTOPOL, CA 95472-3452
TEL 707-829-5480

CA CONTEMPORARY CRAFTS ASSOC.
PO BOX 2060
SAUSALITO, CA 94966-2060
TEL 415-927-3158

CALIFORNIA ART GALLERY
305 N COAST HWY #A
LAGUNA BEACH, CA 92651-1681

CALIFORNIA CONTEMPORARY CRAFT
109 CORTE MADERA AVE
TOWN CENTER
CORTE MADERA, CA 94925-1304
TEL 415-927-3158

CALIFORNIA CRAFT MUSEUM
GHIRADELLI SQUARE
900 N POINT ST
SAN FRANCISCO, CA 94109
TEL 415-774-1919

CALIFORNIA PACIFIC DESIGNS
2060 LINCOLN AVE
ALAMEDA, CA 94501-2713

CARD DE A
1570 Q ROSECRANS AVE
MANHATTAN BEACH, CA 90266

CARR & ASSOCIATES
2 HENRY ADAMS ST #333
SAN FRANCISCO, CA 94103-5025
TEL 415-861-1021

CASKEY LEES GALLERY
PO BOX 1409
TOPANGA, CA 90290-1409
TEL 310-455-2886

CAVANAUGH GALLERY
415 MAIN ST
HALF MOON BAY, CA 94019-1749
TEL 415-726-7771

CECILE MOOCHNEK GALLERY
1809D 4TH ST
BERKELEY, CA 94710-1910
TEL 510-549-1018

CEDANNA GALLERY
400 MAIN ST
HALF MOON BAY, CA 94019-1725
TEL 415-726-6776

CEDANNA GALLERY & STORE
1925 FILLMORE ST
SAN FRANCISCO, CA 94115-2744
TEL 415-474-7152

CELEBRATE LIFE
6201 W SUNSET BLVD #129
LOS ANGELES, CA 90028-8704
TEL 818-585-0690

CHAN SCHATZ
626 E HALEY ST #630
SANTA BARBARA, CA 93103-3110
TEL 805-962-3720

CHAPSON ARTSVISION
1750 UNION ST
SAN FRANCISCO, CA 94123-4407
TEL 415-292-6560

CHEZ MAC
812 POST ST
SAN FRANCISCO, CA 94109-6013
TEL 415-775-2515

CHRISTINE OF SANTA FE
220 FOREST AVE
LAGUNA BEACH, CA 92651-2114
TEL 714-494-3610

CLAUDIA CHAPLINE GALLERY
3445 SHORELINE HWY
PO BOX 946
STINSON BEACH, CA 94970
TEL 415-868-2308

CLOSETS & CLOTHS
617 BLUE SPRUCE DR
DANVILLE, CA 94506-4524

CLYDE STREET GALLERY
34 CLYDE ST
SAN FRANCISCO, CA 94107-1718
TEL 415-546-5185

COAST GALLERY
HIGHWAY 1
BIG SUR, CA 93920
TEL 408-667-2301

CODA GALLERY
73151 EL PASEO
PALM DESERT, CA 92260-4217
TEL 619-346-4661

COMPOSITIONS GALLERY
317 SUTTER ST
SAN FRANCISCO, CA 94108-4301
TEL 415-693-9111

CONCEPTS
PO BOX 301
SIXTH AND MISSION ST
CARMEL, CA 93921
TEL 408-624-0661

CONTEMPORARY CRAFTS
ASSN GALLERY
109 CORTE MADERA TOWN CENTER
CORTE MADERA, CA 94925
TEL 415-331-8520

COONLEY GALLERY
325 STANFORD SHOPPING CTR
PALO ALTO, CA 94304-1413
TEL 415-327-4000

COURTYARD GALLERY
1349 PARK ST
ALAMEDA, CA 94501-4533
TEL 415-521-1521

COUTURIER GALLERY
166 N LA BREA AVE
LOS ANGELES, CA 90036-2912
TEL 213-933-5557

CRAFT & FOLK ART MUSEUM
5800 WILSHIRE BLVD
LOS ANGELES, CA 90036-4500
TEL 213-937-9099

CRAFTSMAN'S GUILD
300 DE HARO ST #342
SAN FRANCISCO, CA 94103-5144
TEL 415-431-5425

CROCK-R-BOX
EL PASEO VILLAGE
73-425 EL PASEO
PALM DESERT, CA 92260
TEL 619-568-6688

DAVID AUSTIN CONTEMPORARY ART
355 W EL PORTAL
PALM SPRINGS, CA 92264-8908
TEL 619-322-7709

DEL MANO GALLERY
33 E COLORADO BLVD
PASADENA, CA 91105-1901
TEL 818-793-6648

DEL MANO GALLERY
11981 SAN VICENTE BLVD
LOS ANGELES, CA 90049-5003
TEL 310-476-8508

DEVERA GALLERY
334 HAYES ST
SAN FRANCISCO, CA 94102-4421
TEL 415-861-8480

DEVORZON GALLERY
2720 ELLISON DR
BEVERLY HILLS, CA 90210-1208
TEL 310-659-0555

DISCOVERIES CONTEMPORARY CRAFT
17350 17TH ST #E
TUSTIN, CA 92680-1956
TEL 714-544-6206

DOLCE VITA
2907 PASATIEMPO LN
SACRAMENTO, CA 95821-4911

DOROTHY WEISS GALLERY
256 SUTTER ST
SAN FRANCISCO, CA 94108-4409
TEL 415-397-3611

EARTH SPIRITS
73130 EL PASEO #N
PALM DESERT, CA 92260
TEL 619-779-8766

EARTHWORKS
290 MAIN ST
LOS ALTOS, CA 94022
TEL 415-948-5141

GALLERY LISTINGS

ECLECTICA
1795 MARKET ST
SAN FRANCISCO, CA 94103
TEL 415-626-6255

EDITIONS LIMITED GALLERY
625 2ND ST #400
SAN FRANCISCO, CA 94107-2050
TEL 415-543-9811

EILEEN KREMEN GALLERY
619 N HARBOR BLVD
FULLERTON, CA 92632-1517
TEL 714-879-1391

ELEGANT EARTH GALLERY
1310í HIGHWAY 9
BOULDER CREEK, CA 95006-9120
TEL 408-338-3646

ELIZABETH FORTNER GALLERY
100 W MICHELTORENA ST
SANTA BARBARA, CA 93101-3019
TEL 805-969-9984

FEINGARTEN GALLERIES
PO BOX 5383
BEVERLY HILLS, CA 90209-5383
TEL 310-274-7042

FERRARI OF CARMEL
SAN CARLOS 5TH & 6TH
PO BOX 3273
CARMEL, CA 93921
TEL 408-624-9677

FINE GALLERY
PO BOX 1494
SUTTER CREEK, CA 95685-1494
TEL 209-267-0571

FINE WOODWORKING GALLERY
1201C BRIDGEWAY
SAUSALITO, CA 94965-1916
TEL 415-332-5770

FINE WOODWORKING OF CARMEL
SAN CARLOS & MISSION
6TH & 5TH·
CARMEL, CA 93921
TEL 408-622-9663

FOLLOWING SEA
8522 BEVERLY BLVD
LOS ANGELES, CA 90048-6204
TEL 213-659-0592

FOX ON THE GREEN
254 MAIN ST
SALINAS, CA 93901-2704

FREDERICK SPRATT GALLERY
920 S 1ST ST
SAN JOSE, CA 95110-3125
TEL 408-294-1135

FREEHAND GALLERY
8413 W 3RD ST
LOS ANGELES, CA 90048-4111
TEL 213-655-2607

FRESNO ART MUSEUM SHOP
2233 N 1ST ST
FRESNO, CA 93703-2364
TEL 209-485-4810

GALLERI ORREFORS KOSTA BODA
3333 BEAR ST, S COAST PLAZA
COSTA MESA, CA 92626
TEL 714-549-1959

GALLERY 912¹/₂
912 ¹/₂ BROADWAY
SANTA MARICE, CA 93454
TEL 805-922-5005

GALLERY ALEXANDER
7850 GIRARD AVE
LA JOLLA, CA 92037-4230
TEL 619-459-9433

GALLERY EIGHT
7464 GIRARD AVE
LA JOLLA, CA 92037-5142
TEL 619-454-9781

GALLERY FAIR
PO BOX 263
MENDOCINO, CA 95460-0263
TEL 707-937-5121

GALLERY FOURTEEN
300 NAPA ST SLIP 21
SAUSALITO, CA 94965-1971
TEL 510-547-7608

GALLERY JAPONESQUE
824 MONTGOMERY ST
SAN FRANCISCO, CA 94133
TEL 415-398-8577

GALLERY OF FUNCTIONAL ART
2429 MAIN ST
SANTA MONICA, CA 90405-3539
TEL 310-450-2827

GALLERY ONE
209 WESTERN AVE
PETALUMA, CA 94952-2909
TEL 707-778-8277

GEORGEO'S COLLECTION
416 N RODEO DR
BEVERLY HILLS, CA 90210-4502
TEL 310-275-7967

GEORGEO'S COLLECTION
1139 PROSPECT ST
LA JOLLA, CA 92037-4534
TEL 619-551-8664

GEORGEO'S COLLECTION
269 FOREST AVE
LAGUNA BEACH, CA 92651-2113
TEL 714-497-0907

GLASS COLLECTION & GALLERY
22 EL PASEO
SANTA BARBARA, CA 93101

GOLDEN EGG GALLERY
540 SOUTH COAST HWY #104
LAGUNA BEACH, CA 92651
TEL 714-376-0063

GOLDEN TULIP
464 1ST ST #E
SONOMA, CA 95476
TEL 707-938-3624

GOOD DAY SUNSHINE
29 E NAPA ST
SONOMA, CA 95476-6708
TEL 707-938-4001

GRAPHICS GALLERY
219 MARINE AVE
BALBOA ISLAND, CA 92662
TEL 714-673-2220

GRAYSTONE
SECOND & F ST
EUREKA, CA 95501

GUMP'S GALLERY
250 POST ST
SAN FRANCISCO, CA 94108-5101
TEL 415-984-9274

HANDWORKS
DOLORES 7 6TH AVE
CARMEL, CA 93921
TEL 408-624-6000

HANK BAUM GALLERY
2842 PIERCE ST
SAN FRANCISCO, CA 94123-3819
TEL 415-752-4336

HARLEEN ALLEN FINE ARTS
427 BRYANT ST
SAN FRANCISCO, CA 94107-1302
TEL 415-777-0920

HARMONY POTTERY
OLD HIGHWAY ONE
HARMONY, CA 93435
TEL 805-927-4293

HENLEY'S GALLERY
ON THE SEA RANCH
1000 ANNAPOLIS RD
THE SEA RANCH, CA 95497
TEL 707-785-2951

HIGHLANDS SCULPTURE GALLERY
DOLORES BETWEEN 5TH & 6TH
CARMEL, CA 93921
TEL 408-624-0535

HIGHLIGHT GALLERY
45052 MAIN ST
MENDOCINO, CA 95460
TEL 707-937-3132

HUMAN ARTS
310 E OJAI AVE
OJAI, CA 93203
TEL 805-646-1525

HUMBOLDT'S FINEST
417 2ND ST
EUREKA, CA 95501-0405
TEL 707-443-1258

HUNTER UNLIMITED
28 EL PASEO
SANTA BARBARA, CA 93101
TEL 805-899-0007

ICAAN GALLERIES
228 MANHATTAN BEACH BLVD #107
MANHATTAN BEACH, CA 90266-5355
TEL 310-376-6171

IMAGE OF THE CULTURE
340 CALIFORNIA AVE
PALO ALTO, CA 94306
TEL 415-342-0621

IMAGES OF THE NORTH
1782 UNION ST
SAN FRANCISCO, CA 94123-4407
TEL 415-673-1273

INTERIA
11404 SORRENTO VALLEY RD
SAN DIEGO, CA 92121-1315
TEL 619-455-7177

INTERNATIONAL GALLERY
643 G ST
SAN DIEGO, CA 92101-7028
TEL 619-235-8255

INTERNATIONAL GLASS & BEAD
317 W IST ST
CLAREMONT, CA 91711
TEL 909-626-0877

IRA WOLK GALLERY
1235 MAIN ST
SAINT HELENA, CA 94574-1902
TEL 707-963-8801

JOAN ROBEY GALLERY
2912 4TH ST
SANTA MONICA, CA 90405-5504

JOANNE CHAPPEL GALLERY
625 SECOND ST
SAN FRANCISCO, CA 94107
TEL 415-777-5711

JOHN NATSOULAS GALLERY
140 F ST
DAVIS, CA 95616-4628
TEL 916-756-3938

JOSLYN STUDIO & ART GALLERY
GENERAL DELIVERY
PO BOX 596
COLOMA, CA 95613-9999
TEL 916-621-2049

JUDITH LITVICH CONTEMP. ARTS
2 HENRY ADAMS ST #M-69
SAN FRANCISCO, CA 94103-5016
TEL 415-863-3329

KALEIDOSCOPE GALLERY
3273 ROGERS AVE
WALNUT CREEK, CA 94596-1846
TEL 510-210-1336

KIMBERLEY'S
25601 PINE CREEK LN
WILMINGTON, CA 90744-1827
TEL 310-835-4169

KIYO HIGASHI GALLERY
8332 MELROSE AVE
LOS ANGELES, CA 90069-5420
TEL 213-655-2482

KONGO SQUARE GALLERY
4334 DEGNAN BLVD
LOS ANGELES, CA 90008
TEL 213-291-6878

LA VAE GALLERY
4703 SPRING ST
LA MESA, CA 91941-5207

LEGENDS — A GALLERY OF AMERICAN ARTISANS
483 FIRST ST W
SONOMA, CA 95476
TEL 707-939-8100

LEONE NII GALLERY
198 CASTRO ST
MOUNTAIN VIEW, CA 94041-1202

LH SELMAN, LTD
761 CHESTNUT ST
SANTA CRUZ, CA 95060-3751
TEL 800-538-0766

LORI'S ART GALLERY
20929 VENTURA BLVD
WOODLAND HILLS, CA 91364-2334
TEL 818-884-1110

LOS ANGELES ART EXCHANGE
2451 BROADWAY
SANTA MONICA, CA 90404-3046
TEL 310-828-6866

LOS GATOS COMPANY
17½ N SANTA CRUZ AVE
LOS GATOS, CA 95030-5916
TEL 408-354-2433

LUNA
4928 E. 2ND ST
LAGUNA BEACH, CA 90803

MADE IN MENDOCINO
PO BOX 510
HOPLAND, CA 95449-0510
TEL 707-744-1300

MAGPIE
1141 HIGHLAND AVE
MANHATTAN BEACH, CA 90266
TEL 310-546-3816

MAIN STREET JEWELERS
125 N MAIN ST
LAKEPORT, CA 95453-4814

MANDEL & COMPANY
8687 MELROSE AVE
LOS ANGELES, CA 90069-5701
TEL 310-652-5025

MANY HANDS CRAFT GALLERY
655 G ST
SAN DIEGO, CA 92101-7028

MANY HANDS GALLERY
1510 PACIFIC AVE
SANTA CRUZ, CA 95060-3903
TEL 408-429-8696

MARCELLA NOON IMPORTS
101 HENRY ADAMS ST #423
SAN FRANCISCO, CA 94103-5214
TEL 415-255-8485

MARTIN LAWRENCE GALLERIES
2855 STEVENS CREEK BLVD
SANTA CLARA, CA 95050-6709
TEL 408-985-8885

MASTER'S MARK GALLERY
3228 SACRAMENTO ST
SAN FRANCISCO, CA 94115-2007
TEL 415-885-6700

MATRIX GALLERY
1725 "I" ST
SACRAMENTO, CA 95814-3001
TEL 916-441-4818

MCGOWAN & CO.
6220 LA SALLE AVE
OAKLAND, CA 94611
TEL 510-339-0814

MEADOWLARK GALLERY
317 CORTE MADERA TOWN CENTER
CORTE MADERA, CA 94925
TEL 415-924-2210

MICHAEL HIMOVITZ GALLERY
1020 10TH ST
SACRAMENTO, CA 95814-3502
TEL 916-448-8723

MICHAELJON WOODWORKER
18663 EAST HWY 88
CLEMENTS, CA 95227-0188
TEL 209-763-5713

MODERN LIVING
8125 MELROSE AVE
LOS ANGELES, CA 90046-7011
TEL 213-655-3898

MUSEUM OF CONTEMPORARY ART
250 S GRAND AVE
LOS ANGELES, CA 90012-3021
TEL 213-621-2766

NADEL PHELAN GALLERY
1245 EL SOLYO HEIGHTS DR
FELTON, CA 95018-9336
TEL 408-426-4980

NATURESQUE
PIER 39, SPACE H-3
SAN FRANCISCO, CA 94133

NEW PIECES GALLERY
1597 SOLANO AVE
BERKELEY, CA 94707-2116
TEL 510-527-6779

NORDSTROM 499 D.C.
37599 FILBERT ST
NEWARK, CA 94560
TEL 510-975-5540

OAK TREE
546 OLD MAMMOTH RD
MAMMOTH LAKES, CA 93546
TEL 619-935-4032

OFF YOUR DOT
2241 MARKET ST
SAN FRANCISCO, CA 94114-1612
TEL 415-252-5642

OUT OF HAND GALLERY
1303 CASTRO ST
SAN FRANCISCO, CA 94114-3620
TEL 415-826-3885

OUTSIDE-IN GALLERY
6909 MELROSE AVE
LOS ANGELES, CA 90038-3305
TEL 213-933-4096

PACIFIC GALLERY
PO BOX 844
DANA POINT, CA 92629-0844
TEL 714-240-9099

PACIFIC GALLERY
228 FOREST AVE
LAGUNA BEACH, CA 92651-2114
TEL 714-494-8732

PAINTED LADY GALLERY
1407 JACKSON GATE RD
JACKSON, CA 95642-9575
TEL 209-223-1754

PALM SPRINGS DESERT MUSEUM
101 N MUSEUM DR
PALM SPRINGS, CA 92262-5659
TEL 619-325-7186

PALUMBO GALLERY
DOLORES ST (AT SIXTH)
PO BOX 5727
CARMEL, CA 93921
TEL 408-625-5727

GALLERY LISTINGS

PASSING GLIMPSE
9219 W PICO BLVD
LOS ANGELES, CA 90035
TEL 310-858-1776

PAZAR GALLERY
23561 MALIBU COLONY RD
MALIBU, CA 90265-4626
TEL 310-456-1142

PIECEMAKERS
1720 ADAMS AVE
COSTA MESA, CA 92626-4890

PINNACLE GROUSE
127 FOREST ST
BOULDER CREEK, CA 95006-8900

PLAZA DESIGN
808 G ST
ARCATA, CA 95521
TEL 707-822-9613

PLUMS CONTEMPORARY ART
5096 N PALM AVE
FRESNO, CA 93704-2201
TEL 209-227-5389

POT-POURRI GALLERY
4100 REDWOOD RD
OAKLAND, CA 94619-2363
TEL 510-531-1503

POWER SEWING
185 5TH AVE
SAN FRANCISCO, CA 94118-1309
TEL 415-386-0400

PRIMAVERA GALLERY
214 E OJAI AVE
OJAI, CA 93023-2737
TEL 805-646-7133

RANDOLPH & HEIN
101 HENRY ADAMS ST #101
SAN FRANCISCO, CA 94103-5211
TEL 415-864-3550

RANDOLPH & HEIN, INC
8687 MELROSE AVE #310
LOS ANGELES, CA 90069-5701
TEL 310-855-1222

RASBERRYS
6540 WASHINGTON ST
YOUNTVILLE, CA 94599
TEL 707-944-9211

RED ROSE GALLERY
2251 CHESTNUT ST
SAN FRANCISCO, CA 94123-2607
TEL 415-776-6871

RITAMARIE SUSTEK & ASSOCIATES
712 BANROFT ROAD #197
WALNUT CREEK, CA 94598
TEL 510-944-4711

ROBERGE GALLERY
73520 EL PASEO
PALM DESERT, CA 92260-4338
TEL 619-340-5045

ROOKIE-TO GALLERY
PO BOX 606
14300 HWY 128
BOONVILLE, CA 95415-0606
TEL 707-895-2204

RUTH BACHOFNER GALLERY
2046 BROADWAY
SANTA MONICA, CA 90404-2910
TEL 310-458-8007

SAFARI COLLECTION
2620 SAN MIGUEL
NEWPORT BEACH, CA 92660
TEL 714-720-9448

SAN ANSELMO ART GLASS GALLERY
245 SAN ANSELMO AVE
SAN ANSELMO, CA 94960
TEL 415-457-2082

SANTA BARBARA STYLE & DESIGN
137 E DE LA GUERRA ST
SANTA BARBARA, CA 93101-2228
TEL 805-965-6291

SAVAS GALLERY
33 MILLER AVE
MILL VALLEY, CA 94941
TEL 415-380-8098

SCHWARTZ CIERLAK GALLERY
26106 PAOLINO PL
VALENCIA, CA 91355-2039
TEL 213-396-3814

SCULPTURE HOUSE & GARDENS
HIGHWAY 1, BOX 247
CARMEL, CA 93923
TEL 408-624-2476

SCULPTURE TO WEAR
9638 BRIGHTON WAY
BEVERLY HILLS, CA 90210-5110
TEL 310-277-2542

SEEKERS COLLECTION & GALLERY
2450 MAIN ST
CAMBRIA, CA 93428-3420
TEL 805-927-8626

SEEKERS GALLERY
4090 BURTON DR
CAMBRIA, CA 93428
TEL 805-927-4352

SHADY LANE CRAFT GALLERY
441 UNIVERSITY AVE
PALO ALTO, CA 94301-1813

SHARON PARK GALLERY
325 SHARON PARK DR
MENLO PARK, CA 94025-6848
TEL 415-854-6878

SHERWOOD GALLERY
460 S COAST HWY
LAGUNA BEACH, CA 92651-2404
TEL 714-497-2668

SHIBUI HOUSE
630 CLIFF DR
APTOS, CA 95003-5312
TEL 408-688-7195

SIGNATURE GALLERY
3693 5TH AVE
SAN DIEGO, CA 92103-4218
TEL 619-297-0430

SIMPSON HELLER GALLERY
2289 MAIN ST
CAMBRIA, CA 93428-3017
TEL 805-927-1800

SOCO GALLERY
101 S COOMBS ST
NAPA, CA 94559-4500
TEL 707-255-5954

SOFT TOUCH ARTISTS
COLLECTIVE GALLERY
1580 HAIGHT ST
SAN FRANCISCO, CA 94117

SOLOMON DUBNICK GALLERY
2131 NORTHROP
SACRAMENTO, CA 95825
TEL 916-920-4547

SOMETHING/ANYTHING
900 NORTHPOINT
SAN FRANCISCO, CA 94109
TEL 415-441-8003

SOPHIA/CHIARA DESIGNER
80 THROCKMORTON
MILL VALLEY, CA 94941

SOUTH BAY BRONZE
PO BOX 3254
SAN JOSE, CA 95156-3254

STARY SHEETS FINE ART GALLERY
14988 SAND CANYON AVE
IRVINE, CA 92718-2107
TEL 714-733-0445

STEVE STEIN GALLERY
13934 VENTURA BLVD
SHERMAN OAKS, CA 91423-3564
TEL 818-990-0777

STILLWATER'S
1228 MAIN ST
SAINT HELENA, CA 94574-1901
TEL 707-963-1782

STONEFLOWER GALLERY
795 BRIDGEWAY
SAUSALITO, CA 94965
TEL 415-332-6832

STUDIO 41
739 1ST ST
BENICIA, CA 94510-3213
TEL 707-745-0254

STUDIO FORTY TWO
23 N SANTA CRUZ AVE
LOS GATOS, CA 95030-5916
TEL 408-395-3191

SUMMER HOUSE GALLERY
14 MILLER AVE
MILL VALLEY, CA 94941-1904
TEL 415-383-6695

SUSAN CUMMINS GALLERY
12 MILLER AVE
MILL VALLEY, CA 94941-1904
TEL 415-383-1512

TAFOYA GALLERY
LINCOLN COURT BLDG #110
2105 S BASCOM ST
CAMPBELL, CA 95008
TEL 408-559-6161

TAKADA FINE ARTS GALLERY
251 POST ST
SIXTH FLOOR
SAN FRANCISCO, CA 94108-5004
TEL 415-956-5288

TARBOX GALLERY
1202 KETTNER BLVD
SAN DIEGO, CA 92101-3338
TEL 619-234-5020

TAYLOR-GRATZER GALLERY
8667 W SUNSET BLVD
WEST HOLLYWOOD, CA 90069-2313
TEL 213-659-6422

TEN DIRECTIONS GALLERY
723 SANTA YSABEL AVE
LOS OSOS, CA 93402-1137
TEL 805-528-4574

TERCERA GALLERY
24 N SANTA CRUZ AVE
LOS GATOS, CA 95030-5917
TEL 408-354-9482

TERRAIN
165 JESSIE ST #2
SAN FRANCISCO, CA 94105-4008
TEL 415-543-0656

TESORI GALLERY
319 S ROBERTSON BLVD
LOS ANGELES, CA 90048-3805
TEL 213-273-9890

TESORI GALLERY
30 E 3RD AVE
SAN MATEO, CA 94401-4011
TEL 415-344-4731

TEXTURES GALLERY
550 DEEP VALLEY DR #135
RLLNG HLS EST, CA 90274-3620
TEL 213-541-1943

THE ART COMPANY
25 W GUTIERREZ ST
SANTA BARBARA, CA 93101-3449
TEL 805-963-1157

**THE CRATE:
AMERICAN HANDCRAFTS**
#9 HYATT REGENCY PLAZA
1200 K ST
SACRAMENTO, CA 95814
TEL 916-441-4136

THE GALLERY
329 PRIMROSE RD
BURLINGAME, CA 94010-4037
TEL 415-347-9392

THE IMP
1413 MONTANA AVE
SANTA MONICA, CA 90403
TEL 310-917-3320

THE LIMN COMPANY
457 PACIFIC AVE
SAN FRANCISCO, CA 94133-4613
TEL 415-986-3884

THE PHOENIX AT NEPENTHE
HIGHWAY 1
BIG SUR, CA 93920
TEL 408-667-2347

THE QUEST
777 BRIDGEWAY
SAUSALITO, CA 94965-2174
TEL 415-332-6832

TOPS MALIBU GALLERY
23410 CIVIC CENTER WAY
MALIBU, CA 90265-4857
TEL 213-456-8677

TROVE GALLERY
343 N ORCHARD TREE LN
PALM SPRINGS, CA 92262-0328
TEL 619-346-1999

ULRICH CREATIVE ARTS
PO BOX 684
VENTURA, CA 93002-0684
TEL 805-643-4160

VALERIE MILLER FINE ARTS
73100 EL PASEO #2
PALM DESERT, CA 92260-4263
TEL 213-467-1511

VAULT GALLERY
2289 MAIN ST
CAMBRIA, CA 93428
TEL 805-927-0300

VERDI
723 BRIDGEWAY
SAUSALITO, CA 94965-2102
TEL 415-331-3009

VICTOR FISCHER GALLERIES
1300 CLAY ST #510
OAKLAND, CA 94612-1427
TEL 510-464-8044

VICTOR FISCHER GALLERIES
1525 SANTANELLA TER
CORONA DEL MAR, CA 92625-1746
TEL 714-644-9655

VIDEOLA
2110 VINE ST #A
BERKELEY, CA 94709-1524
TEL 510-549-3373

VIEWPOINT GALLERY
224 THE CROSSROADS
CARMEL, CA 93923-8648
TEL 408-624-3369

VIEWPOINTS ART GALLERY
315 STATE ST
LOS ALTOS, CA 94022-2816
TEL 415-941-5789

VIEWPOINTS GALLERY
11315 HWY 1
PO BOX 670
POINT REYES STATION, CA 94956
TEL 415-663-8861

VILLAGE ARTISTRY GALLERY
DOLORES (BETWEEN. OCEAN & 7TH)
PO BOX 5493
CARMEL, CA 93921
TEL 408-624-7628

VIRGINIA BREIER GALLERY
3091 SACRAMENTO ST
SAN FRANCISCO, CA 94115-2016
TEL 415-929-7173

WALTER WHITE FINE ARTS
107 CAPITOLA AVE
CAPITOLA, CA 95010-3202
TEL 408-476-7001

WALTER WHITE GALLERY
SAN CARLOS AT 5TH
BOX 4834
CARMEL, CA 93921
TEL 408-624-4957

WELLSPRING GALLERY
120 BROADWAY #105
SANTA MONICA, CA 90401-2385
TEL 310-451-1924

WILD BLUE GALLERY
7220 MELROSE AVE
LOS ANGELES, CA 90046-7620
TEL 213-939-8434

WOLFORD & CO.
2408 MAGOWAN DR
SANTA ROSA, CA 95405
TEL 707-542-7426

Z GALLERY
5500 W 83RD ST
LOS ANGELES, CA 90045-3309
TEL 310-410-6655

21ST CENTURY GALLERY
235 FILLMORE ST
DENVER, CO 80206-5023
TEL 303-320-0926

A SHOW OF HANDS GALLERY
2440 E 3RD AVE
DENVER, CO 80206-4704
TEL 303-920-3071

ABBEY LANE GALLERY
131 MAIN ST
CREEDE, CO 81130
TEL 719-658-2736

AMEN WARDY HOME
405 E COOPER AVE
ASPEN, CO 81611
TEL 303-920-7700

ANN HYDE ART & ANTIQUES
302 E HOPKINS AVE
ASPEN, CO 81611-1906
TEL 303-925-7904

ART OF CRAFT
1736 WAZEE ST
DENVER, CO 80202
TEL 303-292-5564

ART WEST DESIGNS LTD
8743 W FLOYD AVE
DENVER, CO 80227-4729
TEL 303-986-1439

ART YARD
1251 S PEARL ST #A
DENVER, CO 80210-1537
TEL 303-777-3219

ARTCYCLE
BOX 344
BOULDER, CO 80306-0344
TEL 303-449-4950

ARTISAN CENTER
2757 E 3RD AVE
DENVER, CO 80206-4802
TEL 303-333-1201

ASPEN MOUNTAIN GALLERY
555 E DURANT AVE
ASPEN, CO 81611
TEL 303-925-5083

BRISTOL GALLERY
1424 P LARIMER
DENVER, CO 80202
TEL 303-620-9822

GALLERY LISTINGS

CANYON ROAD GALLERY
257 FILLMORE ST
DENVER, CO 80206-5003
TEL 303-321-4139

COMMONWHEEL ARTIST CO-OP
102 CANON AVE
MANITOU SPRINGS, CO 80829-1708
TEL 719-685-1008

DAVID FLORIA GALLERY
6 WOOD CREEK PL
WOOD CREEK, CO 81656
TEL 303-923-5705

DIAMOND TANITA GALLERY
303 ELK AVE #4
PO BOX 2293
CRESTED BUTTE, CO 81224
TEL 303-349-0940

GINGERBREAD SQUARE GALLERY
649 QUINCE CIR
BOULDER, CO 80304-1030
TEL 303-443-3180

GOTTHELFF GALLERY
122 E MEADOW DR
VAIL, CO 81657-5330
TEL 303-476-1777

HABATAT GALLERIES
213 S MILL ST
ASPEN, CO 81611-1926
TEL 303-920-9098

HEATHER GALLERY
555 E DURANT AVE
ASPEN, CO 81611-1856
TEL 303-925-6641

HIBBERD MCGRATH GALLERY
GENERAL DELIVERY
PO BOX 7638
BRECKENRIDGE, CO 80424-9999
TEL 303-453-6391

HOWELL GALLERY
1420 LARIMER ST
DENVER, CO 80202-1705
TEL 303-820-3925

J COTTER GALLERY
234 WALL ST
PO BOX 385
VAIL, CO 81657-4538
TEL 303-476-3131

KINKOPH GALLERY
220 S MAIN ST BOX 1717
BRECKENRIDGE, CO 80424
TEL 303-453-9095

LUMA
1 LAKE AVE
COLORADO SPRINGS, CO 80901
TEL 719-634-7711

MAXIMS ART GALLERY
818 9TH ST
GREELEY, CO 80631-1104

MILL STREET GALLERY
112 S MILL ST
ASPEN, CO 81611-1976
TEL 303-925-4988

MOLE HOLE
130 CROSSROADS MALL
1700 28TH ST
BOULDER, CO 80301
TEL 303-440-9131

NANCY LEE, LTD
DENVER MERCHANDISE MART #1508
DENVER, CO 80216
TEL 303-295-1283

NEW WEST GALLERY
747 MAIN ST
DURANGO, CO 81301
TEL 303-259-5777

PANACHE CRAFT GALLERY
315 COLUMBINE ST
DENVER, CO 80206-4223
TEL 303-321-8069

PISMO
2727 E 3RD AVE
DENVER, CO 80206-4802
TEL 303-333-7724

RACHAEL COLLECTION
433 E COOPER ST
ASPEN, CO 81611-1831
TEL 303-920-1313

REISS GALLERY
429 ACOMA ST
DENVER, CO 80204
TEL 303-778-6924

SANDY CARSON GALLERY
1734 WAZEE ST
DENVER, CO 80202-1232
TEL 303-297-8585

SHANAHAN COLLECTIONS
595 S BROADWAY #100S
DENVER, CO 80209-4072
TEL 303-778-7088

SKILLED HANDS GALLERY
GENERAL DELIVERY
PO BOX 5048
BRECKENRIDGE, CO 80424-9999
TEL 303-453-7818

SPIRITS IN THE WIND GALLERY
708 13TH ST
GOLDEN, CO 80401
TEL 303-279-1192

SQUASHBLOSSOM
198 GORE CREEK DR
VAIL, CO 81657-4511

STEAMBOAT ART COMPANY
903 LINCOLN AVE
STEAMBOAT SPRINGS, CO
  80487-5002

SUSAN DUVAL GALLERY
525 E COOPER ST
ASPEN, CO 81611-1860
TEL 303-925-9044

TAPESTRY, LTD
2859 E 3RD AVE
DENVER, CO 80206-4905
TEL 303-393-0535

TAVELLI GALLERY
555 N MILL ST
ASPEN, CO 81611-1509
TEL 303-920-3071

**TELLURIDE GALLERY
OF FINE ART**
GENERAL DELIVERY
PO BOX 1900
TELLURIDE, CO 81435-9999
TEL 303-728-3300

TERMAR GALLERY
780 MAIN AVE
PO BOX 3269
DURANGO, CO 81302
TEL 970-247-3728

TERRA VERDE
208 N. TEJON
COLORADO SPRINGS, CO 80903
TEL 719-444-8621

TOH-ATIN GALLERY
145 W 9TH ST
DURANGO, CO 81301-5431
TEL 800-525-0384

UPPER EDGE GALLERY
303 E MAIN ST
ASPEN, CO 81611-1929
TEL 303-923-5373

WHITE HART GALLERY
843 LINCOLN AVE
STEAMBOAT SPRINGS, CO 80487-5001
TEL 303-879-1015

CONNECTICUT

A TOUCH OF GLASS
PO BOX 433
N MOODUS RD
MOODUS, CT 06469-0433
TEL 203-873-9709

AMERICA WORKS INC
29 SANDY BEACH RD
MIDDLEBURY, CT 06762-1322

AMERICAN HAND
125 POST RD E
WESTPORT, CT 06881-3410
TEL 203-226-8883

ARTISTIC SURROUNDINGS
40½ PADANARAM RD
DANBURY, CT 06811-4840
TEL 203-798-0361

ATELIER STUDIO GALLERY
27 EAST ST
NEW MILFORD, CT 06776-3028
TEL 203-354-7792

BARBARA BAKER'S ONE ROOM
AT A TIME
PO BOX 1724
DARIEN, CT 06820
TEL 203-866-7978

BROWN GROTTA GALLERY
39 GRUMMAN HILL RD
WILTON, CT 06897-4504
TEL 203-834-0623

COMPANY OF CRAFTSMEN
43 W MAIN ST
MYSTIC, CT 06355-2545
TEL 203-536-4189

ENDLEMAN GALLERY
1014 CHAPEL ST
NEW HAVEN, CT 06510-2402
TEL 203-776-2517

FISHER GALLERY
25 BUNKER LN
AVON, CT 06001
TEL 203-678-1867

HERON AMERICAN CRAFT GALLERY

MAIN ST
PO BOX 535
KENT, CT 06757
TEL 203-927-4804

MENDELSON GALLERY

TITUS SQUARE
WASHINGTON DEPOT, CT 06794
TEL 203-868-0307

NEW HORIZONS GALLERY

122 GARWOOD RD
TRUMBULL, CT 06611-2220
TEL 203-261-6767

SILO GALLERY

44 UPLAND RD
NEW MILFORD, CT 06776-2104
TEL 203-355-0300

STARSHINE GALLERY

319 HORSE HILL RD
WESTBROOK, CT 06498-1402
TEL 203-399-5149

VARIATIONS GALLERY

PO BOX 246
RT 20
RIVERTON, CT 06065-0246
TEL 203-379-2964

WAVE

1046 CHAPEL ST
NEW HAVEN, CT 06510

WHITNEY MUSEUM OF ART

FAIRFIELD COUNTY
ONE CHAMPION PLAZA
STAMFORD, CT 06921-0001
TEL 203-358-7652

WHYEVERNOT

17 WEST MAIN ST
MYSTIC, CT 06355

WOODEN LEATHER

760 MAIN ST
PLANTSVILLE, CT 06479-1536

DELAWARE

BLUE STREAK GALLERY

1723 DELAWARE AVE
WILMINGTON, DE 19806-2342
TEL 302-429-0506

CRAFT COLLECTION

129D REHOBOTH AVE
REHOBOTH BEACH, DE 19971-2138
TEL 302-227-3640

CREATIONS FINE WOODWORKING

GALLERY
2890 CREEK RD
VORKLYN, DE 19736
TEL 302-234-2350

DELAWARE CENTER FOR THE ARTS

103 E 16TH ST
WILMINGTON, DE 19801
TEL 302-656-6466

STATION GALLERY

3922 KENNETT PIKE
GREENVILLE, DE 19807-2304
TEL 302-654-8638

TIDELINE GALLERY

135 REHOBOTH AVE
REHOBOTH BEACH, 1, DE 19971
TEL 302-227-4444

TIDELINE GALLERY

1 GREENVILLE CROSSING
4019 B KENNETT PIKE
GREENVILLE, DE 19807
TEL 302-651-9444

DISTRICT OF COLUMBIA

AMERICAN HAND PLUS

2906 M ST NW
WASHINGTON, DC 20007-3713
TEL 202-965-3273

ANNE O'BRIEN GALLERY

4829 BENDING LN NW
WASHINGTON, DC 20007-1527
TEL 202-265-9697

APPLACHIAN SPRING

1415 WISCONSIN AVE NW
WASHINGTON, DC 20007
TEL 202-342-5578

DUPONT PLAZA HOTEL

1500 NEW HAMPSHIRE AVE NW
WASHINGTON, DC 20036
TEL 202-797-0160

COLLECTORS CABINET

1023 CONNECTICUT AVE NW
WASHINGTON, DC 20036-5403

FARRELL COLLECTION

2633 CONNECTICUT AVE NW
WASHINGTON, DC 20008-1522
TEL 202-483-8334

GAZELLE GALLERY

5335 WISCONSIN AVE NW
WASHINGTON, DC 20015-2030
TEL 202-686-5656

INDIAN CRAFT SHOP

1050 WISCONSIN AVE NW
WASHINGTON, DC 20007-3633
TEL 202-342-3918

INDIAN CRAFT SHOP

DEPT OF THE INTERIOR
1849 C ST NW #1023
WASHINGTON, DC 20240-0001
TEL 202-737-4381

JACKIE CHALKLEY GALLERY

5301 WISCONSIN AVE NW
WASHINGTON, DC 20015-2015
TEL 202-537-6100

JACKIE CHALKLEY GALLERY

3301 NEW MEXICO AVE NW
WASHINGTON, DC 20016-3622
TEL 202-686-8882

JACKIE CHALKLEY GALLERY

1455 PENNSYLVANIA AVE NW
WASHINGTON, DC 20004-1008
TEL 202-683-3060

JEWELER'S WERK GALERIE

2000 PENNSYLVANIA AVE NW
WASHINGTON, DC 20006
TEL 202-293-0249

KELLOGG COLLECTION

3424 WISCONSIN AVE NW
WASHINGTON, DC 20016-3009
TEL 202-363-6878

LIPERT INTERNATIONAL

2112 M ST NW
WASHINGTON, DC 20007
TEL 202-625-0541

MAURINE LITTLETON GALLERY

1667 WISCONSIN AVE NW
WASHINGTON, DC 20007-2721
TEL 202-333-9307

MIYA GALLERY

410 8TH ST NW
WASHINGTON, DC 20004
TEL 202-347-6330

MOON BLOSSOMS & SNOW

225 PENNSYLVANIA AVE SE
WASHINGTON, DC 20003
TEL 202-543-8181

NATIONAL BUILDING MUSEUM

401 F ST NW
WASHINGTON, DC 20001-2728
TEL 202-272-2448

OUTSIDE DESIGN

CHEVY CHASE PAVILLION
5335 WISCONSIN AVE NW
WASHINGTON, DC 20007
TEL 202-363-3841

PIRJO

1044 WISCONSIN AVE NW
WASHINGTON, DC 20007
TEL 202-337-1390

RENWICK GALLERY

PENNSYLVANIA AVE AT 17 ST NW
WASHINGTON, DC 20006

SANSAR GALLERY

4200 WISCONSIN AVE NW
WASHINGTON, DC 20016-2143
TEL 202-244-4448

STUDIO DESIGN INC

1508 19TH ST NW
WASHINGTON, DC 20036-1102
TEL 202-667-6133

TOUCHSTONE GALLERY

2009 R ST NW
WASHINGTON, DC 20009-1011
TEL 202-797-7278

UPTOWN ARTS

3236 P ST NW
WASHINGTON, DC 20007-2755
TEL 202-337-0600

VERY SPECIAL ARTS GALLERY

1331 F ST NW
WASHINGTON, DC 20016
TEL 202-628-0800

FLORIDA

5G COLLECTION, ART PLUS

4534 COCOPLUM WAY
DELRAY BEACH, FL 33445-4304
TEL 407-637-8899

A PLACE ON EARTH

29 SW OSCEOUA
STUART, FL 34994
TEL 407-283-9556

A STEP ABOVE GALLERY

500 N TAMAMI TR
SARASOTA, FL 34236
TEL 813-955-4477

GALLERY LISTINGS

AHAVA
MIZNER PARK
414 PLAZA REAL
BOCA RATON, FL 33433
TEL 407-395-5001

ALBERTSON PETERSON GALLERY
329 S PARK AVE
WINTER PARK, FL 32789-4390
TEL 407-628-1258

ALEXANDERS — A FINE ART SHOWCASE
3225 S MACDILL AVE #107
TAMPA, FL 33629-8171
TEL 813-839-6088

AMERICAN CRAFTWORKS
5050 TOWN CENTER CIRCLE
BOCA RATON, FL 33486
TEL 407-362-4220

ART GLASS ENVIRONMENTS, INC
174 NW 13TH ST
BOCA RATON, FL 33432-1605
TEL 407-391-7310

ART LEAGUE OF MARCO ISLAND
1010 WINTERBERRY DR
MARCO ISLAND, FL 33937
TEL 813-394-4221

ART UPTOWN, INC.
1367 MAIN ST
SARASOTA, FL 34236
TEL 813-955-5409

ARTCETERA
640 E ATLANTIC AVE
DELRAY BEACH, FL 33483-5353

ARTSI PHARTSI
2820 S MACDILL AVE
TAMPA, FL 33629
TEL 813-832-2787

BARBARA GILLMAN GALLERY
939 LINCOLN RD
MIAMI BEACH, FL 33139-2601

BAYFRONT GALLERY
713 S PALAFOX ST
PENSACOLA, FL 32501-5935
TEL 904-438-7556

BELVETRO GLASS GALLERY
934 LINCOLN RD
MIAMI BEACH, FL 33139
TEL 305-673-8300

CASA RODRIGUEZ
52 ST. GEORGE ST
ST. AUGUSTINE, FL 32084
TEL 904-824-2305

CENTER STREET GALLERY
136 S PARK AVE
WINTER PARK, FL 32789-4396
TEL 407-644-1545

CHRISTY TAYLOR ART GALLERY
MIZNER PARK
410 PLAZA REAL
BOCA RATON, FL 33433
TEL 407-394-6387

CLAY SPACE GALLERY
924 LINCOLN RD
MIAMI BEACH, FL 33139-2609
TEL 305-534-3339

CLAYTON GALLERIES
4105 S MACDILL AVE
TAMPA, FL 33611-1936
TEL 813-831-3753

COLLECTORS GALLERY
213 W VENICE AVE.
VENICE, FL 34285-2002
TEL 813-488-3029

CONCEPTS 3 INTERNATIONAL
1133 LOUISIANA AVE #105
WINTER PARK, FL 32789-2350
TEL 407-740-0645

CREATIVE INSPIRATIONS GALLERY
718 E LAS OLAS BLVD
FT. LAUDERDALE, FL 33301

CROSSED PALMS GALLERY
8315 MAIN ST
BOKEELIA, FL 33922
TEL 913-283-2283

EG CODY GALLERY
80 NE 40TH ST
MIAMI, FL 33137-3510
TEL 305-374-4777

EXIT ART
THE CENTRE
5380 GULF OF MEXICO DR
LONGBOAT KEY, FL 34228
TEL 813-383-4099

FLORIDA CRAFTSMEN GALLERY
501 CENTRAL AVE
SAINT PETERSBURG, FL 33701-3703
TEL 813-821-7391

GALERIA OF SCULPTURE, INC.
VIA PARIGI #11 WORTH AVE
PALM BEACH, FL 33480
TEL 407-659-7557

GALLERY CAMINO REAL
GALLERY CENTER
608 BANYAN TR
BOCA RATON, FL 33428
TEL 407-241-1606

GALLERY CONTEMPORANEA
526 LANCASTER ST
JACKSONVILLE, FL 32204-4138
TEL 904-359-0016

GALLERY FIVE
363 TEQUESTA DR
TEQUESTA, FL 33469-3027
TEL 407-747-5555

GALLERY ONE
1301 3RD ST S
NAPLES, FL 33940-7203
TEL 813-263-0835

GRAND CENTRAL GALLERY
442 W GRAND CENTRAL AVE #100
TAMPA, FL 33606-1926
TEL 813-254-4977

GREEN GALLERY
1541 BRICKELL AVE #1503
MIAMI, FL 33129-1213
TEL 305-858-7868

GREYWOLF GALLERY
3044 SCHERER DR N
SAINT PETERSBURG, FL 33716-1027

HB BRICKELL GALLERY
905 S BAYSHORE DR
MIAMI, FL 33131-2935
TEL 305-358-2088

HABITAT GALLERIES
GALLERY CENTER
608 BANYAN TRAIL
BOCA RATON, FL 33428
TEL 407-241-4544

HARPER COMPANY
4 VIA PARIGI
PALM BEACH, FL 33480-4613

HARRISON GALLERY
825 WHITE ST
KEY WEST, FL 33040
TEL 305-294-0609

HEARTWORKS
820 LOMAX ST
JACKSONVILLE, FL 32204-3902
TEL 904-355-6210

HELANDER GALLERY
350 SOUTH COUNTY RD
PALM BEACH, FL 33480
TEL 407-659-1711

HELIUM
760 OCEAN DR
MIAMI, FL 33139-6273
TEL 305-538-4111

HELLER GALLERY PALM BEACH
203 WORTH AVE
PALM BEACH, FL 33480-4614
TEL 407-833-4457

HODGELL GALLERY
46 PALM AVE S
SARASOTA, FL 34236
TEL 813-366-1146

HOFFMAN GALLERY
4070 NE 15TH TER
FORT LAUDERDALE, FL 33334-4647
TEL 305-561-7300

IMAGES ART GALLERY
7400 TAMIAMI TRL N #101
NAPLES, FL 33963-2855
TEL 813-598-3455

J LAWRENCE GALLERY
535 W EAU GALLIE BLVD
MELBOURNE, FL 32935-6506
TEL 407-728-7051

JAY MOOS GALLERY
355 NE 59TH TERR
MIAMI, FL 33137
TEL 305-754-9373

LEWIS CHARLES GALLERY
1627 W SNOW CIR
TAMPA, FL 33606-2562
TEL 813-254-8700

LUCKY STREET GALLERY
919 DUVAL ST
KEY WEST, FL 33040-7407
TEL 305-294-3976

MARGEAUX
2808 BIRD AVE
MIAMI, FL 33133-4605
TEL 305-444-8343

MASTERPIECE GALLERY
449 PLAZA REAL
BOCA RATON, FL 33432-3942
TEL 407-394-0070

MELANGE
11440 SOUTH TROPICAL TR
MERRITT ISLAND, FL 32952
TEL 407-779-1115

MODERN ART GALLERY
1469 MAIN ST
SARASOTA, FL 34236
TEL 813-366-3494

MOLE HOLE OF FORT MYERS
13499 U.S. 41 SE #100
FORT MYERS, FL 33907

NANCY KAYE GALLERY
201 E PALMETTO PARK RD
BOCA RATON, FL 33432-5013
TEL 407-392-8220

NEWBILL COLLECTION
309 RUSKIN PL
PO BOX 4809
SEASIDE, FL 32459
TEL 904-231-4500

OEHLSCHLAEGER GALLERY II
253 BIRD KEY DR
SARASOTA, FL 34236-1601
TEL 813-366-0652

OVERWHELMED
445 PLAZA REAL
MIZNER PARK
BOCA RATON, FL 33432-3942
TEL 407-368-0078

PARK SHORE GALLERIES
501 GOODLETTE RD N #8-204
NAPLES, FL 33940-5661
TEL 813-434-0833

PASSAGE WEST FINE ART GALLERY
3020 N FEDERAL HWY
FORT LAUDERDALE, FL 33306-1417
TEL 305-565-8009

PLANTATION POTTERS
521 FLEMING ST
KEY WEST, FL 33040-6824
TEL 305-294-3143

PRESIDIO GALLERY
36 SPANISH ST
SAINT AUGUSTINE, FL 32084-3612
TEL 904-826-1758

PRODIGY GALLERY
4320 GULF SHORE BLVD N #206
NAPLES, FL 33940-2662
TEL 813-263-5881

RAIN BARREL
86700 OVERSEAS HWY
ISLAMORADA, FL 33036-3138
TEL 305-852-3084

RALEIGH GALLERY
1855 GRIFFIN RD
DANIA, FL 33004-2242
TEL 305-922-3330

RICK MOORE FINE ART GALLERY
5455 TAMIAMI TRL N
NAPLES, FL 33963-2870
TEL 813-592-5455

RICK SANDERS GALLERIES
1310 BAY RD
SARASOTA, FL 34239-6801
TEL 813-364-9911

ROBERT WINDSOR GALLERY
1855 GRIFFIN RD
DANIA, FL 33004-2200
TEL 305-923-9100

SCOTT LAURENT GALLERIES
348 PARK AVE
WINTER PARK, FL 32789
TEL 407-629-1488

SELDOM SEEN
820 E LAS OLAS BLVD
FT. LAUDERDALE, FL 33301
TEL 305-764-5590

SIMONS & GREEN
5842 SUNSET DR
S. MIAMI, FL 33143
TEL 305-667-1692

SOKOLSKY GALLERY FOR FINE ARTS
942 LINCOLN RD
SOUTH FLORIDA ART CENTER
MIAMI BEACH, FL 33139-2602
TEL 305-674-8278

SPECTRUM OF AMERICAN ARTISTS
3101 PGA BLVD #B117
PALM BEACH GARDENS, FL 33410
TEL 407-622-2527

STATE STREET GALLERY
1517 STATE ST
SARASOTA, FL 34236-5808
TEL 813-362-3767

TEQUESTA GALLERIES, INC
361 TEQUESTA DR
TEQUESTA, FL 33469-3027
TEL 407-744-2534

TURNBERRY ART GALLERY
19707 TURNBERRY WAY
MIAMI, FL 33180-2566
TEL 305-931-5272

VINCENT WILLIAM GALLERY INC.
348 COREY AVE
ST. PETE BEACH, FL 33706
TEL 813-363-1334

ZOO GALLERY
1209 AIRPORT RD #3
DESTIN, FL 32541-2933

ZOO GALLERY
186 MIRACLE STRIP PKWY
FT WALTON BEACH, FL 32548
TEL 904-243-6702

GEORGIA

ADVENTURES
2626 AUBURN AVE #G
COLUMBUS, GA 31906-1330

ALIYA, GALLERY AT MORNINGSIDE
1402 N HIGHLAND AVE NE #6
ATLANTA, GA 30306-3301
TEL 404-892-2835

AURUM STUDIOS
125 E CLAYTON ST
ATHENS, GA 30601
TEL 706-546-8826

BY HAND SOUTH
W PONCE PLACE
308 W PONCE DE LEON AVE #E
DECATUR, GA 30030
TEL 404-378-0118

CITY ARTWORKS
2140 PEACHTREE RD NW
ATLANTA, GA 30309
TEL 404-605-0786

CONNELL GALLERY
333 BUCKHEAD AVE NE
ATLANTA, GA 30305-2305
TEL 404-261-1712

D. MORGAN GALLERY
909 COMMERCIAL ST
CONYERS, GA 30207
TEL 404-922-4554

DEAN MOSS GALLERY
308 WEST PONCE DE LEON AVE
DECATUR, GA 30030
TEL 404-377-4705

DIASPRORA ART GALLERY
232 AUBURN AVE
ATLANTA, GA 30303
TEL 404-525-7900

EVE MANNES GALLERY
116 BENNETT ST NW #A
ATLANTA, GA 30309-1267
TEL 404-351-6651

FAY GOLD GALLERY
247 BUCKHEAD AVE NE
ATLANTA, GA 30305-2237
TEL 404-233-3843

FRAGILE
175 MT VERNON HIGHWAY
ATLANTA, GA 30328
TEL 404-257-1323

HEATH GALLERY, INC
416 E PACES FERRY RD NE
ATLANTA, GA 30305-3307
TEL 404-262-6407

ILLUMINA
3500 PEACHTREE RD NE #A24
PHIPP'S PLAZA
ATLANTA, GA 30326-1251
TEL 404-233-3010

LAGERQUIST GALLERY INC
3235 PACES FERRY PL NW
ATLANTA, GA 30305-1308
TEL 404-261-8273

LOWE GALLERY
75 BENNETT ST NW #A-7
ATLANTA, GA 30309-1275
TEL 404-352-8114

MAIN STREET GALLERY
MAIN ST
CLAYTON, GA 30525
TEL 404-782-2440

MCINTOSH GALLERY
ONE VIRGINIA HILL
587 VIRGINIA AVE
ATLANTA, GA 30306
TEL 404-892-4023

RED DOOR GALLERY
BANKHEAD HWY
CARROLTON, GA
TEL 404-830-0025

GALLERY LISTINGS

SIGNATURE SHOP & GALLERY
3267 ROSWELL RD NE
ATLANTA, GA 30305-1840
TEL 404-237-4426

SOUTHERN ACCESSORIES TODAY
ATLANTA MERCHANDISE MART #12A2
ATLANTA, GA 30303
TEL 404-581-0811

THE CREATIVE MARK
130 W WASHINGTON ST
MADISON, GA 30650-1216
TEL 404-342-2153

TRINITY GALLERY
940 MYRTLE ST NE APT 8
ATLANTA, GA 30309-4144
TEL 404-525-7546

TULA GALLERIES
75 BENNETT ST NW #D1
ATLANTA, GA 30309-1275
TEL 404-351-6724

UP THE CREEK GALLERY
HWYS 115 & 105
DEMOREST, GA 30535
TEL 404-754-4130

VERONICAS ATTIC
220 SANDY SPRING #181
ATLANTA, GA 30328
TEL 404-257-1409

VESPERMANN GLASS GALLERY
2140 PEACHTREE ST NW
ATLANTA, GA 30309-1314
TEL 404-350-9698

WINN/REGENCY GALLERY
2344 LAWRENCEVILLE HWY
ATLANTA, GA 30033
TEL 404-633-1789

HAWAII

BEADS OF PARADISE
120 HANA HWY. #7
PAIA MAUI, HI 96779
TEL 808-579-9459

COAST GALLERY
PO BOX 565
HANA, HI 96713-0565
TEL 808-248-8636

COLLECTOR'S FINE ART
1571 POIPU RD
KOLOA, HI 96756
TEL 808-700-8431

CONTEMPORARY MUSEUM SHOP
2411 MAKIKI HEIGHTS DRIVE
HONOLULU, HI 96822
TEL 808-523-3447

DREAMS OF PARADISE
308 KAMEHAMEHA AVE #106
HILO, HI 96720-2960
TEL 808-935-5670

**FINE ART ASSOC.
THE ART LOFT**
1020 AUAHI ST #4
HONOLULU, HI 96814-4133
TEL 808-523-0489

MADALINE MICHAELS GALLERY
108 LOPAKA PL
KULA, HI 96790-9504
TEL 800-635-9369

RAKU INTERNATIONAL
331 KAMANI ST
HONOLULU, HI 96813-5324
TEL 808-537-4181

SANDPEOPLE
5-5161 KUHIO HWY
HANALEI, HI 96714
TEL 808-826-7848

THE FOLLOWING SEA
4211 WAIALAE AVE
HONOLULU, HI 96816-5311
TEL 808-734-4425

VILLAGE GALLERY
120 DICKENSON ST
LAHAINA, HI 96761-1203
TEL 808-669-0585

VOLCANO ART CENTER
PO BOX 104
HAWAII NATIONAL PARK, HI
   96718-0104
TEL 808-967-8222

IDAHO

ANNE REED GALLERY
620 SUN VALLEY RD
PO BOX 597
KETCHUM, ID 83340
TEL 208-726-3036

GAIL SEVERN GALLERY
620 SUN VALLEY RD
PO BOX 1679
KETCHUM, ID 83340
TEL 208-726-5079

RICHARD KAVESH GALLERY
PO BOX 6080
KETCHUM, ID 83340-6080
TEL 208-726-2523

RIVER RUN GALLERY
291 1ST AVE
KETCHUM, ID 83340
TEL 208-726-8878

SLEEPING BEAR GALLERY
601 SUN VALLEY RD
PO BOX 2395
KETCHUM, ID 83340
TEL 208-726-3059

ILLINOIS

A UNIQUE PRESENCE
2121 N CLYBOURN AVE
CHICAGO, IL 60614-4031
TEL 312-929-4292

ANN NATHAN GALLERY
210 W SUPERIOR ST
CHICAGO, IL 60610-3508
TEL 312-664-6622

ANNELEE GALLERY
37 E MINE ST
GLENWOOD, IL 60425
TEL 708-757-7100

ART & INTERIOR DESIGN
4826 5TH AVE
MOLINE, IL 61265-1962
TEL 309-762-1135

ART CONCEPTS
2411 S MACARTHUR BLVD
SPRINGFIELD, IL 62704-4505
TEL 217-793-1600

ART EFFECT
641 W ARTMITAGE
CHICAGO, IL 60614
TEL 312-664-0997

ART SCAPE
1625 N ALPINE RD
ROCKFORD, IL 61107-1414
TEL 815-397-1223

ARTISAN SHOP & GALLERY
1515 SHERIDAN RD
PLAZA DEL LAGO
WILMETTE, IL 60091-1822
TEL 312-251-3775

ARTISAN'S GALLERY
PLAZA DEL LAGO
1515 SHERIDAN RD
WILMETTE, IL 60091
TEL 708-251-3775

ARTS AND ARTISANS, LTD.
36 S WABASH #604
CHICAGO, IL 60603
TEL 312-855-9220

ATLAS GALLERIES
549 N MICHIGAN AVE
CHICAGO, IL 60611-1201
TEL 800-423-8702

CALLA LILY
5901 N PROSPECT RD
PEORIA, IL 61614
TEL 309-693-2988

CALLARD & OSGOOD
1611 MERCHANDISE MART
CHICAGO, IL 60654
TEL 312-670-3640

CAREY GALLERY
1062 W CHICAGO AVE
CHICAGO, IL 60622-5416
TEL 312-942-1884

CARL HAMMER GALLERY
200 W SUPERIOR ST
CHICAGO, IL 60610-3532
TEL 312-226-8512

**CENTER FOR
CONTEMPORARY ART**
325 W HURON ST
CHICAGO, IL 60610-3617
TEL 312-944-0094

CHIAROSCURO GALLERY
700 N MICHIGAN AVE
CHICAGO, IL 60611
TEL 312-988-9253

CHICAGO STREET GALLERY
143 11TH AVE
LINCOLN, IL 62656-1505
TEL 217-732-5937

CITYWOODS
659 CENTRAL AVE
HIGHLAND PARK, IL 60035
TEL 708-432-9393

CYRNA INTERNATIONAL
12-101 MERCHANDISE MART
CHICAGO, IL 60654
TEL 312-329-0906

DOUGLAS DAWSON GALLERY
222 W HURON ST
CHICAGO, IL 60610-3613
TEL 312-751-1961

DREAM FAST GALLERY
2035 W WABANSIA AVE
CHICAGO, IL 60647-5501
TEL 312-235-4779

EJ MIRAGE
3260 TIMBERWOOD LN
RIVERWOODS, IL 60015
TEL 708-945-3692

ECLECTIC JUNCTION
1630 N DAMEN
CHICAGO, IL 60647
TEL 312-342-7865

EVA COHON GALLERY
301 W SUPERIOR 2ND FLR
CHICAGO, IL 60610
TEL 312-664-3669

EXPRESSLY WOOD
605 DEMPSTER ST
EVANSTON, IL 60201
TEL 708-869-7060

FUMIE GALLERY
126 S FRANKLIN ST
CHICAGO, IL 60606-4606
TEL 312-726-0080

GALLERIE STEPHANIE
2405 N CLYBOURN
CHICAGO, IL 60614
TEL 312-880-0995

GALLERY MOYA
835 N MICHIGAN AVE
CHICAGO, IL 60611-2203
TEL 312-337-2900

GOOD WORKS GALLERY
485 N MAIN ST
GLEN ELLYNE, IL 60137
TEL 708-858-6654

GWENDA JAY GALLERY
301 W SUPERIOR ST FL 2
CHICAGO, IL 60610-3515
TEL 312-664-3406

HELTZER DESIGN
4853 N RAVENSWOOD AVE
CHICAGO, IL 60640-4409
TEL 312-561-5612

HOKIN KAUFMAN GALLERY
PO BOX 14761
CHICAGO, IL 60614-0761
TEL 312-266-1212

ILLINOIS ARTISANS GALLERY
100 W RANDOLPH ST
CHICAGO, IL 60601-3218
TEL 312-814-5321

IMAGES IN GLASS
719 NORTH CONVENT
BOURBANNAIS, IL 60914
TEL 815-939-3719

JACQUELINE LIPPITZ ART TO WEAR
431 LAKESIDE TER
GLENCOE, IL 60022-1760
TEL 312-835-2666

JAYSON GALLERY
1915 N CLYBOURN AVE
CHICAGO, IL 60614-4903
TEL 312-525-3100

JEAN ALBANO GALLERY
215 WEST SUPERIOR
CHICAGO, IL 60610
TEL 312-440-0770

JOY HORWICH GALLERY
226 E ONTARIO ST
CHICAGO, IL 60611-3205
TEL 312-787-0171

KALEIDOSCOPE GALLERY
205 S COOK ST
BARRINGTON, IL 60010-4313
TEL 708-381-4840

KLEIN ART WORKS
400 N MORGAN ST
CHICAGO, IL 60622-6538
TEL 312-243-0400

LILL STREET GALLERY
1021 W LILL AVE
CHICAGO, IL 60614-2205
TEL 312-477-6185

LINDSEY GALLERY
146 N OAK PARK AVE
OAK PARK, IL 60301-1321
TEL 708-386-5272

LOVELY FINE ARTS, INC
18 W 10022ND ST
OAKBROOK TERRACE, IL 60181
TEL 708-369-2999

LYMAN HEIZER ASSOCIATES
325 W HURON ST #407
CHICAGO, IL 60610-3617
TEL 312-751-2985

MANDEL & COMPANY
1600 MERCHANDISE MART
CHICAGO, IL 60654
TEL 312-644-8242

MARX GALLERY
230 W SUPERIOR ST
CHICAGO, IL 60610-3536
TEL 312-573-1400

MARY BELL GALLERIES
740 N FRANKLIN ST
CHICAGO, IL 60610
TEL 312-642-0202

MERRILL CHASE GALLERIES
1090 JOHNSON DR
BUFFALO GROVE, IL 60089-6918
TEL 708-215-4900

MINDSCAPE
1506 SHERMAN AVE
EVANSTON, IL 60201-4407
TEL 708-864-2660

PAUL STUART
JOHN HANCOCK CENTER
875 MICHIGAN AVE
CHICAGO, IL 60611
TEL 312-640-2650

PEARLMAN GALLERY
474 N LAKE SHORE DR #5806
CHICAGO, IL 60611-3400
TEL 312-467-0144

PERIMETER GALLERY
750 N ORLEANS ST
CHICAGO, IL 60610-3540
TEL 312-266-9473

PERLMAN FINE JEWELRY
1322 SPRINGHILL MALL
DUNDEE, IL 60118-1262

PIECES
644 CENTRAL AVE
HIGHLAND PARK, IL 60035-3222
TEL 708-432-2137

PISTACHIOS
ONE EAST DELAWARE
CHICAGO, IL 60611
TEL 312-988-9433

PLUM LINE GALLERY
1511 CHICAGO AVE
EVANSTON, IL 60201-4405
TEL 708-328-7586

PORTIA GALLERY
1702 N DAMEN AVE
CHICAGO, IL 60647-5509
TEL 312-862-1700

PRESTIGE ART GALLERIES
3909 HOWARD ST
SKOKIE, IL 60076-3793
TEL 708-679-2555

PRESTIGE ART PLUS
8800 GROSS POINT RD
SKOKIE, IL 60077-1809
TEL 708-966-4020

PRINCETON ART GALLERY
1844 1ST ST
HIGHLAND PARK, IL 60035-3102
TEL 708-432-1930

R.C. DANON GALLERY
1224 W LUNT AVE #1
CHICAGO, IL 60626-3030
TEL 312-262-9222

SCHNEIDER GALLERY
230 W SUPERIOR ST
CHICAGO, IL 60610-3536
TEL 312-988-4033

SEO GALLERIA
2655 N CLARK ST
CHICAGO, IL 60614
TEL 312-477-1030

SPECIAL EFFECTS INTERIORS
405 LAKE COOK RD
DEERFIELD, IL 60015-4918
TEL 708-480-1973

STUDIO OF LONG GROVE GALLERY
360 N OLD MCHENRY RD
LONG GROVE, IL 60047-8077
TEL 708-634-4244

GALLERY LISTINGS

SUNRISE ART GALLERY
227 S 3RD ST
GENEVA, IL 60134-2778
TEL 708-232-0730

SWANK
401 N MILWAUKEE AVE
CHICAGO, IL 60610-3914
TEL 312-942-0444

TEXTILE ARTS CENTRE
916 W DIVERSEY PKY
CHICAGO, IL 60614-1429
TEL 312-929-5655

THEA BURGER
223 E STATE ST
PO BOX 182
GENEVA, IL 60134-2335
TEL 708-232-8006

UNIQUE ACCENTS
3137 DUNDEE RD
NORTHBROOK, IL 60062-2402
TEL 708-205-9400

VALE CRAFT GALLERY
207 W SUPERIOR ST
CHICAGO, IL 60610-3507
TEL 312-337-3525

WENTWORTH GALLERY
835 N MICHIGAN AVE
FIFTH LEVEL
CHICAGO, IL 60611-2203
TEL 312-944-0079

WHIMSY
3234 N SOUTHPORT AVE
CHICAGO, IL 60657-3227
TEL 312-665-1760

WOOD STREET GALLERY
1239 N WOOD ST
CHICAGO, IL 60622-3252
TEL 312-227-3306

INDIANA

ARTIFACTS
6327 GUILFORD AVE
INDIANAPOLIS, IN 46220-1709
TEL 317-255-1178

ARTISANS
721 W MULBERRY ST
PO BOX 1222
KOKOMO, IN 46901-4482
TEL 317-452-5505

BY HAND GALLERY
104 E KIRKWOOD AVE
BLOOMINGTON, IN 47408-3330
TEL 812-334-3255

CENTRE ART GALLERY
301B E CARMEL DR
CARMEL, IN 46032-2809
TEL 317-844-6421

CHESTERTON ART GALLERY
115 FOURTH ST
CHESTERTON, IN 46304
TEL 219-926-4711

CORNERSTONE GALLERY
176 W MAIN ST
GREENWOOD, IN 46142-3126
TEL 317-887-2778

DETAILS
1516 WEST 86TH ST
INDIANAPOLIS, IN 46206
TEL 317-872-2626

EARTHLY DESIGNS
8701 KEYSTONE XING
INDIANAPOLIS, IN 46240-4626
TEL 317-580-1861

FABLES GALLERY
317 LINCOLN WAY E
MISHAWAKA, IN 46544-2012
TEL 219-255-9191

FORM & FUNCTION
5449 YELLOW BIRCH WAY
INDIANAPOLIS, IN 46254
TEL 317-328-2949

JM MALLON GALLERIES
EDITIONS LIMITED
4040 E 82ND ST
INDIANAPOLIS, IN 46250
TEL 317-253-7800

JUBILEE GALLERY
121 W COURT AVE
JEFFERSONVILLE, IN 47130-3527
TEL 812-282-9997

KATHERINE TODD FINE ARTS
5356 HILLSIDE AVE
INDIANAPOLIS, IN 46220-3446
TEL 317-253-0250

**PATRICK KING
CONTEMPORARY ART**
PO BOX 44261
INDIANAPOLIS, IN 46244-0261
TEL 317-634-4101

SIGMAN'S GALLERY
930 BROAD RIPPLE AVE
INDIANAPOLIS, IN 46220-1938
TEL 317-253-9953

THE GALLERY
109 E 6TH ST
BLOOMINGTON, IN 47408-3363
TEL 812-336-0564

THE PICTURE SHOW
409 SOUTH MAIN ST
ELKHART, IN 46516
TEL 219-294-3166

TRILOGY GALLERY
120 E MAIN ST, BOX 200
NASHVILLE, IN 47448
TEL 812-988-4030

TULIP TREE ART GALLERY
2525 WEST WASHINGTON ST
MUNCIE, IN 47303
TEL 317-284-4987

IOWA

AGORA ARTS
224 WEST WATER ST
DECORAH, IA 52101
TEL 319-382-8786

ARTISTIC ACCENTS
3405 MT VERNON RD SE
CEDAR RAPIDS, IA 52403
TEL 319-366-8881

ARTISTS CONCEPTS, LTD
7 LONGVIEW KNLS NE
IOWA CITY, IA 52240-9148
TEL 319-337-2361

**CORNERHOUSE
GALLERY & FRAME**
2753 1ST AVE SE
CEDAR RAPIDS, IA 52402-4804
TEL 319-365-4348

FROM GIFTED HANDS
400 MAIN (ON THE PARK)
AMES, IA 50010
TEL 515-232-5656

IOWA ARTISANS GALLERY
117 E COLLEGE ST
IOWA CITY, IA 52240-4002
TEL 319-351-8686

JEAN SAMPLE STUDIO GALLERY
3111 INGERSOLL AVE
DES MOINES, IA 50312-3909

SIGNATURE
132 FIFTH ST
WEST DES MOINES, IA 50265
TEL 515-277-5865

THE LAGNIAPPE
114 5TH ST
WEST DES MOINES, IA 50265-4716
TEL 515-277-0047

KANSAS

GALLERY AT HAWTHORNE
4833 W 119TH ST
OVERLAND PARK, KS 66209-156C
TEL 913-469-8001

SANTA FE CONNECTION
4563 INDIAN CREEK PKY
SHAWNEE MISSION, KS 66207-4004
TEL 913-897-2275

SILVER WORKS & MORE
715 MASSACHUSETTS ST
LAWRENCE, KS 66044-2345
TEL 913-842-1460

KENTUCKY

AFFINITY
2030 TYLER LN
LOUISVILLE, KY 40205-2904

APPALACHIAN FIRESIDE
182 MAIN ST
BEREA, KY 40403-1763
TEL 606-986-9013

ART BIZ GALLERY
414 BAXTER AVE
LOUISVILLE, KY 40204-1160
TEL 502-585-2809

ARTIQUE GALLERY
410 W VINE ST
FIRST LEVEL
LEXINGTON, KY 40507-1616
TEL 606-233-1774

BENCHMARK GALLERY
I-75 INTERCHANGE
BEREA, KY 40403
TEL 606-986-9413

CHESTNUT STREET GALLERY
3409 NICHOLASVILLE RD
LEXINGTON, KY 40503-3605

COMMON WEALTH GALLERY
313 S 4TH AVE
LOUISVILLE, KY 40202-3001
TEL 502-589-4747

COMPLETELY KENTUCKY
235 W BROADWAY ST
FRANKFORT, KY 40601-1956
TEL 502-223-5240

CONTEMPORARY ARTIFACTS
128 N BROADWAY ST
BEREA, KY 40403-1504
TEL 606-986-1096

EDENSIDE GALLERY
1422 BARDSTOWN RD
LOUISVILLE, KY 40204-1419
TEL 502-459-2787

KENTUCKY ART & CRAFT
609 W MAIN ST
LOUISVILLE, KY 40202-2951
TEL 502-589-0102

LIBERTY GALLERY
416 W JEFFERSON ST
LOUISVILLE, KY 40202-3202
TEL 502-566-2081

NASH COLLECTION
843 LANE ALLEN RD
LEXINGTON, KY 40504-3605
TEL 606-276-0161

PERSIMMON TREE GALLERY
3936 CHENOWETH SQUARE
LOUISVILLE, KY 40207

PROMENADE GALLERY
204 CENTER ST
BEREA, KY 40403-1733
TEL 606-986-1609

SWANSON-CRALLE GALLERY
1377 BARDSTOWN RD
LOUISVILLE, KY 40204
TEL 502-452-2904

ZEPHYR GALLERY
812 W MAIN ST
LOUISVILLE, KY 40202-2620
TEL 502-585-5646

LOUISIANA

**ARIODANTE:
CONTEMPORARY CRAFT**
535 JULIA ST
NEW ORLEANS, LA 70130-3623
TEL 318-524-3233

ARTIFACTS
5515 MAGAZINR ST
NEW ORLEANS, LA 70115
TEL 504-899-5505

ARTISTS ALLIANCE
125 W VERMILION ST
LAFAYETTE, LA 70501-6915
TEL 318-233-7518

BATON ROUGE GALLERY
1442 CITY PARK AVE
BATON ROUGE, LA 70808-1037
TEL 504-383-1470

CAROL ROBINSON GALLERY
4537 MAGAZINE ST
NEW ORLEANS, LA 70115-1542
TEL 504-895-6130

GALLERIE I/O
1812 MAGAZINE ST
NEW ORLEANS, LA 70130-5014
TEL 800-875-2113

HILDERBRAND GALLERIES
4524 MAGAZINE ST
NEW ORLEANS, LA 70115
TEL 504-895-3313

LASTING INDULGENCE
628 TOULOUSE ST
NEW ORLEANS, LA 70130
TEL 504-525-2440

MOREHEAD FINE ARTS GALLERY
603 JULIA ST
NEW ORLEANS, LA 70130-3709
TEL 504-568-5470

NEW ORLEANS SCHOOL OF GLASS
727 MAGAZINE ST
NEW ORLEANS, LA 70130
TEL 504-529-7277

RIGSBYS GALLERY
7520 PERKINS RD
BATON ROUGE, LA 70808
TEL 504-769-7903

STONER ARTS CENTER
614 EDWARDS ST
SHREVEPORT, LA 71101-3641
TEL 318-222-1780

MAINE

ABACUS HANDCRAFTERS GALLERY
8 MCKOWN ST
BOOTHBAY HARBOR, ME 04538-1012
TEL 207-633-2166

ARIES FINE AMERICAN CRAFTS
22-A MAIN ST
OGUNQUITI, ME 03907
TEL 207-646-5597

BENSON'S FIBER & WOOD, ETC
59 MOUNTAIN ST
CAMDEN, ME 04843-1635
TEL 207-236-6564

BLUE HERON GALLERY
CHURCH ST
DEER ISLE, ME 04627
TEL 207-348-6051

COMPLIMENTS GALLERY
PO BOX 567
KENNEBUNKPORT, ME 04046-0567
TEL 207-967-2269

EARTHLY DELIGHTS
81 WATER ST
HALLOWELL, ME 04347-1411
TEL 207-622-9801

EDGECOMB POTTERS
RT 27, BOX 2104
EDGECOMB, ME 04556
TEL 207-882-6802

ELEMENTS GALLERY
190 DANFORTH ST
PORTLAND, ME 04102-3828
TEL 207-729-1108

ETIENNE & CO
20 MAIN ST
CAMDEN, ME 04843-1704
TEL 207-236-9696

FRICK GALLERY
139 HIGH ST
BELFAST, ME 04915-1539
TEL 207-338-3671

GREEN HEAD FORGE
OLD QUARRY RD
STONINGTON, ME 04681
TEL 207-367-2632

HANDWORKS
MAIN ST
BLUE HILL, ME 04614
TEL 207-374-5613

HARBOR SQUARE GALLERY
374 MAIN ST
ROCKLAND, ME 04841

**HARBORSQUARE
GALLERY/GOOD HAND**
BAYVIEW ST
CAMDEN, ME 04843
TEL 207-236-8700

LEIGHTON GALLERY
PARKER POINT RD
BLUE HILL, ME 04614
TEL 207-374-5001

LIVING ARTS
17 WESTON AVE
KENNYBUNK, ME 04043
TEL 508-349-9803

MAINE COTTAGE FURNITURE
LOWER FALLS LANDING
YARMOUTH, ME 04046
TEL 207-846-0602

NANCY MARGOLIS GALLERY
367 FORE ST
PORTLAND, ME 04101-5010
TEL 207-775-3822

PHILIP STEIN GALLERY
20 MILK ST
PORTLAND, ME 04101-5024
TEL 207-772-9072

SHORE ROAD GALLERY
112 SHORE RD
OGUNQUIT, ME 03907
TEL 207-646-5046

THOSMAS MOSER
415 CUMBERLAND AVE
PORTLAND, ME 04101
TEL 207-774-3791

TURTLE GALLERY
39 MORNING ST
PORTLAND, ME 04101-4481
TEL 207-774-0621

VICTORIAN STABLE GALLERY
WATER ST
PO BOX 728
DAMARISCOTTA, ME 04543
TEL 207-563-1991

GALLERY LISTINGS

MARYLAND

ART INSTITUTE & GALLERY
RTE 50 & LEMMON HILL LN
SALISBURY, MD 21801
TEL 301-546-4748

ARTISANS COLLECTION, LTD
11216 OLD CARRIAGE RD
GLEN ARM, MD 21057-9415
TEL 301-661-1118

AURORA GALLERY
67 MARYLAND AVE
ANNAPOLIS, MD 21401-1629
TEL 301-263-9150

BARBARA FENDRICK GALLERY
4104 LELAND ST
BETHESDA, MD 20815-5034
TEL 301-226-3881

BRASSWORKS COMPANY, INC
1641 THAMES ST
BALTIMORE, MD 21231-3430
TEL 301-327-7280

CALICO CAT
2137 GWYNN OAK AVE
BALTIMORE, MD 21207
TEL 410-944-2450

CAROLYN'S INTERIORS
7 LOCKS PLAZA
ROCKVILLE, MD 20854
TEL 301-340-2346

CATHY HART POTTERY STUDIO
MILL CENTRE STUDIO #221
BALITMORE, MD 21211
TEL 301-467-4911

CHESAPEAKE EAST
GENERAL DELIVERY
UPPER FAIRMOUNT, MD 21867-9999
TEL 301-543-8175

DISCOVERIES
COLUMBIA MALL
COLUMBIA, MD 21044
TEL 410-740-5800

FINE WARES
7042 CARROLL AVE
TAKOMA PARK, MD 20814
TEL 301-270-3138

FINER SIDE
209B NORTH BLVD
SALISBURY, MD 21801-6252
TEL 410-749-4081

GAZELLE GALLERY
5100 FALLS RD
BALTIMORE, MD 21210-1935
TEL 301-433-3305

GLASS GALLERY
4720 HAMPDEN LN
BETHESDA, MD 20814-2910
TEL 301-657-3478

GRAND JURY
10301 OLD GEORGETOWN RD
BETHESDA, MD 20814
TEL 301-530-7982

JURUS, LTD
5618 NEWBURY ST
BALTIMORE, MD 21209-3604
TEL 410-542-5227

MARGARET SMITH GALLERY
8090 MAIN ST
ELLICOTT CITY, MD 21043-4617
TEL 410-461-0870

MEREDITH GALLERY
805 N CHARLES ST
BALTIMORE, MD 21201-5307
TEL 301-837-3575

PICTURE THIS
9202 BROADWATER DR
GAITHERSBURG, MD 20879
TEL 301-977-6897

PIECES OF OLDE
716 W 36TH ST
BALTIMORE, MD 21211-2505
TEL 301-366-4949

PRESENCE
7718 WOODMONT AVE
BETHESDA, MD 20814
TEL 301-986-4710

ZYZYX
10301A OLD GEORGETOWN RD
BETHESDA, MD 20814
TEL 301-493-0297

ZYZYX
1809 REISTERSTOWN RD
BALTIMORE, MD 21208-6329
TEL 410-486-9785

MASSACHUSETTS

ALIANZA CONTEMPORARY CRAFTS
154 NEWBURY ST
BOSTON, MA 02116-2838
TEL 617-262-2385

ANDREA MARQUIT FINE ARTS
38 NEWBURY ST
BOSTON, MA 02116-3210
TEL 617-859-0190

ARTFUL HAND GALLERIES
MAIN ST SQUARE
PO BOX 131
ORLEANS, MA 02653
TEL 617-255-2969

ARTFUL HAND GALLERY
36 COPLEY PL
100 HUNTINGTON AVE
BOSTON, MA 02116-6514
TEL 617-262-9601

ARTIQUE GALLERY
400 COCHITUATE RD
FARMINGHAM MALL
FRAMINGHAM, MA 01701-4655
TEL 508-872-3373

ARTISAN GALLERY
150 MAIN ST
NORTHAMPTON, MA 01060-3131
TEL 413-586-1942

ARTISTS & CRAFTSMEN GALLERY
72 MAIN ST
WEST HARWICH, MA 02671-1115
TEL 508-432-7604

ARTS & CRAFTS GALLERY
27 WHITEHAVEN WAY
SOUTH DENNIS, MA 02660-2681
TEL 508-385-4414

ARTWORK GALLERY
261 PARK AVE
WORCESTER, MA 01609-1919
TEL 508-755-7808

ATELIER GALLERY
200 BOYLSTON ST #405
CHESTNUT HILL, MA 02167-2008
TEL 617-965-5757

BARACCA GALLERY
PO BOX 85
NORTH HATFIELD, MA 01066-0085
TEL 413-247-5262

BARBARAS TWO GALLERY
58 GREENLAWN AVE
NEWTON CENTER, MA 02159-1714

BLACKS HANDWEAVING SHOP
597 MAIN ST
WEST BARNSTABLE, MA 02668-1128
TEL 508-362-3955

BLAIR HOUSE ANTIQUES
1 FRONT ST
BEVERLY, MA 01915

BOSTON CORPORATE ART
470 ATLANTIC AVE
BOSTON, MA 02210-2208
TEL 617-426-8880

BRAMHALL & DUNN
BOX 923 MAIN ST
VINEYARD HAVEN, MA 02568
TEL 508-693-6437

BRAMHALL & DUNN GALLERY
16 FEDERAL ST
NANTUCKET, MA 02554-3568
TEL 508-228-4688

CLARK GALLERY
PO BOX 339
LINCOLN STATION
LINCOLN, MA 01773-0339
TEL 617-259-8303

CRAFTY YANKEE
1838 MASSACHUSETTS AVE
LEXINGTON, MA 02173-5303
TEL 617-863-1219

CROMA GALLERY
94 CENTRAL ST
WELLESLEY, MA 02181-5714
TEL 617-235-6230

DANCO FURNITURE
ROUTES 5 & 10
WEST HATFIELD, MA 01088
TEL 413-247-5681

DESIGNERS GALLERY LTD
1 DESIGN CENTER PL #329
BOSTON, MA 02210-2313
TEL 617-426-5511

DON MULLER GALLERY
40 MAIN ST
NORTHAMPTON, MA 01060
TEL 413-586-1119

FESTIVE CREATIONS
55 LOVE LN
WESTON, MA 02193
TEL 617-894-5139

FIRE OPAL
7 POND ST
JAMAICA PLAIN, MA 02130-2502
TEL 617-524-0262

FULLER MUSUEM OF ART
MUSEUM SHOP
455 OAK ST
BROCKTON, MA 02401
TEL 508-588-6000

GALLERIE OCEANNA
18 N SUMMER ST
EDGARTOWN, MA 02539
TEL 508-627-3121

GALLERY NAGA
67 NEWBURY ST
BOSTON, MA 02116-3010
TEL 617-267-9060

GIFTED HAND GALLERY
32 CHURCH ST
WELLESLEY, MA 02181-6322
TEL 617-235-7171

GM GALLERIES
MAIN ST
WEST STOCKBRIDGE, MA 01266
TEL 413-232-8519

HALF MOON HARRY
19 BEARSKIN NCK
ROCKPORT, MA 01966-1666
TEL 508-546-6601

HAND OF MAN CRAFT GALLERY
THE CURTIS SHOPS
WALKER ST
LENOX, MA 01240
TEL 413-637-0632

HAND OF MAN CRAFT GALLERY
29 WENDELL AVE
PITTSFIELD, MA 01201-6311
TEL 413-443-6033

HANDWORKS INC
157 GREAT RD #2A
ACTON, MA 01720-5712
TEL 508-263-7107

HOADLEY GALLERY
66 CHURCH ST
LENOX, MA 01240
TEL 413-637-2814

HOLSTEN GALLERIES
GENERAL DELIVERY
STOCKBRIDGE, MA 01262-9999
TEL 413-298-3044

HOORN ASHBY GALLERY
10 FEDERAL ST
NANTUCKET, MA 02554-3514
TEL 508-228-9314

ICARUS
5 STATE ST
NEWBURY PORT, MA 01950
TEL 508-463-9246

IMPULSE
188 COMMERCIAL ST
PROVINCETOWN, MA 02657-2117
TEL 508-487-1154

JOHN LEWIS, INC
97 NEWBURY ST
BOSTON, MA 02116-3086
TEL 617-266-6665

JUBILATION
91 UNION ST
PICADILLY STATION
NEWTON, MA 02159-2224
TEL 617-965-0488

LA RUCHE
168 NEWBURY ST
BOSTON, MA 02116
TEL 617-536-6366

LACOSTE GALLERY
39 THOREAU ST
CONCORD, MA 01742
TEL 508-369-0278

LEFT BANK GALLERY
COMMERCIAL ST
WELLFLEET, MA 02667
TEL 508-349-9451

LIMITED EDITIONS, INC
1176 WALNUT ST
NEWTON HIGHLANDS, MA 02161-1224
TEL 617-965-5474

MDF
19 BRATTLE ST
CAMBRIDGE, MA 02138-3709
TEL 617-491-2789

MOBILIA
358 HURON AVE
CAMBRIDGE, MA 02138-6828
TEL 617-876-2109

NEAL ROSENBLUM GOLDSMITHS
287 PARK AVE
WORCESTER, MA 01609-1846
TEL 508-755-4244

NORTHSIDE CRAFT GALLERY
933 MAIN ST
YARMOUTH PORT, MA 02675-2124
TEL 508-362-5291

ORIEL
17 COLLEGE ST
SOUTH HADLEY, MA 01075-1403
TEL 413-532-6469

QUADRUM
THE MALL AT CHESTNUT HILL
CHESTNUT HILL, MA 02167
TEL 617-262-9601

RICE POLAK GALLERY
432 COMMERCIAL ST
PROVINCETOWN, MA 02657-2426
TEL 508-487-1052

SALMON FALLS ARTISANS SHOWROOM
PO BOX 17
ASHFIELD RD
SHELBURNE FALLS, MA 01370-0017
TEL 413-625-9833

SIGNATURE GALLERY
10 STEEPLE ST
MASHPEE, MA 02657-2117
TEL 508-539-0029

SIGNATURE GALLERY DOCK SQUARE
24 NORTH ST
BOSTON, MA 02109
TEL 617-227-4885

SILVERSCAPE DESIGNS
264 N PLEASANT ST
AMHERST, MA 01002-1725
TEL 413-253-3324

SILVERSCAPE DESIGNS
1 KING ST
NORTHAMPTON, MA 01060-3221
TEL 413-253-3324

SIOUX EAGEL DESIGNS
80 MAIN ST
VINEYARD HAVEN, MA 02568
TEL 508-693-6537

SKERA GALLERY
221 MAIN ST
NORTHAMPTON, MA 01060-3122
TEL 413-586-4563

SOCIETY OF ARTS & CRAFTS
175 NEWBURY ST
BOSTON, MA 02116
TEL 617-266-1810

SPECTRUM OF AMERICAN ARTISTS
369 MAIN ST
BREWSTER, MA 02631-1036
TEL 508-385-3322

SPECTRUM OF AMERICAN ARTISTS
26 MAIN ST
NANTUCKET, MA 02554-3531
TEL 508-228-4606

STEPHEN FELLERMAN
534 SOUTH MAINE ST
SHEFFIELD, MA 01257
TEL 413-229-8533

SWEET PEAS
232 NEWBURY ST
BOSTON, MA 02116
TEL 617-247-2828

TERRA COTTA
765 MASSACHUSETTS AVE
CAMBRIDGE, MA 02139
TEL 617-864-1454

TERRA FIRMA
49 LEONARD ST
BELMONT, MA 02178
TEL 617-489-5353

THE BALCONY
PO BOX 489
VINEYARD HAVEN, MA 02568-0489
TEL 508-693-5127

THE SPECTRUM
369 OLD KLUGS HWY
BREWSTER, MA 02631
TEL 508-385-3322

WAYSIDE GALLERY
512 MAIN ST
CHATHAM, MA 02033
TEL 508-945-0749

WHIPPOORWILL CRAFTS GALLERY
126 S MARKET ST
FANEUIL HALL MARKET
BOSTON, MA 02109-1626
TEL 617-523-5149

WICKER LADY INC.
925 WEBSTER ST
NEEDHAM, MA 02192
TEL 617-449-1172

GALLERY LISTINGS

WILD GOOSE CHASE
1431 BEACON ST
BROOKLINE, MA 02146
TEL 617-738-8020

WOLOV GALLERY
94 SEAVIEW AVE
MARBLEHEAD, MA 01945-1732
TEL 617-426-5511

MICHIGAN

16 HANDS GALLERY
216 S MAIN
ANN ARBOR, MI 4104
TEL 313-761-1110

ACKERMAN GALLERY
327 ABBOTT RD
EAST LANSING, MI 48823-4309
TEL 517-332-6818

ALICE SIMSAR GALLERY
PO BOX 7089
ANN ARBOR, MI 48107-7089
TEL 313-665-4883

ANDERSON GALLERY
7 NORTH SAGINAW ST
PONTIAC, MI 48342
TEL 810-335-4611

ANDY SHARKEY GALLERY
204 WEST FIFTH AVE
ROYAL OAK, MI 48067
TEL 313-546-6770

ANIMALIA
403 WATER ST
SAUGATUCK, MI 49453
TEL 616-857-3227

ANN ARBOR ART ASSOCIATION
117 W LIBERTY ST
ANN ARBOR, MI 48104-1380
TEL 313-994-8004

ARIANA GALLERY
119 S MAIN ST
ROYAL OAK, MI 48067-2610
TEL 810-546-8810

ART LEADERS GALLERY
26111 NOVI RD
NOVI, MI 48375-1140
TEL 810-348-5540

ART RAGE
815 FIRST ST
MENOMINEE, MI 49858
TEL 906-864-7243

ARTISANS GALLERY
2666 CHARLEVOIX AVE
PETOSKEY, MI 49770-9707
TEL 616-347-6466

BELL GALLERY
257 E MAIN ST
HARBOR SPRINGS, MI 49740-1511
TEL 616-526-9855

BOYER GLASSWORKS
207 N STATE ST
HARBOR SPRINGS, MI 49740
TEL 616-526-6359

CAROL HOOBERMAN GALLERY
124 S WOODWARD AVE #12
BIRMINGHAM, MI 48009-6119
TEL 313-647-3666

CAROL JAMES GALLERY
301 S MAIN ST
ROYAL OAK, MI 48067-2613
TEL 313-541-6216

CHAMELEON GALLERY
370 S MAIN ST
PLYMOUTH, MI 48170

COURTYARD GALLERY
813 E BUFFALO ST
NEW BUFFALO, MI 49117-1522
TEL 616-469-4110

DECO ART
815 1ST ST
MENOMINEE, MI 49858-3231
TEL 906-863-3300

DELL PRYOR GALLERY
HARMONIE PARK
1452 RANDOLPH
DETROIT, MI 48226
TEL 313-963-5977

DETROIT GALLERY OF
CONTEMPORARY CRAFTS
104 FISHER BLDG
DETROIT, MI 48202
TEL 313-873-7888

DONNA JACOBS GALLERY, LTD
574 N WOODWARD AVE
SECOND FLOOR
BIRMINGHAM, MI 48009-5375
TEL 313-540-1600

FRIENDS FURNISHINGS
& DESIGN
126 MAINCENTRE
NORTHVILLE, MI 48167-1562
TEL 313-380-6930

GALLERIE 454
15105 KERCHEVAL ST
GROSSE POINTE, MI 48230-1389
TEL 313-822-4454

GALLERY FOUR FOURTEEN
414 DETROIT ST
ANN ARBOR, MI 48104-1118
TEL 313-747-7004

GALLERY ON THE ALLEY
611 BROAD ST
SAINT JOSEPH, MI 49085-1257
TEL 616-983-6161

GALLERY ONE
3201 SUNSET LN
ODEN ISLAND
PETOSKEY, MI 49770
TEL 616-347-4634

GARDEN HOUSE INTERIORS
9426 BIRCH RUN RD
BIRCH RUN, MI 48415-9442
TEL 517-624-9649

GOOD GOODS
106 MASON ST
SAUGATUCK, MI 49453
TEL 616-857-1557

GREAT FRAME UP
2876 WASHTENAW RD
YPSILANTI, MI 48197-1507
TEL 313-434-8556

HABITAT GALLERIES
TRIATRIA BLDG #45
32255 NORTHWESTERN HWY
FARMINGTON HILLS, MI 48334
TEL 313-851-9090

HANDIWORKS, LTD
5260 HELENA ST
ALDEN, MI 49612
TEL 616-331-6787

HOOVER HOUSE GALLERY
8730 CURTIS LN
PETOSKEY, MI 49770-9789
TEL 616-526-9819

HUZZA
136 E MAIN ST
HARBOR SPRINGS, MI 49740-1510
TEL 616-526-2128

JOYCE PETTER GALLERY
134 BUTLER ST
DOUGLAS/SAUGATUCK, MI 49453
TEL 616-857-7861

JUDITH RACHT GALLERY, INC
GENERAL DELIVERY
HARBERT, MI 49115-9999
TEL 517-469-1080

KENNEDY FLORAL
4665 CASCADE RD SE
GRAND RAPIDS, MI 49546-3766

KOUCKY GALLERY
319 BRIDGE ST
CHARLEVOIX, MI 49720-1414
TEL 616-547-2228

LAKESIDE STUDIO
15251 LAKESHORE RD
LAKESIDE, MI 49116-9712
TEL 616-469-1377

LINDA HAYMAN GALLERY
5 PINE GATE CT
BLOOMFIELD HILLS, MI 48304-2111
TEL 810-433-3430

MACKEREL SKY GALLERY
217 ANN ST
E. LANSING, MI 48823
TEL 517-351-2211

ATTIE FLYNN
1033 E FULTON ST
GRAND RAPIDS, MI 49503-3608
TEL 616-454-8775

MESA ARTS GALLERY
32800 FRANKLIN RD
FRANKLIN, MI 48025-1111
TEL 313-851-9949

NICOL STUDIO & GALLERY
2531 CHARLEVOIX AVE
PETOSKEY, MI 49770-8524
TEL 616-347-0227

PAINTED BIRD
216 ST. JOSEPH'S AVE
SUTTON'S BAY, MI 49682
TEL 616-271-3050

PDA ASSOCIATES
1019 WEST KILGORE
KALAMAZOO, MI 49008
TEL 616-342-0103

PEACEABLE KINGDOM
210 S MAIN ST
ANN ARBOR, MI 48104-2106

PELLETIER GALLERY
414 DETROIT ST
ANN ARBOR, MI 48104-1118
TEL 313-741-0571

PENNIMAN SHOWCASE
827 PENNIMAN AVE
PLYMOUTH, MI 48170-1621
TEL 313-455-5531

PERRY SHERWOOD FINE ART
200 HOWARD ST
PETOSKY, MI 49770
TEL 616-348-5079

PINE TREE GALLERY
824 E CLOVERLAND DR
US HWY 2
IRONWOOD, MI 49938-1502
TEL 906-932-5120

POSNER GALLERY
32407 N WESTERN HWY
FARMINGTON HILLS, MI 48332
TEL 313-626-6450

PRESTON BURKE GALLERY
37622 W 12 MILE RD
FARMINGTON HILLS, MI 48331-3074
TEL 313-963-2350

PRIVATE COLLECTION GALLERY
6736A ORCHARD LAKE RD
WEST BLOOMFIELD, MI 48322-3411
TEL 313-737-4050

REVOLUTION
23257 WOODWARD AVE
FERNDALE, MI 48220-1361

RICHARD BERK GALLERY
7056 SPRINGRIDGE
SPRINGRIDGE, MI 48322
TEL 810-851-0739

ROBERT KIDD GALLERY
107 TOWNSEND ST
BIRMINGHAM, MI 48009-6001
TEL 313-642-3909

RUSSELL KLATT GALLERY
1467 S WOODWARD AVE
BIRMINGHAM, MI 48009-5125
TEL 313-647-6655

SANDRA COLLINS, INC
470 N WOODWARD AVE
BIRMINGHAM, MI 48009-5372
TEL 313-642-4795

SAPER GALLERY
433 ALBERT AVE
EAST LANSING, MI 48823-4406
TEL 517-351-0815

SELO SHEVEL GALLERY
301 S MAIN ST
ANN ARBOR, MI 48104-2107
TEL 313-761-4620

SELO SHEVEL GALLERY
335 S MAIN ST
ANN ARBOR, MI 48104
TEL 313-761-6263

SPITLER GALLERY
2007 PAULINE CT
ANN ARBOR, MI 48103-5185
TEL 313-662-8914

SUZIE VIGLAND GALLERY
1047 MICHIGAN AVE
BENZONIA, MI 49616
TEL 616-882-7203

SYBARIS GALLERY
202 E 3RD ST
ROYAL OAK, MI 48067-2620
TEL 313-544-3388

T'MARRA GALLERY
111 N 1ST ST
ANN ARBOR, MI 48104-1301
TEL 313-769-3223

TAMARACK CRAFTSMEN
GENERAL DELIVERY
OMENA, MI 49674-9999
TEL 616-386-5529

TOUCH OF LIGHT GALLERY
23426 WOODWARD AVE
FERNDALE, MI 48220-1344
TEL 313-543-1868

TRULY GIFTED
515 S WASHINGTON AVE
ROYAL OAK, MI 48067-3825

URBAN ARCHITECTUR INC
15 E KIRBY ST
DETROIT, MI 48202-4047
TEL 313-873-2707

WETSMAN COLLECTION
132 N WOODWARD AVE
BIRMINGHAM, MI 48009-3375
TEL 810-645-6212

WOODWARD GALLERY
1357 DAVIS
BIRMINGHAM, MI 48009
TEL 313-642-1357

YAW GALLERY
550 N WOODWARD AVE
BIRMINGHAM, MI 48009-5375
TEL 313-747-5470

MINNESOTA

ANDERSON & ANDERSON GALLERY
414 1ST AVE N
MINNEAPOLIS, MN 55401-1702
TEL 612-332-4889

ART LENDING GALLERY
25 GROVELAND TER
MINNEAPOLIS, MN 55403-1104
TEL 612-377-7800

ART RESOURCES GALLERY
3245 GALLERIA
EDINA, MN 55345

ART RESOURCES GALLERY
494 JACKSON ST
SAINT PAUL, MN 55101-2320
TEL 612-222-4431

BLANC DE BLANC
691 LAKE ST
WAYZATA, MN 55391
TEL 612-473-8275

BOIS FORT GALLERY
130 E SHERIDAN ST
ELY, MN 55731-1215
TEL 218-365-5066

CALLAWAY GALLERIES
101 SW FIRST AVE
ROCHESTER, MN 55902
TEL 507-287-6525

CELEBRATION DESIGNS
1089 GRAND AVE
SAINT PAUL, MN 55105-3002
TEL 612-690-4344

FORUM GALLERY
1235 YALE PL #1308
MINNEAPOLIS, MN 55403-1947
TEL 612-333-1825

GLASSPECTACLE
402 MAIN ST N
STILLWATER, MN 55082-5051
TEL 612-439-0757

GOLDSTEIN GALLERY
250 MCNEAL HALL
1985 BUFORD AVE
SAINT PAUL, MN 55108
TEL 612-624-7434

GRAND AVENUE FRAME & GALLERY
964 GRAND AVE
SAINT PAUL, MN 55105-3014
TEL 612-224-9716

MC GALLERY
400 1ST AVE N #336
THIRD FLOOR
MINNEAPOLIS, MN 55401-1721
TEL 612-339-1480

M LAVINE
PO BOX 315
COLD SPRING, MN 56320
TEL 612-685-3071

MADE IN THE SHADE GALLERY
600 E SUPERIOR ST
DULUTH, MN 55802-2230
TEL 218-722-1929

NORTHERN CLAY CENTER
2375 UNIVERSITY AVE W
SAINT PAUL, MN 55114-1603
TEL 612-642-1735

NORTHFIELD ARTS GUILD
304 DIVISION ST
NORTHFIELD, MN 55057
TEL 507-645-8877

OUT OF THE ORDINARY
8800 HIGHWAY 7
SAINT LOUIS PARK, MN 55426-3908

PETER M DAVID GALLERY
3351 SAINT LOUIS AVE
MINNEAPOLIS, MN 55416-4394
TEL 612-339-1825

RAYMOND AVENUE GALLERY
761 RAYMOND AVE
SAINT PAUL, MN 55114-1522
TEL 612-644-9200

ROOMERS GALLERY
5632 SANIBEL DR
MINNETONKA, MN 55343-9428
TEL 612-822-9490

ROURKE'S GALLERY
523 4TH ST S
MOORHEAD, MN 56560-2620
TEL 218-236-8861

GALLERY LISTINGS

SAYER STRAND GALLERY
275 MARKET ST #222
MINNEAPOLIS, MN 55405-1623
TEL 612-375-0838

SONIA'S GALLERY, INC
400 1ST AVE N #318
MINNEAPOLIS, MN 55401-1721
TEL 612-338-0350

**SUPERIOR LAKE—
N AMERICA, INC**
716 E SUPERIOR ST
DULUTH, MN 55802-2210
TEL 218-722-6998

SUZANNE KOHN GALLERY
1690 GRAND AVE
SAINT PAUL, MN 55105-1806
TEL 612-699-0417

TECHNIC GALLERY
400 SELBY AVE #B
SAINT PAUL, MN 55102-4508
TEL 612-222-0188

TEXTILE ARTS INTERNATIONAL
PO BOX 52063
MINNEAPOLIS, MN 55402-5063
TEL 612-338-6776

THOMAS BARRY FINE ARTS
400 1ST AVE N #304
MINNEAPOLIS, MN 55401-1721
TEL 612-338-3656

WHITE OAK GALLERY
3939 W 50TH ST
EDINA, MN 55424-1244
TEL 612-927-3575

MISSISSIPPI

BRYANT GALLERIES
2845 LAKELAND DR
JACKSON, MS 39208-8831
TEL 601-932-1993

CHIMNEYVILLE CRAFTS
1150 LAKELAND DR
JACKSON, MS 39216-4701
TEL 601-988-9253

EARTH TRADERS INC
1060 E COUNTY LINE RD
RIDGELAND, MS 39157-1900

OLD TRACE GALLERY, LTD
200 E WASHINGTON ST
KOSCIUSKO, MS 39090-3746
TEL 601-289-9170

SERENITY GALLERY
126½ MAIN ST
BAY SAINT LOUIS, MS 39520-4526
TEL 601-467-3061

THIRD DIMENSION GALLERY
201 BANNER HALL
4465 I-55 N
JACKSON, MS 39206
TEL 601-366-3371

MISSOURI

AUSTRAL GALLERY
2115 PARK AVE
SAINT LOUIS, MO 63104-2539
TEL 314-776-0300

BARUCCI GALLERY
8101 MARYLAND AVE
CLAYTON, MO 63105-3720
TEL 314-727-2020

BERRYBRIDGE FOR THE BIRDS
17 DEVON RD
SAINT LOUIS, MO 63122
TEL 314-725-1177

CENTRAL PARK GALLERY
1644 WYANDOTTE ST
KANSAS CITY, MO 64108-1224
TEL 816-471-7711

CRAFT ALLIANCE GALLERY
6640 DELMAR BLVD
SAINT LOUIS, MO 63130-4503
TEL 314-725-1151

**GLYNN BROWN DESIGN
GALLERY**
420 W 7TH ST
KANSAS CITY, MO 64105-1407
TEL 816-842-2115

**HELLA'S ART TO WEAR
& FIBERS**
9769 CLAYTON RD
SAINT LOUIS, MO 63124-1503
TEL 314-997-9696

INTERWOVEN DESIGNS
4400 LACLEDE AVE
SAINT LOUIS, MO 63108-2204
TEL 314-531-6200

LEEDY VOULKOS GALLERY
2012 BALTIMORE AVE
KANSAS CITY, MO 64108-1914
TEL 816-474-1919

LITHOS GALLERY
6301 B DELMAR
UNIVERSITY CITY, MO 63130
TEL 314-862-0674

MELI-MELO
6635 DELMAR BLVD
ST. LOUIS, MO 63130
TEL 314-725-4285

MORGAN GALLERY
412 DELAWARE ST #A
KANSAS CITY, MO 64105-1269
TEL 816-842-8755

NANCY SACHS GALLERY
7700 FORSYTH BLVD
SAINT LOUIS, MO 63105-1810
TEL 314-727-7770

PORTFOLIO GALLERY
3514 DELMAR BLVD
SAINT LOUIS, MO 63103-1003
TEL 314-533-3323

PRIVATE STOCK GALLERY
4550 WARWICK BLVD
KANSAS CITY, MO 64111-7725
TEL 816-561-1191

RANDALL GALLERY
999 N 13TH ST
SAINT LOUIS, MO 63106-3836
TEL 314-231-4808

STYLE WORKS
6934 DARTMOUTH AVE
SAINT LOUIS, MO 63130-3132
TEL 314-531-3900

TRADITIONS
GRAND VILLAGE SHOPS
2800 W 76 COUNTRY BLVD
BRANSON, MO 65616
TEL 417-336-7235

UNION HILL ARTS GALLERY
3013 MAIN ST
KANSAS CITY, MO 64108-3323
TEL 816-561-3020

MONTANA

ACCENTS WEST
42 W MAIN ST
BOZEMAN, MT 59715
TEL 406-586-4185

ART FOCUS
215 W MAIN ST
HAMILTON, MT 59840
TEL 406-363-3292

ARTIFACTS GALLERY
403 N 9TH ST
LIVINGSTON, MT 59047-1734
TEL 406-922-8465

ARTISTIC TOUCH
209 CENTRAL AVE
WHITEFISH, MT 59937-2661
TEL 406-862-4813

CHANDLER GALLERY
FRONT ST
MISSOULA, MT 59802
TEL 406-721-5555

FURNITURE, ETC.
17 MAIN ST
KALISPELL, MT 59901-4449
TEL 406-756-8555

SQUIRREL NEST
1332 LEWIS AVE
BILLINGS, MT 59102-4238
TEL 406-259-5461

NEBRASKA

ADAM WHITNEY GALLERY
8725 SHAMROCK RD
OMAHA, NE 68114-5238
TEL 402-393-1051

ANDERSON O'BRIEN GALLERY
8724 PACIFIC ST
OMAHA, NE 68114-5232
TEL 402-390-0717

CORNERSTONE INTERIORS
745 "D" ST
LINCOLN, NE 68502
TEL 402-474-6780

HAYMARKET GALLERY
728 Q ST
LINCOLN, NE 68508-1330
TEL 402-475-1061

LEWIS ART GALLERY
8025 W DODGE RD
OMAHA, NE 68114-3413
TEL 402-391-7733

UNIVERSITY PLACE ART CENTER
2601 N 48TH ST
LINCOLN, NE 68504-3632
TEL 402-466-8692

WHITE CRANE GALLERY
1032 HOWARD ST
OMAHA, NE 68102
TEL 402-345-1066

NEVADA

MARK MASUOKA GALLERY
1149 S MARYLAND PKY
LAS VEGAS, NV 89104-1738
TEL 702-366-0377

MOONSTRUCK GALLERY
6368 W SAHARA AVE
LAS VEGAS, NV 89102-3050
TEL 702-364-0531

ONE WORLD
THE FORUM AT CEASAR'S PALACE
LAS VEGAS, NV 89109

SHUTLER-ZIV ART GROUP
3119 W POST RD
LAS VEGAS, NV 89118-3840
TEL 702-896-2218

STREMMEL GALLERY
1400 S VIRGINIA ST
RENO, NV 89502-2889
TEL 702-786-0558

NEW HAMPSHIRE

ART 3 GALLERY
44 WEST BROOK ST
MANCHESTER, NH 03101-1215
TEL 603-668-6650

ARTISANS GROUP
GENERAL DELIVERY
DUBLIN, NH 03444-9999
TEL 603-563-8782

AVA GALLERY
4 BANK ST
LEBANON, NH 03766-1730
TEL 603-448-3117

CRAFTINGS
72 HANOVER ST
MANCHESTER, NH 03101-2212
TEL 603-623-4108

GALLERY THIRTY THREE
111 MARKET ST
PORTSMOUTH, NH 03801-3703
TEL 603-431-7403

JEWELRY CREATIONS
388 CENTRAL AVE
DOVER, NH 03820-3411
TEL 603-749-3129

LEAGUE OF NH CRAFT CENTER
36 N MAIN ST
CONCORD, NH 03301-4912
TEL 603-228-8171

LEAGUE OF NH CRAFTS CENTER
13 LEBANON ST
HANOVER, NH 03755-2124
TEL 603-643-5050

MCGOWAN FINE ART, INC
10 HILLS AVE
CONCORD, NH 03301-4803
TEL 603-225-2515

NEW JERSEY

ALICE WHITE GALLERY
105 PULIS AVE
FRANKLIN LAKES, NJ 07417-2710
TEL 201-848-1855

ART DIRECTIONS
38 WILCOX DR
MOUNTAIN LAKES, NJ 07046-1148
TEL 201-263-1420

ARTFORMS
16 MONMOUTH ST
RED BANK, NJ 07701-1614
TEL 908-530-4330

CBL FINE ART
459 PLEASANT VALLEY WAY
WEST ORANGE, NJ 07052-2919
TEL 201-736-7776

CONTRASTS
49 BROAD ST
RED BANK, NJ 07701-1902
TEL 908-741-9177

DESIGN QUEST LTD.
3 GRAND AVE
ENGLEWOOD, NJ 07631-3508
TEL 201-568-7001

DEXTERITY, LTD
26 CHURCH ST
MONTCLAIR, NJ 07042-2702
TEL 201-746-5370

EAST WEST CONNECTION
1274 ROUTE 31
LEBANON, NJ 08833
TEL 908-713-9655

ELEANOR'S CRAFT GALLERY
32-40 N DEAN ST
ENGLEWOOD, NJ 07631
TEL 201-816-7376

ELVID GALLERY
PO BOX 5267
ENGLEWOOD, NJ 07631-5267
TEL 201-871-8747

F. GERALD NEW
1107 MOUNT KEMBLER AVE
MORRISTOWN, NJ 07960
TEL 201-425-4485

GALERIE ATELIER
347 KINGS HWY W
HADDONFIELD, NJ 08033-2103
TEL 609-627-3624

GALLERY AT BRISTOL-MEYERS
PO BOX 4000
PRINCETON, NJ 08543-4000
TEL 609-921-5896

GOLDSMITHS
26 N UNION ST
LAMBERTVILLE, NJ 08530-2140
TEL 609-398-4590

KIMBERLY DESIGNS
1111 PARK AVE
PLAINFIELD, NJ 07060-3006
TEL 201-561-5344

LA GALLERIE DU VITRAIL
216 LINCOLN AVE
HADDONFIELD, NJ 08033-1851
TEL 609-428-6712

LIMITED EDITIONS, INC
2200 LONG BEACH BLVD
SURF CITY, NJ 08008-5555
TEL 609-494-0527

MARGARET'S CRAFT SHOP
413 RARITAN AVE
HIGHLAND PARK, NJ 08904-2739
TEL 908-247-2210

MATREX DALTON
485 BERGEN BLVD
RIDGEFIELD, NJ 07657-2803
TEL 201-945-8077

MELME GALLERY
BRIDGEWATER COMMONS
400 COMMONS WAY #256
BRIDGEWATER, NJ 08807
TEL 908-722-0933

NK THAINE GALLERY
150 KINGS HWY E
HADDONFIELD, NJ 08033-2004
TEL 609-428-6961

NATHANS GALLERY
1205 MCBRIDE AVE
WEST PATERSON, NJ 07424-2540
TEL 201-785-9119

PETERS VALLEY GALLERY
19 KUHN RD
LAYTON, NJ 07851
TEL 201-948-5202

POTTERY INTERNATIONAL
28 PARK PL ON THE GREEN
MORRSTOWN, NJ 07960
TEL 201-538-1919

SCHERER GALLERY
93 SCHOOL RD W
MARLBORO, NJ 07746-1572
TEL 201-536-9465

SHEILA NUSSBAUM GALLERY
341 MILLBURN AVE
MILLBURN, NJ 07041-1609
TEL 201-467-1720

SIGNATURE DESIGNS
5 W MAIN ST
MOORESTOWN, NJ 02649
TEL 609-778-8657

STRAND GALLERY
9209 VENTNOR AVE
MARGATE CITY, NJ 08402-2447
TEL 609-822-8800

THE QUEST
38 MAIN ST
CHESTER, NJ 07930-2535
TEL 908-879-8144

**WALKER-KORNBLUTH
ART GALLERY**
7-21 FAIR LAWN AVE
FAIR LAWN, NJ 07410-1823
TEL 201-791-3374

WILLIAMS GALLERY
8 CHAMBERS ST
PRINCETON, NJ 08542-3708
TEL 609-921-1142

NEW MEXICO

ANDREWS PUEBLO GALLERY
400 SAN FELIPE ST NW
ALBUQUERQUE, NM 87104-1462
TEL 505-243-0414

BAREISS CONTEMPORARY ART
PO BOX 2739
TAOS, NM 87571-2739
TEL 505-776-2284

GALLERY LISTINGS

BELLAS ARTES
653 CANYON RD
SANTA FE, NM 87501-2762
TEL 505-274-1115

CLAY & FIBER GALLERY
126 W PLAZA
TAOS, NM 87571-5923
TEL 505-758-8093

CONTEMPORARY SOUTHWEST GALLERY
123 W PALACE AVE
SANTA FE, NM 87501-2045
TEL 800-283-0440

DEARING GALLERIES
132 KIT CARSON RD
TAOS, NM 87571

EL PRADO GALLERY
112 W SAN FRANCISCO ST
SANTA FE, NM 87501-2068
TEL 505-988-2906

FAIRCHILD & CO.
110 WEST SAN FRANCISCO ST
SANTA FE, NM 87501
TEL 505-984-1419

GALLERY A
105 KIT CARSON RD
TAOS, NM 87571
TEL 505-758-2343

GARLAND GALLERY
125 LINCOLN AVE #113
SANTA FE, NM 87501-2005
TEL 505-984-1555

GERALD PETERS GALLERY
PO BOX 908
SANTA FE, NM 87504-0908
TEL 505-988-8961

HANDSEL GALLERY
306 CAMINO DEL MONTE SOL
SANTA FE, NM 87501-2824
TEL 505-988-4030

HANDWOVEN ORIGINALS
211 OLD SANTA FE TRL
SANTA FE, NM 87501-2160
TEL 505-982-4118

JOAN CAWLEY GALLERY
133 W SAN FRANCISCO ST
SANTA FE, NM 87501-2111
TEL 505-984-1464

JOHNSON BENKERT
128 W WATER ST
SANTA FE, NM 87501-2137
TEL 505-984-2768

KENT GALLERIES
130 LINCOLN AVE
SANTA FE, NM 87501-2069
TEL 505-988-1001

LA MESA OF SANTA FE
225 CANYON RD
SANTA FE, NM 87501-2755
TEL 505-984-1688

LAURA CARPENTER FINE ART
309 READ ST
SANTA FE, NM 87501-2628
TEL 505-986-9090

LEWALLEN GALLERY
129 W PALACE AVE
SANTA FE, NM 87501-2045
TEL 505-988-5387

LIGHTSIDE GALLERY
225 CANYON RD
SANTA FE, NM 87501-2755
TEL 505-982-5501

MABEL'S WEST
201 CANYON RD
SANTA FE, NM 87501-2714
TEL 505-986-9105

MADE IN THE USA GALLERY
110 W SAN FRANCISCO ST
SANTA FE, NM 87501-2189
TEL 505-982-3232

MARIPOSA GALLERY
225 CANYON RD
SANTA FE, NM 87501-2755
TEL 505-982-3032

MICHAEL WIGLEY GALLERIES, LTD
1111 PASEO DE PERALTA
SANTA FE, NM 87501-2737
TEL 505-984-8986

MISI LAKIA-BI KISI GALLERY
312 READ ST
SANTA FE, NM 87501-2629
TEL 505-984-0119

NEW TRENDS GALLERY
225 CANYON RD
SANTA FE, NM 87501-2755
TEL 505-988-1199

OFF THE WALL
616 CANYON RD
SANTA FE, NM 87501
TEL 505-983-8337

OKUN GALLERY
301 N GUADALUPE ST
SANTA FE, NM 87501-5502
TEL 505-989-4300

OOT'I GALLERY
708 CANYON RD
SANTA FE, NM 87501-2751
TEL 505-984-1676

ORIGINS
135 SAN FRANCISCO ST
SANTA FE, NM 87501
TEL 505-988-2323

ORNAMENT GALLERY
209 W SAN FRANCISCO ST
SANTA FE, NM 87501-2128

POST WESTERN
201 GALISTEO ST
SANTA FE, NM 87501-2125
TEL 505-984-9195

QUILTS, LTD
625 CANYON RD
SANTA FE, NM 87501-2721
TEL 505-988-5888

ROBERGE GALLERY
702 1/2 CANYON RD
SANTA FE, NM 87501
TEL 505-820-2008

RUNNING RIDGE GALLERY
640 CANYON RD
SANTA FE, NM 87501-2722
TEL 505-988-2515

SANTA FE EAST
200 OLD SANTA FE TRL
SANTA FE, NM 87501-2107
TEL 505-988-3103

SANTA FE WEAVING GALLERY
124 1/2 GALISTEO ST
SANTA FE, NM 87501-2124
TEL 505-982-1737

SHIDONI CONTEMPORARY GALLERY
GENERAL DELIVERY
PO BOX 250
TESUQUE, NM 87574-9999
TEL 505-988-8001

SKY'S THE LIMIT
1031 MECHEM DR
RUIDOSO, NM 88345-7064

TAOS BLUE
1014 BENT ST
TAOS, NM 87571
TEL 505-758-3561

TEXTILE ARTS, INC
1571 CANYON RD
SANTA FE, NM 87501-6135

TWINING WEAVERS
135 N PUELBO RD
TAOS, NM 87571
TEL 505-758-9000

WEAVING SOUTHWEST GALLERY
216B PASEO DEL PUEBLO SUR
TAOS, NM 87571-5960
TEL 505-758-0433

WEEMS GALLERY
2801 M EUBANK BLVD NE
ALBUQUERQUE, NM 87112-1300
TEL 505-293-6133

WEEMS GALLERY
303 ROMERO NW
ALBUQUERQUE, NM 87104
TEL 505-764-0302

WEYRICH GALLERY
2935D LOUISIANA BLVD NE
ALBUQUERQUE, NM 87110-3537
TEL 505-883-7410

WORTH GALLERY
112A CAMINO DE LA PLACITA
TAOS, NM 87571-5939
TEL 505-751-0816

NEW YORK

15 STEPS
CENTER ITHACA
171 E STATE ST
ITHACA, NY 14850
TEL 607-272-4902

4W
704 FULTON ST
BROOKLYN, NY 11217
TEL 718-875-6500

AB IMPORTS
122 W 26TH ST
NEW YORK, NY 10001-6804
TEL 212-633-6010

AARON FABER GALLERY
666 5TH AVE
NEW YORK, NY 10103-0001
TEL 212-586-8411

ADIRONDACK ARTWORK
RT 3, MAIN ST
NATURAL BRIDGE, NY 13665

AFTER THE RAIN
149 MERCER ST
NEW YORK, NY 10012-3240
TEL 212-431-1044

AMERICA HOUSE
466 PIERMONT AVE
PIERMONT, NY 10968-1038
TEL 914-359-0106

AMERICAN CRAFT MUSEUM
GIFTSHOP
40 W 53RD ST
NEW YORK, NY 10019
TEL 212-956-3535

AN AMERICAN CRAFTSMAN
217 BLEEKER ST
NEW YORK, NY 10014
TEL 212-727-0841

AN AMERICAN CRAFTSMAN
478 6TH AVE
NEW YORK, NY 10019
TEL 212-399-2555

ANTHONY GARDEN BOUTIQUE LTD
1190 LEXINGTON AVE
NEW YORK, NY 10028-1405

ARCHETYPE
115 MERCER ST
NEW YORK, NY 10012-3805
TEL 212-334-0100

ARRANGEMENTS
172 MERRICK RD
MERRICK, NY 11566-4532
TEL 516-378-4820

ARTCRAFTERS
472 ELMWOOD AVE
BUFFALO, NY 14222
TEL 716-881-4320

ARTISANS ALLEY
10 RAINBOW BLVD. AT 1ST ST
NIAGARA FALLS, NY 14303
TEL 716-282-0196

ARTISANS GALLERY
6 BOND ST
GREAT NECK, NY 11021-2409
TEL 516-829-6747

ARTISANS INTERNATIONAL
89 MAIN ST
WESTHAMPTON BEACH, NY 11978-2607
TEL 516-288-2222

ASHLEY COLLECTION
322 W 57TH ST #19S
NEW YORK, NY 10019-3716
TEL 212-247-7294

ATMOSPHERE
81 GREENE ST
NEW YORK, NY 10012-4374
TEL 212-343-9115

AUSTIN HARVARD GALLERY
NORTHFIELD COMMON
50 STATE ST
PITTSFORD, NY 14534
TEL 716-383-1472

BABCOCK GALLERIES
724 5TH AVE
NEW YORK, NY 10019-4106
TEL 212-767-1852

BALAMAN CRAFT GALLERY
1031 LEXINGTON AVE
NEW YORK, NY 10021-3504
TEL 212-472-8366

BARRY PALUM GALLERY
21 PRINCE ST
ROCHESTER, NY 14607-1405
TEL 716-244-9407

BELLARDO, LTD
100 CHRISTOPHER ST
NEW YORK, NY 10014-4201
TEL 212-675-2668

BEN JANE ARTS
PO BOX 298
WEST HEMPSTEAD, NY 11552-0298
TEL 516-483-1330

BERNICE STEINBAUM GALLERY
132 GREENE ST
NEW YORK, NY 10012-3242
TEL 212-431-4224

BILHUBER INC
330 E 59TH ST
NEW YORK, NY 10022
TEL 212-308-4888

CARRIAGE HOUSE STUDIO
79 GUERNSEY ST
BROOKLYN, NY 11222-3111
TEL 718-629-2337

CASCABEL
10 CHASE RD
SCARSDALE, NY 10583
TEL 914-725-8922

CERAMICS & MORE
197 HAWKINS ST
BRONX, NY 10464-1443
TEL 718-885-0319

CHARLES COWLES GALLERY
420 W BROADWAY
NEW YORK, NY 10012-3764
TEL 212-925-3500

CHRIS CREATIONS
645 VANDERBILT AVE
BROOKLYN, NY 11238
TEL 718-783-6420

CIMARRON
64 S BROADWAY
NYACK, NY 10960-3837

COE KERR GALLERY
49 E 82ND ST
NEW YORK, NY 10028-0387
TEL 212-628-1340

CONTEMPORARY PORCELAIN GALLERY
105 SULLIVAN ST
NEW YORK, NY 10012-3669
TEL 212-219-2172

COUNTRY GEAR, LTD
GENERAL DELIVERY
BRIDGEHAMPTON, NY 11932-9999
TEL 516-537-1032

CRAFT CO NO 6
785 UNIVERSITY AVE
ROCHESTER, NY 14607
TEL 716-473-3413

CRAFTS PEOPLE
424 SPILLWAY RD
WEST HURLEY, NY 12491-5114

DAWSON GALLERY
17 SELDEN ST
ROCHESTER, NY 14605-2921
TEL 716-454-6966

DESIGNERS' STUDIO
492 BROADWAY
SARATOGA SPRINGS, NY 12866-2207
TEL 518-584-0987

DESIGNERS, TOO
8037 JERICHO TNPK
WOODBURY, NY 11797
TEL 516-921-8080

DISTANT ORIGIN GALLERY
150 MERCER ST
NEW YORK, NY 10012-3212
TEL 212-941-0024

ELAINE BENSON GALLERY
PO BOX 3034
2317 MONTAUK HWY
BRIDGEHAMPTON, NY 11932-3034
TEL 516-537-3233

ENCHANTED FOREST
85 MERCER ST
NEW YORK, NY 10012-4438
TEL 212-431-1045

ENGEL GALLERY
51 MAIN ST
EAST HAMPTON, NY 11937-2701
TEL 516-324-6462

ENTREE LIBRE GALERIE CONTEMPORAINE
110 WOOSTER ST
NEW YORK, NY 10012
TEL 212-431-5279

ERIC ZETTERQUIST GALLERY
24 E 81ST ST APT 5C
NEW YORK, NY 10028-0227
TEL 212-988-3399

EUREKA CRAFTS
210 WALTON ST
SYRACUSE, NY 13202-1227
TEL 315-471-4601

FABULOUS FURNITURE, INC
RTE 28
BOICEVILE, NY 12412
TEL 914-657-6317

FAST FORWARD GALLERY
580 5TH AVE
PENTHOUSE
NEW YORK, NY 10036-4701
TEL 212-302-5518

GALLERY LISTINGS

FINE CONTEMPORARY CRAFTS
246 SOUTHDOWN RD
LLOYD HARBOR, NY 11743-1719
TEL 516-549-3078

FIRSTHAND GALLERY
MAIN ST
SAG HARBOR, NY 11963
TEL 516-725-3648

FRANKLIN PARRASCH GALLERY
584 BROADWAY
NEW YORK, NY 10012-3229
TEL 212-925-7090

GALLERY 514, LTD
98 WHEATLEY RD
OLD WESTBURY, NY 11568-1212
TEL 516-626-0387

GALLERY AT THE COURTYARD
223 KATONAH AVE
KATONAH, NY 10536-2139
TEL 914-232-9511

GALLERY AUTHENTIQUE
1499 OLD NORTHERN BLVD
ROSLYN, NY 11576-2146
TEL 516-484-7238

GALLERY MUHR
PO BOX 572
PORT WASHINGTON, NY 11050-0105
TEL 516-883-0571

GALLERY NINETY ONE
91 GRAND ST
NEW YORK, NY 10013-2612
TEL 212-966-3722

GALLERY NORTH
90 N COUNTRY RD
SETAUKET, NY 11733-1345
TEL 516-751-2676

GALLERY TEN
7 GREENWICH AVE
NEW YORK, NY 10014-3512
TEL 212-206-1058

GARGOYLES, LTD
138 W 25TH ST
NEW YORK, NY 10001-7405
TEL 212-255-0135

GARTH CLARK GALLERY
24 W 57TH ST
NEW YORK, NY 10019-3918
TEL 212-246-2205

GAYLE WILLSON GALLERY
16 JOBS LN
SOUTHAMPTON, NY 11968-4807
TEL 516-283-7430

GIFT GALLERY
6584 NASH RD
NORTH TONAWANDA, NY 14120-1234

GIMPEL WEITZENHOFFER GALLERY
PO BOX 20006
NEW YORK, NY 10011-0001
TEL 212-925-9060

GLASS MENAGERIE
37 EAST MARKET ST
CORNING, NY 14830

GLORIA PLEVIN GALLERY
PO BOX 188
CHAUTAUQUA, NY 14722-0188

GRAHAM GALLERY
1014 MADISON AVE
MAIN FLOOR
NEW YORK, NY 10021-0103
TEL 212-535-5767

GREENHUT GALLERIES
STUYVESANT PLAZA
ALBANY, NY 12203
TEL 518-482-1984

GUESS WHAT? LTD
STUYUESANT PLAZA
ALBANY, NY 12203
TEL 518-482-5619

GUGGENHEIM MUSEUM
575 BROADWAY FOURTH FLOOR
NEW YORK, NY 10012

HAMMER GALLERY
33 W 57TH ST
NEW YORK, NY 10019-3499
TEL 212-644-4400

HAND OF THE CRAFTMAN
5 S BROADWAY
NYACK, NY 10960-3117
TEL 914-358-3366

HELLER GALLERY
71 GREENE ST
NEW YORK, NY 10012-4338
TEL 212-966-5948

HENOCH GALLERY
80 WOOSTER ST
NEW YORK, NY 10012-4347
TEL 212-966-0303

HUDSON RIVER GALLERY
217 MAIN ST
OSSINING, NY 10562-4704
TEL 914-762-5300

HUDSON RIVER MUSEUM
GIFT SHOP
511 WARBURTON AVE
YONKERS, NY 10701
TEL 914-963-4550

HUMMINGBIRD DESIGNS
29 3RD ST
TROY, NY 12180-3205
TEL 518-272-1807

HUMMINGBIRD JEWELERS
20 W MARKET ST
RHINEBECK, NY 12572-1403
TEL 914-876-4585

HYACINTH CONTEMPORARY CRAFTS
4004 BELL BLVD
BAYSIDE, NY 11361-2063
TEL 718-224-9228

IMAGES ART GALLERY
1157 PLEASANTVILLE RD
BRIARCLIFF MANOR, NY 10510-1603
TEL 914-762-3000

IMPORTANT AMERICAN CRAFT
70 RIVERSIDE DR
NEW YORK, NY 10024-5714
TEL 212-496-1804

IMPRESSIVE INTERIOR GALLERY
14 OLD INDIAN TRL
MILTON, NY 12547-5114
TEL 914-795-5101

INTERART CENTER
167 SPRING ST
SECOND FLOOR
NEW YORK, NY 10012-3842
TEL 212-431-7500

JARO ART GALLERIES
955 MADISON AVE
NEW YORK, NY 10021-2702
TEL 212-734-5475

JEWELLRY 10
11625 UNION TPKE
FOREST HILLS, NY 11375-6058
TEL 718-793-4225

JEWELRY PROJECT
9A 59 WEST 71ST ST
NEW YORK, NY 10023
TEL 212-877-0573

JEWISH MUSEUM
1109 5TH AVE
NEW YORK, NY 10128
TEL 212-423-3201

JOHN CHRISTOPHER GALLERY
43 MAIN ST
COLD SPRING HARBOR, NY 11724-1401
TEL 516-367-3978

JOHN CHRISTOPHER GALLERY
131 MAIN ST
STONY BROOK, NY 11790-1911
TEL 516-689-1601

JULIE ARTISANS GALLERY
687 MADISON AVE
NEW YORK, NY 10021-8042
TEL 212-688-2345

KATE'S PAPERIE
561 BROADWAY
NEW YORK, NY 10012
TEL 212-941-9816

KELMSCOTT GALLERY
131 MAIN ST
COLD SPRING, NY 10516-2813
TEL 914-265-2379

LANDING GALLERY
7956 JERICHO TPKE
WOODBURY, NY 11797-1204
TEL 516-364-2787

LEE GALLERY
83 MAIN ST
SOUTHAMPTON, NY 11968-4808
TEL 516-287-2361

LEO KAPLAN MODERN
965 MADISON AVE
NEW YORK, NY 10021-2702
TEL 212-535-2407

LEWIS DOLIN GALLERY, INC
PO BOX 239
KATONAH, NY 10536-0239
TEL 212-941-8130

LIMESTONE GALLERY
205 THOMPSON ST
FAYETTEVILLE, NY 13066-1911
TEL 315-637-0460

MANGO TREE OF NEW YORK
191-195 S MAIN ST
NEW YORK, NY 10956
TEL 914-638-9668

MARI GALLERIES OF WESTCHESTER
133 E PROSPECT AVE
MAMARONECK, NY 10543-3710
TEL 914-698-0008

MARK MILLIKEN GALLERY
1200 MADISON AVE
NEW YORK, NY 10128-0507
TEL 212-534-8802

MAX PROTECH GALLERY
560 BROADWAY
NEW YORK, NY 10012-3938
TEL 212-966-5454

MELE GALLERY
6 TERRACE CT
OLD WESTBURY, NY 11568-1302
TEL 212-486-8304

MICHAEL INGBAR GALLERY OF ART
568 BROADWAY
NEW YORK, NY 10012-3225
TEL 212-334-1100

MICHELE MOSKO MILLER FINE ART
59 GRAND ST 2ND FLOOR
NEW YORK, NY 10013
TEL 212-226-0166

MILLER GALLERY
560 BROADWAY (AT PRINCE ST)
FOURTH FLOOR
NEW YORK, NY 10012
TEL 212-226-0702

MODERN STONE AGE, LTD
111 GREENE ST
NEW YORK, NY 10012-3803
TEL 212-966-2570

MOOSE RIVER TRADING COMPANY
419 MANDEVILLE ST
UTICA, NY 13502-4609

MUD SWEAT & TEARS EAST
1566 2ND AVE
NEW YORK, NY
TEL 212-570-6868

NAN MILLER GALLERY
3450 WINTON PL
ROCHESTER, NY 14623-2805
TEL 716-292-1430

NANCY MARGOLIS GALLERY
560 BROADWAY
NEW YORK, NY 10012
TEL 212-255-0386

NEW GLASS GALLERY
345 W BROADWAY
NEW YORK, NY 10013-2238
TEL 212-431-0050

NOHO GALLERY
168 MERCER ST
NEW YORK, NY 10012-3284
TEL 212-219-2210

OBJECTS OF BRIGHT PRIDE
455A COLUMBUS AVE
NEW YORK, NY 10024-5129
TEL 212-721-4579

OF CABBAGES & KINGS
587 E BOSTON POST RD
MAMARONECK, NY 10543-3740
TEL 914-698-0445

OFFERINGS
59 KATONAH
KATONAH, NY 10536
TEL 914-232-9643

ONE OF A KIND, LTD
978 BROADWAY
THORNWOOD, NY 10594-1139
TEL 914-769-5777

PETER JOSEPH GALLERY
9 WINDMILL LN
SOUTHAMPTON, NY 11968

PETER JOSEPH GALLERY
745 5TH AVE
NEW YORK, NY 10151-0407
TEL 212-751-5500

POTTERY A LA CARTE
616A PITTSFORD-VICTOR RD
PITTSFORD, NY 14534

PRITAM & EAMES GALLERY
27-19 RACE LN
EAST HAMPTON, NY 11937-2445
TEL 516-324-7111

PROGRESSIVE UNLIMITED
14 EAST 125TH ST
NEW YORK, NY 10035
TEL 212-517-0135

RAKU GALLERY
171 SPRING ST
NEW YORK, NY 10012-3843
TEL 212-226-6636

RANDOLPH & HEIN INC
232 E 59TH ST # 234
NEW YORK, NY 10022-1464
TEL 212-826-9878

RICE GALLERY
135 WASHINGTON AVE
ALBANY, NY 12210-2202
TEL 518-463-4478

ROBERTA WOOD GALLERY
6907 E GENESEE ST
LYNDON PLAZA
FAYETTEVILLE, NY 13066-1012
TEL 315-445-0423

ROCHESTER MEMORIAL GALLERY
500 UNIVERSITY AVE
ROCHESTER, NY 14607-1415
TEL 716-473-7720

RUTH RAIBLE GALLERY
41 FOREST AVE
HASTINGS ON HUDSON, NY 10706-1203
TEL 914-478-0585

SCOTT JORDAN FURNITURE
137 VARICK AT SPRING
NEW YORK, NY 10013
TEL 212-620-4682

SCULPTURE FIELDS GALLERY
PO BOX 94
KENOZA LAKE, NY 12750-0094
TEL 914-482-3669

SEDONI GALLERY
304 A NEW YORK AVE
HUNTINGTON, NY 11743
TEL 516-547-4811

SOTHEBY'S
1334 YORK AVE
NEW YORK, NY 10021
TEL 212-606-7170

SOUTHWEST STUDIO CONNECTION
65 MAIN ST
SOUTHAMPTON, NY 11968-4808
TEL 516-283-9649

STEINHARDT GALLERY
370 NEW YORK AVE
HUNTINGTON, NY 11743
TEL 516-549-4430

SWEETHEART GALLERY
34C TINKER ST
WOODSTOCK, NY 12498-1233
TEL 914-679-2622

SYMMETRY GALLERY
348 BROADWAY
SARATOGA SPRINGS, NY 12866-3110
TEL 518-584-5090

TERRCOTTA GALLERY
259 W 4TH ST
NEW YORK, NY 10014-3205
TEL 212-243-1952

THE CRAFTSMEN
RT 9 SOUTH RD
POUGHKEEPSIE, NY 12601
TEL 914-454-2336

THE DAVID COLLECTION
161 W 15TH ST
NEW YORK, NY 10011-6720
TEL 212-929-4602

TRACKSIDE EMPORIUM LTD
14 E BROADWAY
PORT JEFFERSON, NY 11777-1400

TURBULENCE
812 BROADWAY
NEW YORK, NY 10003-4804

UNIQUE GALLERY
5701 TRANSIT RD
EAST AMHERST, NY 14051-1805
TEL 716-689-2160

VICTRIX GALLERY
77 W MARKET ST
CORNING, NY 14830-2526

VISUAL JAPAN
860 BROADWAY FL 5
NEW YORK, NY 10003-1228
TEL 212-254-1229

WARD MASSE GALLERY
178 PRINCE ST
NEW YORK, NY 10012-2905
TEL 212-925-6951

WARES FOR ART
421 HUDSON ST #220
NEW YORK, NY 10014-3647
TEL 212-989-7845

WEST END GALLERY
87 W MARKET ST
CORNING, NY 14830-2526
TEL 607-962-8692

GALLERY LISTINGS

WHEELER-SEIDEL GALLERY
606 3RD ST
BROOKLYN, NY 11215-3004
TEL 212-533-0319

WHITE BUFFALO GALLERY
13 MILL RD
WOODSTOCK, NY 12498
TEL 800-724-2113

WILLIAM BARTHMAN GALLERY
174 BROADWAY
NEW YORK, NY 10038-2503
TEL 212-227-3524

WINSTON & COMPANY
97A 7TH AVE
BROOKLYN, NY 11215-1305
TEL 718-638-7942

WINTER TREE GALLERY
147 SPRING ST
NEW YORK, NY 10012-3860
TEL 212-343-2220

WOODSTOCK GUILD CRAFT SHOP
34 TINKER ST
WOODSTOCK, NY 12498-1233
TEL 914-679-2079

NORTH CAROLINA

ACCIPITER
2046 CLARK AVE
RALEIGH, NC 27605
TEL 919-755-9309

ALLANSTAND
MILEPOST 382 BLUERIDGE PKWY
ASHEVILLE, NC 28815
TEL 704-298-7928

AMERICAN CRAFT SHOWROOM
DESIGN CNTR D-408
INT'L HOME FURNITURE
HIGH POINT, NC 27260
TEL 910-889-2933

ART
502 POLLOCK ST
NEW BERN, NC 28562-5612
TEL 919-636-2120

ART ON THE WALL
16 WALL ST
ASHEVILLE, NC 28801-2710

BALSAM GALLERY
119 N MAIN ST
WAYNESVILLE, NC 28786
TEL 704-452-2524

BELLAGIO
5 BILTMORE PLZ
ASHEVILLE, NC 28803-2628
TEL 704-277-8100

BIZARRE DUCK BAZAAR
16 WALL ST
ASHEVILLE, NC 28801-2710

BLUE SPIRAL 1
38 BILTMORE AVE
ASHEVILLE, NC 28801-3625
TEL 704-251-0202

BROADHURST GALLERY
800 MIDLAND RD
PINEHURST, NC 28374-8215
TEL 910-295-2296

BROWNING ARTWORK
PO BOX 275
HWY 12
FRISCO, NC 27936-0275
TEL 919-995-5538

CEDAR CREEK GALLERY
RR 2 BOX 420
1150 FLEMING RD
CREEDMOOR, NC 27522-9641
TEL 919-528-1041

COMPTON ART GALLERY
409 W FISHER AVE
GREENSBORO, NC 27401-2039
TEL 919-370-9147

CONTINUITY, INC
PO BOX 999
US HWY 19
MAGGIE VALLEY, NC 28751-0999
TEL 704-926-0333

CREATED WITH CLAY
120 WEST LEXINGTON
HIGH POINT, NC 27262
TEL 919-841-8792

DANICAARTWEAR
406 STATE ST STATION
GREENSBORO, NC 27405
TEL 910-271-0871

FINE LINE
304 S STRATFORD RD
WINSTON SALEM, NC 27103-1820
TEL 919-723-8066

FIRST LIGHT GALLERY
7631 PINEVILLE-MATTHEWS RD
CHARLOTTE, NC 28226
TEL 704-542-9449

FIRST LIGHT GALLERY
8508 PARK RD #123
CHARLOTTE, NC 28210-5803
TEL 704-543-9939

FOLK ART CENTER
MILEPOST 382
BLUE RIDGE PKWY
ASHEVILLE, NC 28805
TEL 704-298-7928

GALLERY OF THE MOUNTAINS
290 MACON AVE
ASHEVILLE, NC 28804-3711
TEL 704-254-2068

GALLERY WDO
2000 SOUTH BOULEVARD
CHARLOTTE, NC 28203
TEL 704-333-9123

GROVEWOOD GALLERY
111 GROVEWOOD RD
ASHEVILLE, NC 28804
TEL 704-253-7651

GUILD CRAFTS
930 TUNNEL RD
ASHEVILLE, NC 28805
TEL 704-298-7903

HARLLEE GALLERY
HIGHWAY 64 EAST
HIGHLANDS, NC 28741
TEL 704-526-2083

HAYDEN GALLERY
7 S MAIN ST
BURNSVILLE, NC 28714-2928
TEL 704-682-7998

HEARTWOOD GALLERY
PO BOX 546
SALUDA, NC 28773-0546

HODGES TAYLOR GALLERY
227 N TRYON ST
CHARLOTTE, NC 28202-2136
TEL 704-334-3799

HORIZON GALLERY
905 W MAIN ST
DURHAM, NC 27701-2054
TEL 919-688-0313

ISLAND ART GALLERY
PO BOX 265
HWY 64
MANTEO, NC 27954-0265
TEL 919-473-2838

JULIA RUSH GALLERY
216 UNION SQ NW
HICKORY, NC 28601-6111
TEL 704-324-0409

LICK LOG MILL STORE
DILLARD RD
HIGHLANDS, NC 28741
TEL 704-526-3934

LITTLE ART GALLERY
NORTH HILLS MALL
RALEIGH, NC 27609
TEL 919-787-6317

LITTLE MOUNTAIN POTTERY
PENIEL RD
RT 2 BOX 60
TRYON, NC 28782
TEL 704-894-8091

MAKADO GALLERY
307 N FRONT ST
THE COTTON EXCHANGE
WILMINGTON, NC 28401-3955
TEL 919-762-8922

MASTER WORKS GALLERY
WRIGHT SQUARE
MAIN ST
HIGHLANDS, NC 28741
TEL 704-526-2633

MORNING STAR GALLERY
RR 1 BOX 292-10
BANNER ELK, NC 28604-9752
TEL 704-963-6902

MOUNTAIN POTTERY
GENERAL DELIVERY
DILLSBORO, NC 28725-9999
TEL 704-586-9183

NEW ELEMENTS GALLERY
216 N FRONT ST
WILMINGTON, NC 28401-3920
TEL 919-343-8997

NEW MORNING GALLERY
7 BOSTON WAY
BILTMORE VILLAGE
ASHEVILLE, NC 28803-2681
TEL 704-274-2831

OAKS GALLERY
RIVERWOOD SHOPS
PO BOX 310
DILLSBORO, NC 28725
TEL 704-586-6542

PEDEN GALLERY II
1316 SAINT ALBANS DR
RALEIGH, NC 27609-6827
TEL 919-834-9800

PICTURE HOUSE, INC
1520 E 4TH ST
CHARLOTTE, NC 28204-3224
TEL 704-333-8235

PIEDMONT CRAFTSMEN, INC
1204 REYNOLDA RD
WINSTON SALEM, NC 27104-1121
TEL 919-725-1516

POTTERS GALLERY
RR 1 BOX 283
BANNER ELK, NC 28604-9736
TEL 704-963-4258

RAINBOW HARVEST
1177 DUCK RD
DUCK, NC 27949
TEL 919-261-5949

RALEIGH CONTEMPORARY GALLERY
134 E HARGETT ST
RALEIGH, NC 27601-1440
TEL 919-828-6500

SECCA, CENTER SHOP
750 MARGUERITE DR
WINSTON SALEM, NC 27106-5861

SEVEN SISTERS GALLERY
117 CHERRY ST
BLACK MOUNTAIN, NC 28711
TEL 704-669-5107

SHADY LANE
MAIN ST
SALUDA, NC 28773
TEL 704-749-1155

SKILLBECK GALLERY
238 S SHARON AMITY RD
CHARLOTTE, NC 28211-2801
TEL 704-366-9613

SOMERHILL GALLERY
3 EASTGATE
EAST FRANKLIN STREET
CHAPEL HILL, NC 27514
TEL 919-968-8868

SOUTHERN EXPRESSIONS GALLERY
2157 NEW HENDERSONVILLE HWY
PISGAH FOREST, NC 28768-8600
TEL 704-884-6242

THE EMPORIUM
128 CHERRY ST
BLACK MOUNTAIN, NC 28711
TEL 704-669-0050

THE FRAME UP
4 WEST MAIN ST
BREVARD, NC 28712
TEL 704-883-2385

THE HERITAGE
8 MARINA ST
WRIGHTSVILLE BEACH, NC 28480
TEL 910-256-7117

THE POLLITT SELECTION
110 WESTWOOD SHOPPING CENTER
FAYETTEVILLE, NC 28314
TEL 910-487-9100

TRILLIUM GALLERY
SWITZERLAND INN
LITTLE SWITZERLAND, NC 28749
TEL 704-765-0024

URBAN ARTIFACTS
413 FORUM IV
GREENSBORO, NC 27408
TEL 919-855-0557

NORTH DAKOTA

ART CONNECTION
624 MAIN AVE
FARGO, ND 58103-1966
TEL 701-237-6655

BROWNING ARTS
22 N 4TH ST
GRAND FORKS, ND 58203-3720
TEL 701-746-5090

OHIO

A SHOW OF HANDS
208 GREAT NORTHER MALL
NORTH OLMSTED, OH 44070
TEL 216-777-2143

A SHOW OF HANDS
CAREW TOWER ARCADE
441 VINE STREET
CINCINNATI, OH 45202
TEL 513-421-7119

AMERICAN CRAFTS GALLERY
13101 LARCHMERE BLVD
CLEVELAND, OH 44120-1148
TEL 216-231-2008

ART AT THE POWERHOUSE
2000 SYCAMORE ST
NAUTICA COMPLEX
CLEVELAND, OH 44113-2340
TEL 216-696-1942

ART BANK GALLERY
317 W 4TH ST
CINCINNATI, OH 45202-2605
TEL 513-621-7779

ARTERNATIVE GALLERY
2034 MADISON RD
CINCINNATI, OH 45208-3238
TEL 513-871-2218

ARTSPACE CENTER FOR COMTEMPORY ART
8501 CARNEGIE AVE
CLEVELAND, OH 44106
TEL 216-421-8671

AVALON GALLERY
20163 LAKE RD
ROCKY RIVER, OH 44116
TEL 216-331-3776

AVANTE GALLERY
2094 MURRAY HILL RD
CLEVELAND, OH 44106-2359
TEL 216-791-1622

BENCHWORKS
2563 N HIGH ST
COLUMBUS, OH 43202-2555
TEL 614-263-2111

BONFOEY COMPANY
1710 EUCLID AVE
CLEVELAND, OH 44115-2106
TEL 216-621-0178

BRENDA KROOS GALLERY
1360 W 9TH ST
CLEVELAND, OH 44113-1254
TEL 216-621-1164

CARGO NET, INC
GENERAL DELIVERY
PO BOX 369
PUT IN BAY, OH 43456-9999
TEL 419-285-4231

CHELSEA GALLERY
23225 MERCANTILE RD
BEACHWOOD, OH 44122
TEL 216-591-1066

COURT STREET COLLECTION
64 NORTH COURT
ATHENS, OH 45701
TEL 614-593-8261

DAYTON ART INSTITUTE
PO BOX 941
DAYTON, OH 45401-0941
TEL 513-223-5277

DECIOCCIO SHOWROOM
LONGWORTH HALL DESIGN CENTER
CINCINNATI, OH 45203
TEL 513-241-9573

DESIGNS OF ALL TIMES
28001 CHAGRIN BLVD
CLEVELAND, OH 44122-4543
TEL 216-831-3010

DRUMM STUDIOS & GALLERY
437 CROUSE ST
AKRON, OH 44311-1220
TEL 216-253-6268

DUDA GALLERY
8912 BRECKSVILLE RD
BRECKSVILLE, OH 44141
TEL 216-526-3210

DUNCAN GALLERY
130 WEST STREETSBORO
HUDSON, OH 44236
TEL 216-650-6199

FACE IT
110 W ASH ST
PIQUA, OH 45356-2304
TEL 513-773-1838

FIORI-OMNI GALLERY, INC
2072 MURRAY HILL RD
CLEVELAND, OH 44106-2359
TEL 216-721-5319

GALLERY 400
4659 DRESSLER RD NW
CANTON, OH 44718-2535
TEL 216-492-2600

GALLERY AT STUDIO B
140 W MAIN ST
LANCASTER, OH 43130-3718
TEL 614-653-8424

GORDON BEALE FRANK GALLERY
12609 LARCHMERE BLVD
CLEVELAND, OH 44120
TEL 216-421-0677

GALLERY LISTINGS

HELIOTROPE ART GALLERY
3001 CALTALPA DR
DAYTON, OH 45405
TEL 513-275-1071

IMAGES GALLERY
3154 MARKWAY RD
TOLEDO, OH 43606-2925

KUSSMAUL GALLERY
103 N PROSPECT ST
GRANVILLE, OH 43023-1336
TEL 614-587-4640

MALTON GALLERY
2709 OBSERVATORY AVE
CINCINNATI, OH 45208-2107
TEL 513-321-8014

MILLER GALLERY
2715 ERIE AVE
HYDE PARK SQUARE
CINCINNATI, OH 45208-2103
TEL 513-871-4420

MURIEL MERAY STUDIO SHOP
537 E MAPLE ST
NORTH CANTON, OH 44720-2603
TEL 216-967-3736

MURRAY HILL ART & CRAFTS
2181 MURRAY HILL RD
CLEVELAND, OH 44106-2338
TEL 216-231-2012

OH DESIGNER CRAFTSMEN GALLERY
1665 W 5TH AVE
COLUMBUS, OH 43212-2315
TEL 614-486-7119

OSHER OSHER GALLERY
5662 MAYFIELD RD
LYNDHURST, OH 44124-2916
TEL 216-646-9191

PM GALLERY
726 N HIGH ST
COLUMBUS, OH 43215
TEL 614-299-0860

PUMP HOUSE ART GALLERY
ENDERLIN CIRCLE
PO BOX 1613
CHILLICOTHE, OH 45601
TEL 614-772-5783

RAINBOWERS
7720 OLDE EIGHT RD
HUDSON, OH 44236-1055
TEL 216-467-0259

RILEY HAWK GALLERIES
2026 MURRAY HILL RD
CLEVELAND, OH 44106
TEL 216-421-1445

RILEY HAWK GLASS GALLERY
642 N HIGH ST
COLUMBUS, OH 43215-2010
TEL 614-228-6554

SANDUSKY CULTURAL CENTER
2130 HAYES AVE
SANDUSKY, OH 44870-4740
TEL 419-625-8097

SANTA CLARA GALLERY
1942 N MAIN ST
DAYTON, OH 45405-3801
TEL 513-279-9100

SCHNEIDER GALLERYY OF ART
23 PUBLIC SQUARE
MEDINA, OH 44256
TEL 216-723-6767

SCULPTURE CENTER
12206 EUCLID AVE
CLEVELAND, OH 44106-4311
TEL 216-229-6527

SILVIA ULLMAN GALLERY
13010 LARCHMERE BLVD
CLEVELAND, OH 44120
TEL 216-231-2008

SOMETHING DIFFERENT
3427 MEMPHIS AVE
CLEVELAND, OH 44109-3264
TEL 216-398-0472

STANLEY KAUFMAN GALLERY
GENERAL DELIVERY
BERLIN, OH 44610-9999
TEL 216-893-2842

THE GALLERY
24 S GAMBLE ST #10
SHELBY, OH 44875-1541
TEL 419-347-4206

THE MODERN OBJECT
641 N HIGH ST #105B
COLUMBUS, OH 43215
TEL 614-461-9114

THREE ELYSABEHE'S
170 CHILLICOTHE RD
AURORA, OH 44202
TEL 216-562-4544

TONI BIRCKHEAD GALLERY
342 W 4TH ST
CINCINNATI, OH 45202-2603
TEL 513-241-0212

VETRO MARMO ARTE GALLERY
77 MILL ST (RT 62)
COLUMBUS, OH 43230
TEL 614-476-2211

VILLAGE ARTISANS COOPERATIVE
220 XENIA AVE
YELLOW SPRINGS, OH 45387-1831
TEL 513-767-1209

WILLIAM BUSTA GALLERY
2021 MURRAY HILL RD
CLEVELAND, OH 44106-2348
TEL 216-231-7363

WOODBOURNE GALLERY
9885 MONTGOMERY RD
CINCINNATI, OH 45242-6424
TEL 513-793-1888

WOODBOURNE GALLEY
175 E ALEX BELL RD #208
DAYTON, OH 45459-2794
TEL 513-434-3565

OKLAHOMA

DORAN GALLERY
3509 S PEORIA AVE
TULSA, OK 74105-2517
TEL 918-748-8700

OREGON

ALDER GALLERY & ART SERVICE
160 E BROADWAY
EUGENE, OR 97401-3140
TEL 503-342-6411

ART DECOR GALLERY
136 HIGH ST SE
SALEM, OR 97301-3608
TEL 503-378-0876

BLUE PEAR
1713 NE 15TH
PORTLAND, OR 97212
TEL 503-284-5497

CHANGES
927 SW JAMHILL
PORTLAND, OR 97205
TEL 503-223-3737

CLOUDTREE & SUN
112 N MAIN
GRESHAM, OR 97030
TEL 503-666-8495

CONTEMPORARY CRAFTS GALLERY
3934 SW CORBETT AVE
PORTLAND, OR 97201-4304
TEL 503-223-2654

DRESHER GALLERY
553 NW HWY 101
LINCOLN CITY, OR 97367
TEL 503-994-7342

EARTHWORKS GALLERY
2222 HIGHWAY 101 N
YACHATS, OR 97498-9435
TEL 503-547-4300

EXCLUSIVE ACCENTS
301 E MAIN ST
MEDFORD, OR 97501
TEL 503-776-1215

GANGO GALLERY
205 SW 1ST AVE
PORTLAND, OR 97204-3502
TEL 503-222-3850

GRAYSTONE GALLERY
3279 SE HAWTHORNE BLVD
PORTLAND, OR 97214-5044
TEL 503-238-0651

INDIGO GALLERY
311 AVE B #B
LAKE OSWEGO, OR 97034
TEL 503-636-3454

ITCHY FINGERS
513 NW 23RD AVE
PORTLAND, OR 97210-3206
TEL 503-222-5237

LAURA RUSSO GALLERY
805 NW 21ST AVE
PORTLAND, OR 97209-1408
TEL 503-635-7419

LAWRENCE GALLERY
PO BOX 187
SHERIDAN, OR 97378-0187
TEL 503-843-3633

MAVEETY GALLERY
PO BOX 148
GLENEDEN BEACH, OR 97388-0148
TEL 503-764-2318

MONTAGE GALLERY
5875 SW ELM AVE
BEAVERTON, OR 97005-4222
TEL 503-643-7513

OPUS 5 GALLERY
136 E BROADWAY
EUGENE, OR 97401
TEL 503-484-1710

**PORTLAND ART MUSEUM
RENTAL SALES GALLERY**
1219 SW PARK AVE
PORTLAND, OR 97205
TEL 503-274-4121

PURPLE PELICAN
210 BROADWAY
SEASICE, OR 97138
TEL 503-738-5743

REAL MOTHER GOOSE GALLERY
927 SW YAMHILL ST
PORTLAND, OR 97205-2532
TEL 503-223-3737

SAXONS
3138 N HIGHWAY 97
BEND, OR 97701-7514
TEL 503-389-6655

SKYLARK GALLERY
130 SPAULDING AVE
BROWNSVILLE, OR 97327-2258
TEL 503-466-5221

SUNBIRD GALLERY
916 NW WALL ST
BEND, OR 97701-2022
TEL 503-389-9196

TOAD HALL
237 W 3RD ST
YACHATZ, OR 97498
TEL 503-547-4044

TWIST
30 NW 23RD PLACE
PORTLAND, OR 97210-3533
TEL 503-224-0334

WEBSTERS
11 NORTH MAIN ST
ASHLAND, OR 97520
TEL 503-482-9801

WHITE BIRD GALLERY
N HEMLOCK RD
PO BOX 502
CANNON BEACH, OR 97145
TEL 503-436-2681

WOOD GALLERY, INC
818 SW BAY BLVD
NEWPORT, OR 97365-4838

PENNSYLVANIA

2 SUSANS
8428 GERMANTOWN AVE
PHILADELPHIA, PA 19118
TEL 215-242-0533

479 GALLERY
55 N 2ND ST
PHILADELPHIA, PA 19106-2229
TEL 215-922-1444

A-MANO
128 S MAIN ST
NEW HOPE, PA 18938-1202
TEL 215-862-5122

AART VARK GALLERY
17TH AT LOCUST
PHILADELPHIA, PA 19103
TEL 215-735-5600

ACCENTS & IMAGES
GENERAL DELIVERY
PO BOX 18931
LAHASKA, PA 18931-9999
TEL 215-794-7660

ART ACCENTS
350 MONTGOMERY AVE
MERION STATION, PA 19066-1202
TEL 215-664-4444

ART EFFECTS GALLERY
277 MONTGOMERY AVE
BALA CYNWYD, PA 19004
TEL 610-668-0992

ARTISANS GALLERY
PEDDLERS VILLAGE
PO BOX 133
LAHASKA, PA 18931
TEL 215-794-3112

ARTISANS THREE
THE VILLAGE CENTER
SPRING HOUSE, PA 19477
TEL 215-643-4504

BACH & COMPANY
447 CHESTNUT ST
EMMAUS, PA 18049-2401

BEST FRIENDS
4329 MAIN ST
PHILADELPHIA, PA 19127-1516
TEL 215-487-1250

CALICO CAT GALLERY
36 W KING ST
LANCASTER, PA 17603-3809
TEL 717-397-6372

CASA
612 S 4TH ST
PHILADELPHIA, PA 19147
TEL 215-238-0707

CAT'S PAW GALLERY
31 RACE ST
JIM THORPE, PA 18229-2003
TEL 717-325-4041

CATHERINE STARR GALLERY
4235 MAIN ST
PHILADELPHIA, PA 19127-1602
TEL 215-482-7755

CHADDS FORD GALLERY
US HWY 1 & 100
PO BOX 179
CHADDS FORD, PA 19317
TEL 610-459-5510

CLAY PLACE GALLERY
MINEO BLDG
5416 WALNUT ST
PITTSBURG, PA 15232
TEL 412-682-3737

CLAY STUDIO
139 N 2ND ST
PHILADELPHIA, PA 19106-2009
TEL 215-925-3453

COUNTRY CLASSICS
36 E. GERMANTOWN PIKE
NORRISTOWN, PA 19401
TEL 215-275-3666

COUNTRY STUDIO
590 GEORGETOWN RD
HADLEY, PA 16130-1098
TEL 412-253-2493

CREATIVE HANDS
PEDDLERS VILLAGE
LAHASKA, PA 18931
TEL 215-794-7012

DESIGN ARTS GALLERY
NESBITT COLLEGE OF DESIGN ARTS
33RD & MARKET STS
PHILADELPHIA, PA 19104
TEL 215-895-2386

DINA PORTER GALLERY
1655 HAUSMAN RD
ALLENTOWN, PA 18104-9345
TEL 215-434-7363

DISCOVERIES
221 CHERRY ST
READING, PA 19602
TEL 215-372-2595

DISCOVERIES
4226 MAIN ST
MANAYUNK, PA 19127
TEL 215-482-1117

DOWNINGTOWN ART GALLERY
305 MANOR AVE
DOWNINGTOWN, PA 19335-2542

EXPRESSIONS GALLERY
84 S MAIN ST
YARDLEY, PA 19067
TEL 215-321-7433

F A N GALLERY
311 CHERRY ST
PHILADELPHIA, PA 19106-1803
TEL 215-922-5155

FABRIC WORKSHOP
1100 VINE ST
THIRTEENTH FLOOR
PHILADELPHIA, PA 19107-1717
TEL 215-922-7303

GALLERIA TRICIA
102 HARRISON DR
NEW CUMBERLAND, PA 17070-1718
TEL 717-691-0263

GALLERIE NADEAU
118 N 3RD ST
PHILADELPHIA, PA 19106-1802
TEL 215-574-0202

GALLERY 500
CHURCH & OLD YORK RDS
ELKINS PARK, PA 19117
TEL 215-572-1203

GALLERY LISTINGS

GALLERY AT THE CLAY LADY
GENERAL DELIVERY
UWCHLAND, PA 19480-9999
TEL 610-458-8262

GALLERY G
211 9TH ST
PITTSBURGH, PA 15222-3501
TEL 412-562-0912

GALLERY OF 1ST IMPRESSIONS
4 E LANCASTER AVE
PAOLI, PA 19301-1402

GALLERY RIGGIONE-FINE CRAFTS
130 ALMSHOUSE RD
RICHBORO, PA 18954
TEL 215-322-5035

GLASS GROWERS GALLERY
701 HOLLAND ST
ERIE, PA 16501-1216
TEL 814-453-3758

GREENE & GREENE GALLERY
88 S MAIN ST
NEW HOPE, PA 18938-1232
TEL 215-862-9620

GUNLEFINGERS
303 W STATE ST
MEDIA, PA 19063-2615

HAHN GALLERY
8439 GERMANTOWN AVE
PHILADELPHIA, PA 19188-0001
TEL 215-247-8439

HELEN DRUTT GALLERY
1721 WALNUT ST
PHILADELPHIA, PA 19103
TEL 215-735-1625

HONEY BROOK WOODS
102 TELEGRAPH RD
HONEY BROOK, PA 19344
TEL 215-273-2680

IMAGINE GALLERY & GIFTS
3330 W 26TH ST
ERIE, PA 16506-2449
TEL 814-858-8077

IRON GLASS & WOOD
605 COLLEGE AVE
PITTSBURGH, PA 15232
TEL 414-661-7550

JAB GALLERY
225 RACE ST
PHILADELPHIA, PA 19106-1909
TEL 215-923-8122

JAMES A. MICHENER ART MUSEUM
128 S PINE ST
DOYLESTOWN, PA 18901-4931
TEL 215-340-9800

JAMES GALLERY
2892 W LIBERTY AVE
PITTSBURGH, PA 15216-2621
TEL 412-343-1366

JUN GALLERY
114 MARKET ST
PHILADELPHIA, PA 19106-3006
TEL 215-627-5020

KAISER NEWMAN GALLERY
134 N 3RD ST
PHILADELPHIA, PA 19106-1814
TEL 215-923-7438

LANGMAN GALLERY
WILLOW GROVE PARK
2500 MORELAND RD
WILLOW GROVE, PA 19090
TEL 215-657-8333

LANNON'S
1007 LANCASTER AVE
BRYN MAWR, PA 19010
TEL 215-525-4526

LARIMORE FURNITURE
160 N 3RD ST
PHILADELPHIA, PA 19106-1814
TEL 215-440-7136

LATITUDES GALLERY
4325 MAIN ST
PHILADELPHIA, PA 19127-1516
TEL 215-482-0417

LOCKS GALLERY
600 S WASHINGTON SQ
PHILADELPHIA, PA 19106-4155
TEL 215-629-1000

MADE BY HAND GALLERY
303 S CRAIG ST
PITTSBURGH, PA 15213-3706
TEL 412-681-8346

MARSHA CHILD CONTEMPORARY
PO BOX 0364
SOLEBURY, PA 18963-9999
TEL 215-297-0414

MEDIA POTTERY
303 W STATE ST
MEDIA, PA 19063-2615

MEDICI CORPORATION
68 N 2ND ST
PHILADELPHIA, PA 19106-4505
TEL 215-627-8109

NEXUS GALLERY
137 N 2ND ST
PHILADELPHIA, PA 19106-2009
TEL 215-629-1103

OLC GALLERY
152 N 3RD ST # 154
PHILADELPHIA, PA 19106-1814
TEL 215-923-6085

OWEN PATRICK GALLERY
4345 MAIN ST
PHILADELPHIA, PA 19127-1415
TEL 215-482-9395

PAINTED BRIDE GALLERY
230 VINE ST
PHILADELPHIA, PA 19106-1213
TEL 215-925-9914

R & R COLLECTIBLES
26 LONESOME RD
NEWVILLE, PA 17241
TEL 717-776-6262

REISBORD GALLERY
4313 MAIN ST #17
PHILADELPHIA, PA 19127-1525
TEL 215-483-3232

RODGER LAPELLE GALLERY
122 N 3RD ST
PHILADELPHIA, PA 19106-1802
TEL 215-592-0232

RUTH ZAFIR GALLERY
13 S 2ND ST
PHILADELPHIA, PA 19106-3003
TEL 215-627-7098

SANDE WEBSTER GALLERY
2018 LOCUST ST
PHILADELPHIA, PA 19103-5614
TEL 215-732-8850

SAVOIR-FAIRE
837 W ROLLING RD
SPRINGFIELD, PA 19064-1133
TEL 215-544-8998

SHOW OF HANDS
1006 PINE ST
PHILADELPHIA, PA 19107-6007
TEL 215-592-4010

SIMCOE GALLERY
1925 MAIN ST
NORTHAMPTON, PA 18067-1313
TEL 215-262-8154

SNYDERMAN GALLERY
303 CHERRY ST
PHILADELPHIA, PA 19106-1803
TEL 215-238-9576

SOCIETY FOR CONTEMPORARY CRAFT
2100 SMALLMAN ST
PITTSBURGH, PA 15222-4430
TEL 412-261-7003

SOMETHING SPECIAL
2 FORMAN ST
BRADFORD, PA 16701-1215
TEL 814-368-6011

STRAWBERRY & COMPANY
79 W KING ST
LANCASTER, PA 17603-3842
TEL 717-392-5345

STUDIO IN SWARTHMORE GALLERY
14 PARK AVE
SWARTHMORE, PA 19081-1723
TEL 215-543-5779

STYLE & SUBSTANCE GALLERY
GREENGATE MALL
GREENSBURG, PA 15601
TEL 412-834-9299

SUNDANCE
PEDDLER'S VILLAGE
PO BOX 311
LAHASKA, PA 18931
TEL 215-794-8871

THE GALLERY AT CEDAR HOLLOW
2447 YELLOW SPRINGS RD
MALVERN, PA 19355-1411
TEL 610-640-2787

TOPEO GALLERY
35 N MAIN ST
NEW HOPE, PA 18938-1339
TEL 215-862-2750

TURTLEDOVE
4373 MAIN ST
PHILADELPHIA, PA 19127-1415
TEL 215-487-7350

WOODMERE ART MUSEUM
9201 GERMANTOWNS AVE
PHILADELPHIA, PA 19118

WORKS GALLERY
319 SOUTH ST
PHILADELPHIA, PA 19147-1518
TEL 215-922-7775

RHODE ISLAND

RAMSON HOUSE ANTIQUES
36 FRANKLIN ST
NEWPORT, RI 02840-3013
TEL 401-847-0555

SPECTRUM OF AMERICAN ARTISTS
306 THAMES ST
NEWPORT, RI 02840-6610
TEL 401-847-4477

SUN UP GALLERY
95 WATCH HILL RD
WESTERLY, RI 02891
TEL 401-596-0800

TROPEA-PUERINI
7 DRESSER ST #2B
NEWPORT, RI 02840-3620
TEL 401-846-3344

VIRGINIA LYNCH GALLERY
4 CORNELL RD
3883 MAIN RD
TIVERTON, RI 02878-3202
TEL 401-624-3392

SOUTH CAROLINA

AMERICAN ORIGINALS
153 EAST BAY ST
CHARLESTON, SC 29401
TEL 803-853-5034

ARTISTS PARLOR
126 LAURENS ST NW
AIKEN, SC 29801-3846
TEL 803-648-4639

BLUE HERON GALLERY
D2 LAGOON RD, COLIGNY PLAZA
HILTON HEAD, SC 29928
TEL 803-785-3788

BOHEMIAN
2112 DEVINE ST
COLUMBIA, SC 29205-2414
TEL 803-256-0629

CAROL SAUNDERS GALLERY
922 GERVAIS ST
COLUMBIA, SC 29201-3128
TEL 803-256-3046

CHECKERED MOON GALLERY
208 WEST ST
BEAUFORT, SC 29902-5559
TEL 803-522-3466

CRAFTSELLER GALLERY
818 BAY ST
PO BOX 1968
BEAUFORT, SC 29902-5566
TEL 803-525-6104

DUKE STREET GALLERY
109 DUKE ST
PENDLETON, SC 29670
TEL 803-646-3469

HARBOUR TOWN CRAFTS
#7 HARBOUR HOUSE, PO BOX 306
HILTON HEAD, SC 29928
TEL 803-671-3643

HAVENS GALLERY
1616 GERVAIS ST
COLUMBIA, SC 29203
TEL 803-256-1616

NINA LIU & FRIENDS
24 STATE ST
CHARLESTON, SC 29401-2815
TEL 803-722-2724

SMITH GALLERIES OF FINE CRAFTS
THE VILLAGE AT WEXFORD #J-11
HILTON HEAD ISLAND, SC 29928
TEL 803-842-2280

SOUTHERN GALLERIES
402 SE MAIN ST
SIMPSONVILLE, SC 29681-2652
TEL 803-963-4893

TENNESSEE

AMERICAN ARTISAN, INC
4231 HARDING RD
NASHVILLE, TN 37205-2076
TEL 615-298-4691

ARTIFACTS GALLERY
1007 OAKHAVEN RD
MEMPHIS, TN 38119-3811
TEL 901-767-5236

BELL GALLERY OF FINE ART
6150 POPLAR AVE #118
MEMPHIS, TN 38119
TEL 901-682-2189

BENNETT GALLERIES
4515 KINGSTON PIKE
KNOXVILLE, TN 37919
TEL 615-584-6791

BOONES CREEK POTTER'S GALLERY
4903 KINGSPORT HWY 36
JOHNSON CITY, TN 37615
TEL 615-282-2801

CUMBERLAND GALLERY
4107 HILLSBORO CIR
NASHVILLE, TN 37215-2742
TEL 615-297-0296

G. WEBB GALLERY
2160 TUDOR MTN RD
GATLINBURG, TN 37738
TEL 615-436-3639

HANSON ARTSOURCE
5607 KINGSTON PIKE
KNOXVILLE, TN 37919-6347
TEL 615-584-6097

KURTS BINGHAM GALLERY
766 S WHITE STATION RD
MEMPHIS, TN 38117-4579
TEL 901-683-6200

RIVER GALLERY
HIGH ST & BLUFF VIEW
CHATANOOGA, TN 37403
TEL 615-267-7353

ROBERT TINO GALLERY
812 OLD DOUGLAS DAM RD
SEVIERVILLE, TN 37876-1676
TEL 615-428-6519

SOHO SOUTH
4713 POPLAR AVE
MEMPHIS, TN 38120
TEL 901-767-7070

THE BROWSERY
424 RIVERMONT DR
CLARKSVILLE, TN 37043-5991
TEL 615-552-2733

VARIATIONS BY VICTORIA
4901 JACKSBORO PIKE
KNOXVILLE, TN 37918
TEL 615-688-4920

TEXAS

ACQUISATORY
3016 GREENVILLE AVE
DALLAS, TX 75206-6030

ADELLE M. GALLERY
3317 MCKINNEY AVE # 203
DALLAS, TX 75204-2336
TEL 214-220-0300

APPLE CORPS
2324 UNIVERSITY BLVD
HOUSTON, TX 77005-2642
TEL 713-524-2221

ART GROUP
1119 N WINDOMERE AVE
DALLAS, TX 75208-3506
TEL 214-942-0258

ARTISANS FINE CRAFTS GALLERY
10000 RESEARCH BLVD
AUSTIN, TX 78759-5801
TEL 512-345-3001

BANKS FINE ART
3316 ROYAL LN
DALLAS, TX 75229-5061
TEL 214-352-1811

BLAIRE CARNAHAN FINE ART
418 LA VILLITA ST
SAN ANTONIO, TX 78205-2906
TEL 210-227-6313

BLUE HAND
2323 UNIVERSITY BLVD
HOUSTON, TX 77005-2641

BOWDEN GALLERY
6981 BLANCO RD
SAN ANTONIO, TX 78216-6164
TEL 512-341-4367

CARLYN GALERIE
6137 LUTHER LN
DALLAS, TX 75225-6202
TEL 214-368-2828

CARSON ART
1444 OAK LAWN AVE #610
DALLAS, TX 75207-3613
TEL 214-747-3055

CIRCA NOW GALLERY
2162 PORTSMOUTH ST
HOUSTON, TX 77098-4057
TEL 713-529-8234

GALLERY LISTINGS

CLARKSVILLE POTTERY
4001 N LAMAR #200
AUSTIN, TX 78756
TEL 512-472-4695

CLARKSVILLE POTTERY
1013 W LYNN ST
AUSTIN, TX 78703-3996
TEL 512-478-9079

CLARKSVILLE POTTERY 2
ARBORETUM MARKET
9722 GREAT HILLS
AUSTIN, TX 78759
TEL 512-794-8580

COUNTERPOINT
2626 N STANTON
EL PASO, TX 79902
TEL 915-545-5073

CREATIVE ARTS GALLERY
11765 WEST AVE #177
SAN ANTONIO, TX 78216-2559
TEL 210-342-8659

CULLER CONCEPTS
1347 CEDAR HILL AVE
DALLAS, TX 75208-2404
TEL 214-942-1646

DEBUSK GALLERIES
3813 N COMMERCE ST
FORT WORTH, TX 76106-2713
TEL 817-625-8476

EVENTS
1966 WEST GRAY
HOUSTON, TX 77019
TEL 713-520-5700

**FINE ART
CONSULTANTS/SOUTHWEST**
1744 NORFOLK ST
HOUSTON, TX 77098-4408
TEL 713-526-5628

FREE FLIGHT GALLERY
13350 DALLAS PARKWAY
DALLAS, TX 75240
TEL 214-701-9566

FREE FLIGHT GALLERY
603 MUNGER AVE #309
DALLAS, TX 75202-2003
TEL 214-720-9147

GOLDEN EYE GALLERY
20035 KATY FWY
KATY, TX 77450-2238
TEL 713-678-2820

GREGORY'S
2 MAIN ST
SALADO, TX 76571
TEL 817-947-5703

HANSON GALLERIES
800 W SAM HOUSTON PKY NE118
HOUSTON, TX 77024-3900
TEL 713-984-1242

HEARTLAND GALLERY
4006 S LAMAR BLVD #950
AUSTIN, TX 78704-7971
TEL 512-447-1171

HIGH GLOSS
515 HEDWIG RD
HOUSTON, TX 77024
TEL 713-468-2915

HUMMINGBIRD ORIGINALS
4319 CAMP BOWIE BLVD
FORT WORTH, TX 76107-3833

IOTA
3107 KNOX ST
DALLAS, TX 75205
TEL 214-522-2999

JACK MEIER GALLERY
2310 BISSONNET ST
HOUSTON, TX 77005-1512
TEL 713-526-2983

JADE EAST
1317 MAHLMAN #610
ROSENBERG, TX 77471
TEL 713-239-8521

JUDY YOUENS GALLERY
3115 DAMICO ST
HOUSTON, TX 77019-1901

KEENE GALLERY
242 LOSOYA ST
SAN ANTONIO, TX 78205-2610
TEL 210-299-1999

KITTRELL RIFFKIND ART GLASS
5100 BELTLINE RD #820
DALLAS, TX 75240
TEL 214-239-7957

KITTRELL RIFFKIND ART GLASS
12215 COIT RD
DALLAS, TX 75251
TEL 214-239-7957

LEGACY'S
1846 ROSE MEAD PKWY #148
CARROLLTON, TX 75007

LYONS MATRIX GALLERY
1712 LAVACA ST
AUSTIN, TX 78701-1316
TEL 512-479-0068

NEW GALLERY
2639 COLQUITT ST
HOUSTON, TX 77098-2117
TEL 713-520-1753

PERIMETER GALLERY
2365 RICE BLVD
HOUSTON, TX 77005
TEL 713-521-5928

POSITIVE IMAGES
1118 W 6TH ST
AUSTIN, TX 78703-5304
TEL 512-472-1831

PRESTON COLLECTION
305 PRESTON ROYAL
DALLAS, TX 75230
TEL 214-373-6065

ROBINS NEST
11700 PRESTON RD #800
DALLAS, TX 75230

ROCK HOUSE GALLERY
1311 W ABRAM ST
ARLINGTON, TX 76013-1704
TEL 817-265-5874

SABLE V FINE ART GALLERY
PO BOX 1792
WIMBERLEY, TX 78676-1792
TEL 512-847-8975

SOL DEL RIO GALLERY
1020 TOWNSEND AVE
SAN ANTONIO, TX 78209-5144
TEL 210-828-5555

SOUTHWEST CRAFT CENTER
300 AUGUSTA ST
SAN ANTONIO, TX 78205-1296
TEL 210-224-1848

SPICEWOOD GALLERY
1206 W 38TH ST
AUSTIN, TX 78705-1018
TEL 512-458-6575

STUDIO B
109 E MAIN
FREDERICKSBURG, TX 78624
TEL 210-997-4547

THE ARRANGEMENT
2605 ELM ST
DALLAS, TX 75226-1423
TEL 214-748-4540

THE OLE MOON
3016 GREENVILLE AVE
DALLAS, TX 75206-6030
TEL 214-827-9921

TWO FRIENDS GALLERY
2301 STRAND ST
GALVESTON, TX 77550-1546
TEL 409-765-7477

URSULINE GALLERY
300 AUGUSTA ST
SAN ANTONIO, TX 78205-1216
TEL 210-224-1848

VILLAGE WEAVERS
418 LA VILLITA ST
SAN ANTONIO, TX 78205-2906
TEL 210-222-0776

VIRTU
4514 TRAVIS ST
DALLAS, TX 33316
TEL 214-520-7817

WEST BANK GALLERY
4201 BEE CAVES RD #A100
AUSTIN, TX 78746-6458
TEL 512-329-8514

**WM CAMPBELL
CONTEMPORARY ART**
4935 BYERS AVE
FORT WORTH, TX 76107-4198
TEL 817-737-9566

UTAH

CARRIBEAN CASTINGS
PO BOX 73
ST. JOHN, UT 00831
TEL 809-693-8520

PHILLIPS GALLERY
444 E 200 S
SALT LAKE CITY, UT 84111-2103
TEL 801-364-8284

**UTAH DESIGNER CRAFTS
GALLERY**
1658 YALECREST AVE
SALT LAKE CITY, UT 84105-1751
TEL 801-359-2770

VERMONT

FROG HOLLOW CRAFT CENTER
1 MILL ST
MIDDLEBURY, VT 05753-1144
TEL 802-388-3177

HAWKINS HOUSE
262 NORTH ST
BENNINGTON, VT 05201-1828
TEL 802-447-1171

JOHN MCLEOD LTD.
PO BOX 338
WILMINGTON, VT 05363
TEL 802-464-8175

MOUNTAIN HIGH AMERICAN CRAFT
THE MARKET PLACE
LUDLOW, VT 05149
TEL 802-228-5216

NORTH WIND ARTISAN GALLERY
81 CENTRAL ST
WOODSTOCK, VT 05091-1145
TEL 802-457-4587

SIMON PEARCE GLASS
GENERAL DELIVERY
QUECHEE, VT 05059-9999
TEL 802-295-2711

SPIRAL GALLERY
PO BOX 29
MARLBORO, VT 05344-0029
TEL 802-257-5696

VERMONT ARTISAN DESIGNS
115 MAIN ST
BRATTLEBORO, VT 05301-3061
TEL 802-257-7044

VERMONT STATE CRAFT CENTER
MAIN ST
PO BOX 1777
WINDSOR, VT 05089
TEL 802-674-6729

WINDHAM ART GALLERY
75 MAIN ST
BRATTLEBORO, VT 05301-3257
TEL 802-257-1881

WOODSTOCK GALLERY OF ART GALLERY PLACE
RT 4 EAST
WOODSTOCK, VT 05091
TEL 802-457-1900

VIRGINIA

19TH ST. GALLERY
700 19TH ST
SUITE 105
VIRGINIA BEACH, VA 23451
TEL 804-425-8224

A TOUCH OF EARTH
6580 RICHMOND RD
WILLIAMSBURG, VA 23188-7200
TEL 804-565-0425

AMERICAN ARTISAN INC
201 KING ST
ALEXANDRIA, VA 22314-3209
TEL 703-548-3431

APPLACHIAN SPRING
102 W JEFFERSON
FALLS CHURCH, VA 22046

ART & SOUL
1127 KING ST
ALEXANDRIA, VA 22314-2924
TEL 703-549-4881

ARTIFAX
1511 COLLEY AVE
NORFOLK, VA 23517
TEL 804-623-8840

ARTISAN'S STUDIO
105 HANOVER AVE
ASHLAND, VA 23005-1813

ARTS AFIRE GLASS GALLERY
112 N. ROYAL ST
ALEXANDRIA, VA 22314
TEL 703-838-9785

BLUE SKIES GALLERY
120 W QUEENS WAY # 201
HAMPTON, VA 23669-4014
TEL 804-727-0028

BREIT FUNCTIONAL CRAFTS
1701 COLLEY AVE
NORFOLK, VA 23517-1610
TEL 804-640-1012

BROADWAY GALLERY
11213J LEE HWY
FAIRFAX, VA 22030-5608
TEL 703-273-2388

CAVE HOUSE CRAFT SHOP
279 E MAIN ST
ABINGDON, VA 24210-2903
TEL 703-628-7721

COUNTRY HERITAGE ANTIQUES & CRAFTS
PO BOX 148
WASHINGTON, VA 22747
TEL 703-675-3738

CRAFTERS' GALLERY
RR 12 BOX 97
CHARLOTTESVILLE, VA 22901-9501
TEL 804-295-7006

CUDAHY'S GALLERY
1314 E CARY ST
RICHMOND, VA 23219-4118
TEL 804-782-1776

D'ART CENTER
125 COLLEGE PL
NORFOLK, VA 23510-1907
TEL 804-625-4211

EBASHAE GALLERY
GENERAL DELIVERY
OCCOQUAN, VA 22125-9999
TEL 703-491-5984

ELECTRIC GLASS GALLERY
823 W PEMBROKE AVE
HAMPTON, VA 23669-3326
TEL 804-722-6300

FENTON GALLERY
110 S HENRY ST
WILLIAMSBURG, VA 23185-4153
TEL 804-253-8700

FIBER DESIGNS
323 KING ST
ALEXANDRIA, VA 22314
TEL 703-548-1461

FIBER WORKS
105 N UNION ST
ALEXANDRIA, VA 22314-3217
TEL 703-836-5807

FISHSCALE & MOUSETOOTH
9406 MAIN ST
MANASSAS, VA 22110
TEL 703-330-1263

FUNCTIONAL ART OF VIRGINIA
1700 DOMINION TOWER
NORFOLK, VA 23570
TEL 800-423-8655

GALLERY FOUR
115 S COLUMBUS ST
ALEXANDRIA, VA 22314-3003
TEL 703-548-4600

GALLERY OF MOUNTAIN SECRETS
RT 250
MAIN ST
MONTEREY, VA 24465
TEL 703-468-2020

GALLERY THREE
213 MARKET ST SE
ROANOKE, VA 24011-1800
TEL 703-343-9698

GLASS REUNIONS
1307 E CARY ST
RICHMOND, VA 23219
TEL 804-643-3233

HARRIET'S ART & ANTIQUES
7306 LANGSFORD CT
SPRINGFIELD, VA 22153-1536
TEL 703-644-1121

MARINA SHORES GALLERY
2100 MARINA SHORES DR
VIRGINIA BEACH, VA 23451-6819
TEL 804-496-7000

MCMANN MCDADE FINE ART
364 WALNUT AVE SW
ROANOKE, VA 24016-4621
TEL 703-345-5123

MELLOWOOD
4313 35TH ST N
ARLINGTON, VA 22207-4470
TEL 703-528-3037

METALLUM
105 N UNION ST
ALEXANDRIA, VA 22314-3217
TEL 703-548-4600

OLD MILL CRAFT GALLERY
EVANS FARM INN
RT 123
MCLEAN, VA 22101
TEL 703-893-2736

ON THE HILL CREATIVE ARTS CTR
121 ALEXANDER HAMILTON BLVD
PO BOX 222
YORKTOWN, VA 23690-3800
TEL 804-898-3076

PALMER RAE GALLERY, INC
112 GRANBY ST
NORFOLK, VA 23510-1656
TEL 804-627-0081

PAULA LEWIS GALLERY
SOURT SQUARE
1924 GREENBRIER DR
CHARLOTTESVILLE, VA 22901-2915
TEL 804-295-6244

POTOMAC CRAFTSMEN
105 N UNION ST #18
ALEXANDRIA, VA 22314-3217
TEL 703-548-0935

GALLERY LISTINGS

PRIMAVERA GALLERY
4216 VIRGINIA BEACH BLVD
VIRGINIA BEACH, VA 23452-1233
TEL 804-431-9393

ROCKY ROAD TO KANSAS
215 SOUTH UNION ST
ALEXANDRIA, VA 22314
TEL 703-683-0116

RUSH RIVER COMPANY
PO BOX 74
GAY ST
WASHINGTON, VA 22747-0074
TEL 703-675-1136

SCOPE GALLERY
TORPEDO FACTORY
105 N UNION ST
ALEXANDRIA, VA 22314
TEL 703-548-6288

SIGNET GALLERY
212 5TH ST NE
PO BOX 753
CHARLOTTESVILLE, VA 22902-5208
TEL 804-296-6463

STARDUST
1774 U INTERNATIONAL DR
MCLEAN, VA 22102

VINCENT'S FINE ART
4429 SHORE DR
VIRGINIA BEACH, VA 23455-2821
TEL 804-464-9380

VISTA FINE CRAFTS GALLERY
5 W WASHINGTON ST
PO BOX 2034
MIDDLEBURG, VA 22117
TEL 703-687-3317

WHISTLE WALK CRAFTS GALLERY
7 S KING ST
LEESBURG, VA 22075-2903
TEL 703-777-4017

YORKTOWN ARTS FOUNDATION
121 ALEXANDER HAMILTON BLVD
PO BOX 244
YORKTOWN, VA 23690-3800
TEL 804-898-3076

WASHINGTON

AMERICAN ART GALLERY
1126 BROADWAY
TACOMA, WA 98402-3503
TEL 206-272-4327

ARTWOOD
1000 HARRIS AVE
BELLINGHAM, WA 98225-7035
TEL 206-647-1628

ARTWORKS GALLERY
155 S MAIN ST
SEATTLE, WA 98104-2571
TEL 206-625-0932

AVOIR GALLERY
216 KIRKLAND AVE
KIRKLAND, WA 98033
TEL 206-827-8349

CARNEGIE ART CENTER, NC
109 S PALOUSE ST
WALLA WALLA, WA 99362-3006
TEL 509-525-4270

CAROLYN PRICE DYER GALLERY
3318 N PROCTOR
TACOMA, WA 98407

CHILDERS/PROCTOR GALLERY
302 1ST ST
PO BOX 458
LANGLEY, WA 98260-8802
TEL 206-221-2978

CHILDHOOD'S END GALLERY
222 4TH AVE W
OLYMPIA, WA 98501-1004
TEL 206-943-3724

CORPORATE ART WEST, INC
12360 NE 8TH ST
BELLEVUE, WA 98005-3188
TEL 206-454-2595

CRACKERJACK GALLERY
WALLINGFORD CENTER
1815 N 45TH #212
SEATTLE, WA 98103
TEL 206-547-4983

CREATIONS GALLERY
7651 COAL CREEK PKY SE
RENTON, WA 98059-3212
TEL 206-624-5578

EARTHENWORKS
713 FIRST ST
PO BOX 702
LA CONNER, WA 98257
TEL 206-466-4422

EARTHENWORKS
702 WATER ST
PORT TOWNSEND, WA 98368-5729
TEL 206-385-0328

ELEMENTS GALLERY
113 SEAFIRST BLDG
10500 NE EIGHTH ST
BELLEVUE, WA 98004
TEL 206-454-8242

ELLIOTT BROWN GALLERY
619 N 35TH ST #101
SEATTLE, WA 98103-8639
TEL 206-547-9740

FIREWORKS GALLERY
PIONEER SQUARE
210 1ST AVE S
SEATTLE, WA 98104
TEL 206-682-8707

FLYING SHUTTLE GALLERY
607 1ST AVE
SEATTLE, WA 98104-2209
TEL 206-343-9762

FOLK ART GALLERY LA TIENDA
4138 UNIVERSITY WAY NE
SEATTLE, WA 98105
TEL 206-634-1795

FOSTER WHITE GALLERY
311½ OCCIDENTAL AVE S
SEATTLE, WA 98104-2839
TEL 206-622-2833

FOSTER WHITE GALLERY
126 CENTRAL WAY
KIRKLAND, WA 98033-6106
TEL 206-822-2305

FRANK DUNYA GALLERY
3418 FREMONT AVE N
SEATTLE, WA 98103-8812
TEL 206-547-6760

FRIESEN GALLERY
1210 2ND AVE
SEATTLE, WA 98101-2926
TEL 206-628-9502

GALLERY ONE
408½ N PEARL ST
ELLENSBURG, WA 98926-3112
TEL 509-925-2670

GARDENS OF ART
2900 SYLVAN ST
BELLINGHAM, WA 98226-4372
TEL 206-671-1069

GLASS EYE
1902 POST ALLEY
SEATTLE, WA 98101
TEL 800-237-6961

GLASS EYE GALLERY
1902 POST ALY
SEATTLE, WA 98101-1015
TEL 206-441-3221

GLASSHOUSE ART GLASS
PIONEER SQUARE
311 OCCIDENTAL AVE S
SEATTLE, WA 98104
TEL 206-682-9939

HIGH SPIRITS
100 N WENATCHEE AVE
WENATCHEE, WA 98801
TEL 509-633-7798

HIGHLY STRUNG
4222 E MADISON ST
SEATTLE, WA 98112-3237
TEL 206-328-1045

IMAGES IN TIME
30 LAKESHORE PLAZA
KIRKLAND, WA 98033
TEL 206-828-6484

JANET HUSTON GALLERY
PO BOX 845
LA CONNER, WA 98257-0845
TEL 206-466-5001

LAKESHORE GALLERY
15 LAKE ST
KIRKLAND, WA 98033
TEL 206-827-0606

LINDA FARRIS GALLERY
320 2ND AVE
SEATTLE, WA 98104

LYNN MCALLISTER GALLERY
1028 LAKEVIEW BLVD E #5
SEATTLE, WA 98102-4400
TEL 206-624-6864

MANDARIN GLASS STUDIO GALLERY
8821 BRIDGEPORT WAY SW
TACOMA, WA 98499-2645
TEL 206-582-3355

MELANGE
120 LAKESIDE AVE
SEATTLE, WA 98122-6548
TEL 206-322-1341

MESOLINI & AMICI
77½ S MAIN ST
SEATTLE, WA 98104-2513
TEL 206-587-0275

MIA GALLERY
512 IST AVE S
SEATTLE, WA 98104-2804
TEL 206-467-8283

MOSS BAY GALLERY
128A PARK LN
KIRKLAND, WA 98033
TEL 206-822-3630

NORTHWEST DISCOVERY
142 BELLEVUE SQ
BELLEVUE, WA 98004-5021
TEL 206-454-1676

NW GALLERY OF FINE WOOD-WORKING
317 NW GILMAN BLVD
ISSAQUAH, WA 98027-2485
TEL 206-391-4221

NW GALLERY OF FINE WOOD-WORKING
202 IST AVE S
SEATTLE, WA 98104-2504
TEL 206-625-0542

PANACA GALLERY
133 BELLEVUE SQ
BELLEVUE, WA 98004-5021
TEL 206-454-0234

PARKLANE GALLERY
130 PARK LN
KIRKLAND, WA 98033
TEL 206-827-8053

PETERSON ART FURNITURE GALLERY
122 CENTRAL WAY
KIRKLAND, WA 98033-6106
TEL 206-827-8053

PHOENIX RISING GALLERY
2030 WESTERN AVE
SEATTLE, WA 98121-2124
TEL 206-728-2332

PROVAN-JONES
94 KIRKLAND AVE
KIRKLAND, WA 98033
TEL 206-827-1878

RAGAZZI'S FLYING SHUTTLE
607 FIRST AVE
SEATTLE, WA 98104
TEL 206-343-9762

RON SEGAL GALLERY
1420 5TH AVE #208
SEATTLE, WA 98101-2333
TEL 800-688-2788

SERENDIPITY
909 COMMERCIAL AVE
ANACORTES, WA 98221-4114

ST HILL ART FACTORY
3509 TENT ST NW
GIG HARBOR, WA 98335
TEL 206-851-8825

STONINGTON GALLERY
2030 IST AVE
SEATTLE, WA 98121-2112
TEL 206-443-1108

THE COLLECTION
118 S WASHINGTON ST
PIONEER SQUARE
SEATTLE, WA 98104-2522
TEL 206-682-6184

THE HOST
SEA-TAC INTERNATIONAL AIRPORT
SEATTLE, WA 98158
TEL 206-433-5122

TOPPERS
1260 CARILLON PT
KIRKLAND, WA 98033-7351
TEL 206-889-9311

WILLIAM TRAVER GALLERY
110 UNION ST
SEATTLE, WA 98101-2028
TEL 206-448-4234

WOOD MERCHANT
707 S FIRST ST
PO BOX 511
LA CONNER, WA 98257
TEL 206-466-4741

WEST VIRGINIA

QUILTS UNLIMITED
203 E WASHINGTON ST
LEWISBURG, WV 24901-1423
TEL 304-647-4208

SANGUINE GRYPHON GALLERY
PO BOX 3120
SHEPHERDSTOWN, WV 25443-3120
TEL 304-876-6569

STUDIO 40
GREENBRIER HOTEL
WH SULPHUR SPRINGS, WV 24986
TEL 304-536-4898

TERRASALIS GARDEN CENTER
PO BOX 60090
MALDEN, WV 25306
TEL 304-925-4754

THE ART STORE
1013 BRIDGE RD
CHARLESTON, WV 25314-1305
TEL 304-345-1038

THE SHOP
THE CULTURAL CENTER
CHARLESTON, WV 25305
TEL 304-348-0690

WISCONSIN

ACCENTRICS LTD
1505 W MEQUON RD
MEQUON, WI 53092
TEL 414-241-9292

AGOSY
18900 W BLUE MOUND RD
WAUKASHA, WI 53188
TEL 414-821-6900

ART ELEMENTS GALLERY
1400 W MEQUON RD
MEQUON, WI 53092-3226
TEL 414-241-7040

ART ELEMENTS GALLERY
10050 NORTH PORT WASHINGTON
MEQUON, WI 53092
TEL 414-241-7040

ART INDEPENDENT GALLERY
623 W MAIN ST
LAKE GENEVA, WI 53147-1907
TEL 414-248-3612

ARTISTRY STUDIO GALLERY
833 E CENTER ST
MILWAUKEE, WI 53212-3047
TEL 414-372-3372

ATYPIC GALLERY
AUDUBON CT
333 W BROWN DEER RD
MILWAUKEE, WI 53217
TEL 414-351-0333

AVENUE ART
10 COLLEGE AVE
APPLETON, WI 54911-5756
TEL 414-734-7710

BERGSTROM MAHLER MUSEUM
165 N PARK AVE
NEENAH, WI 54956-2956
TEL 414-751-4658

BREAKWATER GALLERY
400 IST ST BOX 325
PEPIN, WI 54759

BRODEN GALLERY, LTD
114 STATE ST
MADISON, WI 53703-2560
TEL 608-256-6100

BY JAMES
115 N 4TH
LA CROSSE, WI 54601
TEL 608-785-2637

CEDAR CREEK POTTERY
N70 W6340 BRIDGE RD
CEDARBURG, WI 53012
TEL 414-375-1226

DELIND FINE ART
801 N JEFFERSON ST
MILWAUKEE, WI 53202-3709
TEL 414-271-8525

EDGEWOOD ORCHARD GALLERIES
W 4140 PENINSULA PLAYERS RD
FISH CREEK, WI 54212
TEL 414-868-3579

FANNY GARVER GALLERY
230 STATE ST
MADISON, WI 53703-2215
TEL 608-256-6755

GALLERY 323 AT RUBINS
323 E WILSON ST
MADISON, WI 53703-3426
TEL 608-255-8998

GRACE CHOSY GALLERY
218 N HENRY ST
MADISON, WI 53703-2204
TEL 608-255-1211

GWENDOLYN'S AT WHISTLING SWAN
PO BOX 617
FISH CREEK, WI 54212
TEL 414-868-3602

HARDWARE DESIGN
438 W NATIONAL AVE
MILWAUKEE, WI 53204-1744
TEL 414-647-8089

JM KOHLER ART CENTER
608 NEW YORK AVE
SHEBOYGAN, WI 53081-4507
TEL 414-458-6144

JOHNSTON GALLERY
245 HIGH ST
MINERAL POINT, WI 53565-1209
TEL 608-987-3787

GALLERY LISTINGS

JURA SILVERMAN GALLERY
143 S WASHINGTON ST
SPRING GREEN, WI 53588
TEL 608-588-7049

KATIE GINGRASS GALLERY
241 NORTH BROADWAY
MILWAUKEE, WI 53202
TEL 414-289-0855

KOHLER ARTS CENTER
725-G WOODLAKE RD
KOHLER, WI 53044
TEL 414-452-8602

MADISON ART CENTER
211 STATE ST
MADISON, WI 53703
TEL 608-257-0158

MAPLE GROVE GALLERY
N9098 COUNTY RD. F
FISH CREEK, WI 54212
TEL 414-839-2693

MCMILLAN GALLERY
AT KNICKERBOCKER PLACE
2701 MONROE ST
MADISON, WI 53711
TEL 608-238-6501

METRO ONE GALLERY
7821 EGG HARBOR RD
EGG HARBOR, WI 54209-9624
TEL 414-868-3399

MINKOFF FINE ART, LTD
10004 N KIRKLAND CT
MEQUON, WI 53092-5444
TEL 414-242-5900

MOYER GALLERY
2351 S WEBSTER AVE
GREEN BAY, WI 54301-2123
TEL 414-435-3388

NEW ORNATE BOX
TURTLE GALLERY
248 E JEFFERSON
SPRING GREEN, WI 53588
TEL 608-274-0528

NEW VISIONS GALLERY, INC
1000 N OAK AVE
MARSHFIELD, WI 54449-5703
TEL 715-387-5562

OCONOMOWOC GALLERY LTD
157 E WISCONSIN AVE
OCONOMOWOC, WI 53066-3033
TEL 414-567-8123

PEDESTRIAN ARTS
11 MERRITT AVE
OSHKOSH, WI 54901-4926
TEL 414-231-9790

PERINE GALLERY
1719 MONROE ST
MADISON, WI 53711-2022
TEL 608-256-4040

PUMP HOUSE
REGIONAL CENTER FOR THE ARTS
119 KING ST
LA CROSSE, WI 54601
TEL 608-785-1434

RAIN FOREST GALLERY
1041 N OLD WORLD 3RD ST
MILWAUKEE, WI 53203-1301

RED BALLOON GALLERY
HWY 35
PO BOX 606
STOCKHOLM, WI 54769
TEL 715-442-2504

SCHRAGER'S
2837 N SHERMAN BLVD
MILWAUKEE, WI 53210-1702

SEEBECK GALLERY
5601 6TH AVE
KENOSHA, WI 53140-4101
TEL 414-657-7172

STONEHILL CRAFTS
GENERAL DELIVERY
EPHRAIM, WI 54211-9999
TEL 414-854-4749

STORNAWAY HOUSE
W62N630 WASHINGTON AVE
CEDARSBURG, WI 53012

STUDIO ON HIGH
154 HIGH ST
MINERAL POINT, WI 53565-1208
TEL 608-987-2834

THE GREAT MIDWEST CRAFTSMARKET
7700 120TH AVE
KENOSHA, WI 53142
TEL 414-857-9448

THE HANG UP GALLERY
204 W WISCONSIN AVE
NEENAH, WI 54956-2502
TEL 414-722-0481

TORY FOLLIARD GALLERY
233 N MILWAUKEE ST
MILWAUKEE, WI 53202-5811
TEL 414-273-7311

WEST BEND GALLERY OF FINE ARTS
300 S 6TH AVE
WEST BEND, WI 53095-3312
TEL 414-334-1151

WISCONSIN ARTISAN GALLERY
6858 PAOLI RD
BELLEVILLE, WI 53508-9223
TEL 608-845-6600

WOODLOT GALLERY
5215 N EVERGREEN DR
SHEBOYGAN, WI 53081-8213
TEL 414-458-4798

WYOMING

ART WEST GALLERY
PO BOX 1248
JACKSON, WY 83001-1248
TEL 307-733-6379

MARGO'S POTTERY & FINE CRAFTS
457 N MAIN ST
BUFFALO, WY 82834-1732
TEL 307-684-9406

CANADA

A SHOW OF HANDS GALLERY
1947 AVENUE RD
TORONTO, ON M5M-4AZ
TEL 416-782-1696

ART GLASS GALLERY
21 HAZLETON AVE
TORONTO, ON M5R-2E1
TEL 416-968-1823

ART ZONE
592 MARKHAM ST
TORONTO, ON M6G-2L8
TEL 416-534-1892

BECKETT GALLERY LIMITED
142 JAMES ST S
HAMILTON, ON L8P-3A2
TEL 905-525-4266

CABBAGES & KING
710 NINTH ST
CANMORE, AB T0L-0M0
TEL 403-678-6915

CANADA'S FOUR CORNERS
93 SPARKS ST
OTTAWA, ON K1P-5B5
TEL 613-233-2322

CANADIAN ART GALLERIES
901 10TH AVE, SW
CALGARY, BC T2R-0B4
TEL 403-290-0203

CHRISTINE PARKER GALLERY
7 PLANK RD
ST. JOHNS, NF A1E-1H3
TEL 709-753-0580

CONFEDERATION OF THE ARTS GALL
PO BOX 848
CHARLOTTETOWN, NS C1A-7M1
TEL 902-628-6131

CRAFTWORKS
35 MCCAUL ST, CHALMERS BLDG
TORONTO, ON M5T-1V7
TEL 416-977-3487

DEVON HOUSE CRAFT GALLERY
59 DUCKWORTH ST
ST. JOHNS, NF A1C-1E6
TEL 709-753-2749

DEXTERITY
173 KING ST E
TORONTO, ON M5A-1J4
TEL 416-367-4775

EQUINOX GALLERY
2321 GRANVILLE ST
VANCOUVER, BC V7C-1C8
TEL 604-736-2405

GALLERY MOOS LTD.
622 RICHMOND W
TORONTO, ON M5V-1Y9
TEL 416-777-0707

GALLEY 78
796 QUEEN ST
FREDERICTION, NB E3B-1C6
TEL 506-454-5192

HAND WAVE GALLERY
BOX 145
MECHAM, SK S0K-2V0
TEL 306-376-2211

HUMANUM ART GALLERY
123 2ND AVE S
SASKATOON, SK S7K-7E6
TEL 306-665-9912

INUIT GALLERY
345 WATER ST
VANCOUVER, BC V6B-1B8
TEL 604-688-7323

LAKELAND ART GALLERY
BOX 180
CHRISTOPHER LAKE, BC S0J-0N0
TEL 306-982-2223

MARIPOSA GALLERY
312 COLLEGE ST
TORONTO, ON M5T-1S3
TEL 416-923-2085

MENDEL ART GALLERY
PO BOX 569
SASKATOON, SK S7K-3L6
TEL 306-975-7610

MOUNTAIN AVENS GALLERY
709 EIGHTH ST, PO BOX 47
CANMORE, BC T0L-0M0
TEL 403-678-4471

MOUNTAIN CRAFT GALLERY
4050 WHISTLER WAY, BOX 1234
WHISTLER WAY, BC V0N-1B0
TEL 604-932-5001

NANCY POOLE'S STUDIO
16 HAZELTON AVE
TORONTO, ON M5R-2E2
TEL 416-964-9050

NB CRAFT GALLERY
103 CHURCH ST
FREDERICTON, NB E3B-4C8
TEL 506-450-8989

NIJINSKA'S
PORTAGE PLACE
WINNIPEG, MB R3B 3H6
TEL 204-956-2552

NIJINSKA'S GALLERY
CAIRBOU ST
BANFF, BC T0L-0C0
TEL 403-762-5006

**ROWLES & PARHAM DESIGN
SANDRA AINSLEY GALLERY**
2 FIRST CANADIAN PLAZA
TORONTO, ON M5X-1G8
TEL 416-362-4480

SNOW GOOSE HANDICRAFTS
83 SPARKS ST
OTTAWA, ON K1P-5A5
TEL 613-232-2213

SYLVAN CRAFTS & POTTERY
3080 EDGEMONT BLVD
NORTH VANCOUVER, BC V7R-2N5
TEL 416-986-4863

THE QUEST
105 BANFF AVE
BANFF, BC T0L-0C0
TEL 403-762-2722

THREE GRACES INC.
1190 VICTORIA DRIVE
VANCOUVER, BC V5L 4G5
TEL 604-254-4212

TRUDY VAN DOP GALLERY
421 RICHMOND ST
NEW WESTMINSTER, BC V3L 4C4
TEL 604-521-7887

UNFUNDI GALLERY
541 SUSSEX DR
OTTAWA, ON K1N-6Z6
TEL 613-232-3975

**VIRGINIA CHRISTOPHER
GALLERIES**
1134 8TH AVE, SW
CALGARY, BC T2P-1S5
TEL 403-263-4346

WEST END GALLERY
12308 JASPER AVE
EDMONTON, AB T5N-3K5
TEL 403-488-4892

**YDESSA HENDELES ART
FOUNDATION**
778 KING WEST
TORONTO, ON M5V-1N6
TEL 416-941-9400

SELECTED ORGANIZATIONS & PUBLICATIONS

ORGANIZATIONS

AMERICAN ASSOCIATION OF WOODTURNERS

3200 LEXINGTON AVE
SHOREVIEW, MN 55126-8118
FAX 612-484-1724
TEL 612-484-9094

Mary Redig, Administrator

The American Association of Woodturners (AAW) is a non-profit organization dedicated to the advancement of woodturning. Seventy-nine chapters throughout the United States provide education and information for those interested in woodturning. Members include hobbyists, professionals, gallery owners, collectors, and wood and equipment suppliers.

AMERICAN CRAFT COUNCIL

72 SPRING ST
NEW YORK, NY 10012-4006
FAX 212-274-0650
TEL 212-274-0630

Hunter Kariher, Executive Director

The American Craft Council (ACC) stimulates public awareness and appreciation of the work of American craftspeople through museum exhibitions and educational programs, visual aids and publications. The American Craft Museum is an affiliate of the ACC; membership is shared.

The ACC consists of four operating units:

1. American Craft Enterprises produces exhibitions of handmade objects made by America's most talented craftspeople to enhance the awareness of American craft and to provide the opportunity for the public to acquire such crafts;

2. American Craft Publishing produces a bi-monthly magazine to enhance the understanding and appreciation of American crafts;

3. American Craft Association produces educational seminars and audio-visual materials to educate craftspeople, and provides support services for craftspeople;

4. American Craft Information Center provides information on American crafts through a book/exhibit catalog collection and unique files on American craftspeople.

AMERICAN SOCIETY OF FURNITURE ARTISTS

PO BOX 7491
HOUSTON, TX 77248-7491
FAX 713-556-5444
TEL 713-556-5444

Adam St. John, President

The American Society of Furniture Artists (ASOFA) is a non-profit organization dedicated to the field of 'art furniture' and to the artists who create it. Organized in 1989, ASOFA is the only national organization of such artists. The Society's nationwide scope promotes the highest professional standards and provides its members with significant avenues for continued artistic and professional development.

AMERICAN TAPESTRY ALLIANCE

128 MONTICELLO RD
OAK RIDGE, TN 37830
TEL 423-483-0772

Marti Fleischer, President

The American Tapestry Alliance was founded in 1982 to: (1) promote an awareness of and an appreciation for tapestries designed and woven in America; (2) establish, perpetuate and recognize superior quality tapestries by American tapestry artists; (3) encourage greater use of tapestries by corporate and private collectors; (4) educate the public about tapestry; and (5) coordinate national and international juried tapestry shows, exhibiting the finest quality American-made works.

CREATIVE GLASS CENTER OF AMERICA

1501 GLASSTOWN ROAD
PO BOX 646
MILLVILLE, NJ 08332-1566
FAX 609-825-2410
TEL 609-825-6800

The Creative Glass Center is a public attraction devoted to increasing know-how of glass works. The Creative Glass Center of America offers insight to glass arts through the Museum of American Glass, an informational resource center providing fellowships; demonstrations in the T.C. Wheaton Glass Factory; and various tours throughout Wheaton Village.

THE EMBROIDERERS' GUILD OF AMERICA, INC.

335 W. BROADWAY #100
LOUISVILLE, KY 40202
FAX 502-584-7900
TEL 502-589-6956

Jeanette Lovensheimer, President

The Embroiderer's Guild of America (EGA) seeks to set and maintain high standards of design, color and workmanship in all kinds of embroidery and canvas work. EGA sponsors lectures, exhibitions, competitions and field trips; offers examinations for teaching certification; and serves as an information source for needlework in the United States. EGA also maintains a comprehensive reference library for research and study, and publishes *Needle Arts*, a quarterly magazine.

GLASS ART SOCIETY

1305 FOURTH AVE #711
SEATTLE, WA 98101-2401
FAX 206-382-2630
TEL 206-382-1305

Alice Rooney, Executive Director

The Glass Art Society (GAS), an international non-profit organization, was founded in 1971 to encourage excellence and advance appreciation, understanding and development of the glass arts worldwide. GAS promotes communication among artists, educators, students, collectors, gallery and museum personnel, art critics, manufacturers and others through an annual conference and through the *Glass Art Society Journal* and newsletters.

HANDWEAVERS GUILD OF AMERICA, INC.

3327 DULUTH HIGHWAY #201
DULUTH, GA 30136-3373
FAX 770-495-7703
TEL 770-495-7702
E-MAIL to Compuserve 73744.202

Sandra Bowles, Executive Director

The Handweavers Guild of America, Inc. (HGA) is an international non-profit organization dedicated to upholding excellence, promoting the textile arts, and preserving our textile heritage. HGA provides a forum for education, opportunities for networking, and inspiration and encouragement for handweavers, handspinners and related fiber artists. HGA publishes a quarterly journal for members, *Shuttle, Spindle & Dyepot*.

INTERNATIONAL SCULPTURE CENTER

1050 17TH ST NW #250
WASHINGTON, DC 20036
FAX 202-785-0810
TEL 202-785-1144

David Furchgott, Executive Director

The International Sculpture Center (ISC) is a non-profit membership organization devoted to the advancement of contemporary sculpture. The ISC publishes *Sculpture* magazine, *Maquette*, and *InSite*. Activities include conferences; workshops; Sculpture Source, a computerized referral service and registry; exhibitions; and various other member benefits.

INTERNATIONAL TAPESTRY NETWORK

PO BOX 203228
ANCHORAGE, AK 99520-3228
FAX 907-346-3316
TEL 907-346-2392

Helga Berry, President

International Tapestry Network (ITNET) is a not-for-profit global network of tapestry artists, teachers, curators and collectors. ITNET works to develop greater awareness of contemporary tapestry as an art form by sponsoring international tapestry exhibitions and by educating the public and encouraging dialogue about tapestry on an international level. ITNET publishes a quarterly newsletter, distributed worldwide. Newsletter correspondents and advisory board members search for and share news of exhibitions, educational opportunities and other tapestry events.

NATIONAL COUNCIL ON EDUCATION FOR THE CERAMIC ARTS

PO BOX 158
BANDON, OR 97411
TEL 503-347-4394
TEL 800-99N-CECA

Regina Brown, Executive Secretary

The National Council on Education for the Ceramic Arts (NCECA) is a professional organization of individuals whose interests, talents, or careers are primarily focused on the ceramic arts. NCECA strives to stimulate, promote and improve education in the ceramic arts, and to gather and disseminate information and ideas that are vital and stimulating to teachers, studio artists and others throughout the creative studies community. NCECA hosts a national conference each spring.

NATIONAL WOODCARVERS ASSOCIATION

PO BOX 43218
CINCINNATI, OH 45243
TEL 513-561-0627

Edward F. Gallenstein, President

The National Woodcarvers Association (NWCA) promotes woodcarving and fellowship among its members; encourages exhibitions and area get-togethers; publishes *Chip Chats*, a bi-monthly magazine; and assists members in finding tool and wood suppliers, as well as markets for their work. Distinguished professional woodcarvers in the United States and abroad share their know-how with fellow members.

SOCIETY OF AMERICAN SILVERSMITHS

PO BOX 3599
CRANSTON, RI 02910-0599
FAX 401-461-3196
TEL 401-461-3156
TEL 800-584-2352
E-MAIL SLVRSMITH@AOL.COM

Jeffrey Herman, Executive Director

The Society of American Silversmiths (SAS) was founded in 1989 to preserve the art and history of contemporary handcrafted hollow-ware, flatware and sculpture. SAS also provides its juried artisan members with support, networking and greater access to the market, partly through its annual traveling exhibitions. The public is welcome to consult SAS with all silver-related questions, including those regarding silversmithing techniques, history and restoration. A unique referral service commissions work from artisan members for collectors, corporations and museums.

SURFACE DESIGN ASSOCIATION

PO BOX 20799
OAKLAND, CA 94620
FAX 707-829-3285
TEL 510-841-2008

Joy Stocksdale, Administrator

The Surface Design Association promotes surface design through education; encouragement of individual artists; communication of technical information and information concerning professional opportunities; and the exchange of ideas through conferences and publications.

TILE HERITAGE FOUNDATION

PO BOX 1850
HEALDSBURG, CA 95448
FAX 707-431-8455
TEL 707-431-8453

Joseph A. Taylor, President

The Tile Heritage Foundation is a national non-profit organization dedicated to promoting awareness and appreciation of ceramic surfaces in the United States. In addition to maintaining a reference and research library, Tile Heritage publishes a biannual magazine and a quarterly newsletter, conducts annual symposiums, and supports research in the field of ceramic history and conservation.

SELECTED ORGANIZATIONS & PUBLICATIONS

PUBLICATIONS

AMERICAN CERAMICS

9 E 45 ST #603
NEW YORK, NY 10017
FAX 212-661-2389
TEL 212-661-4397

$28/year

American Ceramics, an art quarterly, was founded to enhance the preservation of ceramics' rich heritage and to document contemporary developments in the field. Articles feature the best and brightest ceramists: rising stars and established luminaries, as well as those early pioneers who transformed ceramics into a genuine art form.

AMERICAN CRAFT

AMERICAN CRAFT COUNCIL
72 SPRING ST
NEW YORK, NY 10012-4019
FAX 212-274-0650
TEL 212-274-0630

$40/year

American Craft, a bimonthly magazine, focuses on contemporary craft through artist profiles, reviews of major shows, a portfolio of emerging artists, a national calendar and news section, and book reviews, as well as illustrated columns reporting on commissions, acquisitions and exhibitions.

CERAMICS MONTHLY

PROFESSIONAL PUBLICATIONS, INC.
1609 NORTHWEST BLVD
PO BOX 12788
COLUMBUS, OH 43212-0788
FAX 614-488-4561
TEL 614-488-8236

$22/year

Ceramics Monthly offers a broad range of articles—including artist profiles, reviews of exhibitions, historical features, and business and technical information—for potters, ceramic sculptors, collectors, gallery and museum personnel, and interested observers.

FIBERARTS

50 COLLEGE ST
ASHEVILLE, NC 28801
FAX 704-253-7952
TEL 704-253-0467
TEL 800-284-3388

$21/year

Five annual issues of *Fiberarts* focus on contemporary textile art, including clothing, quilts, baskets, paper, tapestry, needlework and surface design. Features include artist profiles, critical essays, book reviews, and extensive listings of opportunities, events and resources.

FINE WOODWORKING

THE TAUNTON PRESS, INC.
PO BOX 5506
NEWTOWN, CT 06470-5506
FAX 203-426-3434
TEL 203-426-8171

$29/year

Fine Woodworking is a bimonthly magazine for all those who strive for and appreciate excellence in woodworking—veteran professional and weekend hobbyist alike. Articles by skilled woodworkers focus on basics of tool use, stock preparation and joinery, as well as specialized techniques and finishing.

GLASS CRAFTSMAN

28 S STATE ST
NEWTOWN, PA 18940
FAX 215-860-1812
TEL 215-860-9947

$25/year

Glass Craftsman is a full-color bimonthly publication featuring articles on the creative use of the glass arts and crafts. In addition to how-to information and artist and studio profiles, each issue contains book reviews, career tips, a home-studio section, and a complete calendar of glass-related events.

GLASS MAGAZINE

THE GLASS WORKSHOP
647 FULTON ST
BROOKLYN, NY 11217
TEL 718-625-3685
TEL 718-625-3889

$28/year

Glass Magazine, a full-color quarterly for design professionals, artists and collectors, features profiles of contemporary artists, an educational directory, and critical reviews of national and international exhibitions.

GLASS ART

TRAVIN INC.
PO BOX 260377
HIGHLANDS RANCH, CO 80163-0377
FAX 303-791-7739
TEL 303-791-8998

$24/year U.S.

Glass Art, published bimonthly, includes business articles geared towards glass retailers and professional studios, as well as features on hot and cold glass techniques and artist profiles.

HOME FURNITURE

THE TAUNTON PRESS, INC.
63 S MAIN ST
NEWTOWN, CT 06470-5506
FAX 203-426-3434
TEL 203-426-8171
TEL 800-888-8286

$20/year

Home Furniture, a full-color quarterly magazine, is both a portfolio of top contemporary furniture makers and a review of furniture design. Articles include artist profiles and discussions of furniture history and design.

METALSMITH

5009 LONDONDERRY DR
TAMPA, FL 33647
FAX 813-977-8462
TEL 813-977-5326

$26/year

Metalsmith, a four-color quarterly, includes artist profiles, critical essays and reviews. Its focus is on contemporary metal artists producing jewelry, small sculpture and objects. *Metalsmith* is published by the Society of North American Goldsmiths. Subscription includes a complimentary issue of a special publication, often an Exhibition in Print.

SELECTED ORGANIZATIONS & PUBLICATIONS

SCULPTURE

INTERNATIONAL SCULPTURE CENTER
1050 17TH ST NW #250
WASHINGTON, DC 20036
FAX 202-785-0810
TEL 202-785-1144

$32/year

Sculpture, a bimonthly, four-color journal, focuses on established and emerging sculptors from the United States and abroad, through profiles, interviews and critical reviews. Each issue also highlights collectors, commissions, opinion pieces, site-specific works and a calendar of exhibitions.

SHUTTLE SPINDLE & DYEPOT

HANDWEAVERS GUILD OF
AMERICA, INC. (HGA)
3327 DULUTH HIGHWAY #201
DULUTH, GA 30136-3373
FAX 770-495-7703
TEL 770-495-7702
E-MAIL to Compuserve 73744.202

$30/year

Shuttle Spindle & Dyepot, a quarterly four-color journal, includes features of historical and technical interest, artists profiles, book reviews, articles in support of HGA-sponsored activities and events, a "Gallery" section featuring the work of contemporary fiber artists, and a calendar of events and opportunities.

TILE HERITAGE

TILE HERITAGE FOUNDATION
PO BOX 1850
HEALDSBURG, CA 95448
FAX 707-431-8455
TEL 707-431-8453

$20/year

Tile Heritage: A Review of American Tile History, a biannual publication, features informative articles on both historic and contemporary ceramic tiles, written from a humanistic perspective and enhanced with large black-and-white photographs. From the time of the earliest cave paintings and molded clay forms, people have sought to conceptualize themselves and inspire others through this decorative art form that today is thoroughly integrated into our daily lives.

WOODSHOP NEWS

SOUNDINGS PUBLICATIONS, INC.
35 PRATT ST
ESSEX, CT 06426
FAX 203-767-1048
TEL 203-767-8227

$15.97/year

Woodshop News, published monthly, includes features and descriptions about new technology, artists and their techniques, trade news and source information.

FIBERARTS

THE MAGAZINE OF TEXTILES

For 20 years, artists and other fiber enthusiasts

have turned to FIBERARTS magazine for

information and inspiration.

Today, more than ever, FIBERARTS brings you

dazzling color, fascinating essays, revealing

artist profiles, insightful exhibition reviews

and valuable resource information.

Discover how exciting fiber art can be —

SUBSCRIBE TODAY

❏ 1 year (5 issues): $22 (outside the US: $27 (includes Canadian GST)

❏ 2 years (10 issues): $40 (outside the US: $50 (includes Canadian GST)

Payment in US funds, please

❏ new subscription ❏ renewal

❏ check enc. ❏ MasterCard ❏ VISA

card #

Exp. Date

Name (please print)

Address

Send To: Fiberarts Magazine
50 College St., Asheville, NC, 28801
or call us **toll-free at 1.800.284.3388**

When filling your clients' art needs, you want:

A. **An extensive selection.**

B. **An unmatched value.**

C. **Art they love!**

D. **All of the above.**

Through ArtSouth's disposition program, you will be able to get all of the above!

ArtSouth offers the broadest grouping of corporate art collections, including the prominent collections of IBM – all selling substantially below the original purchase price. Collections include valuable and rare pieces, out-of-print as well as original art.

CALL TODAY to inquire about ArtSouth's disposition program and the additional art services we provide.

Valuable Corporate Art Collections
Available Now

1 800 977 1152

ArtSouth Inc.
4401 Cresson Street
Philadelphia, PA 19127

INDEX OF ADVERTISERS BY STATE

INDEX OF ARTISTS AND COMPANIES

INDEX OF ARTISTS AND COMPANIES

INDEX OF ARTISTS AND COMPANIES